Mrs Beeton's
COOKERY IN COLOUR

Mrs Beeton's
COOKERY
IN COLOUR

WARD LOCK LIMITED ·LONDON

Introduction

Some names have a tried and tested reliability, and Isabella Beeton's is one of them. In compiling *Mrs Beeton's Cookery in Colour,* the editors have taken care to preserve both the substance and spirit of the Beeton tradition, and the direct Beeton style with its clear approach to the subject. Though necessarily selective, the recipes are rich in their variety and colourful appeal, while special mention is made of those advances which modern science has made and put at our disposal in the culinary arts.

This work can be confidently used by English-speaking people in many parts of the world where 'Imperial' measures are standard. There are, however, many millions of people in the English-speaking world who use American measures, and even more who are accustomed to seeing American cook-books. For all who want to cook the British way, the following information shows how to convert the recipes in this 'classic' book to American usage.

The 'Imperial' ½ pint is 10 fluid ounces, which is 2 fluid ounces more than the American ½ pint contained in a standard American cup; 1¼ American cups should be used for ½ pint liquid in the following recipes or where a British cupful is mentioned.

A British tablespoon and teaspoon hold more than the American standard ones; 1 American tablespoon plus 1 scant American teaspoon should be used for 1 tablespoonful of liquid in our recipes, and 1¼ American teaspoons instead of 1 British teaspoon.

For dry measures, use 1 American cup for 4 ounces of flour, or 4 tablespoons for 1 ounce. Other useful equivalents are:

Black molasses and syrups	1 cup	=	12 oz
Cheese, blue or cottage	,,	=	6 oz
Cheese, hard (e.g. Cheddar)	,,	=	5 oz
Dried fruits	,,	=	6-8 oz
Fats (butter, margarine, etc.)	,,	=	8 oz
Fats, whipped or soft	,,	=	6 oz (about)
Rice, dried beans	,,	=	7 oz ,,
Sugar, castor	,,	=	5 oz ,,
,, confectioner's	,,	=	3 oz ,,
,, Demerara and loaf	,,	=	6 oz ,,
,, granulated	,,	=	8 oz ,,

In using tablespoons and teaspoons, substitute 3 American tablespoons of cornflour for 2 British tablespoons, and 5 teaspoons of powdered gelatine for 4 British teaspoons or ½ oz.

The editors have geared 'Mrs Beeton's' recipes to modern teaching syllabuses in features such as the use of convenience foods and new low-cost products, and are constantly testing and re-testing these recipes.

There is a strong possibility that Britain will 'go metric' in the same way as she has 'gone decimal'. But when this book was prepared there was no firm, final standard of conversion. As most people are still using 'Imperial' measures and will be for some time, we have used them in this edition. But our re-testing will enable us to convert the text to metric measures as soon as our readers require it.

A word or two about Trimmings, Sauces and Flavourings: these, *where not described as part of a specific recipe,* are the subject of a separate section (the last, No. 9) where the various items will be found arranged in strict alphabetical order for easy reference.

Some people like to browse through their cook-book hoping to light on a recipe that takes their fancy. Others are more methodical and look for specific recipes, and for them this book is equipped with a systematic and comprehensive index.

Contents

© **Ward Lock Limited 1971**
Reprinted 1972
Reprinted 1973
ISBN 0 7063 1425 5

Text filmset in 10/11 pt and 11/12 pt Century and
Univers Display by FILMTYPE SERVICES LIMITED,
Scarborough.

**Here are brief descriptions of the decorative
pictures on the six introductory pages:**

Page 1   *Chilled consommé with summer vegetables*
Page 2   *Gay summer dinner ready for the table*
Page 3   *Decorative open fruit tart*
Page 4   *Piled glazed fruit in a tartlet*
Page 5   *Currant bread in two shapes of loaf*
Page 6   *Fruit preserves and chutneys*

Printed in Hong Kong

Our modern meal patterns are becoming more informal daily. Housewives who go out to work have neither the wish nor time to organise formal meals. Television has made fork or finger food useful for many main meals as well as for packed lunches, picnics and late-night snacks. Many types of dishes are therefore used more flexibly than in the past. We do not serve soup at the end of a meal because its purpose is to stimulate our appetites; but a first course may equally be a conventional hors d'œuvre, a soup or a light savoury dish which would once have been served at the end of a formal meal. It may be composed of vegetables or fruit, a salad, eggs or cheese, fish or meat. It may be cold or hot and may or may not need a sauce.

Served in bite-sized portions, many of these dishes make good cocktail appetisers and snacks. Others, served in larger portions, can serve as main supper dishes.

A hearty soup can also be used as a supper dish. But most soups are specialised 'starters'; all consommés come into this class. Almost all soups have a basis of meat or vegetable stock or sauce, just as many salads are 'dressed' with French Dressing, Vinaigrette Sauce, or some form of mayonnaise. These basic stocks and sauces are given below or in the special section on Trimmings, Sauces and Flavourings, so that you can check all your basic cookery processes, quickly and easily.

Vegetables served as an hors d'œuvre or first

SIMPLE HORS D'ŒUVRE SELECTION
Cauliflower sprigs with paprika; smoked salmon, rolled, with soft cheese; salami horns; cucumber and cottage cheese rounds; apple wedges and grated carrot salad

course may be raw, blanched or fully cooked. The techniques of blanching and of cooking vegetables and other foods to retain their food value are also described in later sections.

Whatever you serve as a first course, light meal or savoury snack, its flavour and appearance are equally important. It must be appetising; something which interests the appetite rather than being cloying. But it will only be really interesting if it tempts the eye as well as the palate.

The pictures which illustrate our recipes are excellent guides to making the simplest ingredients decorative, for use by themselves as hors d'œuvres or party snacks, or as garnishes for other dishes.

HORS D'ŒUVRES

Simple vegetables, fruits (such as apples) and pickles make a colourful selection of hors d'œuvres. They may be uncooked, blanched, or cooked and served cold, and are usually presented in separate small dishes on a tray.

Raw and blanched vegetables should be cut up finely. Carrots should be grated, cabbage finely chopped and cauliflower broken into small sprigs. Other vegetables and fruits often served as part of an hors d'œuvre selection are:

sliced tomatoes	diced apple with
sliced cucumber	walnut fragments
diced cooked	tossed in lemon
beetroot	juice
finely sliced raw	diced new potatoes,
onion rings	'dressed' while still
cooked green peas	warm, and cooled
with tinned	celery curls
sweetcorn	gherkin fans
shredded green	radish roses
peppers	tomato lilies

Small slices or cubes of continental sausage, pâtés or meat may be included. So may sardines and similar fish, and hard-boiled eggs cut in segments. Meat and fish are often sprinkled with chopped parsley to add colour.

The recipes for chopping parsley, and for making celery curls, gherkin fans, radish roses and tomato lilies are given in our special section on Trimmings, Sauces and Flavourings.

Most fruit and vegetable salads are tossed in French Dressing just before serving, to give flavour and to make them more digestible. The recipe for this is also given in the special section on Trimmings, Sauces and Flavourings. So are the recipes for Mayonnaise, Vinaigrette Sauce and various other dressings and sauces.

Cooked vegetables used as hors d'œuvres should be cooled completely before dressing and serving. They should, like all vegetables, be cooked in as little water as possible and only for just long enough to make them tender. In this way, they retain as much food value as possible, and are crisper and more attractive when mixed with apples and other fruits or meat.

HORS D'ŒUVRE TRAY

Use the following hors d'œuvres for a well-balanced selection:
1 Sardines sprinkled with lemon juice, salt and ground black pepper.
2 Canned asparagus tips, rolled up in thin ham slices, seasoned, and garnished with pineapple.
3 Russian salad, fresh or canned, mixed with mayonnaise and seasoning.
4 Canned tuna fish sprinkled with capers, lemon juice, salt and freshly ground black pepper.
5 Hard-boiled eggs coated with aspic mayonnaise and sprinkled with paprika and salt.
6 Cooked cold green beans mixed with vinaigrette sauce and chopped chives.
7 Canned kipper fillets mixed with diced cucumber, lemon juice, salt and freshly ground black pepper.

SPICED GRAPEFRUIT

2 large grapefruit	Cherries, glacé or
1 oz butter	Maraschino to
1–2 oz brown sugar	decorate
½–1 teasp mixed spice	

Halve the grapefruit and loosen the pulp from the skins, discarding pips and pith. Spread with the softened butter and sprinkle sugar and spice over the top. Cook for about 4 min under a hot grill or for 10 min in a fairly hot oven (200°C, 400°F, Gas 6). Decorate with cherries and serve at once.

4 helpings

AVOCADO PEARS AND PRAWNS

2 large Avocado pears	Crisp lettuce leaves
2 tablesp olive oil	Lemon
2 tablesp vinegar	Pinch of sugar
Good pinch of salt	(optional)
Good pinch of pepper	¼ crushed clove of
A little made mustard	garlic (optional)
2 teacups (about ½ pt)	
shelled prawns, fresh,	
frozen or canned	

Halve the pears. Blend the oil, vinegar and seasonings together. Toss the prawns in this, and then spoon into the pear halves. Put on crisp lettuce leaves and garnish with wedges of lemon. A pinch of sugar can be added to the dressing if wished, also a little garlic.

4 helpings

HORS D'ŒUVRE TRAY
Sardines with lemon juice, asparagus tips rolled in ham, Russian salad, tuna with capers, hard-boiled eggs in aspic mayonnaise, green beans vinaigrette and kipper fillets with cucumber

EGGS A LA DIJON

4 hard-boiled eggs	Tomato garnish

FILLING

4 oz cooked ham	Seasoning
2 oz cooked mushrooms	

Cut the eggs in halves, remove the yolks and cut small thin slices off the bottom to make them stand properly. Make a purée of the minced or chopped ham, and mix with the egg yolks and chopped mushrooms and season. Fill the egg whites with the mixture. Garnish with tiny pieces of tomato and serve.

8 savouries

ROLLMOP HERRINGS

6 large herrings	2 bay leaves
2 oz kitchen salt	4–6 small gherkins
1 pt water	Chillies
1 pt malt vinegar	1 tablesp pickling
2 large onions	spice

Clean, bone and fillet the herrings. Mix the salt and water together and put the herrings to soak in this for 2 hr. Lift out of the brine, drain and put into a shallow dish, covering with the vinegar and leaving for several hours. Shred the onions finely. Drain the herring fillets, reserving the vinegar, put 1 tablesp of onion on each fillet and roll firmly. Secure with small wooden cocktail sticks if possible. Put into jars with bay leaves, gherkins and chillies (use 1 per jar). Pour the vinegar from the dish into a saucepan and boil for a few minutes with the pickling spice. Cool and strain over the herrings. Cover the jars and store in a cool place. They will keep for 2–3 weeks prepared in this way. Note that the herrings are NOT cooked for this dish.

6–12 helpings—or fillets can be divided into halves for part of a mixed hors d'œuvre

SMOKED FISH

Smoked salmon, trout, buckling, kipper fillets and other smoked fish can be bought at many delicatessen. They make excellent hors d'œuvres.

Have smoked salmon cut thinly from the centre of the salmon. Serve spread on a plate with thin brown bread and butter and lemon wedges. Smoked trout, buckling, etc, are usually served whole but with the heads removed. Sometimes the skin is removed from the top side of the fish too. They are served with salad, bread and butter or toast and lemon wedges.

Kipper fillets, frozen or fresh, are served raw, arranged attractively on a plate, with fresh cream and a garnish of watercress.

ASPARAGUS WHOLE OR AU NATUREL

1 bundle of asparagus	2 oz butter
Salt	Lemon juice

Trim the hard white ends of the asparagus to suit-

Globe artichokes 'au naturel'

Asparagus salad with shrimps

able lengths for serving. Scrape the stalks with a sharp knife, working downwards from the head. Wash them well in cold water. Tie them into small bundles with the heads in one direction. Re-trim the stalks evenly. Keep them in cold water until ready to cook. Cook very gently, with the heads above the source of heat, in just enough salted boiling water to cover. When tender (in about 15–20 min) drain and serve in a folded table napkin. Serve with melted butter, seasoned and lightly flavoured with lemon.

To ensure that the tender points of the asparagus are not overcooked by the time the stems are ready, the asparagus should be cooked 'standing'. This can be achieved by using a bottling jar half-filled with boiling water, stood in a deep saucepan of boiling water. The asparagus is placed stems down in the jar and the points cook more slowly in steam only.

Allow 30 min for this method of cooking
Allow 6 or 8 medium-sized heads per person

CUCUMBER AND SEAFOOD ROLLS

1 large thin *or* 2 small thin cucumbers	Mayonnaise
Oil	1 2-oz can anchovy fillets
Vinegar	Stuffed olives
Seasoning	Parsley
1 teacup crab *or* lobster meat	

Peel the cucumbers and cut them into 1-in thick slices. Cut out the centre portion, place rings on a dish, and pour over a little oil and vinegar. Season well. Pound the crab or lobster meat or blend in an electric blender. Mix the meat with mayonnaise. Drain the cucumber shapes and fill each cavity with this mixture. Twist a whole anchovy fillet round each and place a slice of stuffed olive on top. Garnish with parsley.

About 10 savouries

GLOBE ARTICHOKES AU NATUREL

6 globe artichokes	½ pt Hollandaise sauce
Salt	*or* 2 oz melted butter
1 tablesp lemon juice	

Soak the artichokes in cold, salt water for at least 1 hr, to ensure the removal of all dust and insects. Wash them well. Cut off the tails and trim the bottoms with a sharp knife. Cut off the outer leaves and

trim the tops of the remaining ones with scissors. Put them into a pan with just sufficient boiling water to cover them, adding salt and the lemon juice. Cook until tender, 15–45 min, according to size and freshness (when cooked leaves pull out easily). Test frequently after 15 min as they are apt to break and become discoloured if overcooked. Remove from water and drain them well by turning them upside down. Serve with Hollandaise sauce or melted butter.

6 helpings

ASPARAGUS SALAD WITH SHRIMPS

1 small *or* ½ a large bundle of green asparagus *or* 1 10 oz can of asparagus	½ pt shrimps (shelled)
	Mayonnaise
	4 hard-boiled eggs

Prepare and cook the asparagus, or drain canned asparagus. When cold, cut the tender portions into small pieces and put them into a bowl with the shrimps. Mix lightly with enough mayonnaise to moisten. Serve on a dish in the centre of a border of sliced hard-boiled egg.

4 helpings

POTTED SHRIMPS

1 pt shrimps—measure when shelled	Pinch of salt
2–3 oz butter	Grating of nutmeg
Good pinch of cayenne pepper	Lettuce
	Lemon

Heat the butter and turn the shrimps in this until they are well coated, but do not cook them. Add the seasonings and nutmeg. Pour into small moulds or dishes and leave until the butter is set. Turn out on to a bed of crisp lettuce and garnish with lemon. Serve with cayenne pepper and crisp toast.

DRESSED CRAB IN SHELL

One 2½–3 lb crab	A little lemon juice (optional)
Salt and pepper	French dressing
Fresh breadcrumbs (optional)	

Pick the crab meat from the shells. Mix the dark crab meat with salt and pepper, fresh breadcrumbs and a little lemon juice if liked. The breadcrumbs are optional but they lessen the richness and give a

Oysters 'au naturel'

firmer texture. Press the mixture lightly against the sides of the previously cleaned shell. Flake up the white meat, mix with French dressing and pile in the centre of the shell. Garnish with sieved egg yolk, chopped egg white, chopped parsley, sieved coral if any, and decorate with small claws. Make a necklace with the small claws, place on a dish and rest the crab on this. Surround with salad.

4 helpings

OYSTERS AU NATUREL

To eat oysters 'au naturel' all that is needed is to place the opened oysters on the upper shell with a little of the liquor; they are then arranged on a dish, garnished with sprigs of fresh parsley, and, if possible, surrounded with ice. Thin slices of buttered brown bread, quarters of lemon and Tabasco sauce can be handed round at the same time; also cayenne pepper and vinegar.

It is advisable to ask the fishmonger to open the shells for you.

Oysters make delicious hot first-course dishes. They can be baked like baked eggs—coquette style, fried in batter or wrapped in strips of bacon, or mixed with a sauce and used as a filling for small vols-au-vent or patty cases. Cheap cooking oysters are not easy to find today, but canned ones can be used instead. Use canned smoked oysters raw as an hors d'œuvre item. Do not cook them.

PRAWN OR SHRIMP COCKTAIL

Heart of a small lettuce	1 teasp chilli vinegar if available
½ pt shelled prawns *or* shrimps	1 teasp tarragon vinegar
⅓ gill mayonnaise	Good pinch of salt
1 tablesp tomato pureé *or* tomato ketchup	Good pinch of cayenne pepper
	4 prawns in their shells
	Brown bread and butter

Wash and dry the lettuce very well—pick out the tiny leaves and break into very small pieces. Arrange in cocktail glasses. Put the prawns or shrimps on top. Mix the mayonnaise with the tomato ketchup or purée. To obtain the latter, rub one large tomato through a fine sieve. Add the vinegars and seasoning. Put over the shellfish and garnish each glass with an unshelled prawn. Serve with brown bread and butter.

4 helpings

EGGS IN ASPIC

3 hard-boiled eggs	Chervil
1 pt aspic jelly (*see* below)	Cress

Coat the bottoms of 6 dariole moulds with jelly, decorate them with chervil; when set, put in slices of egg and aspic jelly alternately, taking care that each layer of jelly is firmly set before adding the egg. When the whole is firmly set, unmould and decorate with chopped aspic and cress.

ASPIC JELLY

2 egg whites and shells	1 onion
1 lemon	1 carrot
2 chicken *or* veal bouillon cubes	2–3 sticks of celery
1 qt water	Bouquet garni (parsley, thyme, bay leaf)
2½ oz gelatine	10 peppercorns
¼ pt malt vinegar	1 teasp salt
1 tablesp tarragon vinegar	

Whisk the egg whites slightly, wash the shells, peel the lemon rind as thinly as possible, and strain the juice; crumble the cubes. Put them with the rest

Eggs in aspic

LIVER PÂTÉ

of the ingredients into a pan, whisk over heat until boiling, then simmer very gently for about 20 min. Strain through a jelly bag.

This jelly is used principally for lining and garnishing moulds. If too stiff, it may be diluted with a little water, or sherry, when additional flavour is desired.

6 helpings

LIVER PÂTÉ

1 lb calf's or pig's liver or the livers from poultry	Pinch of mixed herbs A few gherkins (optional)
4 oz very lean ham or bacon	1–2 hard-boiled eggs (optional)
1 small onion	A little cream (optional)
3 oz butter	Extra butter
Seasoning	

Cut the liver, ham and onion into small pieces. Heat the butter in a pan and cook the liver, ham and onion for about 6 min—no longer. Put through a very fine mincer twice to give a very smooth mixture. Add the seasoning, herbs and chopped gherkins or chopped hard-boiled eggs too if wished. For a very soft pâté also add a little cream. Put into a dish and cook for about ½ hr in a moderate oven (180°C, 350°F, Gas 4), covered with buttered paper and standing in a dish of hot water to prevent the mixture becoming dry. When the pâté is cooked, cover with a layer of melted butter.

Serve cut in slices on a bed of crisp lettuce and accompanied by hot toast and butter.

4–6 helpings

CHOPPED LIVER

½ lb chicken or calves' liver	1 hard-boiled egg
2 tablesp chicken fat	Salt and pepper
1 small onion	Lettuce leaves

Fry the liver gently in the chicken fat until tender, then remove from the pan. Skin and chop the onion and fry this until soft but not brown. Put the liver and hard-boiled egg through the finest cutter of the mincing machine, then add the onion with the fat in which it was cooked, season with salt and pepper and mix to a paste. Serve on lettuce leaves garnished with hard-boiled egg, as an hors d'œuvre or as a spread for canapés or sandwiches.

4–5 helpings

CHEESE CREAM, COLD

1 oz grated Parmesan cheese	Cayenne pepper
1–2 oz grated Cheddar or Gruyère cheese	Pinch of salt ½ gill aspic jelly (see Eggs in Aspic)
Made mustard	1 gill cream
	Watercress

Season the cheese with the mustard, a good pinch of salt and cayenne pepper. Stir the aspic jelly, which should be quite cold, and just beginning to stiffen slightly, into the cheese. Add the lightly whipped cream. Put the mixture into a glass dish or individual soufflé dishes and allow to set. Garnish with a light dusting of cayenne pepper and watercress. If preferred the mixture can be put into small dariole moulds, previously coated with aspic jelly and decorated with tiny pieces of tomato, gherkin, etc.

This dish can be served either as a cold hors d'œuvre or a savoury.

4 helpings

MAKING COLD MOUSSES

A cold savoury mousse makes an excellent first course. It may be made with a custard base alone or have cream added. If it contains cream, avoid a creamy main course. A mousse or soufflé may be made in one big mould or in individual ones, in all the recipes below. In general, mousses are made with pounded or puréed cooked fish, meat or vegetables usually mixed with a starchy substance or panada, and a liquid thickened with egg yolks, and sometimes with gelatine. The stiffly whipped egg whites may then be added, and the mixture is then poured into the carefully prepared mould or moulds to set.

HAM MOUSSE

¼ lb cooked ham	2 tablesp white stock
Salt and pepper	1 drop cochineal
Grated nutmeg	1½ gills cream or milk
½ pt rich brown stock or consommé	1 tablesp chopped mushroom
½ oz gelatine	½ gill firm aspic jelly (see Eggs in Aspic)
¼ pt aspic jelly (see Eggs in Aspic)	

Tie a band of stiff paper round a china soufflé dish about 5-in diameter so that it stands about 2 in higher than the dish.

Pass the ham twice through the mincer, and sieve it; or blend in an electric blender. Season with salt, pepper and nutmeg. Add the brown stock or consommé which should be well coloured and flavoured with a little tomato paste or purée. Dissolve the gelatine in the aspic, together with the white stock. Colour with cochineal, and add to the ham. Whip the cream lightly, fold it into the mixture. When it is just beginning to set, pour it into the prepared soufflé dish. Allow to set. Add the chopped mushroom to the firm aspic, cold but liquid, and pour over the top of the mould. When set, remove the paper. Serve with green salad.

SALMON MOUSSE

2 eggs	1 dessertsp lemon juice
1 lb canned or cooked salmon	1 tablesp chopped parsley
½ teacup milk	Hard-boiled egg
1 teacup breadcrumbs	Sliced cucumber
Salt and pepper	

Mousse in the making

Ham mousse

Drain the fish, remove the skin and bone and flake. Put the milk and breadcrumbs into a pan and add the juice from the canned fish (or ½ teacup liquid in which the fish was cooked). Put this over a low heat for 5 min, stirring occasionally. Then add the fish, salt and pepper, lemon juice and parsley. Mix, and leave to cool slightly.

Separate the eggs; add the lightly beaten yolks to the fish mixture and stir well, beat the whites until stiff and fold them in thoroughly. Pour into a well-greased mould, cover with greaseproof paper and place in a tin of hot water reaching quarter-way up the side of the mould. Bake in a cool oven (150°C, 310°F, Gas 2) for 40–45 min. During the last 10 min cooking have the mould uncovered. When cold, turn out and serve garnished with hard-boiled egg and cucumber.

4 generous helpings

SMOKED HADDOCK SOUFFLÉ

1 small cooked smoked haddock	1 egg white
1½ oz butter	Pinch of pepper
2 eggs	Cayenne pepper

Flake the fish while still hot and when quite smooth beat in most of the butter and the yolks of the eggs. Use the rest of the butter to grease a soufflé dish. Add all the stiffly beaten egg whites and pepper and cayenne pepper. It should not be necessary to add salt but it is advisable to taste the mixture, as the saltiness of smoked haddock varies a good deal. Put the mixture into the soufflé dish and bake for about 15–20 min in the centre of a moderate oven (180°C, 350°F, Gas 4). Serve at once.

SPINACH SOUFFLÉ

3 level tablesp cooked sieved spinach *or* frozen creamed spinach	2 tablesp grated mild Cheddar *or* Edam cheese
1 tablesp cream	Seasoning
	1 egg

Mix spinach, cream and cheese together. Season well. Add the beaten egg yolk. Fold in the stiffly-beaten egg white. Pour into an individual buttered soufflé dish. Bake for about 20 min in a moderate oven (180°C, 350°F, Gas 4). Serve at once.

1 helping

DEVILLED CRAB

1 medium-sized crab	Cayenne pepper
1 teacup breadcrumbs	Salt to taste
1 teasp made mustard	Cream *or* milk
1 teasp Worcester sauce	2 tablesp browned breadcrumbs
1 tablesp oiled butter	Extra butter

Remove the crab meat from the shell and claws, clean the shell and put it aside. Chop the meat of the crab, add the breadcrumbs, mustard sauce, butter and a very liberal seasoning of cayenne pepper and salt. Mix well, if necessary moisten with a little milk or cream, then turn the whole into the prepared shell. Cover lightly with breadcrumbs, add a few small pieces of butter, and bake in a fairly hot oven (190°C, 375°F, Gas 5) until heated through (about 10 min).

3 helpings

SCALLOPS AU GRATIN

4 scallops	1 oz grated cheese
½ pt milk	1 level tablesp browned
1 oz margarine	breadcrumbs
1 oz flour	Chopped parsley
Salt and pepper	
Creamed potatoes,	
home-made *or*	
'instant'	

Simmer the scallops in the milk until tender, about 15 min. Drain carefully, place each in a deep shell and keep hot. Melt the margarine in a saucepan, stir in the flour and cook for 2 min. Add the milk in which the scallops were cooked, season to taste and boil for 3 min. Pipe a firm border of creamed potatoes round each shell and pour sauce over the fish. Mix the cheese with the crumbs and spread over the top of each scallop. Reheat in a hot oven or under the grill until lightly browned. Sprinkle with chopped parsley and serve at once.

4 helpings

BAKED OR SCALLOPED HERRING ROES

1½ oz butter *or*	A few drops anchovy
margarine	essence
4 small mushrooms	Seasoning
1 small shallot *or*	½ gill thick white sauce
onion	8 fresh soft herring roes
¼ teasp chopped parsley	2 tablesp breadcrumbs
Lemon juice	

Brush the inside of 8 small ramekin dishes or individual scallop shells with a little butter. Chop the shallot or onion finely. Heat 1 oz butter in a saucepan, put in the mushrooms, shallot and parsley and cook gently. When tender, remove from the pan, leaving any surplus butter in the pan, and put the mixture into the dishes or shells. Add a little lemon juice, anchovy essence and seasoning to the white sauce and pour a little over the mushroom mixture. Reheat the butter in the pan and cook the roes until tender. Put on top of the mixture in the dishes and top with breadcrumbs and knobs of butter. Bake in a hot oven for 7 min or under a hot grill until the crumbs are brown.

Make scalloped lobster in the same way, using canned meat.

8 helpings

SCAMPI OR DUBLIN BAY PRAWNS PROVENÇALE

8 oz frozen *or* fresh	2 tomatoes
scampi or Dublin Bay	2–3 large mushrooms
prawns (weight when	Seasoning
peeled)	2 teasp chopped
1 oz butter	parsley
1–2 tablesp olive oil	Lemon juice
1 small onion	
½ clove garlic	

Separate frozen scampi. Heat the butter and oil together, then fry the thinly sliced onion, crushed clove of garlic (½ clove is sufficient for most people). Skin and slice the tomatoes, slice the mushrooms and add to the onion with the shellfish and fry together until just tender. Season well, then add the parsley and lemon juice and serve at once.

For a more substantial dish serve on a bed of boiled rice.

2–3 helpings

CREAMED KIPPER FILLETS

One 8 oz pkt kipper	¼ pt single cream
fillets	Pepper
½ oz butter	Chopped parsley
1 level tablesp finely	
chopped onion	

Melt the butter in a frying-pan and sauté the onion until soft but not browned. Add the cream, bring to the boil and then add the kipper fillets and simmer for 5 min. Season with pepper and serve sprinkled with chopped parsley.

Meats and vegetable ingredients for soups

Consommé Rosé

SOUPS AND CONSOMMÉS

Soup can be a light appetiser with little food value, a hearty first course for the hungry, or even a main course for lunch or supper with the right accompaniments. It is the most economical of all types of food too, since the main ingredients are cheap and many leftovers can be used up.

Soup as a first course should be a contrast in flavour and texture to the following one. Consommés are typical light soups which can precede any rich or solid dish at a dinner; they are designed to stimulate rather than satisfy the appetite.

Main-course soups should contain a fair amount of solid ingredients, such as diced fish, meat or vegetables.

The main ingredients of all classes of soups should be stock of one kind or another (*see* below) and flavouring matter. The water in which vegetables have been boiled should always be used to make stocks, or instead of plain water if you have no stock on hand.

The classes into which we divide soups are:

Broths Unstrained soups, not thickened but containing bits of meat, vegetables, barley, rice, etc, used in the making of the soup.

Clear Soups Strained and 'cleared' liquids (*see* below) sparkling and decoratively garnished.

Purées Soups in which the main ingredients are sieved or put through an electric blender to make them thick; not garnished but usually served with croûtons, bread, savoury biscuits or rusks.

Thickened Soups Liquids thickened by added ingredients. These are usually starchy, such as flour, cornflour, ground rice or semolina, roux (mixed, cooked fat and flour) or beurre manié (kneaded raw butter and flour). But luxury soups are sometimes thickened with cream or egg yolks and cream. They can then be called 'cream soups'.

STOCK FOR CONSOMMÉ, ETC.

2–3 lb veal and beef bones mixed (for brown stock) *or* veal and chicken bones (for white stock)	1½ teasp salt
	1 carrot (brown stock only)
	1 onion (peeled for white stock)
3 qt cold water	1 stick celery *or* 1 leek
Small strip lemon rind (white stock only)	6 peppercorns
	1 bay leaf

Scrape the bones if required, and wash them. Put into a pan and add the water and salt. Soak for 1 hr. Bring very slowly to simmering point, and simmer for 1 hr. Add the vegetables, whole, and the remaining ingredients. Simmer for 3–4 hr. Strain and use.

TO 'CLEAR' STOCK FOR CONSOMMÉ, (AND FOR ASPIC JELLY, ETC)

1 qt clear stock, free from fat	¼ pt water
	2 tablesp sherry
1 small onion, peeled and parboiled	1 egg white
1 small carrot, scraped	¼ teasp salt and pepper mixed
1 small stick celery	Small pinch nutmeg *or* mace
¼ lb lean shin of beef *or* skirt	

Scrub the vegetables and chop roughly. Chop or mince the beef finely and soak it for ¼ hr in the cold water. Beat the egg white until stiff. Put all the ingredients into a pan and bring them slowly to simmering point. Simmer very gently without touching the pan for 1 hr. Strain very carefully through a woollen or cotton cloth. This method gives an excellent flavour if not quite as clear a stock as the more 'classic' method.

CONSOMMÉ ROSÉ

4 raw beetroots	1 onion
Sugar	1 bay leaf

CONSOMME ROYALE

1 qt vegetable water *or* stock	1 clove garlic
3 carrots	1 clove
1 stick of celery	1 egg white
1½ lb tomatoes *or* 1 large can tomatoes	Salt and pepper

Scrub and peel the beetroots, slice and sugar them and cook in the water or stock till soft. Then lift them out to be used in salad. Cool the stock, add the other vegetables and spices. Beat the egg white and add to the stock. Bring slowly to simmering point and simmer very gently for 1 hr. Strain through a linen cloth. Season and reheat. This soup can be served hot or cold. If cold, ¾ oz gelatine should be dissolved in a little stock and added to the whole before cooling.

6 helpings

CONSOMMÉ ROYALE

1 qt consommé

ROYALE CUSTARD SHAPES

2 egg yolks	1 tablesp milk *or* stock
Salt and pepper	

To make the custard, mix the egg yolks with the seasoning and the milk or stock. Strain it into a small greased basin. Stand the basin in hot water and steam the custard until it is firm. Turn out the custard, cut it into thin slices, and from these cut tiny fancy shapes with a 'brilliant' cutter. Add them to the hot consommé.

6 helpings

CONSOMMÉ À LA JULIENNE

1 qt consommé

GARNISH

1 tablesp shreds of carrot	1 tablesp finely chopped onion
1 tablesp shreds of turnip	1 tablesp shreds of celery
1 tablesp shreds of green leek	

Cut the shreds 1/16-in thick and 1–1¼-in long. Boil them separately for a few min till just tender, then drain them and pour on to them the hot consommé.

6 helpings

CONSOMMÉ MADRILÈNE

1 qt brown stock	1 bay leaf
1 lb tomatoes	¼–½ lb lean beef
1 green pepper	1 carrot
1 clove of garlic	1 egg white
Parsley stalks	1 onion
Thyme	1 stick of celery

Cut up the tomatoes and green pepper. Tie the herbs together in a small piece of muslin. Shred and soak the beef in ¼ pt water. Whip the egg white slightly. Put all ingredients into a pan and simmer very gently for 1 hr. Strain as usual. To garnish cut tiny dice from the firm flesh of skinned tomato. Serve the consommé hot or iced; if iced, it should be almost liquid and may therefore need whisking a little.

6 helpings

BEEF BROTH WITH GOLDEN ROLL SLICES

1 carrot	Salt and pepper
1 turnip (small)	½ small cabbage
1 onion	A sprig of parsley

1 clove of garlic (optional)	A few chives
1 oz butter *or* margarine	Grated nutmeg
	6 thin slices of French bread
1 qt brown stock	

Scrub and peel the carrot and turnip, peel the onion and crush the garlic (if used). Slice the vegetables in thin rounds. Melt the fat and in it cook the vegetables gently for 10 min with a lid on the pan. Add the stock (boiling) and ½ teasp salt. Simmer the whole for 30 min.

Meanwhile wash the cabbage, shred it finely and chop the parsley and chives. Add the cabbage to the broth and simmer for 20 min longer; then add seasoning, a little grated nutmeg, and the chopped parsley and chives. Toast or bake the slices of French bread till golden brown and put one in each soup plate or cup; pour the hot soup over them. If liked, grated cheese may be handed round with this soup.

4–6 helpings

CHICKEN BROTH

1 small boiling fowl	Lemon rind
3–4 pt water to cover	1 bay leaf
Salt and pepper	1 tablesp long-grain rice (optional)
1 onion	
Pinch of mace	1 tablesp finely chopped parsley
A bunch of fresh herbs (thyme, marjoram, parsley stalks)	

Wash and joint the fowl, break the carcase bones, scald and skin the feet and wash the giblets. Put the pieces of fowl and the giblets into a pan and cover them with cold water. Add ½ teasp salt to each quart of water and bring the whole very slowly to simmering point. Add the onion, skinned but still whole, the mace, herbs, lemon rind and bay leaf. Simmer very gently for 3–4 hr. Strain the broth through a colander, return it to the pan and sprinkle into it the washed rice, if used. Simmer for a further 20 min.

Meanwhile, the meat may be removed from the chicken bones and cut into small cubes, to be returned to the broth before serving. Just before serving the broth, season to taste and add the chopped parsley.

8 helpings

POT-AU-FEU (a broth and a meat dish)

2 lb brisket, topside *or* boned top ribs of beef	2 turnips
	1 small parsnip
½ lb broken beef bones	2 leeks
	4 onions stuck with one clove each
2 teasp salt	6 peppercorns
2 qt water	¼ cabbage
Bunch of fresh herbs— parsley stalks, chervil, thyme, garlic, bayleaf	2 tomatoes
	Potatoes (optional)
	6 toasted slices of French bread
4 carrots	

Wipe the meat with a damp cloth and remove some of the outside fat if excessive. Tie the meat into shape. Wash the bones. Put meat and bones in a large strong pan, add the salt and the cold water, and soak for ½ hr. Bring very slowly to simmering point, add the herbs and simmer very gently for 1 hr.

Meanwhile, scrub and peel the root vegetables; keep the onions whole but cut the others into large pieces and add these to the broth after the first hour's simmering. Put on the lid but leave it slightly tilted

French onion soup

to allow steam to escape, and simmer very gently for another 2½ hr. Soak, wash and finely shred the cabbage, scald and skin the tomatoes and cut them into small pieces. Add these to the broth and, if liked, sufficient medium-sized peeled potatoes to serve with the meat. Continue simmering gently for ½ hr.

To serve Strain the broth through a colander, return it to the pan, and keep it hot. Dish the meat with the potatoes, some of the large pieces of vegetable round it and a little of the broth to moisten; keep this covered and hot. Remove the bones and herbs from the broth, cut 1 tablesp of ¼ in cubes from the carrot, leek, parsnip and turnip and add these to 1 qt of the broth. Reheat. Serve the broth with the toasted bread floating in it. There will be some broth left to use as stock, and the bones can be reboiled for stock too.

Broth—6 helpings
A meat dish—6 helpings
Stock—about 1¼ pt

FRENCH ONION SOUP

2 oz fat bacon	**¼ pt white wine *or***
6 medium-sized onions	**cider**
½ oz flour	**6 small slices of bread**
Salt and pepper	**2 oz cheese: Gruyère**
½ teasp French	***or* Parmesan**
mustard	**A little butter**
1½ pt stock	

Chop the bacon and heat it gently in a deep pan till the fat runs freely. Slice the onions thinly and fry them slowly in the bacon fat till golden. Add the flour, salt and pepper to taste and continue frying for a few minutes. Stir in the mustard, the stock and the wine or cider. Simmer till the onions are quite soft. Toast the bread, grate the cheese. Butter the toast and spread the slices with grated cheese. Pour the soup into individual fireproof soup bowls, float a round of toast on each and brown it in a very hot oven or under the grill.

6 helpings

COCK-A-LEEKIE

1 small boiling fowl	**Salt and pepper**
¼ lb prunes	**1 lb leeks**

Soak the prunes for 12 hr in ½ pt water. Clean the fowl and truss it: wash the giblets, scald and skin the feet. Put the fowl, giblets and enough cold water to cover them in a pan. Bring very slowly to simmering point. Add 2 teasp salt. Wash and trim the leeks thoroughly and cut them into thin rings. Add the leeks to the broth after 1 hr cooking and simmer for 2–3 hr more. Half an hour before serving add the soaked prunes; simmer till they are just tender but not broken. Lift out the fowl and the giblets and feet. Cut some of the flesh of the fowl into small cubes and return them to the broth. Season the broth carefully and serve it with the prunes.

CHICKEN PURÉE

FOR THE STOCK

1 boiling fowl *or*	**A bunch of herbs:**
carcass, giblets, skin	**parsley, thyme,**
and legs of a fowl	**marjoram**
¼ lb lean bacon	**1 bay leaf**
2 onions	**¼ teasp mace**
1 carrot	**6 peppercorns**
3 qt water	**Lemon juice**
Salt and pepper	**A strip of lemon rind**

FOR EACH QUART OF CHICKEN STOCK

1 oz butter *or*	**Lemon juice**
margarine	**Nutmeg**
1 oz flour	**½ gill cream *or milk***

Prepare the fowl, chop the bacon, peel and slice the vegetables; put into a large pan with the water, salt, herbs, spice, lemon juice and rind. Cook until the flesh of the chicken is absolutely white; the addition of lemon juice makes the flesh tender more quickly. Cool the stock and skim off all fat. Mince 4 oz of the cooked chicken and moisten it with a little stock. Rub it through a coarse wire sieve. Melt

the fat, stir into it the flour, then the stock, a little at a time; boil well. Stir the hot soup gradually into the chicken purée. Season lightly with lemon juice, salt, pepper and a trace of nutmeg. Add the cream or milk and re-heat without boiling.

4–6 helpings

VEGETABLE PURÉES AND CREAM SOUPS
BASIC RECIPE (1)

1 lb vegetables	$\frac{1}{4}$ pt milk (*or* $\frac{1}{8}$ pt milk
Vegetables to flavour	and $\frac{1}{8}$ pt cream for
$\frac{1}{2}$–1 oz butter,	light-coloured soups)
margarine *or* other	$\frac{1}{2}$ oz starchy thickening,
suitable fat	e.g. flour, cornflour,
1 pt stock; white for	ground rice, tapioca
white and pale green	*or* potato to each pint
vegetables; brown for	of sieved soup
dark-coloured	Salt and pepper
vegetables; *or*	Other flavouring or
vegetable water	colouring if required
Flavouring herbs	
(optional)	

For a cream soup add $\frac{1}{8}$–$\frac{1}{4}$ pt cream (this may replace some of the milk), sometimes also 1 egg yolk.

Slice or chop the main and flavouring vegetables. Melt the fat in a deep pan and cook the vegetables in it over a gentle heat for 10 min. Keep the lid on the pan and shake it vigorously from time to time. Boil the stock, add it to the vegetables with the herbs and other flavouring (if used) and simmer the whole until the vegetables are quite soft. This cooking time should be as short as possible but will vary with the kind and age of the vegetables used. Remove the herbs, rub or press the vegetables through a sieve (wire for soft, pulpy or very firm vegetables; nylon if a very smooth purée is needed). Mix the liquid with the purée and measure the soup. Weigh or measure the thickening in the proportion given above. Blend the starch powder with the cold milk, stock or water and stir it into the soup. Cook the soup until the starch is thickened and no longer tastes raw. Season carefully to taste.

FOR A CREAM SOUP

After the starch thickening has been cooked, remove the pan from the heat. Mix the egg yolk and cream together, stir them into the soup, which should be well below boiling point. Stir over gentle heat till the egg yolk thickens, but *do not boil*. Serve the soup at once; cream and eggs cannot be kept hot.

Cream when used alone may be stirred into the soup just at boiling-point, as it is removed from the heat. It must not itself be allowed to boil.

Serve separately: fried croûtons, pulled bread or Melba toast.

BASIC RECIPE (2)

1 lb vegetables	1 pt thin sauce, i.e.
1$\frac{1}{2}$–1 oz butter	1 oz fat and flour to
margarine *or* fat	1 pt white stock for
and/*or* $\frac{1}{8}$ pt boiling	light-coloured
stock *or* vegetable	purées, *or* brown-
water	stock sauce for
	dark-coloured purées

Cook the vegetables as in Basic Recipe (1), adding only sufficient boiling liquid to moisten the mixture. Cook very carefully without allowing it to evaporate or burn. Rub this concentrated purée through a sieve and whisk it into the hot sauce. Boil the soup, and if, you wish, convert it to a cream soup as in the previous recipe.

Typical vegetable purées are artichoke (Jerusalem) purée, broad bean purée, chestnut purée, leek purée, parsnip purée, peapod soup and tomato soup.

CHESTNUT PURÉE

1 lb chestnuts after	Salt and pepper
peeling (about 1$\frac{1}{2}$ lb	A little yeast extract
in shells)	*or* meat extract
1 onion	A pinch of sugar
1 oz butter	A pinch of cinnamon
1 qt stock	Grated nutmeg
Lemon juice	$\frac{1}{4}$ pt cream (optional)

Make an incision in the rounded sides of the chestnuts then drop them into fast boiling water and boil for 15 min. Drain them, and while still warm remove shells and brown skins. Proceed as for basic recipe (see above). Add the spices so sparingly that they cannot be recognised but merely enhance the chestnut flavour. No added thickening is required except the cream which is optional.

CUCUMBER CREAM SOUP

1 lb cucumber	Lemon juice
1 oz butter	Green colouring
6 spring onions	A sprig of mint

1 oz flour
1 pt white stock
Salt and pepper

A sprig of parsley
$\frac{1}{8}$ pt cream

Peel the cucumber, reserve a 2-in length for garnish. Slice the rest. Melt the butter in a deep pan and cook the onion gently, without browning for 10 min. Stir in the flour, then the stock and bring to boiling point. Add the sliced cucumber and cook till tender. Sieve through a nylon sieve. Season and add lemon juice to taste. Cut the 2-in piece of cucumber into $\frac{1}{4}$-in dice and boil these in a little stock or water till just tender. Add them to the finished soup. Five minutes before serving the soup, add the mint and parsley. Tint the soup pale green. Stir the cream into the hot soup immediately before serving.

4 helpings

PEA POD SOUP

2 lb pea pods
1 sliced lemon
A few sprigs of mint
   and parsley
1$\frac{1}{2}$ pt white stock *or*
   vegetable water
$\frac{3}{4}$ oz flour

$\frac{3}{4}$ oz butter *or* margarine
Salt and pepper
Sugar to taste
4 tablesp small cooked
   peas
Chopped mint

Wash the pods and boil them with the onion, mint and parsley in the stock until the outer flesh of the pods is soft. Cook the flour in the butter for 2–3 min without browning it. Sieve the pulp from the pea pods. Stir the purée into the butter and flour, and bring it to boiling point. Season and sugar to taste. Just before serving, add the cooked peas and chopped mint. Serve garnished with frankfurters for a hearty meal.

TOMATO SOUP

1 lb tomatoes, fresh *or*
   canned
1 onion
1 carrot
$\frac{1}{2}$ oz margarine
1 oz bacon scraps, rind
   or bone
1 pt white stock *or*
   juice from canned
   tomatoes

Grated nutmeg
Lemon juice
A bunch of herbs
Minute tapioca *or*
   cornflour
Salt and pepper
Red colouring, if
   needed

Slice the tomatoes, onion and carrot. If canned tomatoes are used, strain them and make the juice up to 1 pt with stock. Melt the margarine in a deep pan and lightly fry the sliced vegetables and chopped bacon for 10 min. Boil the stock or tomato juice and add to the vegetables with the nutmeg, lemon juice and herbs and cook for $\frac{3}{4}$–1 hr. Sieve and thicken the soup with $\frac{1}{2}$ oz cornflour or minute tapioca to each 1 pt soup, blended with a little cold milk, stock or water. Stir into the soup, cook till clear, season, add sugar to taste and colouring if needed. Serve garnished like French Onion Soup for a hearty dish.

4–6 helpings

MINESTRONE

$\frac{1}{4}$ lb haricot beans
3 pt water
2 onions
1–2 cloves of garlic
1 oz lean bacon scraps
2 tablesp olive oil
A bunch of herbs
2 large tomatoes
1 glass red wine

2 carrots
1 small turnip
2 sticks of celery
2 small potatoes
$\frac{1}{2}$ small cabbage
2 oz macaroni or fancy
   shapes of Italian pasta
Salt and pepper
Grated cheese

Vegetable purées

Minestrone

ONION SOUP

Soak the beans overnight in ½ pt of the water. Slice the onions, crush the garlic, chop the bacon. Heat the oil in a deep pan and fry the onion very gently for 10 min. Add the garlic, bacon, herbs, cut-up tomatoes and the wine. Reduce this mixture by rapid boiling for 5 min. Add the haricot beans and all the water and simmer for 2 hr. Dice the carrots, turnip and celery and add them to the soup; simmer for a further ½ hr. Add the potatoes, diced, and simmer for another ½ hr. Add the shredded cabbage and the macaroni and simmer for a final 10–15 min. Season the soup, stir into it a little grated cheese and hand the rest round separately.

Different mixtures of vegetables may be used when they are in season.

6 helpings

ONION SOUP

3 large Spanish onions (about 2 lb)	1 clove
1 oz butter *or* margarine *or* dripping	1 bay leaf
	¼ teasp mace
	Flour to thicken
1 qt white stock *or* 1 pt stock and 1 pt milk	Salt and pepper
	¼ pt milk *or* cream

Peel and slice the onions. Melt the fat in a deep pan and lightly fry the onion for 10 min; cook slowly to prevent the onions colouring. Boil the stock, add it to the onions with spices, and simmer until the onions are tender. Rub through a fine sieve, return the purée to the pan and add milk if used. To each 1 pt of soup allow ½ oz flour, blend the flour with a little cold milk, water or stock and stir into the soup. Cook until the soup thickens, season to taste. If cream is used, add it to the soup just before serving.

For Brown Onion soup use brown stock, and brown the onions very slowly in the fat (about 20 min) before adding the stock.

6 helpings

Mulligatawny soup

BORTSCH, POLISH OR RUSSIAN BEETROOT SOUP

4 raw beetroots	Salt and pepper
1 qt brown stock	Grated nutmeg
1 onion stuck with 1 clove	¼ pt sour cream *or* 1 bottle yogurt
Bunch of herbs	Caraway seeds
1 oz goose fat *or* bacon fat	
Shredded white leek, cabbage, beetroot, celery to make ½ pt in all	

Slice 3 of the beetroots and simmer them in the stock with the onion, clove, herbs and caraway seeds for about 1 hr or until the colour has run into the soup and the flavour is no longer raw. Melt the fat and in it cook the shreds of vegetable and the finely-grated 4th beetroot very gently for 10–15 min. Strain the stock and press the juice out of the beetroots into it. Add the shreds of vegetable and finish cooking them in the soup. Season, add a trace of nutmeg to the soup. Beat the sour cream or yogurt into the hot soup but do not allow it to boil; or put a spoonful of yogurt or sour cream into each soup plate before pouring in the soup.

4 helpings

MULLIGATAWNY SOUP

1 lb lean mutton *or* rabbit *or* stewing veal *or* shin of beef *or* oxtail	Salt
	1 carrot
	½ small parsnip
1 onion	A bunch of herbs
1 small cooking apple	Lemon juice
1 oz butter *or* margarine	¼ teasp black treacle
½ oz curry powder	2 oz long-grain rice
1 oz flour	¼ pt water
1 qt bone stock *or* water	¼ teasp salt

Cut the meat in small pieces. Chop the onion finely, and the apple. Heat the butter in a deep pan and in it quickly fry the onion, then the curry powder. Add

*Angels on horseback
with sausage 'spiral' rolls
and cocktail sausages*

the apple and cook it gently for a few minutes, then stir in the flour. Add the liquid, meat and salt, and bring slowly to simmering point, stirring all the time. Add the other vegetables, the herbs tied in muslin, and a few drops of lemon juice. Simmer until the meat is very tender. This will take between 2 hr for rabbit and 4 hr for shin of beef. Taste the soup and add more lemon juice, then add enough black treacle to obtain a flavour that is neither predominantly sweet nor acid. Strain the soup, cut some of the meat into neat cubes and re-heat them in the soup. Bring rice, water and salt to the boil and simmer, covered, for 15 min. Hand it with the soup. The amount of curry powder may be varied to taste; the quantity given is for a mild-flavoured soup.

4–6 helpings

BOUILLABAISSE

This, the most famous of all fish soups, is made chiefly in the South of France, different districts having particular recipes. It is a kind of thick stew of fish which should include a very wide mixture of different kinds of fish. In order to get a wide enough variety, a large quantity must be made.

A mixture of 8 to 10 different kinds of fish, e.g.

Whiting	John Dory
Red mullet	Monk fish
Crawfish *or* lobster	Crab
Conger eel *or* eel	Bass
Gurnet	Sole

To every 2 lb fish allow

1 large onion	A sprig of fennel *or*
1 leek	tarragon
1 clove of garlic	⅛ teasp saffron
2 tomatoes	Salt and pepper
1 bay leaf	¼ pt olive oil

A sprig of parsley	¼ pt white wine
A sprig of savory	

To each portion of bouillabaisse allow

1 thick slice of French bread

Clean the fish, cut them into thick slices and sort them into 2 groups, the firm-fleshed kind and the soft kind. Chop the onion; slice the leek; crush the garlic; scald, skin and slice the tomatoes. In a deep pan, make a bed of the sliced vegetables and the herbs; season this layer. Arrange on top the pieces of firm-fleshed fish; season them and pour over them the oil. Add to the pan the wine and enough cold water or fish stock barely to cover the top layer of fish. Heat as quickly as possible to boiling point and boil briskly for 8 min. Now add the soft pieces of fish, forming a fresh layer. Boil for a further 5 min. Meanwhile toast the slices of bread and arrange them in the bottom of the soup tureen or individual bowls. Pour the liquid over the bread and serve it as a fish bouillon. Serve the mixture of fish separately. The vegetables and herbs are for flavour only, and need not be served.

LIGHT SAVOURY DISHES

ANGELS ON HORSEBACK

12 oysters	½ teasp chopped shallot
A little thick white sauce	*or* onion
12 small thin slices of	½ teasp chopped parsley
bacon	Lemon juice
Paprika *or* cayenne	12 small rounds of fried
pepper	bread *or* 4 slices of
	toast

21

BACON OLIVES

Beard the oysters, and roll in sauce. Trim the bacon, cutting each piece just large enough to roll round an oyster, season with paprika or cayenne pepper, sprinkle on a little shallot and parsley. Lay an oyster on each, add a few drops of lemon juice, roll up tightly and secure the bacon in position with a fine skewer. Cook in a frying-pan, under the grill or in a hot oven. (220°C, 425°F, Gas 7) *just long enough to crisp the bacon* (further cooking would harden the oysters). Remove the skewers and serve on the croûtes.

4 helpings or 12 small savouries

Cooking time 5–10 min

BACON OLIVES

3 oz finely chopped cooked *or* canned meat	½ teasp finely chopped parsley
1 oz finely chopped cooked ham *or* tongue	¼ teasp powdered mixed herbs
1½ tablesp bread-crumbs	Nutmeg
½ teasp finely chopped onion	Salt and pepper
	1 egg
	8 small thin rashers of bacon

Mix the meat, ham, breadcrumbs, onion, parsley and herbs together; add a pinch of nutmeg, season to taste with salt and pepper. Stir in gradually as much egg as is necessary to bind the mixture together. Leave for ½ hr, then divide into 8 portions. Form each portion into a cork shape, roll in a rasher of bacon, and secure with string or small skewers. Bake in a fairly hot oven (190°C, 375°F, Gas 5) for about ½ hr. Serve on toast.

DEVILS ON HORSEBACK

1–2 chickens' livers *or* the same amount of calf's liver	8 well-drained prunes
	8 short thin rindless rashers streaky bacon
Butter	4 small bread squares
Salt and pepper	Olives stuffed with pimento
Cayenne pepper	

Gently cook the liver in a little butter, then cut it into 8 pieces. Season well and dust with a few grains of cayenne pepper. Stone the prunes and stuff with the liver. Stretch the bacon to double its size with the flat of a knife. Encircle each prune in a piece of bacon, secure with a wooden cocktail stick and bake in a very hot oven. Fry the bread in shallow bacon fat and drain well. Remove sticks and place the 'devils' on the bread. Garnish each with a pimento-stuffed olive.

DEVILLED CHICKEN LIVERS

4 chickens' livers	Pinch of salt
1 shallot *or* small onion	8 small rashers of bacon
½ teasp chopped parsley	4 croûtes of fried bread
Pinch of cayenne pepper	

Wash and dry the livers; cut them in halves. Finely chop the shallot or onion and mix with the parsley, cayenne pepper and salt. Sprinkle this mixture over the livers. Wrap the rashers of bacon round the livers, and fasten them in position with skewers. Bake in a moderate oven (180°C, 350°F, Gas 4) for 7–8 min or cook under the grill. Remove the skewers, put 2 bacon rolls on each croûte and serve as hot as possible.

4 helpings

SAVOURY STUFFED HAM ROLLS

5 thin slices of ham	4 oz cream cheese
2 pears	Endive
Juice of 1 lemon	Half slices of tomato
1 oz almonds, blanched and roasted	

Peel the pears, core and cut into dice. Marinate in lemon juice. Chop most of the almonds and combine with the cream cheese and diced pears. Reserve the unchopped almonds. Place a little filling on each slice of ham and roll the ham slices neatly. Arrange on a serving dish and garnish with the endive, tomato and whole roasted almonds.

5 helpings

MADRAS FRITTERS

20 rounds of brown bread 1½-in diameter	10 rounds of cooked *or* cooked, canned ham 1½-in diameter
Chutney	Egg and breadcrumbs
2 apples, peeled, cored and chopped	Frying fat

Butter all the rounds of brown bread and spread with a layer of chutney. Place apple chips on 10 rounds of bread; cover with ham and the remaining rounds of bread, press together lightly. Coat with egg and breadcrumbs, then fry in hot fat until golden brown.

4–5 helpings

BLUE CHEESE AND APPLE SAVOURIES

3 oz blue-veined cheese, crumbled	Salt and pepper
1 oz butter or margarine	2–3 cooking apples
Flour for dredging	Tarragon butter, shaped into small balls
1 oz breadcrumbs	

Cream together the cheese and butter or margarine. Mix in the breadcrumbs, using a fork. Core the apples but do not peel them. Cut each one into 3 or 4 thick rounds. Lay them on a baking sheet or grilling tray. Season. Dredge with flour to dry, then spread each round with cheese mixture all over. Smooth the surface. Grill under high heat until the cheese bubbles and browns. Leave in a warm place until the apple slices begin to soften. Top each slice just before serving with a small chilled ball of tarragon butter.

WELSH RAREBIT

1 oz butter *or* margarine	A few drops of Worcester sauce
1 level tablesp flour	4–6 oz grated Cheddar cheese
5 tablesp milk: *or* 3 tablesp milk and 2 tablesp ale *or* beer	Salt and pepper
1 teasp mixed mustard	4 slices of buttered toast

Heat the fat in a pan and stir in the flour. Cook for several minutes, stirring well. Add the milk and stir well over the heat until a smooth thick mixture, then add the ale, mustard, Worcester sauce, cheese and a good pinch of salt and pepper. Do not overcook the mixture otherwise the cheese will become 'oily'. Spread on the slices of buttered toast and put under a hot grill until golden brown. Serve at once.

A larger quantity of Welsh Rarebit mixture can be made and stored in the fridge to be used as required.

4 helpings or 8 small savouries

Blue cheese and apple savouries

Stuffed ham rolls

Cheese fondue

BUCK RAREBIT

As for Welsh Rarebit, but top each slice of cooked Welsh Rarebit with a poached egg and serve at once.

YORKSHIRE RAREBIT

As for Welsh Rarebit, but add 4 rashers cooked rinded bacon.

The bacon can either be cut into 4 thin pieces, put on the toast and crisped under the grill before putting on top of the cheese mixture, or it can be diced and mixed with the cheese, etc.

SEPARATED EGGS

Recipes often call for the use of egg yolks or whites alone, resulting in one or the other remaining unused.

EGG YOLKS

Whole yolks will keep for 2–3 days if covered with cold water and placed in a screw-top jar in a refrigerator.

To use them: add an extra egg yolk or two to scrambled eggs and custards, it will make them more creamy. Or add them to a cream sauce or soup,

but do not let the liquid boil after adding the yolks. Or poach them hard and put through a sieve, then use the shreds to garnish salads, rice dishes and soups.

EGG WHITES

Place in a covered bowl in a fridge (well away from the ice-box), and they will keep for 5–6 days.

To use them: add an extra egg white to a mousse, meringue or soufflé. Or whisk the white and fold it into a jelly just before it sets. Or give a meringue top to plain milk puddings or tarts; a few minutes in a hot oven, just long enough to set the meringue is sufficient.

CHEESE MERINGUES

2 egg whites	Deep fat for frying
Pinch of cayenne pepper	A little Parmesan
Pinch of salt	cheese for garnish
2 oz grated Parmesan cheese	

Whisk the egg whites to a very stiff froth. Add a good seasoning of cayenne and a little salt to the cheese, then stir it lightly into the whisked egg whites. Have ready a deep pan of hot fat, drop in the mixture in small teaspoonfuls, and fry until nicely browned. Drain well, and serve sprinkled with Parmesan cheese and more cayenne pepper.

About 14 savouries

CHEESE FONDUE

10–14 oz Emmentaler cheese	2–4 teasp lemon juice
10–14 oz Gruyère cheese	1 heaped teasp cornflour *or* potato flour
1 clove garlic	1 liqueur glass kirsch
4 glasses white wine	Pepper, nutmeg or paprika to taste

Rub round the inside of an earthenware casserole with garlic and warm up the wine together with the lemon juice. Add the cheese gradually, stirring all the time. Boil up on a good heat, then add the kirsch mixed to a smooth paste with the cornflour. Continue to cook for a short time, stirring the fondue all the time in the form of the figure '8', with a whisk. Stand the fondue on a spirit-stove which can be regulated, so that it continues to boil very slowly. Each person serves himself from the casserole. The creamy cheese mixture is eaten by spearing a cube of bread on a fork, stirring it in the mixture several times, and then transferring the cube to the mouth.

If you have no kirsch at hand, gin or brandy can be used instead. The fondue will of course have quite a different taste, but it will be just as good.

4 helpings

Baked egg

BAKED EGGS

Heat one cocotte (a special little dish manufactured for this purpose) for each person. Add a little butter or cream, break an egg into each, season to taste, and place the cocottes in a pan of boiling water to come half way up their sides. Cover the pan and place in a moderate oven (180°C, 350°F, Gas 4). Cooking time when the eggs are in thin china dishes will be 6–7 min; allow 8–9 min with thicker dishes.

BAKED EGGS—COQUETTE STYLE

6 eggs	Salt and pepper
1 oz butter	Cayenne pepper
6 dessertsp cream	2 oz finely chopped ham
Nutmeg	*or* tongue

Liberally butter 6 ramekin cases, divide the remainder of the butter into 6 portions and place a portion in each case. To each add 1 dessertsp cream, a pinch of nutmeg and salt and pepper, and place on a baking-sheet on the oven. When the contents begin to simmer, break an egg into each case, add a pinch of cayenne pepper to the centre of each yolk and replace in an oven set at a low heat. When cooked, sprinkle the ham or tongue lightly on the white of each egg, taking care to keep the yolk uncovered. Serve hot.

6 helpings

SWISS EGGS

1½ oz butter *or* margarine	Good pinch of salt
2 tablesp grated cheese	Pinch of pepper
4 eggs	Cayenne *or* paprika pepper

Well grease 4 small dishes. Put ½ the cheese at the bottom of the dishes. Carefully break the eggs and put one into each dish on top of the cheese. Cover with seasoning, cheese and butter. Bake for about 10 min in a fairly hot oven (200°C, 400°F, Gas 6). Garnish with pepper and serve at once with hot rolls or crisp toast.

4 helpings

FRIED EGGS

Method 1 For eggs fried on one side only. Melt a little bacon fat or butter in a frying-pan, break the eggs and slip them carefully into the pan. Cook over a gentle heat, basting the eggs with some of the hot fat, until the white is opaque and the yolk is set. Season with pepper and salt.

Method 2 For eggs fried on both sides. Each takes less than one min. Put a teacupful of oil into a small pan so that the egg will actually swim in the oil. Heat until the oil begins to smoke lightly, then maintain this temperature. Break the egg into a cup or saucer and season the yolk with salt and pepper. Slip it quickly into the oil, putting the edge of the cup to the surface of the oil. Dip a smooth wooden spoon into the hot oil, then pull the white over the yolk so as to cover it completely. Then turn the egg over in the oil and leave for a second only. It will then be done.

POACHED EGGS

To poach well, eggs must be fresh. They should be broken into a cup or saucer and then slipped into boiling salted water to which 1 tablesp vinegar has

Fried egg and bacon

been added. The water will cease to boil when the eggs are added: do not let it boil again. An average egg will take about 3 min to poach: it is ready when the white has enveloped the yolk and may be touched without breaking. Remove with a perforated spoon.

If you like poached eggs round in shape, boil them for ½ min before breaking into the poaching pan.

POACHED EGGS WITH SPINACH

6 eggs	Nutmeg
1 pt spinach purée (fresh *or* frozen)	Salt and pepper
1 oz butter	Croûtons of toast *or* fried bread

Prepare the spinach purée (*see* Vegetable Purées), place it in a saucepan, add the butter, a good pinch of nutmeg, salt and pepper. Heat through thoroughly. Meanwhile, poach the eggs and trim them neatly. Turn the spinach on to a hot dish, flatten the surface slightly and on it place the eggs. Garnish with croûtons and serve a good gravy or brown sauce separately.

6 helpings

SCRAMBLED EGGS

The secret of serving good scrambled eggs lies in slow cooking over a very low heat (a double saucepan is useful for this), continuous stirring, and

Scrambled eggs with fillings

immediate serving as the eggs go on cooking in their own heat. It is helpful to add a little butter, or cream, when the scrambling is almost finished: this stops the cooking and improves the flavour, as well as making the texture creamier.

4 eggs	½ tablesp butter *or*
Salt and pepper	cream
1 tablesp butter	

Break the eggs into a bowl, add seasonings and beat eggs lightly. Meanwhile melt the 1 tablesp butter in the bottom of a pan and roll it around. Before it begins to sizzle pour the eggs into the pan. Reduce the heat to very low, and stir the mixture evenly and constantly with a wooden spoon. When almost ready add about ½ tablesp butter or cream. Remove from the heat as soon as the eggs are set to a soft creamy consistency. Serve immediately.

2 helpings

EGGS MORNAY

4–5 hard-boiled eggs	1½ oz grated cheese
1 oz butter	¼ pt white sauce
Nutmeg	Salt and pepper

Cut the eggs into thick slices, place them on a well-buttered fireproof dish, sprinkle them lightly with nutmeg and more liberally with salt and pepper. Add 1 oz cheese to the sauce and pour it over the eggs. Sprinkle thickly with cheese, and add a few tiny pieces of butter. Brown the surface in a hot oven or under the grill and serve.

4–5 helpings

CHEESE SOUFFLÉ (HOT)

A little butter for	3 oz grated cheese
greasing	Pinch of salt
1 oz butter	Pinch of cayenne
1 oz flour	pepper
¼ pt milk	1–2 egg whites
2 eggs	

Coat a soufflé dish well with butter and tie round it a well-buttered thickly folded piece of paper to support the soufflé when it rises above the level of the dish. Melt the 1 oz butter in a pan, stir in the flour, add the milk and bring to the boil. Remove from the heat, and mix in the 2 egg yolks, beat well, then stir in the cheese, add seasoning to taste. Whisk the egg whites to a stiff froth, add them lightly to the rest of the ingredients. Pour the mixture into the soufflé dish, and bake in a moderate oven (180°C, 350°F, Gas 4) for 30–35 min. Serve at once, in the dish in which it was baked.

5–6 helpings

COLD CHEESE SOUFFLÉ

¼ pt cream	2 egg whites
1 oz grated Parmesan	Good pinch of salt
cheese	Good pinch of cayenne

1 oz grated Cheddar	pepper
or Gruyère cheese	Tomato
½ gill aspic jelly	Gherkin

Whip the cream lightly, fold in all the cheese, the cold but not set aspic jelly, the stiffly-beaten egg whites and the seasoning. Pour into a small prepared soufflé dish and when set garnish with tiny pieces of tomato and gherkin.

4 helpings

OMELETS

There are two types of omelet: the French, which is flat and generally served folded into three, and the English which is fluffy and more like a soufflé.

The essentials in making either type are a thick, clean and dry omelet pan of the right size, i.e. 6–7 in diameter for a 2 or 3 egg omelet; butter; eggs; and seasoning.

For recipes for sweet omelets, use one of alternate basic recipes, and fill with fruit purée, jam or a liqueur-flavoured sweet butter.

For savoury omelets, use one of the two basic types, and fill or stuff the omelet before folding with a small amount of grated cheese, cooked meat or fish, with a little creamy sauce if liked.

FRENCH OMELETTE

2–3 eggs	½ oz butter
Salt and pepper	

Break the eggs into a basin. Add salt and pepper to taste. Beat the eggs with a fork until they are lightly mixed. Heat the butter in the pan and slowly let it get hot, but not so hot that the butter browns. Without drawing the pan off the heat, pour in the egg mixture. It will cover the pan and start cooking at once.

Shake the pan and stir the eggs with a fork away from the side to the middle. Shake again. In about 1 min the omelette will be soft but no longer runny. Let it stand for 4 or 5 seconds for the bottom to brown slightly. Then remove from the heat. Using a palette knife, fold the omelette from two sides over the middle. Then slip on to a hot dish, or turn it up-side down on to the dish.

This omelette can be eaten plain, or it can be filled. There are two methods of filling; flavouring such as herbs or cheese can be added to the eggs after they are beaten, or they can be added to the omelette just before it is folded.

Suggested savoury fillings (quantities given are for 2 egg omelettes)

Cheese Grate 2 oz hard cheese finely. Add most of it to the mixed eggs, saving a little to top the finished omelette.

Fines Herbes Finely chop 1 tablesp parsley and a few chives, and add this to the mixed eggs before cooking.

Onion Sauté a large onion in a little butter but do not get it too greasy. When cool, add to the egg mixture, saving a few hot morsels for garnishing the omelette.

Kidney Peel, core and cut 2 lamb's kidneys into smallish pieces, and sauté them in a little butter with a small chopped onion or shallot. Pile this mixture along the centre of the omelette after cooking but before folding.

Mushroom Wash and chop 2 oz mushrooms, sauté them in a little butter until tender. Put them along the centre of the cooked omelette.

Shellfish Shrimps, prawns, crayfish, lobster or crab, fresh or canned, can be used. Chop if necessary and warm slowly through in a little white sauce (or butter) so they are hot when the omelette is cooked. Then pile the mixture along the centre.

Spanish Make a mixture of chopped ham, tomato, sweet pepper, a few raisins, 1 or 2 mushrooms, and sauté in a little butter or olive oil. Add this to the egg before cooking; serve this omelette flat.

ENGLISH OMELET

Separate the eggs. Add half an egg-shell of water for each egg, to the yolks: beat them with a wooden spoon until creamy. Whisk the whites until they stay in the basin when turned upside down. Gently fold the whites into the yolks. Have the butter ready in the pan as for the French omelette. Pour in the egg mixture, and cook until it is golden brown on the underside. Then put the pan under the grill and lightly brown the top. Fillings are usually spread over the cooked omelet. Now run a palette knife round the edge of the pan. Fold the omelet over and slip on to a hot dish.

Savoury omelet with fish filling

SAVOURY BATTER

4 oz flour	Salt and pepper
1 egg	1 teasp finely chopped
½ pt milk	parsley
4 tablesp finely chopped	½ teasp mixed herbs
beef *or* mutton	

Mix the flour, egg, milk, salt and pepper into a smooth batter, let it stand for ½ hr. Then add the meat, parsley and herbs. Melt a little dripping in a Yorkshire pudding tin. Pour in the batter, and bake in a fairly hot oven (190°C, 375°F, Gas 5) until set.

For Yorkshire Pudding, use the batter without meat and herbs.

SAVOURY PANCAKES (1)

Batter as for	4 bacon rashers
Savoury Batter	Dripping

SAVOURY PANCAKES

Whilst the batter is standing for ½ hr, remove the rind from the bacon, cut the bacon into small pieces and fry gently. Remove from frying-pan and stir into the batter. Put a little dripping into the frying-pan and heat until smoking hot. Quickly pour in enough batter to coat the bottom of the pan evenly. Cook until brown underneath, turn and brown on the other side. Serve immediately.

4 helpings

SAVOURY PANCAKES (2)

1 small onion	2 tablesp milk
2 oz cheese	Salt and pepper
½ oz butter *or* margarine	Batter as for Savoury Batter

Grate the onion and cheese. Put into a saucepan, add the butter or margarine and stir in the milk. Season to taste. Heat gently until thoroughly hot.

Make the pancakes, spread with the hot filling and roll up. Serve immediately.

Use the same fillings for savoury pancakes as for omelets, see above.

4 helpings

CAULIFLOWER BEIGNETS OR FRITTERS

2 large cauliflowers	A few sprigs of parsley
1 tablesp salt to 2 qt water	Salt and pepper
Olive oil	Coating batter
	Frying fat

Trim and wash the cauliflowers and parboil them in salt and water. Drain thoroughly, divide into sprigs, place in a dish, sprinkle with olive oil, chopped parsley and seasoning. Allow to stand for 10–15 min. Then dip them in the batter below, and fry in lightly-smoking deep fat, taking care that they do not stick together.

Serve in pyramidal shape garnished with sprigs of parsley and lemon wedges.

Savoury pancakes with prawns

COATING BATTER

4 oz plain flour	1 gill warm water (approx)
Pinch of salt	
1 tablesp salad oil *or* melted butter	1 teasp baking powder

Sift together the flour and salt. Mix with the oil and water until the mixture is smooth and thick enough to beat. Beat well; then add water until the mixture is of a consistency to coat the back of a wooden spoon. Leave to stand for at least 30 min. Just before using, stir in the baking-powder.

Other vegetable beignets or fritters can be made and served in the same way. They make an attractive first course or light main-course supper dish.

8 helpings

SAVOURY PANCAKES WITH TUNA

1 large green pepper	4–5 oz commercial soured cream
1 oz butter	
1 oz flour	3 tablesp single fresh cream
1 7-oz can tuna fish, flaked	
4 oz prawns, peeled	Batter as for Savoury Batter
Salt and pepper	

Remove the stalk and seeds from the pepper. Cut into ¼ in pieces, and blanch in boiling salted water for 1 min. Drain. Melt the butter, add the flour and cook over moderate heat for 2 min. Blend in the flaked tuna, the prawns, blanched pepper, soured and single cream. Stir over gentle heat until hot but not boiling. Season to taste, and keep warm.

Make the pancakes. Heat a little dripping in a frying pan, pour in enough batter to coat the bottom and shake. Cook until brown, turn and brown the second side. Spread the pancakes with the filling, roll or fold them, and serve while hot.

4 helpings

SAUSAGES (COCKTAIL, FRANKFURTER AND LARGE)

Cocktail sausages are best baked. Separate the sausages, prick them with a fork and lay in a baking-tin. Bake without extra fat at 180°C, 350°F, Gas 4 for about 10 min until brown on top. Turn, and bake a further 7–10 min to brown the underneath.

Frankfurters are treated like large sausages (*see* below). Alternatively, they can be pricked and simmered in white wine with a pinch of thyme until tender (about 10 min).

Large sausages Prick large sausages first with a fork, throw into boiling water and simmer for 15 min. Put into a frying-pan containing a little hot fat, and fry gently, turning to brown on all sides. To fry large sausages heat slowly to prevent the sausages bursting.

SAUSAGE AND APPLE MASH

½ lb sausages	Pinch of curry powder
3 tomatoes, halved	1 teasp lemon juice
1 lb potatoes	Salt and pepper
1 oz butter	Chopped parsley
¼ pt apple purée	

Fry the sausages gently until brown all over and cooked thoroughly. Add the tomatoes to the pan and cook gently. Meanwhile, boil the potatoes, drain and mash well. Add the butter, heated apple purée, curry powder, lemon juice and seasoning and mix well. Spoon or pipe on to a warm serving dish, arrange the

Sausage and apple mash

MEAT BALLS

sausages and tomatoes on top and decorate with parsley.

Alternatively, leave out the tomatoes, and instead of adding apple purée to the potato, use plain mashed potato and add grilled apple slices to the dish as a garnish.

2 helpings

MEAT BALLS

1 small onion	1 teasp potato flour
A little lard	1½ teasp salt
4 oz raw beef	¼ teasp white pepper
2½ oz pork	1 teasp sugar
1–1½ cups milk	1–2 tablesp butter *or*
1 egg	cream (optional)
2 tablesp breadcrumbs	

Peel, slice and fry onions slightly in a little lard. Wash meat and pass 3 times through mincer, together with the fried onion or blend in an electric blender for a few seconds. Mix milk and egg; soak breadcrumbs and flour in this, add salt, pepper, sugar, cream or butter (if used) and finally the meat. Mix well. Make into small balls and fry brown, in butter or fat.

Meat balls are a favourite dish in Sweden and can be eaten fried or boiled with potato salad with various sauces; mushroom and tomato, etc.

4 helpings

'CREAM' CHEESE FLAN

Short crust pastry,	2 teasp sugar
frozen *or* using 6 oz	4 oz full fat soft cheese
flour, etc if home-made	¼ teasp grated lemon
¼ oz gelatine	rind
2 tablesp water	1 tablesp lemon juice
⅛ pt milk	¼ pt cream
1 egg yolk	

Line an 8-in flan ring with the pastry and bake 'blind'. Soak the gelatine in the water for 2–3 min. Heat the milk and dissolve the gelatine in it. Beat together the egg yolk and sugar and add the hot milk. Combine with the cheese, stir in the lemon rind and juice. Cool. Whip the cream and fold into cheese mixture. Pour into baked flan case; chill for 2 hr.

CHEESE AND ONION PIE

Short crust pastry,	½ oz flour
frozen *or* using 8 oz	Salt and pepper
flour, etc if home-	4 oz cheese
made	2 tablesp milk
3 small onions	

Parboil the onions whilst making the pastry. Line an 8-in fireproof plate with half the pastry. Mix the salt and pepper with the flour. Slice the onions and dip in the seasoned flour, spread them over the bottom of the lined plate. Grate the cheese and sprinkle it over the onion, add the milk. Wet the edge of the pastry, put on the cover and press the edges firmly together. Knock up the edges, decorate as desired and brush over with milk. Bake in a hot oven (220°C, 425°F, Gas 7) for about 40 min.

This can be made as an open tart if liked, using 4 oz flour, etc, for the pastry.

6–8 helpings

SCOTCH EGGS

3 hard-boiled eggs	Egg and breadcrumbs
½ lb sausage meat	Frying fat

Seafood flan

Shell the eggs and cover each egg with sausage meat. If liked, a little finely chopped onion can be mixed with the sausage meat before using. Coat carefully with beaten egg and breadcrumbs, fry in hot fat until nicely browned. Cut each egg in half. Scotch eggs can be served either hot or cold.

3 helpings

SEA FOOD FLAN

2 oz butter *or*	4 oz crushed plain
margarine	biscuits (cream
¼ teasp salt	crackers)
1 oz grated cheese	

FILLING

1 dessertsp gelatine	1 teasp finely chopped
½ 3 oz-can pink salmon	onion
or tuna	1 teasp finely chopped
6 sardines	parsley
1 gill mayonnaise	Salt and pepper to
2 tablesp tomato	taste
ketchup	

To make the flan case. Cream fat, salt and cheese together and knead in the crushed biscuits. Place mixture on a plate and mould it into a greased 7-in flan ring. Put into refrigerator until firmly set. Remove flan ring.

Cheese flan

Macaroni au gratin with bacon rolls

Dissolve gelatine in 3 tablesp hot water. Flake the salmon or tuna and sardines (free from bones) and mix together all ingredients for filling. When beginning to set, pour into prepared flan case. Decorate with hard-boiled egg and shelled prawns.

CHEESE FLAN

CHEESE PASTRY	FILLING
8 oz plain flour	1 egg
Pinch of salt and	$\frac{1}{4}$ pt milk
cayenne pepper	3 oz grated Cheddar
4 oz butter	cheese
4 oz grated Cheddar	Pinch of salt
cheese	A few grains cayenne
1 egg yolk	pepper
Little cold water to mix	

Sieve flour and seasonings into a basin. Rub in the butter until mixture resembles fine breadcrumbs. Stir in cheese, and bind together with egg yolk and water. Roll out on a floured board to $\frac{1}{4}$-in thick and line a greased sandwich tin, approx 8 in long and 1 in deep. Bake 'blind' filled with baking beans in a fairly hot oven (200°C, 400°F, Gas 6) for 20 min. Remove beans and greaseproof paper and return to oven for further 5 min. Cool, and remove flan from tin.

To make the filling, beat the egg, milk, most of the grated cheese and the seasoning together. Pour into the flan case, sprinkle with the remaining cheese, and bake in a fairly hot oven (200°C, 400°F, Gas 6) for about 20 min until the top is golden-brown. Serve hot.

4 helpings

SPAGHETTI WITH TOMATO SAUCE

1 lb spaghetti	1 lb fresh tomatoes *or*
1 large clove garlic	1 14 oz can tomatoes
(peeled)	Salt
2 tablesp oil	Sugar
Salt and pepper	

GARNISH
$\frac{1}{2}$ green pepper

Cook the spaghetti in a large saucepan of boiling, salted water until tender but still firm—about 12 min.

Meanwhile, heat the oil and fry crushed garlic gently without browning. Skin tomatoes if fresh or drain the can. Add to the pan with seasoning and a little sugar, cook for 5–7 min until thick.

Remove the seeds from pepper and cut into strips. Fry gently without browning. Place drained spaghetti in a hot dish, pile sauce in centre and garnish with pepper. Grated cheese can be served separately.

MACARONI AU GRATIN WITH BACON ROLLS

4 oz macaroni	Salt and pepper
1 pt white sauce	Browned breadcrumbs
4 oz grated cheese	*or* 1 oz finely grated
Bacon rashers	Cheddar cheese
	Butter

Break the macaroni into pieces about $1\frac{1}{2}$ in long, put them into rapidly boiling salted water and boil for about 20 min, or until the macaroni is tender. (If not required for immediate use, cover the macaroni with cold water to prevent the pieces sticking together.) Cover the bottom of a well-buttered baking-dish with white sauce, sprinkle liberally with cheese, seasoning to taste, and add a layer of macaroni. Repeat the layers, cover the last layer of macaroni thickly with sauce, sprinkle the surface lightly with breadcrumbs or extra grated cheese and add a few small pieces of butter. Bake in a hot oven (220°C, 425°F, Gas 7) for about 20 min.

Cut the rind off the rashers, roll each one up and place in a baking-tin with the cut ends underneath. Bake under the macaroni dish for 10–15 min until the bacon rolls are crisp. Use as a garnish, or serve separately.

6–7 helpings

RISOTTO

4 oz long-grain rice	Salt and pepper
1 small onion	2 tablesp grated
2 oz butter	Parmesan cheese
1 pt vegetable stock *or*	
water	

Wash and dry the rice thoroughly. Chop the

BAKED STUFFED POTATOES

onion finely; heat the butter and fry the onion until lightly browned. Then add the rice and fry it until brown. Put in the stock or water, add salt and pepper to taste, boil rapidly for 10 min and afterwards simmer slowly until the rice has absorbed all the liquid. Stir in the cheese, add more seasoning if necessary, then serve.

ALTERNATIVELY

½ lb long-grain rice	1 teasp salt
2 oz butter	¼ teasp pepper
1 small onion, finely chopped	Stock
½ teasp saffron	1 pt tomato sauce
Nutmeg	2 oz grated Parmesan cheese

Wash, drain and dry the rice thoroughly in a clean cloth. Heat the butter in a saucepan, put in the onion, and when lightly browned add the rice, and shake the pan over the heat for about 10 min. Then sprinkle in the saffron, a good pinch of nutmeg, salt and pepper. Cover with stock, and cook gently for about 1 hr adding meanwhile the tomato sauce and as much stock as the rice will absorb, the sauce being added when the rice is about half cooked. Just before serving stir in the cheese.

This savoury rice is frequently used for borders instead of plainly boiled rice or mashed potatoes.

Either of these recipes can be used as a main dish, accompanied by small bowls of chutney, cooked shrimps, shredded green peppers or canned red pimentos, sliced hard-boiled eggs and other hors d'oeuvre or salad ingredients. Each person can then choose which garnishes he prefers.

2–3 helpings

BAKED STUFFED POTATOES

6 large potatoes
CHOICE OF STUFFING

1 3 oz grated cheese; 1 oz butter *or* margarine; a little milk; seasoning; nutmeg
2 3 oz chopped, fried bacon; a little milk; seasoning
3 3 oz mashed, cooked smoked haddock; chopped parsley; lemon juice; a little milk; nutmeg

Baked stuffed potatoes

Sausage rolls

4 2 boned kippers, cooked and mashed; a little milk
5 2 oz grated cheese; 1 oz butter; chopped parsley; a little mild seasoning; 2 egg yolks stirred into the filling; 2 egg whites folded in at the end
6 3 oz minced meat, ½ small minced onion and seasoning, sautéed and mixed.

Scrub, rinse and dry the potatoes and grease them. With a small sharp knife, cut through the skin of the potatoes to give the appearance of a lid. Bake for about 1½ hr at 190°C, 375°F, Gas 5 until tender. Cool slightly. Lift off lids carefully, scoop out cooked potato from skins, including lids, taking care not to split the skins. Mash the potato in a basin and add the ingredients of any one of the stuffings listed above. Mix well and season thoroughly. Fill the potato skins with the mixture, piling it high. Fork the tops and brush with a little egg or sprinkle the tops with a little grated cheese (if an ingredient of the stuffing). Put back in the oven and bake till thoroughly hot and golden brown. Serve in a hot dish garnished with parsley and with the skin 'lids' replaced, if liked.

A stuffing consisting of cooked minced meat in a sauce or gravy, *or* of cooked mixed vegetables *or* flaked fish in a sauce may replace the floury meal of the potato entirely. The latter should then be mashed and served separately *or* mashed and piped round the opening of the potato after it has been stuffed and before returning it to the oven.

6 helpings

PARTY AND TV FOOD

SAUSAGE ROLLS

Puff pastry, frozen *or* using 4 oz of flour etc if home-made	½ lb sausages
	Egg yolk to glaze

Roll out the pastry and cut into 8 even-sized squares. Skin the sausages. Divide the sausage meat into 8 portions and make each piece into a roll the same length as the pastry. Place the sausage meat on the pastry, wet the edge and fold over leaving the ends open. Knock up the edges with the back of a knife. Make three incisions on top. Brush over with beaten egg and place on a baking-sheet. Bake in a hot oven (220°C, 425°F, Gas 7) until the pastry is well risen and brown. Reduce the heat and continue baking till the pastry is cooked.

Small sausage rolls can be quickly made by rolling the pastry into an oblong. Form the sausage meat into long rolls the length of the pastry, then divide the pastry into strips wide enough to encircle the meat. Damp one edge of each strip, fold over and press together firmly. Cut into rolls of the desired length, and finish as above.

Home-made sausage 'spiral' rolls are a decorative alternative. Use whole small sausages with skins. Roll out the pastry into a long strip about ½ in wide. Wrap pastry strip diagonally round and round each sausage leaving a small gap between strip edges. Bake as above.

HAMBURGERS

1 lb minced beef	Salt and pepper
½ cup dry breadcrumbs	1 small onion, minced
½ cup milk	

Mix together all the ingredients. Form mixture into 6 patties, brown quickly on both sides in hot fat, reduce heat and cook more slowly until done, turning occasionally. Serve in split toasted rolls.

CORNISH PASTIES

¼ lb raw meat	2 tablesp gravy or
¼ lb potatoes	water
½ teasp finely chopped	Short crust pastry,
onion	using 8 oz flour etc
Mixed herbs to taste	if home-made
Salt and pepper	

Mince the meat finely. Dice the potatoes. Add the onion, herbs, salt, pepper and gravy to the meat and potatoes, and mix well together. Divide the pastry into 8 equal portions and roll them out ¼-in thick, keeping the portions as round as possible. Pile the mixture in the centre of each piece of pastry, wet the edges and join them together on the top to form an upstanding frill, prick them with a fork. Bake in a

Sausage snacks

hot oven (220°C, 425°F, Gas 7) for 10 min, then reduce heat to moderate (180°C, 350°F, Gas 4) and cook for about 50 min longer.

5–6 helpings

SAUSAGE SNACKS

Cooked whole or halved, small sausages make attractive snacks when brightly garnished. Halve sausages crosswise and set each, cut side down, on a small toasted croûte. Spear whole sausages on wooden cocktail picks, and stick these into a large grapefruit or small melon with a thin slice cut from the bottom so that it stands level. Top sausages with maraschino cherries, pickled onions, cheese cubes and chunks of canned pineapple.

Frankfurter sausages can be treated in the same way, or can be split lengthwise and filled with cream cheese before being speared on cocktail sticks.

PASTRY CASES

Vol-au-vent or patty cases filled with savoury mixtures are excellent for first courses and also for TV suppers and for buffet parties. They can be served hot or cold. If a mixture is being put into cold pastry cases, make sure it is quite cold. If, on the other hand, it is being put into hot pastry cases, heat the filling and the pastry separately, and put together at the last minute, so that the filling does not make the pastry soft.

Vol-au-vent cases can be bought uncooked, frozen, or ready to use. They can also, of course, be made at home, using frozen or home-made puff pastry.

HOT VOL-AU-VENT OR TOASTED SANDWICH FILLINGS

Hot vols-au-vent and toasted sandwiches (see below) cannot have fillings which melt easily and run out of the casing. Here are types of fillings from which you can develop others:

CHICKEN FILLING

1 × 3 oz pkt full fat soft	1 small onion, peeled
cheese	and sliced
1 chicken joint, cooked	

Divide the cheese into six portions (for two sandwiches or 6 vols-au-vent). Cut the chicken into bite-sized pieces. Fry the onion rings gently until tender.

On two slices of bread or in six vols-au-vent, lay (a) onion rings (b) a little cheese. Lay on these two more slices of bread if making sandwiches. Add the chicken and remaining cheese. Top sandwiches with a third slice of bread each, vols-au-vent with 'hats'. Toast sandwiches on both sides, and heat vols-au-vent in a gentle oven.

BACON AND MUSHROOM FILLING

6 rashers streaky bacon	¼ lb mushrooms,
1 × 3 oz pkt full fat soft	sautéed in butter
cheese	Salt and pepper

Chop the bacon and fry until crisp. Chop the mushrooms and add them. Season, and cool.

Mix half the cheese with the bacon bits, and half with the mushrooms. Spread bacon and cheese between two slices of bread or in the lower halves of 6 vols-au-vent. Top each second slice of bread or fill the upper half of each vol-au-vent with the mushroom-cheese mixture. Top with two more slices of bread or vol-au-vent 'hats'. Toast or heat as in previous recipe.

SANDWICHES

SAUSAGE AND APPLE FILLING

2 medium onions, peeled and chopped	2 teasp mixed herbs
1 lb sausage meat	Salt and pepper
2 apples, peeled, cored and chopped	1 beaten egg
1 tablesp chopped parsley	Melted butter

Sauté the onions in the butter for 4–5 min. Add sausage meat, apples, parsley, herbs and seasoning, and fry a further 3 min. Cool slightly, and add the beaten egg. Pile on toasted bread or in vol-au-vent or patty cases and bake in a moderate oven (350°F, Gas 4) for 10–15 min or until just set. Top with toasted bread or a pastry 'hat' if appropriate.

4 savouries

SANDWICHES

The term 'sandwich' has a much wider meaning today than when it was first introduced by the Earl of Sandwich, and applied only to slices of meat placed between bread and butter. We have now 'Open' or Continental sandwiches, Club or Two-decker sandwiches, Toasted sandwiches and attractively-shaped Party sandwiches. Their fillings are now immensely varied, savoury or sweet, minced, or shredded and mixed with various butters, sauces and seasonings.

Making sandwiches requires little skill, just plenty of imagination and an eye for colour.

For sandwiches the bread should be fresh but not too new; French rolls, Vienna rolls, wholemeal or milk bread make an interesting change from ordinary loaves. Creamed butter is more easily spread than ordinary butter. When ordinary butter is used it should first be beaten to a cream (add 1 teasp hot water to ½ lb butter) to make spreading easier. Savoury butters give piquancy and variety to other fillings, and can be used alone for rolled sandwiches.

Sandwiches simplify entertaining, for they can be prepared well in advance and can be served buffet-style, leaving the hostess free to mix with her guests. If prepared some time before required, sandwiches keep fresh and moist if wrapped in greaseproof paper and then in a damp cloth, or if put into a polythene bag, or wrapped in waxed paper or aluminium foil, and kept in the fridge or a cool place. Sandwiches with different fillings should be wrapped separately to prevent the flavours mixing.

SANDWICH FILLINGS
SAVOURY FILLINGS

1 Anchovies mixed with hard-boiled egg yolk, cheese and butter, with a sprinkling of cayenne. Spread the bread with curry butter.

2 Canned tuna fish mixed with salad cream, and chopped parsley, with a dash of cayenne.

3 Canned salmon, mashed with lemon juice and

Apple-peanut open sandwich

Cold table with
open sandwiches

chopped chives, spread on a bed of cucumber slices.

4 Minced cooked smoked haddock, seasoned and mixed to a smooth paste with butter and anchovy paste.

5 Very thin slices of cooked chicken and ham, seasoned and placed between bread spread with curry butter.

6 Very finely shredded celery, moistened slightly with canned or double cream, seasoned to taste.

7 Finely grated cheese, mixed to a smooth paste with a little seasoning, anchovy essence or paste, and butter.

8 A layer of finely chopped gherkin, olives and capers, mixed with mayonnaise sauce, covered with a layer of full-fat soft cheese.

9 Mashed sardines, a little lemon juice and seasoning, mixed to a smooth paste with butter.

10 Sardines mashed with an equal amount of grated cheese until smooth; seasoned to taste, with a little lemon juice or vinegar added and sufficient cream or milk to moisten.

11 Minced cooked chicken and ham or tongue, combined with full-fat soft cheese and egg yolk, seasoned and moistened with oil.

12 Finely shredded lettuce and watercress, seasoned with salt and mixed with mayonnaise.

13 Thin slices of Gruyère cheese on slices of bread and butter, spread with French mustard, seasoned with pepper.

14 Slices of hard-boiled egg, seasoned, covered with watercress or mustard and cress, sprinkled with equal quantities of oil and vinegar.

15 Canned foie gras.

16 Minced cooked chicken and ham or tongue, moistened with a little liquid butter and mayonnaise.

17 Lightly spread caviare, sprinkled with lemon juice and a little cayenne. The bread may be spread with shrimp butter.

SWEET FILLINGS

1 Bananas mashed with lemon juice and ground almonds and sprinkled with sugar.

2 A layer of full-fat soft cheese or cottage cheese, covered with a layer of fresh strawberries or raspberries sprinkled with castor sugar.

3 Softened creamed cheese, mixed with canned crushed pineapple and finely chopped preserved ginger.

4 Chocolate spread, mixed with chopped walnuts and cottage cheese.

5 Chopped pears, dates and walnuts, mixed with golden syrup.

6 Thick slices of banana sprinkled with coarsely grated chocolate.

OPEN SANDWICHES

Use $\frac{1}{4}$-in thick slices of white or brown bread. Spread with softened butter, and with any of the party sandwich fillings below. Garnish with stuffed olives, slices of hard-boiled egg, small pieces of tomato, watercress, piped cream cheese, etc.

The appeal of these sandwiches lies in the artistic way in which the garnish is arranged. They must look colourful, fresh and tempting. Remember that garnishes stay fresher if arranged vertically, and if kept under damp paper or cloth until serving time.

SAVOURY SCANDINAVIAN GARNISHES

1 Samsoe cheese with radish.

2 Tongue with Russian salad, cucumber and a twist of tomato.

3 Egg and crisply fried bacon, with cucumber and a twist of tomato.

4 Liver pâté with mushrooms sautéed in butter, shreds of crisply fried bacon, tomato, lettuce and gherkin.

5 Pork luncheon meat with horseradish cream, and an orange butterfly.

6 Danish blue cheese with black grapes.

7 Salami (without garlic) with raw onion rings and chopped parsley.

8 Pork luncheon meat with young carrots, peas in

HOT SAVOURY TOASTS

mayonnaise and cucumber.

9 Danish blue cheese with chopped apple coated with French dressing, topped with a parsley sprig.

TWO-DECKER SANDWICHES

Either brown or white bread may be used for club or double-decker sandwiches. Cut the slices thinly—three slices for each sandwich. Butter the slices thickly—the middle slice should be buttered on both sides—spread with 2 fillings and sandwich together. Press together firmly so that the layers stick to each other. These sandwiches may be served plain or toasted, hot or cold, and knives and forks should be provided.

FILLINGS

1 *1st layer* Slices of cold roast beef, seasoned and spread with horseradish sauce.

2nd layer Watercress with thin slices of drained, pickled beetroot.

2 *1st layer* A slice of Cheddar cheese spread with mango chutney.

2nd layer A mixture of grated raw apple and mayonnaise.

3 *1st layer* Cooked skinless pork sausage split lengthwise.

2nd layer Grilled mushrooms.

TOASTED SANDWICHES

Toasted sandwiches make excellent dishes for TV or late-night suppers, and are economical to produce since leftovers can often be used.

To make them, you can toast the bread on both sides, butter one side of each slice and fill with a hot or cold, separately prepared filling.

Alternatively, toast the bread slices by grilling, on one side only. Spread a suitable filling, such as grated cheese mixed with apple slices and peanut butter, all over the untoasted side. Make sure the filling covers the bread. Grill the filling until crisp or bubbling. Top with a piece of bread toasted on both sides and decorate to choice; for instance, with fried or raw onion rings, tomato slices and watercress. (See also Hot Vol-au-Vent fillings above.)

HOT SAVOURY TOASTS

1½ lb chipolata sausages	6 slices bread
5 rashers bacon	1 oz melted butter
2 tomatoes, sliced	Sprigs of parsley
2 ripe dessert apples, cored and sliced	

Line a grill pan with foil. Cook the sausage and bacon rashers (rolled up) slowly for 10 minutes under the grill. Add the tomatoes and apple rings. Cut rings from the slices of bread with a plain cutter, and toast them. Brush the tomato and apple slices with melted butter and return to the grill until the apple rings are soft and the whole dish is cooked. Arrange two sausages on each round of toast, top with an apple ring and a slice of tomato. Serve garnished with the bacon rolls and with sprigs of parsley.

3 helpings

Hot savoury toasts

Section 2
Fish Dishes

Fish is rich in protein, essential minerals and some vitamins. It is excellent food value, and most kinds of fish are cheap compared with meat.

We eat less fish than we should because it must be transported home and cooked while as fresh as possible, which may be a nuisance. It can also be messy to handle and, if it is carelessly cooked, may be tasteless. However, today, many people can get prepared frozen fish which (although more expensive than fresh fish) lessens these difficulties; and all fish is quick, cheap and easy to cook well. It can be used with many different easily obtained flavourings, or with small amounts of sauce or a garnish which may be leftovers; there is no excuse for either sea- or fresh-water fish dishes to be dull.

All fish can be used for breakfasts, midday meals and evening ones alike.

White fish, being almost fatless, is easily digested and is excellent food for children, invalids and slimmers.

CHOOSING FRESH FISH
Check on these points for freshness

1 that the flesh is firm, not flabby

2 that the fish does not smell stale

3 that the eyes are bright (not sunken) and the gills (of most kinds) are red

4 that the skin is moist (but not with yellowish, smelly slime, signalling decay)

BUYING FISH
The price of fish varies widely with the weather and the fishermen's luck. The boats must find shoals of sea fish at a place and time when they can get them back to port. So a particular kind of fish may be scarce and costly when others are cheap.

Luckily for housewives, many white fish are interchangeable, so if you cannot get one kind, buy a similar cut of some other.

When buying, check

1 that whole fish are not over-large (they may be old and coarse)

2 that flat fish are thick for their size

3 that the cut chosen has little bone and waste tissue (such as fins)

When having fish prepared by a fishmonger, ask for the bones and head for stock. You have paid for them.

STORING FISH
1 If you *must* refrigerate fresh fish, cover it; the smell taints other food.

2 Do not re-freeze thawed frozen fish. Packets still frozen hard will keep in the freezer compartment of the fridge for a short time; follow the 'star rating' on the refrigerator, or the manufacturer's directions.

CLEANING AND PREPARING FISH
Scrape off any scales on both sides. Hold the fish by the tail and scrape downwards, from tail to head, with the back of a knife. Rinse often to remove loose scales.

Make a semi-circular cut below the head if you wish to remove it. Cut it off.

Round fish With scissors or a sharp knife, slit the belly from just below the head to halfway to the tail. Remove the entrails and discard them. Keep the roe. Wash the fish, and rub with a little salt to remove any black tissues. Take out the eyes if the head is left on.

Flat fish Cut off the fins, remove the gills. Cut open the belly just below the head on the dark side. Remove and throw away the entrails. Rinse the fish well.

37

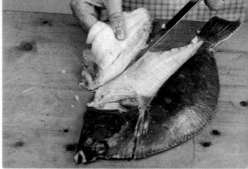

FILLETING PLAICE
Left, *slitting*
flesh
Right, *removing*
first fillet

SKINNING FISH

Keep the fish wet. Cut off a narrow strip of skin over and along the backbone near the tail. Make another cut just below the head and loosen the skin below the head with the point of a sharp knife. Dip the fingers in salt to give a better grip and gently pull off the skin, working towards the tail. Keep the thumb of the right hand well pressed over the backbone to prevent the removal of the flesh with the skin. Remove the skin from the other side in the same way.

To skin whole flat fish The dark skin of sole is always removed but not necessarily the white. The skin of turbot is usually cut off after filleting.

Keep the fish wet. With whole flat fish begin at the tail. Cut the skin across, but do not cut into the flesh. Loosen the skin along the fins on either side with the fingers. Then tear off the skin with the left hand, keeping the thumb of the right hand well pressed over the backbone to prevent the removal of the flesh with the skin.

CUTTING STEAKS FROM FISH

Middle cuts are the most fleshy, and best. Pat the fish dry with a cloth or absorbent paper. Hold firmly, using a little salt or a cloth to help you grip the fish. Use a sharp knife, and cut through the fish with a sawing movement, especially to cut through the backbone. Trim any flakes or scraps of skin from the cut sides with scissors.

FILLETING FISH

A fillet is virtually a whole piece of fish taken from shoulder to tail; if a fillet is cut up, the resulting pieces are, correctly speaking, called 'pieces' or 'portions'. Four fillets are obtained from flat fish and two from round fish.

Flat fish Place the fish flat on a board or table, and with the point of a sharp, flexible knife cut the flesh from head to tail down the

backbone. Next insert the knife in the slit made, and carefully separate the flesh from the bone, keeping the knife pressed lightly against the bone meanwhile. Remove the fillet, turn the fish round, remove the second fillet from tail to head, then turn the fish over and remove the other two fillets in the same way.

Round fish With a sharp knife slit the fish down the centre back to the bone. Working from head to tail, cut along the belly, cutting the flesh cleanly from the bones by keeping the knife pressed against the bones. Remove the fillet from the other side in the same way.

To skin fillets place them on a board skin side down. Rub a little salt on the fingers of the left hand, take a firm hold of the tail in the left hand, and with a knife in the right hand, and using a 'sawing' movement, peel the flesh away from the skin, working from tail to head.

Always use the skin and bones for making fish stock.

BAKING FISH

Baking is a good way of cooking almost any whole round white fish of small or medium size, or a middle cut from a larger one, or steaks or fillets.

Place the cleaned and washed fish in a well-greased baking-tin or oven-proof dish, with a little fat or oil brushed over it. Cover with greased greaseproof paper. Bake in a fairly hot oven (about 190°C, 375°F, Gas 5).

Cooking time will depend on the size and thickness of the fish. Average times are:

Fillets 10–20 min, depending on thickness.

Whole fish and cuts 10 min per lb and 10 min over for weights up to 4 lb. Frozen fish can be baked like fresh fish, but, if still frozen, allow 10–20 min longer, according to the thickness of the fish. Thaw fillets enough to separate before cooking.

FILLETING PLAICE
Left, *slitting*
second side.
Right, *removing*
third fillet

Top, *coating fillets with batter*
Below, *egging and crumbing*

Oiling cod steaks for grilling

STEAMING FISH

Stuffed fish take a little longer to cook than unstuffed fish.

To stuff fish enlarge the belly cavity if required but do not cut through the backbone. Fill the cavity with the stuffing. Either leave the cavity sides open, or skewer or sew them together to hold in the stuffing. Do not stuff the cavity full if the stuffing is likely to swell.

Baked fish can be served with its cooking liquor or with any of the sauces recommended in the special section. Choose a mild sauce for delicately flavoured fish, and a stronger one such as mustard sauce for river fish which may have a muddy flavour in themselves (e.g. carp).

BOILING AND POACHING FISH

The term 'boiled' fish is really a misnomer. Strictly speaking, fish should *never be boiled*; the water should just simmer gently *below boiling* point.

The ideal way to poach fish is to use a fish kettle, i.e. a large pan fitted with a strainer, so that the fish can be gently lifted out without breaking. If no fish kettle is available, use a large saucepan. Tie the fish loosely in clean muslin, for easy removal, and place on a plate on the bottom of the pan.

Salmon and salmon trout should be put into boiling salted water, to preserve their colour; but other kinds of fish should be placed in warm water, because boiling water has a tendency to break the skin, and cold water extracts much of the flavour.

Cook the fish in just sufficient water to cover the fish (this should afterwards be used as a basis for fish soup or fish sauce) as soluble nutrients diffuse out into the cooking water. For each quart of water add 1 tablesp vinegar and 2 level teasp salt. Lemon juice added to the water when cooking white fish tends to improve its whiteness.

When boiling point is reached, reduce the heat immediately and allow the fish to simmer gently in water just below the boil. The time required for cooking depends more on the thickness than on the weight of the fish. Allow 10–15 min per lb.

STEAMING FISH

Steaming is an excellent way of cooking fish: although it is slower than boiling, the flavour is better preserved, and the danger of the fish being broken is much less. If using a steamer, a piece of greased greaseproof paper placed in the bottom will make it easier to remove the fish after cooking. Season the prepared fish and sprinkle with lemon juice.

When a small quantity of fish has to be steamed, the following very easy method gives

SKINNING FISH

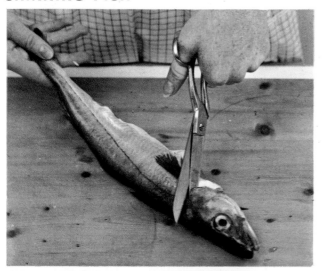

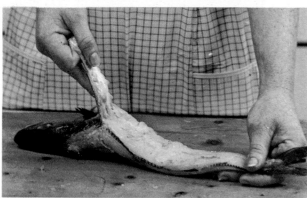

SKINNING FISH
Reading from top: 1, cutting skin.
2, loosening skin. 3, stripping skin.
4, stripping second side off

excellent results. Place the fish on a well-greased soup plate. Sprinkle lightly with salt, pepper and lemon juice, and cover with a piece of oiled greaseproof paper. Place the plate over a saucepan of boiling water (or over the pan of potatoes if serving potatoes with the fish) and cover with another plate or the lid of the saucepan. Steam for 10–25 min, depending on the thickness of the fish. Turn the fish once during cooking. Serve with the fish liquor or a fish sauce made from the liquor.

STEWING FISH

Stewing should be a gentle simmering in a small quantity of fish stock made from bone and fish trimmings, or in milk and water, until the flesh comes easily away from the bones. The liquid in which the fish has been simmered may be flavoured and thickened and used as a sauce. This is one of the most economical and flavoursome ways of cooking fish. Fish should invariably be stewed in a fireproof or earthenware dish.

GRILLING FISH

This method of cooking is an extremely simple one. It is suitable for steaks, cutlets or fillets and small whole fish, such as herring, plaice and sole.

The fish should be thoroughly dried, then liberally brushed over with a little oil or melted fat and seasoned with salt and pepper. Score deep gashes across whole fish to allow the heat to penetrate, or the outside may dry up before the fish is cooked.

Heat the grill and grease the grill rack to prevent the fish sticking. Cook the fish rather slowly, turning carefully until done. Allow 7–8 min for thin fillets and 10–15 min for steaks and thicker pieces of fish.

FRYING FISH

This method is suitable for fillets, steaks and small whole fish.

The fish to be fried should be well dried after washing or wiping, and should first be coated to prevent the fat from soaking into the fish. It may be coated with egg and breadcrumbs, milk or beaten egg and seasoned flour, or, if to be fried in deep fat, it may be coated with batter.

Shallow frying is better for thick slices or steaks, which require longer cooking to ensure that they are cooked through.

There should be enough fat in the pan to come half-way up the fish. Heat the fat, put in the coated fish and fry until golden-brown on one side, then turn and brown the other side. Allow 6–8 min for fillets and 8–12 min for larger pieces.

Deep frying requires a deep frying-pan with a frying basket or deep heavy pan with a per-

Oily fish gashed for grilling

forated spoon to remove the fish from the hot fat. The fat should be very hot, but its temperature must be slightly lower when frying fish fillets than when frying croquettes, rissoles, etc., which are usually composed of cooked fish. When the surface of a small piece of bread immediately hardens and slightly changes its colour on being immersed in the fat, the temperature is correct for raw food or anything thickly coated with batter, but when frying anything of which the exterior only has to be cooked, it is better to have the fat sufficiently hot to brown at once whatever is immersed in it. Heat the basket, if used, in the fat, but gently drop the coated fish into the fat—do not place directly on the basket or the coating will stick to the wires of the basket.

Do not try to fry too much fish at a time as this reduces the temperature of the fat and the result will be pale, greasy fish.

Anything fried should afterwards be well drained on kitchen paper.

Fish is usually garnished with lemon and parsley; croquettes with parsley alone.

CARVING FISH

Brill and John Dory, *see* Turbot.

Cod Cut in fairly thick slices through to the centre bone and detach just above it. The parts about the backbone and shoulders are the firmest.

Eel The thickest parts are considered the best.

Mackerel First cut along the backbone of the fish. Then insert the fish-knife at this part and cut through, separating the upper half of the fish, which may be divided; when the fish is of moderate size, serve for two helpings only. Next remove the backbone, tail and head, and divide the lower half.

Plaice First run the knife down the centre of the fish. Then cut downwards to the bone and remove 'fillets' from each side. Next take away the backbone and head of the fish, and divide the lower half in the same way.

Salmon First run the knife down the centre of the back and along the whole length of the fish. Then cut downwards from the backbone to the middle of the fish, cut through the centre and remove the pieces from the back. Next cut the lower part of the fish in the same way. A slice of the thick part should always be accompanied by a smaller piece of the thin from the belly, where the fat of the fish lies.

Sole The usual way of serving the fish is to cut quite through, bone and all, distributing it in neat pieces. The middle part is generally thought better than either head or tail. The head must be discarded.

Turbot First slice down the thickest part of the fish, quite through to the bone, and then cut slices out towards the sides of the fish. When the carver has removed all the meat from the upper side of the fish, the backbone should be raised, and the under side served in portions.

Whiting, Haddock, etc. Whiting, pike, haddock and similar fish, when sufficiently large, may be carved in slices from each side of the backbone in the same way as salmon, each fish serving for four or more slices. When small, they may be cut through, bone and all, and helped in pieces. A small whiting is served whole; a middle-sized fish in two pieces.

Crab, lobster and other shellfish cannot be carved, but for most dishes the meat is taken out of the shell. The method of doing this is described under the appropriate heading below.

BAKED FISH DISHES

BAKED BREAM OR HADDOCK WITH RICE AND OLIVE STUFFING

1 × 2–3 lb fresh sea bream or haddock—cleaned

STUFFING

2 oz butter	¼ level teasp thyme
1 onion	1½ oz stuffed olives,
2 sticks celery	chopped
4 oz cooked rice	Salt and pepper to
¼ level teasp sage	taste

GARNISH

Cooked rice	Creamed potatoes
Tomatoes	Parsley
Lemon	Streaky bacon

Scale the haddock and trim the fins and tail. Leave the head on, but remove the eyes. To make the stuffing, melt the butter in a pan, add the finely chopped onion and celery and sauté for about 3 min. Add the rice and the remaining ingredients and cook gently for a further 3 min. Stuff the fish with this mixture then place the fish, with the tail curled inwards, in a well-greased baking tin. Cover with greased paper or strips of bacon and bake in a fairly hot oven (190°C, 375°F, Gas 5) for 30–40 min. Serve on a bed of rice garnished with quarters of tomatoes, lemon wedges, creamed potatoes and parsley.

4–6 helpings

BAKED STUFFED CONGER EEL

2 lb conger eel	Butter *or* fat
Veal forcemeat	Flour

Wash and dry the fish thoroughly, skin and stuff it with the forcemeat and bind it with tape. Melt the butter or fat in a baking-dish or tin, put in the fish and baste well. Bake gently for 1 hr, basting occasionally with fat and dredging the surface with flour. Serve with the gravy poured round, or if preferred with tomato or caper sauce.

4–5 helpings

FISH CREAM

3 oz cooked *or* uncooked	½ oz flour
white fish (whiting,	½ gill milk
fresh haddock, cod,	1 egg yolk
all suitable)	2 tablesp cream *or*
½ oz butter	evaporated milk
Salt and pepper	

Chop, mince or pound the fish until very smooth. Heat the butter in a saucepan. Add the flour and cook for 2 min. Gradually add the milk and cook until mixture thickens, stirring well. Add fish, egg yolk, cream and seasoning. Put into a greased basin or mould and steam for 45 min or cover with buttered paper and bake in a warm oven (170°C, 335°F, Gas 3), for same time. Serve with white sauce. This dish is suitable for invalids.

1 helping

GREY MULLET OR TROUT EN PAPILLOTES

4 grey mullet *or* trout	1 tablesp lemon juice
Salt and pepper	

Prepare the fish, sprinkle the insides with salt and pepper and wrap carefully in well-oiled greaseproof paper or aluminium foil, twisting the ends securely. Place on a baking-sheet and bake for about 15–20 min in a fairly hot oven (190°C, 375°F, Gas 5). When cooked, loosen the paper carefully and place the fish on a hot dish. Add the lemon juice to the liquid which has collected in the paper, pour this over the fish and serve. Garnish with slices of lemon and sprigs of parsley.

If liked, the mullet or trout may be stuffed with a mixture of 1 oz fresh breadcrumbs, 1 level tablesp grated onion, 1 level dessertsp chopped parsley, salt and pepper to taste, moistened with a little milk. Allow a little longer cooking time.

4 helpings

BAKED HADDOCK AND ORANGE

1 orange	Juice of 1 lemon
1½ lb fillet of haddock	2 level teasp cornflour
Salt	½ level teasp sugar

Grate the rind from the orange, remove the pith and cut pulp across into slices. Cut the fish into convenient portions for serving. Arrange in a greased dish. Sprinkle with a little salt, add the lemon juice and arrange the slices of orange over the top. Cover with greased paper and cook in a fairly hot oven (200°C, 400°F, Gas 6) for 15–20 min. Strain off the liquor and make up to ¼ pt with water. Blend the cornflour with this, add the grated orange rind and sugar, and bring to the boil, stirring constantly. Boil gently for 3 min, correct the seasoning and serve with the fish.

4 helpings

BAKED HADDOCK WITH VEAL FORCEMEAT STUFFING

1 medium-sized fresh	1 egg
haddock	Browned breadcrumbs
"Veal forcemeat" *(page 248)*	Fat for basting

Wash, clean and scale the fish. Stuff the forcemeat inside the haddock and sew up the opening. Skewer the fish into the shape of the letter 'S' and brush over with beaten egg, coat lightly with browned breadcrumbs and bake in a moderate oven (180°C, 350°F, Gas 4–5) for 30–40 min, basting occasionally

Preparing trout en papillotes

Baked haddock with forcemeat stuffing

with hot fat. Serve with anchovy, tomato or melted butter sauce.

4 helpings

BAKED FROZEN HADDOCK FILLETS WITH CUCUMBER SAUCE

1 × 13-oz carton frozen haddock fillets	½ pt milk
	Salt and pepper
	Cucumber sauce

Partially thaw and separate the fillets into suitable portions for serving. Place in a baking-tin, cover with the milk, season and bake for 20 min in a fairly hot oven (190°C, 375°F, Gas 5). When cooked, place the fillets on a serving-dish and keep warm while making the Cucumber Sauce. Pour the sauce over the fish before serving.

BAKED FRESH HERRINGS WITH SUET STUFFING

6 herrings	¼ teasp grated lemon rind
2 tablesp breadcrumbs	
1 tablesp finely chopped suet	Salt and pepper
	Milk
1 teasp chopped parsley	

Sole à la Portugaise

Sole à la Portugaise

SOLE À LA PORTUGAISE

TOPPING

1 tablesp melted butter	2 tablesp breadcrumbs

Wash and split the herrings and remove the backbone. Mix together the breadcrumbs, suet, parsley and lemon rind, season to taste and add enough milk to moisten. Season each herring with salt and pepper, spread on a thin layer of the forcemeat and fold up in original shape. Pack closely in a greased pie-dish, and top each with a liberal spoonful of breadcrumbs. Sprinkle with melted butter. Cover with greased paper and bake for 20 min in a moderate oven (180°C, 350°F, Gas 4). Serve hot, with buttered toast and grilled tomatoes.

5 helpings

HERRINGS TAILS-IN-AIR

4 herrings	1 green pepper, seeded and sliced
2 oz fresh breadcrumbs	
1 small onion, grated	A little milk if needed
1 level tablesp chopped parsley	Salt and pepper to taste
1 small tomato, chopped	¼–½ pt tomato soup, fresh or canned
1 onion, sliced	

Scale the herrings and remove the heads, then clean and bone them but leave the tails on. Keep the roes. Trim the tails and cut off the fins with kitchen scissors. Chop the roes and mix with the crumbs, grated onion, chopped parsley and tomato; season and bind with milk if needed. Lay the herrings flat on a board, put 1 tablesp stuffing on the head end of each and roll up towards the tail. Place tightly in a deep fireproof dish, and scatter over the sliced onion and green pepper. Pour the soup over. Cover the dish, and bake in a fairly hot oven (200°C, 400°F, Gas 6) for 30 min.

4 helpings

BAKED MACKEREL

2 large-sized mackerel	Flour
"Veal" forcemeat	Salt and pepper
1 oz butter or sweet dripping	

Clean the fish and take out the roes. Stuff with the forcemeat and sew up the opening. Put them with the roes into a fireproof dish. Add the butter or dripping, dredge with flour, sprinkle well with salt and pepper and bake in a moderate oven (180°C, 350°F, Gas 4) for 30–40 min, basting occasionally. Serve with parsley sauce, or melted butter with a little lemon juice added, and with finely chopped parsley. A 2–3 lb shad can be cooked in the same way, topped with 2–3 rashers of bacon. Scale before baking, and bake for about 30 min.

3–4 helpings

SOLE À LA PORTUGAISE

1 medium-sized sole	1 onion
1 oz butter	2–3 tomatoes
1 shallot	1 dessertsp grated Parmesan cheese
1 teasp finely chopped parsley	
½ teasp anchovy essence	1 dessertsp browned breadcrumbs
Salt and pepper	Extra butter

Skin the sole and make an incision down the centre as for filleting; raise the flesh from the bone on each side as far as possible. Mix the butter, finely chopped shallot, parsley and anchovy essence well together, and stuff the mixture inside the sole. Place the fish in a buttered fireproof dish, season. Arrange slices of onion and tomato alternately and overlapping each other, on top of the fish; or if less onion is preferred, surround each slice of tomato with a single ring of onion. Mix together the cheese and breadcrumbs and sprinkle over the fish. Place small pieces of butter on top, cover with lid or greased paper and bake for about 20 min in a moderate oven (180°C, 350°F, Gas 4).

Fillets of sole can be laid on a bed of the stuffing and cooked in the same way. Omit the onion and tomato rings if desired.

2 helpings

BAKED SOLE WITH SHRIMPS

1 medium-sized sole	1 egg
¼ pt shelled shrimps	A little white sauce or
1 dessertsp white	milk
breadcrumbs	Pale brown
Cayenne pepper	breadcrumbs
Salt	A little butter
1 teasp anchovy essence	

Remove the skin from the sole, make an incision down the centre back as for filleting, and raise as far as possible the flesh on each side. Chop the shrimps coarsely, add the breadcrumbs, cayenne, salt (if necessary), anchovy essence, half the egg and sufficient white sauce or milk to moisten. Press the mixture lightly inside the fish, and instead of drawing the two sides together, fill the gap between them with forcemeat and flatten the surface of it to the level of the fish. Brush over with the remainder of the egg, coat lightly with pale brown breadcrumbs. Place in a fireproof dish, dot with a few small pieces of butter and bake for about 20–25 min in a fairly hot oven (190°C, 375°F, Gas 5).

2–3 helpings

FILLETS OF SOLE WITH SUET FORCEMEAT

4 fillets of sole or plaice	¼ teasp mixed herbs
or whiting	1 egg
2 tablesp breadcrumbs	Salt and pepper
1 tablesp finely chopped	Pale brown
suet	breadcrumbs
1 dessertsp finely	Butter
chopped parsley	

Wipe fillets with a clean damp cloth. Mix the other ingredients together with sufficient beaten egg to moisten. Spread a thin layer of forcemeat on each fillet and fold in two. Place the fillets in a fireproof baking-dish and fill up the spaces between with the rest of the forcemeat. Sprinkle lightly with pale brown breadcrumbs, add a few small pieces of butter and bake for about 30 min in a moderate oven (180°C, 350°F, Gas 4). Serve in the cooking dish.

4 helpings

SOLE AU GRATIN

2 fillets or 1 large sole	Canned mushrooms,
Salt and pepper	sliced
¼ glass white wine	White Italian sauce
Lemon juice	Browned breadcrumbs
Mushroom liquor	Butter
1 teasp chopped parsley	

If using a whole sole, skin both sides, cut off the head and fins and make several incisions with a knife across one side of the fish. Place fish on a well-buttered fireproof dish (if using whole fish place cut side uppermost), season with pepper and salt, add the white wine, a few drops of lemon juice, a little mushroom liquor and some chopped parsley. Slice

the mushrooms and place in a row down the centre of the fish. Cover with White Italian Sauce. Cover with browned breadcrumbs, dot a few tiny bits of butter on top of the fish and bake in a moderate oven (180°C, 350°F, Gas 4) for 20–30 min, according to size of sole.

2–3 helpings

SOLE OR PLAICE AUX FINES HERBES

Eight 2 oz fillets of sole	½ pt white wine sauce
or plaice	1 tablesp finely chopped
4 tablesp fish stock or	fresh herbs
court bouillon	Salt and pepper

Wipe the fillets with a clean, damp cloth, season with salt and pepper and fold them in three. Place in a greased fireproof dish, add the stock or court bouillon, and cook in a fairly hot oven (190°C, 375°F, Gas 5) for 15–20 min. Drain the fillets well and place on a dish, coat with white wine sauce and sprinkle with the finely chopped fresh herbs. Whole skinned whiting can also be used for this dish.

4 helpings

TURBOT WITH AUBERGINES

2½–3 lb turbot (middle	3 aubergines
cut)	Olive oil
Salt and pepper	Clarified butter
Milk	Juice of ½ lemon
Flour	1 tablesp finely chopped
2 oz butter	parsley

Remove the dark skin from the fish, free it from bones. Cut the fish into 6 or 7 even-sized slices. Trim the slices neatly, season with salt and pepper, dip them into milk and then into flour. Melt about 1½ oz of butter in a sauté-pan, put in the fillets, cover with greased greaseproof paper, and cook in the oven for 15 min, or longer if required, basting occasionally. Meanwhile remove the skin from the aubergines, cut them into slices, dip in flour and fry in a mixture of equal amounts of olive oil and clarified butter, until golden-brown. Drain and season with salt. Serve the turbot on an oblong dish, sprinkle with a little lemon juice, then the parsley and lastly some nut-brown clarified butter. Garnish with the fried aubergines.

6 helpings

BAKED WHITING, WHOLE OR FILLETED, WITH WINE

4 fillets or 1 large	A few canned sliced
whiting	mushrooms
Salt and pepper	1 teasp chopped parsley
½ glass white wine	White Italian sauce
Lemon juice	Brown breadcrumbs
Mushroom liquor	

If using a whole whiting, skin both sides, cut off the head and fins and make several incisions with a knife across one side of the fish. Place fish on a well-buttered fireproof dish (if using a whole fish place cut side uppermost), season with pepper and salt, add the white wine, a few drops of lemon juice, a little mushroom liquor and some chopped parsley. Slice the mushrooms and place in a row down the centre of the fish or fillets; cover with White Italian Sauce. Sprinkle with brown breadcrumbs, dot a few tiny bits of butter on top of the fish and bake at 180°C, 350°F, Gas 4 (20–30 min for a whole whiting, 12–15 min for fillets).

2–3 helpings

BOILED, POACHED AND STEAMED FISH DISHES

COD À LA PROVENÇALE

2 lb middle cut cod (approx)	A small bunch of parsley
Salt and pepper	Bouquet garni
½ pt Velouté or other rich white sauce	1 egg yolk
1 gill white stock	2 oz butter
2 small shallots	1 teasp anchovy paste
	1 teasp chopped parsley
	2 teasp capers

Wash and wipe the fish well and place in a saucepan. Season with pepper and salt, and add the sauce, stock, finely chopped shallots, bunch of parsley and the bouquet garni. Simmer slowly until the fish is done, basting occasionally. Remove the fish to a hot dish, and keep it warm. Reduce the sauce until the desired consistency is obtained. Remove the herbs, add the egg yolk, work in the butter, and pass through a strainer. Return to a smaller saucepan, add the anchovy paste, chopped parsley and capers, stir over heat for a few minutes but do not allow to boil, then pour over the fish.

5–6 helpings　　　　**Cooking time 35–40 min**

HASHED COD

2 lb cooked cod or similar fish	¼ pt shelled shrimps, fresh or canned
1½ oz butter	Salt and pepper
1½ oz flour	½ lb mashed potatoes
1 pt milk	Chopped parsley

Remove skin and bone and flake the fish into small pieces. Blend the butter and flour in a saucepan, and fry for a few minutes without browning. Add the milk and stir until boiling. Then put in the cod and the shrimps. Cook until thoroughly hot and season carefully. Make a deep border of mashed potatoes on a hot dish, pour the hash in the centre and sprinkle a little chopped parsley over the top.

4–5 helpings　　　　**Cooking time ½ hr**

FISH PUDDING

1 lb any kind of white fish	Salt and pepper
4 oz finely chopped suet	A few drops of anchovy essence
2 oz breadcrumbs	2 eggs
1 teasp finely chopped parsley	¼ pt milk or stock made from fish bones

Grease well a plain mould or basin. Free the fish from skin and bones, chop the fish finely and rub through a fine sieve. Add to the suet with the breadcrumbs, parsley, salt, pepper and anchovy essence, and mix well. Beat the eggs slightly, add the milk or fish stock and stir into the mixture. Put into the mould or basin, cover with greased paper, and steam gently for nearly 1½ hr.

4–5 helpings

POACHED HALIBUT OR TURBOT STEAKS WITH PRAWN SAUCE

3–4 halibut or turbot steaks	½ pt anchovy, prawn or shrimp sauce
Salt	

Add salt to hot water in the proportion of 1 oz to 1 qt, and put in the fish. Bring slowly to boiling point and simmer very gently until cooked through, about 12–15 min. Drain well, arrange in a hot dish and pour the sauce over. Garnish with unshelled, cooked prawns or shrimps if desired.

3–4 helpings

BOILED OR POACHED SALMON AND SALMON TROUT

Make a court bouillon in a fish-kettle or large pan, using just enough water to cover the fish. Wash, clean and scale the fish. Remove the gills, intestines and eyes, but leave on the head and tail. Tie loosely in a piece of muslin if using a stewpan. Remove any scum on the court bouillon, then gently put in the fish and boil (or rather poach) until cooked through. The time will depend on the size and thickness of the fish. Allow 10 min per lb for a thick fish, or whole

Poached halibut with prawn sauce

SEAFOOD CHOWDER

salmon trout, and 7 min for a tail piece of salmon.

To serve hot

Arrange on a flat dish, garnish with sliced cucumber, parsley, lemon and new potatoes. Serve with melted butter or Hollandaise sauce.

SEAFOOD CHOWDER

1–1¾ lb smoked haddock *or* cod	1 tablesp flour
1–2 finely chopped onions	3–4 tablesp dried skim milk made up as liquid
1 breakfast cup instant mashed potato prepared with dried skim milk made up as liquid	Salt and pepper
	½ 10-oz can or pkt sweet corn kernels
2–3 skinned tomatoes	¼ pt shelled prawns
1–1½ oz butter *or* margarine	1 dessertsp finely chopped parsley

Cover the haddock or cod with ¾ pt water, and bring gently to the boil. Remove the fish, skim any scum off the stock. Simmer the onions in a little of this stock until tender, and reserve the rest. Make up the potato if required. Cut the tomatoes into eighths and discard the seeds. Simmer them in the remaining stock until tender, then add them to the onions with the potato. Reserve the tomato stock. Free the fish of skin and bones. Melt the fat, add the flour and cook gently for 2–3 min without browning. Remove from the heat and slowly stir in the tomato stock. Cook for a few moments. Add the vegetables, fish stock and sweet corn. Then add the fish and most of the shellfish. Reserve a few prawns for garnish if liked. Heat the whole dish through without boiling. Turn into a serving dish, sprinkle with parsley, and garnish with the remaining shellfish if desired.

4–5 helpings

SKATE AU BEURRE NOIR

1¼ lb skate wing (approx)	1 tablesp vinegar
1½ oz butter	Chopped parsley

COURT BOUILLON

1 small carrot	1 level teasp salt
1 small onion	½ bay leaf
1 pt water	Sprig of parsley
1 dessertsp vinegar	2 peppercorns

Peel and slice the carrot and onion. Place all the ingredients for the court bouillon in a pan, bring to the boil and boil for 5 min, strain and return to the pan. Cut the skate into convenient portions for serving and poach in the court bouillon for 10–15 min. Remove the pieces of fish carefully, drain and place on a hot dish. Heat the butter in a small, strong pan until it begins to turn brown, remove from the heat and add the vinegar very gradually to prevent spluttering. Pour over the fish, sprinkle with a little chopped parsley and serve.

4 helpings

FILLETS OF SOLE BONNE FEMME

4 fillets of sole	Salt and pepper
4 oz mushrooms	¼ pt white wine
1 shallot	¼ pt Velouté sauce
1 teasp chopped parsley	A little butter

Wipe the fillets with a clean damp cloth. Put them flat in a shallow pan with the sliced mushrooms, sliced shallot, parsley and seasoning. Add the wine, cover and poach for 10–15 min. Drain the fish from the wine, place on a fireproof dish and keep warm.

Boil the wine rapidly until it is reduced by half, then stir it into the hot Velouté sauce and thicken with a little butter. When thoroughly blended pour the sauce over the fillets and place under a hot grill until lightly browned. Serve at once in a border of sliced, steam potatoes.

4 helpings

TROUT 'AU BLEU'

One 6–8 oz trout	Salt
Vinegar	Parsley

The essential factor of this famous dish is that the trout should be alive until just before cooking. In restaurants they are often kept in a tank from which the customer selects his fish. The fish should be stunned, cleaned (gutted) and immediately plunged into a pan of boiling salted water to which a little vinegar has been added. (The fish are not scaled or washed as this would spoil the blue colour.) Draw the pan aside, or reduce the heat, and poach the fish for about 10–12 min. Drain, and serve garnished with parsley and accompanied by melted butter, Hollandaise sauce and small boiled potatoes.

POACHED OR BOILED WHITE FISH

1 brill *or* other white fish	Salt
	Vinegar
Lemon juice	Sauce

Clean and skin the fish, and rub a little lemon juice over it to preserve its whiteness. Barely cover the fish with warm water, add salt and vinegar to taste and simmer gently until done (allow about 10 min per lb). Garnish with cut lemon and parsley, and serve with anchovy, prawn, Hollandaise or melted butter sauce.

Allow 4–6 oz per helping

STEAMED WHITING

1 whiting	Lemon juice
Salt and pepper	White sauce

Skin the whiting and curl it with its tail in its mouth. (Your fishmonger will do this for you.) Place it in a well-buttered soup plate, sprinkle lightly with salt, pepper and lemon juice, and cover with a generously buttered paper. Have ready a saucepan containing boiling water, place the plate on top of it and cover with another plate or the lid of the saucepan. Cook for 20–25 min, turning the fish once during the process. Serve with its own liquid or with white sauce.

Sole or plaice can be steamed in the same way, but take only 10–12 min. These are suitable dishes for invalids.

1 helping

GRILLED AND FRIED FISH DISHES

CAPKIN OR MIXED FISH GRILL

Four 4–5 oz portions sea bream, coley, hake, brill *or* cod	1 level dessertsp chopped pickled capers
2 tablesp salad oil	1 level dessertsp chopped pickled gherkins
1 tablesp vinegar	
Salt and pepper to taste	1 level dessertsp chopped parsley

Prepare the fish and place skin side uppermost in the grill pan. Mix together all the other ingredients except the parsley, and pour over the fish. Grill for about 12–15 min, turning once and basting frequently with the sauce. Serve hot, sprinkled with parsley.

4 helpings

FRIED COD STEAKS

Four 4–6 oz cod steaks	**Fat for frying**
Flour	**Fried parsley**
Salt and pepper	

Make a rather thin batter of flour and water, season well with salt and pepper. Melt sufficient clarified fat or dripping in a frying-pan to form a layer about $\frac{1}{2}$ in deep. Wipe the fish, dip each piece separately in the batter, place these at once in the hot fat, and fry until light brown, turning once during the process. Drain well, and serve garnished with crisply fried parsley. (If preferred, the fish may be coated with egg and breadcrumbs and fried in deep fat.) Serve with anchovy or tomato sauce.

4 helpings

GOLDEN GRILLED COD

3 *or* 4 cutlets *or* steaks of cod about $1\frac{1}{2}$ in thick	**1–2 oz grated cheese *or* fine white breadcrumbs**
1 oz margarine	**Salt and pepper**

Place the prepared fish in a greased fireproof dish and grill quickly for 8–10 min on one side. Meanwhile soften the margarine, cream the cheese and margarine together, and season to taste, or toss the breadcrumbs in the melted fat. Turn the fish over and spread the cheese mixture or breadcrumbs over the uncooked side and return to the grill. Reduce the heat slightly and cook gently for a further 4–5 min

Seafood chowder

JUGGED KIPPERS

until the coating is brown and the fish cooked through. Serve at once, garnished with lemon wedges and pats of parsley butter.

JUGGED AND GRILLED KIPPERS

1–2 kippers per person	Slices of lemon
Butter *or* margarine	Parsley sprigs

TO JUG KIPPERS

Simply place the kippers in a tall jug and cover with boiling water. Cover the jug and stand it in a warm place for 5–10 min. Drain, and serve with a knob of butter or margarine on each kipper. This method produces plump, juicy kippers, though some say a little flavour is lost.

TO GRILL KIPPERS

Remove the heads and lay the kippers flat, skin side up, on the grid. Cook for about 3 min each side, adding a dab of butter or margarine when they are turned over. Top with a slice of lemon decorated with parsley. Serve alone or on a slice of toast.

Alternatively, place a pair of kippers, flesh sides together, and grill under medium heat first on one side then on the other; to serve, separate and top each with a slice of lemon or nut of butter.

GRILLED MACKEREL WITH GOOSEBERRY SAUCE

2 large mackerel	½ lb gooseberries *or* a
1 tablesp seasoned	small bottle *or* 10-oz
flour	can of gooseberries
1 oz margarine	¼ level teasp grated
2 *or* 3 tomatoes	nutmeg

Trim, clean and fillet the mackerel. Dip each fillet in seasoned flour. Melt the margarine in the bottom of the grill pan, add the fillets, brush them with the melted fat and grill for 8–10 min, turning once. Cut the tomatoes in half and grill at the same time, for garnish.

Meanwhile prepare the gooseberries. Stew in a

Fried plaice with lemon

very little water, or in their own juice if bottled or canned. Sweeten slightly if necessary, rub through a sieve and return the purée to the pan. Stir in the grated nutmeg and reheat (reduce by rapid boiling if necessary). Serve the fillets on a hot dish, garnished with the tomatoes and serve the sauce separately.

Grilled mackerel may be served with Maître d'Hôtel butter or Maître d'Hôtel sauce if preferred to gooseberry sauce.

4 helpings

GRILLED HERRINGS WITH MUSTARD SAUCE

1 onion	½ pt vinegar
1 oz butter	4 fresh herrings
½ oz flour	Melted butter *or*
1 teasp dry mustard	cooking oil

Wipe and dry the herrings, remove the heads and score across the back and sides. Avoid cutting the roe. Sprinkle with salt and pepper, brush very lightly with melted butter or oil and grill under a very hot grill for 8–12 min, turning once. Place on a hot dish and garnish with lemon wedges and fresh green parsley. Serve the sauce separately.

TO MAKE THE SAUCE

Chop the onion finely and fry in the butter until lightly browned. Put in the flour and mustard, add the vinegar and ¼ pt water. Stir until boiling and simmer gently for 15 min.

3–4 helpings

FILLETS OF PLAICE WITH LEMON DRESSING

4 fillets of plaice (4 oz	1 oz butter *or*
each approx)	margarine
Seasoning	Juice of ½ lemon
	Chopped parsley

Season the fish. Melt the fat in the grill pan and place the fish skin side uppermost in the pan. Cook for 1 min, then turn with flesh side up and grill steadily until golden-brown and cooked, about 5–8 min, depending on thickness of fillets. Remove to a

Grilled herrings with mustard sauce

hot serving dish, keep hot. Add the lemon juice to the remaining fat in the pan, reheat and pour over the fish. Sprinkle liberally with chopped parsley.

4 helpings

GRILLED SALMON

2–3 slices of salmon (middle cut) about ¾ in thick	1 tablesp (about 1 oz) Maître d'Hôtel or anchovy butter
2 tablesp olive oil or oiled butter (approx)	Parsley
Salt and pepper	Lemon (optional)

Wipe the fish with a damp cloth, then brush over with oil or oiled butter. Season to taste with salt and pepper and place the slices on a well-greased grill rack. Grill each side for 6–8 min, according to the thickness of the slices. When done, place the fish on a flat dish, and place pat of Maître d'Hôtel or anchovy butter on each slice. Garnish with sprigs of fresh parsley. Serve hot.

4–6 helpings

FILLETS OF SOLE À LA ORLY

Six 4 oz fillets of sole	Fried parsley
Deep fat for frying	Batter for coating

MARINADE

1 tablesp lemon juice	1 teasp chopped onion or shallots
1 tablesp salad oil	
1 teasp finely chopped parsley	Salt and pepper

Wipe the fillets with a clean damp cloth and place in a deep dish with the marinade. Soak for 1 hr, then drain well. Meanwhile mix the batter; blend the flour and salt smoothly with the water and oil, then add the stiffly whisked egg white. Dip the fillets in the batter, drop them carefully into a deep pan of hot fat and fry until golden-brown. Serve garnished with fried parsley. Serve with tomato sauce.

6 helpings

FILLETS OF SOLE MEUNIÈRE

4 large or 8 small fillets of sole	1 tablesp lemon juice
A little seasoned flour	1 level tablesp chopped parsley
3 oz butter	Lemon 'butterflies'

Dredge the fillets lightly, but thoroughly, with seasoned flour. Heat the butter in a frying-pan and when hot fry the fillets until golden-brown and cooked through—about 7 min. Arrange the fillets on a hot dish. Reheat the fat until it is nut brown in colour and then pour it over the fish. Sprinkle the lemon juice and parsley over the fillets, and serve.

4 helpings

FRIED SPRATS

3 doz sprats (approx)	½ oz cooking fat
2 tablesp flour	Lemon wedges
Salt and pepper	

Wash and dry the sprats thoroughly, mix the flour with the salt and pepper to season. Dip the sprats in the seasoned flour and fry them in the hot fat for 10 to 15 min. Serve as quickly as possible on a hot dish with a wedge of lemon per helping.

5 helpings

TROUT MEUNIÈRE

4 large or 8 small trout	A little seasoned flour
	3 oz butter

1 tablesp lemon juice	1 level tablesp chopped parsley
Lemon 'butterflies'	

Dredge the trout lightly, but thoroughly, with seasoned flour. Heat the butter in a frying-pan and when hot fry the trout until golden-brown and cooked through. Arrange the trout on a hot dish. Reheat the fat until it is nut brown in colour and then pour it over the fish. Sprinkle the lemon juice and parsley over the fish, garnish with lemon 'butterflies' and serve at once.

4 helpings

Grilled salmon cutlets

FRIED WHITEBAIT

Whitebait is seasonable from February to July

Whitebait	Cayenne or black pepper
Ice	
Flour	Salt
Deep fat for frying	Lemon

Frying whitebait is a difficult task for inexperienced cooks. The following is a well-tried method which, if carefully followed, usually produces satisfactory results. Put the whitebait with a piece of ice in a basin, which must be kept cool. When required for cooking, spread the fish on a cloth to dry, dredge well with flour, place in a wire basket and shake off the superfluous flour. Plunge the basket into a pan of clean, very hot lard and fry rapidly for 3–4 min. Keep moving the basket all the time while frying. Lift the basket, shake it to strain off the fat, and turn the fish on to greaseproof paper. Place on a warm dish and repeat until all the whitebait are fried. Season with cayenne or black pepper and fine salt. Serve garnished with quarters of lemon.

FISH IN CREAM AND CHEESE SAUCES

COD IN CREAM SAUCE

2 lb cod	Salt and pepper
2 oz butter	1 oz flour

COD STEAKS

½ pt fish stock *or* milk
2 tablesp cream
1 teasp lemon juice

Wash and dry the fish thoroughly. Melt 1½ oz butter in a saucepan, put in the cod and fry quickly on both sides without browning. Add the stock or milk, cover closely and simmer gently for about 20 min. Drain the fish then place on a hot dish. Melt the remaining ½ oz butter, stir in the flour, add the stock or milk in which the fish was cooked and enough milk to make up the original quantity (½ pt). Boil up and simmer for about 4 min to cook the flour. Add the cream and lemon juice, season to taste and strain over the fish.

5–6 helpings

Cod steaks—Cardinal style

COD STEAKS—CARDINAL STYLE

2 cod steaks 1¼–1½ in thick
Salt and pepper
1½ oz butter
1 oz flour
¼ pt milk
2 tomatoes
A few drops cochineal
A little finely chopped parsley

Wipe the cod steaks with a clean damp cloth, place them in a baking-dish and sprinkle with salt and pepper. Place ½ oz butter in small pieces on the top of the fish, cover with greased paper and bake for 20–25 min in a moderate oven (180°C, 350°F, Gas 4). Meanwhile melt the remaining 1 oz of butter in a saucepan, stir in the flour, add the milk and boil 2–3 min. Sieve the tomatoes and add the purée to the contents of the saucepan. When the fish is done, remove it to a hot dish, strain the liquor from it and add it to the sauce. Season to taste, add carmine or cochineal until a bright-red colour is obtained and pour it over the fish. Sprinkle on a little parsley and serve.

3–4 helpings

COQUILLES OF COOKED HALIBUT OR TURBOT

½ pt white sauce
¾ lb cooked halibut *or* turbot
Grated cheese
Browned breadcrumbs
Salt and pepper
Butter

Flavour the sauce with grated cheese to taste. Divide the fish into large flakes, put into 6 buttered

scallop shells, cover with sauce and sprinkle thickly with browned breadcrumbs. Season, put 1 or 2 small pieces of butter on each, cook for 15–20 min in a moderate oven (180°C, 350°F, Gas 4).

6 helpings

PLAICE MORNAY

Four 4 oz fillets of plaice, fresh *or* frozen

SAUCE

1 oz butter
1 rounded tablesp flour
Salt and pepper
½ pt milk and fish stock mixed
2 tablesp grated Gruyère *or* Cheddar cheese
Mustard
Grated nutmeg

Fold the fillets in half and steam between 2 plates. Meanwhile make the sauce by melting the fat in a small saucepan, adding the flour, a pinch of salt and pepper, and cooking for 2–3 min without browning. Remove from heat and stir in the liquid gradually, mixing well to prevent lumpiness. Bring to the boil, still stirring, and cook for 5 min. Add most of the cheese and season with mustard and nutmeg. Arrange the cooked fish in a shallow fireproof dish, coat with sauce and sprinkle with the remaining cheese. Place under a hot grill until golden brown. Serve with grilled or baked tomatoes and mashed potatoes.

4 helpings

SALMON CUTLETS MORNAY

2 slices of salmon ¾–1 in thick
1 onion
2½ oz butter
½ pt fish stock
Bouquet garni
Salt and pepper
1 oz flour
¼ pt cream
1 tablesp grated Parmesan cheese
1 dessertsp lemon juice

Chop the onion coarsely. Melt half the butter in a shallow saucepan, fry the onion and the salmon quickly on both sides, then add the stock (boiling), the bouquet garni and salt and pepper. Cover closely, and simmer gently for 20 min. Meanwhile, melt the remainder of the butter in another saucepan, add

Plaice mornay

Codfish breakfast with West Indian Relish

the flour and cook for 4 min. When the fish is done, transfer it to a hot dish and keep warm. Strain the stock on to the flour and butter and stir until boiling. Simmer for 5 min, then add the cream, cheese, lemon juice and seasoning to taste. Pour the mixture over the fish and serve.

5–6 helpings

SOLE A LA MAÎTRE D'HÔTEL

As Sole with Cream Sauce, but stir 1 dessertsp finely chopped parsley and 1 teasp lemon juice into the sauce just before serving.

FILLETS OF SOLE WITH CREAM SAUCE

1 large sole	1 pt milk *or* milk and
Salt and pepper	fish stock
Lemon juice	2 oz butter
1 small piece of onion	1½ oz flour
¼ teasp ground mace	Parsley to garnish
	2 tablesp cream

Wash, skin and fillet the sole, and divide each fillet lengthwise into two. Tie each strip loosely in a knot, or fold the ends over each other. Place in a greased tin, season with salt and pepper, sprinkle with lemon juice, cover with a greased paper and bake for 10–15 min in a moderate oven (180°C, 350°F, Gas 4). Simmer the bones of the fish, the onion and mace in the milk for about 15 min, then strain and season to taste. Melt the butter in a saucepan, add the flour,

cook for 3–4 min, then pour in the flavoured milk and stir until boiling. Let the sauce simmer for 10 min at least then add cream; arrange the fish fillets on a hot dish, either in a circle or forming 2 rows, and strain the sauce over. Decorate with a little chopped parsley.

4 helpings

MISCELLANEOUS FISH DISHES

CODFISH BREAKFAST WITH WEST INDIAN RELISH

2 lb salted cod	4 ripe bananas
6 medium-sized potatoes	2 avocado pears
or one 1-pt pkt instant	Lemon juice
mashed potato	West Indian Relish

Soak the codfish for 6–8 hr. Drain thoroughly. Shred, then simmer slowly for 1·–15 min in fresh water. Boil whole potatoes and mash them, or make up the instant potato as directed. Peel and slice the fruit, and sprinkle with lemon juice to prevent discolouration. Pipe a border of potato round a heated serving dish. Arrange the fish with a few slices of fruit in the centre. Serve hot, with the remaining fruit in small side dishes, and with West Indian Relish. (*Page 52, top of Column 1.*)

CURRIED COD

WEST INDIAN RELISH

2 teasp dry mustard	Juice of 1 lime
2 tablesp butter	Juice of ½ lemon
½ teasp Tabasco sauce	1 teasp Angostura
2 tablesp grated onion	bitters (optional)
Garlic salt to taste	

Mix all the ingredients together. Keep to serve with fish.

6 helpings

CURRIED COD, HADDOCK, ETC

2 lb cod	1 tablesp flour
2 oz butter	1 pt fish stock
1 medium-sized onion	1 tablesp lemon juice
1 dessertsp curry	Salt and pepper
powder	Cayenne pepper

Wash and dry the cod, and cut into pieces about 1½ in square. Melt the butter in a saucepan, fry the cod slightly, then take out and put aside. To make the sauce: add the sliced onion, flour and curry powder to the butter in the saucepan and fry for 15 min, stirring constantly to prevent the onion becoming too brown. Then pour in the stock. Stir until boiling then simmer gently for 20 min. Strain and return to the saucepan, add lemon juice and seasoning to taste, bring nearly to boiling point, then put in the fish. Cover closely, and heat gently until the fish becomes thoroughly impregnated with the flavour of the sauce. An occasional stir must be given to prevent the fish sticking to the bottom of the saucepan.

Remains of cold fish may be used for this dish, in which case the preliminary frying is omitted.

5–6 helpings

FISH CAKES

1 lb cooked fish	2 eggs
1 oz butter or margarine	Salt and pepper
½ lb mashed potatoes	Breadcrumbs

Remove skin and bones and chop fish coarsely. Heat the butter in a saucepan, add the fish, potatoes, yolk of 1 egg, salt and pepper. Stir over heat for a few minutes, then turn on to a plate and allow to cool. When cold, shape into round flat cakes, brush over with beaten egg, coat with breadcrumbs and fry in hot fat. The fish may be made into one large cake instead of several small ones, in which case grease a fish mould or flat tin and shape the mixture as much like a fish as possible. Brush over with egg, cover with slightly browned breadcrumbs and bake for about 20 min in a fairly hot oven (190°C, 375°F, Gas 5).

3–7 helpings

QUICK FISH CAKES

One 1-pt pkt instant	½ lb cooked cod or
mashed potato,	haddock
suitable for frying	1 tablesp tomato sauce

Make up the potato as directed on the packet. Remove any skin and bones from the fish, flake and mix with the potato. Stir in the tomato sauce. Press or roll out the mixture to just over ¼ in thick and cut out with a plain cutter, about 2½ ins in diameter. Fry in deep or shallow fat until golden brown. Garnish with lemon curls and parsley.

10–12 fish cakes

SMOKED HADDOCK

Smoked haddocks are best cooked either in the oven or on the top of the cooker in a dish with a little water to create steam, and so to prevent the surface of the fish becoming hardened. Medium-sized haddocks should be cooked whole, and before serving an incision should be made from head to tail and the backbone removed. The fish should be liberally spread with butter, sprinkled with pepper and served as hot as possible.

SMOKED HADDOCK AND TOMATOES

1 small smoked	1 teasp finely chopped
haddock or 1 lb	onion
smoked haddock	½ teasp finely chopped
or cod fillet	parsley
2–3 small tomatoes	Salt and pepper
1 oz butter	Boiled rice

Place the haddock in a dish with a little water and bake for 10 min. Remove skin and bones and separate the fish into large flakes. Slice the tomatoes. Melt the butter in a saucepan, fry the onion slightly, add the tomatoes and cook until soft. Put in the fish and parsley, season to taste, and stir gently over a low heat until the fish is thoroughly hot. Arrange the boiled rice in a circle on a hot dish and serve the fish in the centre.

JOHN DORY

This fish is dressed in the same way as turbot, which it resembles in firmness but not in richness. Wash it thoroughly, cut off the fins but not the head, place in a pan and cover with warm water, adding salt to taste. Bring gradually to near boiling point and simmer gently for 20–30 min for a 2–3 lb fish. Small John Dorys are excellent baked.

KEDGEREE

1 lb cold cooked fish	2 hard-boiled eggs
(smoked haddock is	2 oz butter
generally preferred)	Salt and pepper
¼ lb rice	Cayenne pepper

Boil and dry the rice. Divide the fish into small flakes. Cut the whites of the eggs into slices and sieve the yolks. Melt the butter in a saucepan, add to it the fish, rice, egg whites, salt, pepper and cayenne and stir until hot. Turn the mixture on to a hot dish. Press into the shape of a pyramid with a fork, decorate with egg yolk and serve as hot as possible.

5–6 helpings   **Cooking time 40–50 min**

COLD FISH DISHES

BROWN STEWED FISH, JEWISH STYLE

2 lb fish fillets or cutlets	Salt
1 onion	2 oz gingerbread or
1 oz sultanas	ginger-nuts
2 bay leaves	2 oz brown sugar or
2 cloves	golden syrup
¼ pt vinegar	2 oz flour

Peel and slice the onion and put it in a saucepan with the sultanas, bay leaves, cloves, ¾ pt water and vinegar. Add salt to taste and bring to the boil. Put in the fish, cover and simmer gently till cooked, then lift the fish on to a serving dish. Remove cloves and bay leaves and add the crumbled gingerbread or ginger-nuts, sugar or syrup and flour blended with cold water to the liquor in the pan. Stir till boiling, simmer for 10 min, then pour over the fish. Serve cold. The amount of sugar and vinegar used can be varied according to taste.

Bream is particularly good cooked like this, but cod, haddock, shad or salmon can all be used.

5–6 helpings   **Cooking time 30–40 min**

CHEQUERBOARD SALAD

1 lb cod fillet *or* **other white fish**	**Salt and pepper**
2 tablesp water	**Lettuce leaves**
2 tablesp lemon juice	**1 small can (2 oz) anchovy fillets**
1 level tablesp chopped parsley	**Hard-boiled egg** *or* **olives**
1 level tablesp chopped chives	

Place the fish in a fireproof dish with the water. Cover and cook in a fairly hot oven (190°C, 375°F, Gas 5) for 20 min. Allow to cool. Remove any skin and bones, flake the fish, then moisten it with the lemon juice and stir in the parsley and chives with seasoning to taste. Arrange neatly on a bed of shredded lettuce, flattening and smoothing the top. Place the anchovy fillets diagonally on top in a squared pattern, filling the spaces with rings of hard-boiled egg or slices of stoned olives. Garnish with radish roses and parsley.

4 helpings

Chequerboard Salad

COOKED FISH MOULD

½ oz gelatine	**1 tablesp chopped parsley**
3 tablesp water	
½ pt fish stock	**1 egg**
3 tablesp evaporated milk	**10 oz minced cooked fish**
Salt and pepper	**1 teasp lemon juice**
Grated nutmeg	**A few drops of red colouring**
	Cayenne pepper

Dissolve gelatine in the water. Put fish stock into a pan, add milk, seasoning, nutmeg and parsley, and simmer for 5 min. Beat egg lightly, pour the fish stock over, then strain back into saucepan. Heat gently, stirring constantly until mixture thickens. Stir in gelatine, add the fish, lemon juice and colouring. Stir gently, allow to cool. When cool pour into a fish-shaped mould, put into refrigerator to set. Garnish with about 4 oz cleaned shrimps or prawns; serve with salad.

4–5 helpings

DARIOLES OF SALMON À LA MOSCOVITE

1 lb cooked salmon (approx)	**Pinch cayenne pepper**
½ pt aspic jelly (approx)	**Salt and pepper**
6–8 button mushrooms	**Grated nutmeg to taste**
Red chillies	**1 teasp tarragon vinegar**
6–8 canned oysters	**2 tablesp cream**
1 hard-boiled egg	**4 filleted anchovies, chopped**
½ oz anchovy paste	**A few slices of cucumber**

Remove all skin and bone and flake the salmon. Line 6–8 small dariole, bouchée or timbale moulds with a thin layer of aspic jelly, decorate with a few thin slices of button mushrooms. Set the garnish with a little aspic and put aside to cool. Pound or blend the remainder of the fish together with the oysters, the hard-boiled egg and the anchovy paste;

season with a pinch of cayenne pepper, salt and a little grated nutmeg. Blend again briefly, or rub through a fine sieve, add the tarragon vinegar, the cream and about 1 gill of liquid aspic jelly. Mix the ingredients well together and half-fill the moulds. Put in the anchovy fillets, then add the rest of the fish mixture. If the mixture does not quite fill the moulds, fill up with aspic jelly. Then put the moulds in the fridge or stand in a cool place until required. For serving, immerse the moulds in tepid water, turn out the contents quickly and place on a round dish. Garnish with chopped aspic and a few fancifully cut slices of cucumber. Serve with a mixed vegetable salad.

6 helpings

Darioles of Salmon à la Moscovite

JELLIED EELS

Live eels are usually purchased. The fishmonger will prepare them for you, but if you prefer to do it at home, this is the method:

Prepare by half-severing the head and slitting down the stomach. Scrape away the gut, etc, and cut off with the head. Cut into 2 ins lengths. Put in a pan with sufficient water to just cover, boil for about ½ hr, turn into a bowl and leave to set. If the liquor does not look thick enough, add a little gelatine, but normally it will 'jell' on its own.

'GEFILTE' FISH

2–2½ lb fish	1 tablesp chopped
2–3 onions	parsley
1–2 sticks of celery	2 eggs
1 large carrot	Fresh breadcrumbs
Salt and pepper	

Remove the skin and bones from the fish and put them in a saucepan with 1 onion, the celery and a piece of carrot, pour 1½ pt water over, season with salt and pepper. Cover and simmer gently for ½ hr, then strain. Put the fish and remaining onion through the mincing-machine or chop finely by hand. Add the parsley and beaten eggs to the chopped fish; season with salt and pepper and add sufficient fresh breadcrumbs to bind. With floured hands roll into balls. Slice the carrot thinly, add to the fish stock and bring to the boil; then put in the fish balls, cover and simmer very gently for 1 hr. Lift the balls out carefully on to a serving dish and place a slice of carrot on top of each. Spoon over a little of the fish stock and serve cold, when the stock should have set in a jelly.

This dish originated in the East, where salt-water fish is in short supply, and was made from pike and carp. But bream, cod, haddock or a mixture can be used.

5–6 helpings   **Cooking time about 1½ hr**

Halibut with Orange and Watercress

HALIBUT WITH ORANGE AND WATERCRESS SALAD

6–7 pieces of halibut	2 bunches watercress
Salt and pepper	
Mayonnaise (optional)	2 oranges

Prepare the fillets, season, fold in half and steam for 10–15 min between 2 plates; allow to cool. Shred about half the watercress leaves and arrange on a dish. Place the cooked fillets on this, and coat them evenly with mayonnaise if desired. Garnish with the remaining watercress and slices of orange. Turbot may also be used for this dish.

6–7 helpings

SOUSED HERRINGS

8 fresh herrings	1 level dessertsp
1 Spanish onion	mixed pickling
Salt and pepper	spice
1 bay leaf	Vinegar

Wash and scale each herring, cut off the head, split open and remove the gut and backbone. Put a slice of onion in the centre of each fish, roll up tightly, beginning with the neck. Pack the herrings closely in a pie-dish, sprinkle with salt, pepper, bay leaf and spice, half fill the dish with equal quantities of vinegar and water, and bake in a moderate oven (180°C, 350°F, Gas 4) for 40 min. Serve cold with salad, or cut up for hors d'œuvre; or eat plain, hot or cold, with bread and butter.

6 helpings

PICKLED MACKEREL

2–3 small mackerel	Allspice
Salt and pepper	12 peppercorns
2 bay leaves	½ pt vinegar

Clean and wash the fish and take out the roes. Place the mackerel in a fireproof dish with the roes (mackerel are best when the roes are not full grown). Sprinkle well with salt and pepper, add the bay leaves, allspice, peppercorns, vinegar and about ¼ pt water. Cover with a greased paper and bake in a cool oven (150°C, 310°F, Gas 2) for nearly 1 hr. Leave in the liquor until required.

2–3 helpings

POACHED SALMON AND SALMON TROUT SERVED COLD

Cool the fish a little after cooking. Neatly remove the skin from one side. Serve quite plain, on a bed of decorated aspic jelly, and garnish with unshelled prawns. Use slices of stuffed olive to fill the eye sockets.

Alternatively, glaze the cold fish with aspic jelly made with liquor in which the fish was cooked. Garnish with chopped aspic, tomato segments and sliced cucumber.

SALMON MAYONNAISE

Cold boiled salmon	Gherkins
Lettuce	Capers
Mayonnaise	Boned anchovies *or*
Aspic jelly (optional)	anchovy fillets
Cucumber	Hard-boiled eggs
Beetroot	

A mayonnaise of salmon may consist of a large centre cut, a thick slice, or the remains of cold salmon cut into pieces convenient for serving. Arrange a bed of shredded lettuce in the bottom of a

Salmon Mousse

salad bowl. Remove the skin and bone from the fish. Flake the fish and place on the lettuce. Mask the fish completely with thick mayonnaise. The sauce may be made stiffer by adding a little liquid, but nearly cold, aspic jelly. When obtainable, a little endive should be mixed with the lettuce, for although the somewhat bitter flavour of this salad plant is disliked by many, its delicate, feathery leaves greatly improve the appearance of a dish. Garnish with the suggested ingredients; or many other garnishings, in addition to those given above, may be used; tarragon and chervil leaves are particularly effective when used to decorate the surface of mayonnaise.

Allow 5–6 oz salmon per helping

SALMON MOUSSE WITH ASPIC

1 lb cooked salmon (approx) or one 16-oz can	1 pt fish stock Salt and pepper
1 oz gelatine	½ cucumber, sliced A few slices tomato

Dissolve the gelatine in the stock and season to taste. Drain the oil from the salmon and remove all skin and bones. Cover the bottom of a mould with the jellied stock, let it set, and then decorate with slices of cucumber. Set the garnish with a little jelly. Allow to set. Add a layer of salmon, cover with jelly and put aside until set. Repeat until the mould is full. Keep in the fridge or in a cool place until wanted, then turn out. Garnish the dish with sliced cucumber and tomato. 1 tablesp sherry or Marsala can be added to the jelly for flavour.

6–8 helpings

SHELLFISH DISHES

CHOOSING A CRAB

Crabs are on sale all the year round, but are at their best from May to October. It is usual to buy crabs which have been boiled by the fishmonger. Choose crabs which are heavy for their size and which are not 'watering' or sound 'watery' when shaken. Avoid crabs which are attracting flies, especially around the mouth, as this is a sign of deterioration; choose a crab which looks and smells fresh. A crab should look clean and wholesome; if the shell is dark, the meat will invariably be dark. The hen crab may be distinguished from the cock crab by its broader tail flap. Normally the flesh of the cock crab is more reliable for quality than the hen; the cock crab is therefore a more economical buy. Avoid crabs that are less than 4½ ins across the shell. An average crab about 6 ins across should weigh 2½–3 lb; this will be found sufficient for 4 people. It is illegal to sell 'berried' or 'rush' crab.

Crab meat can also be bought in cans, or frozen. Frozen meat may be brown, white or mixed. It is economical and labour-saving to use for made-up dishes and for sauces.

PREPARING FOR THE TABLE

After wiping well with a damp cloth, place the crab on its back with the tail facing you, and remove claws and legs by twisting them in the opposite way to which they lie. Place the thumbs under flap at tail and push upwards, pull flap away upwards so that the stomach contents are not drawn over the meat, and lift off. (The fishmonger will do this on request.) Reverse the crab so that the head is facing, then press on the mouth with the thumbs, pushing down and forward; the mouth and stomach will then come away in one piece. Remove the meat from the shell by easing round the inside edge of the shell to loosen the tissues with the handle of a plastic teaspoon, and the meat will then come away easily. Keep the dark and the white meat separate. With the handle of a knife, tap sharply over the false line round the shell cavity, press down and it will come away neatly. Scrub and dry the shell, then rub over with a little oil. Remove the 'dead-men's fingers' (the lungs) and discard, then scoop out the meat from the claw sockets. Scoop out as much as possible but keep it free of bone. Twist off first joint of large claws and scoop out meat. Tap sharply round the broad shell with back of knife and halves fall apart. Cut the cartilage between the pincers, open pincers and meat will come away in one piece.

CURRIED CRAB

1 good-sized crab	1 oz butter *or* other
Mustard	good cooking fat
1 shallot *or* onion	½ pt curry sauce
½ apple	4 oz plain boiled rice

Remove the meat from the crab, including the claws, flake it up and sprinkle a little dry mustard over it. Peel and finely chop the shallot or onion; peel, core and chop the apple. Melt the butter in a saucepan and lightly fry the shallot and apple. Fry for a few minutes only, then add the curry sauce and lastly the crab meat. Re-heat and serve on a hot dish in the centre of a border of rice.

3–4 helpings

SCALLOPED CRAB

1 medium-sized crab	Vinegar
Fine breadcrumbs	A little white sauce
Salt and pepper	Butter
Mustard	

Remove the meat from the claws and body of the crab. Add about half its bulk in breadcrumbs, season with salt, pepper and mustard, and stir in a few drops of vinegar. Add white sauce to moisten, then turn into buttered scallop shells and sprinkle the surface lightly with breadcrumbs. Place small pieces of butter on top and bake in a moderate oven (180°C, 350°F, Gas 4) until nicely browned—about 15 min.

4–5 helpings

PREPARING AND COOKING CRAWFISH AND CRAYFISH

Crawfish are what the French call *langoustes*. They are treated just like lobsters. Crayfish are fresh-water shellfish, also like lobsters but much smaller. They are greenish-brown above, yellowish beneath, but turn red when boiled. They are in season from June–March. The French call them *écrevisses*. To cook crayfish, wash thoroughly, remove intestinal cord and throw the fish into boiling, salted water. Boil for 10–15 min according to size. If wanted for a made-up dish, pick the meat from the shell and dice it or pound it to a paste as required.

HOW TO CHOOSE A LOBSTER

Lobsters can be obtained all the year round, but are scarce from December to March. They are cheapest during the summer months. Lobsters are usually bought already boiled, but live lobsters can be obtained to order if a few days' notice is given to the fishmonger. Choose one of medium size and heavy in weight. If fresh, the tail of a cooked lobster will be stiff; if gently raised, it will return with a spring. The narrowness of the back part of the tail and the stiffness of the two uppermost fins (swimmerettes) in the tail distinguish the cock lobster from the hen.

BOILING A LOBSTER

There are two methods of boiling lobsters, each method having points in its favour.

Method 1

Wash the lobster well before boiling, tie the claws securely. Have ready a saucepan of boiling water, salted in the proportion of ¼ lb salt to 1 gallon water. Throw the lobster head first into the water (this instantly destroys life), keep it boiling for 20–45 min, according to size, and skim well. Allow 20 min–½ hr for small lobsters and ½–¾ hr for large lobsters. If

boiled too long the meat becomes thready, and if not done enough, the coral is not red. If serving in the shell, rub the shells over with a little salad oil to brighten the colour.

Method 2

Put the lobsters into warm water, bring the water gradually to the boil and boil as above. This is believed by many to be a more humane method of killing, as the lobster is lulled to sleep and does not realise it is being killed.

PREPARING A LOBSTER

Wipe the lobster well with a clean damp cloth and twist off claws and legs. Place lobster on a board parallel to the edge with back uppermost and head to the left. Cut along the centre of back, from junction of head with body to tail, using a sharp, stainless knife. Reverse so that tail is to left and cut along head; the stomach, which lies just behind the mouth, is not cut until last. Remove intestinal cord, remove stomach and coral (if any) and keep for garnish. The meat may be left in the shell or removed and used as required. To remove the meat, knock tips of the claws with the back of a knife and drain away any water. Tap sharply round the broadest part of each claw and the shell should fall apart. Cut the cartilage between pincers, open the pincers and the meat can be removed in one piece. Remove the meat from the smaller joints of claws.

DEVILLED LOBSTER

1 boiled lobster	2 tablesp white sauce
Butter	*or* cream
3 tablesp white	Cayenne pepper
breadcrumbs	A few browned
	breadcrumbs

Cut the lobster in two lengthwise, remove the meat carefully, as the ½ shells must be kept whole, and chop the meat finely. Melt 1½ oz butter and pour it on the lobster. Add the white breadcrumbs, and the sauce, season rather highly with cayenne and mix well. Press the mixture lightly into the shells, cover with browned breadcrumbs, put 3 or 4 pieces of butter on top and bake for about 20 min in a moderate oven (180°C, 350°F, Gas 4). Serve hot or cold.

2 helpings

SCALLOPED LOBSTER

1 cooked hen lobster	Pinch of pepper
(*see* note below)	Pinch of salt
¼ pt white sauce	1–2 egg yolks
½ teasp anchovy essence	2 tablesp breadcrumbs
Pinch of cayenne pepper	½–1 oz butter

A hen lobster can be recognised by its broad back —it gives a better colour to this dish to use the hen, since the red coral gives a delicious flavour as well as tinting the fish pale pink.

Remove the coral from the lobster meat, and pound this well until very smooth. Remove all the lobster flesh from the body and claws and mix with the white sauce, together with the coral, anchovy essence and seasonings. Put into a saucepan and heat gently for several minutes, then add the egg yolk or yolks and continue cooking, *without* letting the mixture boil, for 2–3 min. Put into 4 small scallop shells or into the 2 halves of the lobster shell, top with breadcrumbs and knobs of butter and brown under a hot grill. Garnish with the small lobster claws, lemon and parsley.

Caribbean crawfish

LOBSTER THERMIDOR

Canned lobster can be used in this dish, in which case increase the amount of anchovy essence slightly.

2 helpings *or* **4 small savouries**

LOBSTER THERMIDOR

2 small boiled lobsters	1 level teasp mixed
1 shallot	mustard
1 wine glass white wine	Pinch of cayenne pepper
1½ oz butter	A little grated cheese
¼ pt Béchamel sauce	Parsley to garnish

Cut the lobsters in half lengthwise and remove the stomach and the intestinal cord. Remove the meat from the shell and cut into slices, keeping the knife on the slant. Chop the shallot very finely. Put the white wine in a small saucepan and cook the shallot until it is tender and the wine reduced to half. Meanwhile, melt the butter and heat the meat very carefully in this. Add the shallot and wine mixture to the lobster meat with the sauce, mustard and pepper, mix and return to the shells. Sprinkle with grated cheese and brown under a hot grill. Serve garnished with parsley and accompanied by a simple salad or plain lettuce.

4 helpings

Lobster thermidor

CHOOSING AND PREPARING MUSSELS

Mussels are bought while still alive and their shells should be tightly shut. Discard any that do not shut immediately when given a sharp tap, as they are probably dead. Mussels are in season from September to March. They can be served cold with vinegar or hot in soups, sauces or pies.

To prepare mussels, allow 1–1½ pt mussels per person. Scrape and clean the shells thoroughly in several lots of cold water. Mussels are not opened with a knife like oysters, but open themselves during cooking. The only part of a mussel which needs to be removed is the breathing apparatus which is found in the form of a black strip known as the 'beard'. This is removed after the shells have been opened.

There are two simple methods of opening mussels:

English method

For a small quantity of 1–2 pt, place the mussels (after cleaning) in a rinsed wide pan and cover them closely with a folded damp teacloth. Heat quickly, shaking the pan at intervals, and at the end of 5–7 min the shells will open. Remove from the heat promptly as overcooking toughens them.

French method

To 3½ pt of cleaned mussels in a wide pan, add 1 shallot, finely chopped, 5–6 stalks of parsley, a sprig of thyme, ⅓ of a bay leaf, a pinch of pepper and ¼ pt dry white wine (½ water and ½ dry cider could be used). Cover the pan tightly and cook over a sharp heat for 5–6 min, shaking the pan from time to time. Remove from the heat as soon as the shells open.

MOULES MARINIÈRES

3½ pt mussels	¼ pt dry white wine
1 finely chopped shallot	(½ water and ½ dry
5–6 stalks of parsley	cider can be used)
½ a bay leaf	1 oz butter
Sprig of thyme	Chopped parsley
Pinch of pepper	

Open the mussels by the French method. Strain the liquid through muslin, to remove any traces of sand, then return the liquid to the pan with the butter and boil rapidly until reduced by half. Meanwhile, remove the beards from the mussels and return the mussels to their half shell, discard empty shells, arrange in soup plates, pour the reduced liquor over the mussels and sprinkle with chopped parsley.

OYSTERS AND THEIR PREPARATION

Oysters have the highest reputation of all shell-fish. English oysters are in season locally from September to the end of April, and the best kind to get, to eat *au naturel* are the large flavoursome, Whitstable or Colchester 'natives'. Smaller foreign oysters are, however, available the year round in Britain, as elsewhere. They are useful for cooked dishes and garnishes.

Canned oysters, both smoked and unsmoked are also available. Smoked oysters are best served alone or with other smoked fish, as an hors d'œuvre. Unsmoked ones can be useful in cooked dishes, although fewer should be used than when using fresh oysters as their flavour is somewhat insistent.

Oysters should be opened as near as possible to the time of eating. Do not try to open them yourself unless you are an expert. Ask your supplier either to loosen the shells or to open them completely, and to supply the deep shells as well as the oysters and their liquor in a container.

Serve oysters *au naturel* with thin slices of brown bread and butter, and quarters of lemon. You can also offer cayenne pepper, Tabasco sauce or vinegar separately.

DEVILLED OYSTERS

1 dozen fresh oysters	Cayenne pepper
Salt	1 oz butter

Open the oysters carefully so as to preserve as much of the liquor as possible, or ask your fishmonger to open them for you and leave them in their shells. Sprinkle lightly with salt, and more liberally with cayenne pepper, and put a small piece of butter on top of each one. Place the oysters on a baking-sheet and put in a hot oven until thoroughly heated. Serve with sliced lemon and thin brown bread and butter.

3–4 helpings   Cooking time 4 min

OYSTERS OR MUSSELS FLORENTINE

12 fresh oysters *or*	1 oz flour
canned mussels	½ pt milk
12 oz spinach	Seasoning
1½ oz butter	A little grated cheese

Cook the spinach. Put the shellfish in a small saucepan and add their liquor, previously strained through muslin. Poach for 2–3 min until the edges just begin to ruffle slightly, then remove from the heat. Melt the butter in a saucepan, stir in the flour and cook for 2 min. Add the milk, stir until boiling and boil for 3 min. Cool slightly, then add the shell-fish and their liquor. Drain the spinach and spread over the bottom of a fireproof dish, pour the sauce on top, sprinkle with finely grated cheese and brown lightly under the grill. Serve immediately.

2–3 helpings

PRAWNS, SHRIMPS AND SCAMPI

Prawns, shrimps and scampi are available all the year. Fresh ones are usually sold cooked; raw or cooked ones are also available in cans, and frozen.

To boil freshly-caught prawns or shrimps

Cooked prawns should be colourful and have no spawn when cooked; much depends on their freshness and the way in which they are cooked. Wash well, then put into boiling salted water and keep them boiling for about 7–8 min. Dublin Bay prawns will take rather longer, shrimps only 5 min. They are ready when they begin to change colour. Do not overboil or they will become tasteless and indigestible.

To shell prawns

To shell prawns, take the head between the right-hand thumb and second finger, take the tip of the tail between the left thumb and forefinger, raise the shell at the knee or angle, pinch the tail and the shell will come apart, leaving the prawn attached to the head.

To shell shrimps

Take the head between the right thumb and fore-finger and with the left forefinger and thumbnail raise on each side the shell of the tail, pinch the tail, and the shell will at once separate.

'Scampi' is the Venetian name for very large prawns, similar to Dublin Bay prawns. They are now very popular as an hors d'œuvre or, grilled or sautéed, as a main course dish. They are usually sold quick-frozen and uncooked, and must be cooked as soon as thawed. Ordinary boiled prawns are *not* suitable for most scampi recipes.

CURRIED PRAWNS

2 doz prawns	1 level dessertsp flour
1½ oz butter	½ pt stock
1 small onion	1 sour apple
1–1½ dessertsp curry powder (depending on strength)	1 tablesp grated coconut
	Salt
	1 teasp lemon juice

Shell the prawns and put them aside. Melt the butter in a saucepan, fry the chopped onion without browning, then add the curry powder and flour and fry slowly for at least 20 min. Add the stock, coarsely chopped apple, coconut and a little salt. Simmer gently for ½ hr, then strain, and return to the saucepan. Season to taste, add the lemon juice, put in the prawns and when heated through serve with plain boiled rice.

CREAMED SCAMPI

One 1-lb pkt small frozen scampi	½ pt thick white sauce
	2 tablesp single cream

Thaw the scampi sufficiently to separate them. Heat the sauce, add the cream and scampi and simmer for 4–5 min. Serve hot.

4 helpings

FRIED SCAMPI WITH TARTARE SAUCE

8 oz frozen *or* fresh Dublin Bay prawns or scampi (weight when peeled)	Fat for frying
	Tartare sauce, hot
	Batter for coating

Separate the frozen prawns or dry the fresh ones. Make the batter. Season well. Dip each prawn in batter and lower into really hot fat. Cook quickly until golden-brown. Drain on crumpled or absorbent kitchen paper. Serve on a hot dish with tartare sauce and serve a plain salad with them.

3–4 helpings

PREPARING SCALLOPS

Scallops are usually opened by the fishmonger and displayed in their flat shells. If the scallops are to be served in their shells ask the fishmonger for the *deep* shells. If however it is necessary to open scallops they should be put over a gentle heat to allow the shells to open. When they have opened, remove from the shells, trim away the beard and remove the black parts. Wash the scallops well, drain and dry. Wash and dry the shells; keep the deep shells for serving dishes. Scallops are in season from November to March. They can be served baked, fried, poached or grilled.

SCALLOPS EN BROCHETTE

4 large scallops	8 small rashers streaky bacon
6 oz rice	4 thick slices pineapple

Cook the rice in fast boiling salted water until just tender. Wash the scallops and cut in half, then roll each half in a rasher of bacon. Impale on a thin skewer with a half slice of pineapple between each. Grill under a moderate heat, turning once, for 8–10 min. Drain the rice when cooked, rinse under running cold water, then spread out on a sieve and reheat. Pile up on a dish and lay the 4 skewers on the rice. Serve hot.

4 helpings

SCALLOPS AU GRATIN

4 scallops	Creamed potatoes
½ pt milk	1 oz grated cheese
1 oz margarine	1 level tablesp browned breadcrumbs
1 oz flour	Chopped parsley
Salt and pepper	

Mussels Florentine

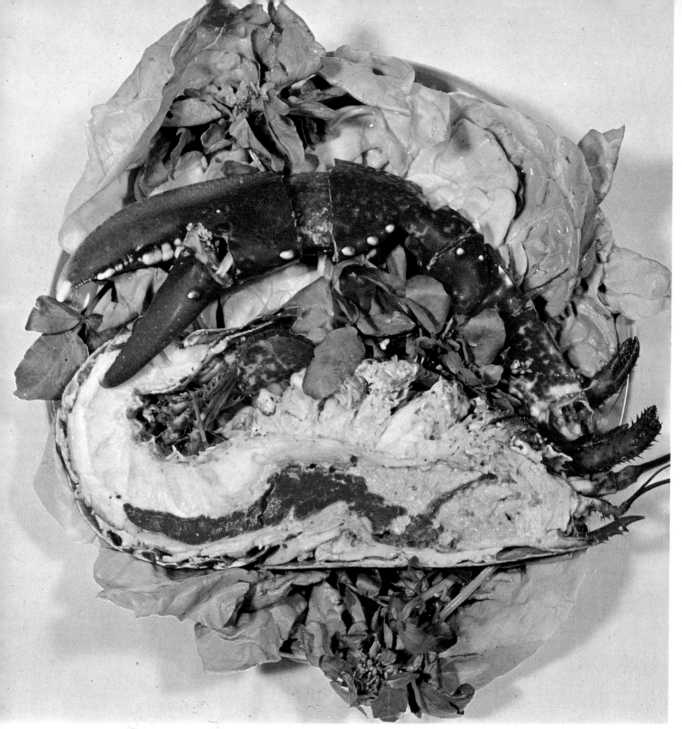

Dressed lobster

Simmer the scallops in the milk until tender—about 15 min. Drain carefully, place each in a deep shell and keep hot. Melt the margarine in a saucepan, stir in the flour and cook for 2 min. Add the milk in which the scallops were cooked, season to taste and boil for 3 min. Pipe a firm border of creamed potatoes round each shell and pour the sauce over the fish. Mix the cheese with the crumbs and spread over the top of each scallop. Reheat in a hot oven or under the grill until lightly browned. Sprinkle with chopped parsley and serve at once.

4 helpings

CRAB SALAD

1 large cooked crab *or*	1 dessertsp chopped
2 small cooked crabs	parsley
or 6 oz crab meat	Salt and pepper

2 celery hearts *or* the	Crisp lettuce leaves
heart of 1 endive	2 hard-boiled eggs
2 tablesp olive oil	1 tablesp capers
2 tablesp tarragon	12 stoned olives
vinegar	Anchovy butter
1 tablesp chilli *or*	
caper vinegar	

Cut the meat of the crabs into convenient-sized pieces. Shred the celery or endive, add to the crab meat and mix lightly with the oil, vinegar, parsley and seasoning. Serve on a bed of lettuce leaves; garnish with slices of hard-boiled egg, capers and olives stuffed with anchovy butter.

6 helpings

DRESSED LOBSTER

Prepare the boiled lobster as described above.

Leave the meat in the shell and arrange each half on a bed of salad. Garnish with the claws. Serve with oil and vinegar handed separately. Piped lobster butter may be used to garnish the shell, if wished. Dressed crab also makes a luxurious main dish for a summer meal. It is prepared and garnished in the same way as lobster.

LOBSTER MAYONNAISE

1 boiled lobster	Salad
Mayonnaise	

Lobster Mayonnaise may be served in any of the following ways:
1 Serve like dressed lobster but with mayonnaise instead of oil and vinegar.
2 Cut the lobster in half lengthways, scoop out the meat from the body, mix with a little mayonnaise and return. Carefully remove the meat from the tail, slice and return to the shell, arranging it in overlapping slices with the red part uppermost. Serve on a bed of salad, garnished with the claws. Serve mayonnaise separately.
3 Remove all the meat from the shell and claws. Arrange on a bed of salad, either cut into slices or roughly flaked and coat with mayonnaise.

The coral can be used, sieved, as a garnish.

LOBSTER SALAD, TWO WAYS

1 (without shell)

1 large cooked lobster	Salt and pepper
1 endive	½ cucumber
1 lettuce	A few radish roses
½ pt mayonnaise	½ bunch watercress

Remove all the meat from the lobster and cut into neat pieces. Break the endive into leaves, shred the lettuce coarsely. Slice the cucumber. Arrange the lobster and salad on a dish. Decorate with watercress. Serve the mayonnaise separately.

2 (served in the shell)

1 cooked lobster	Salt and pepper
⅛ pt tartare sauce or	1 lettuce
⅛ pt mayonnaise	1 lemon

Split the lobster, remove all the meat. Cut the meat into small dice, season it and mix with the tartare sauce and a little shredded lettuce. Fill the cleaned, trimmed lobster shells with the mixture. Decorate a dish with the crisp, inner lettuce leaves and slices of lemon and arrange the shells on the dish.

SHRIMP OR PRAWN SALAD

1 pt shelled shrimps or	Slices of cucumber
prawns	Crisp, inner lettuce
2–3 tablesp mayonnaise	leaves

Mix shrimps or prawns lightly with the mayonnaise and pile in a salad bowl. Garnish with shreds of lettuce and cucumber.

5–6 helpings

SHRIMP AND ASPARAGUS SALAD

25 cooked heads of	3 tablesp mayonnaise
asparagus	2 hard-boiled eggs
1 pt cooked, shelled	
shrimps	

Cut the green part of the asparagus into ½ in pieces. Mix very lightly with the shrimps and mayonnaise sauce. Pile on a salad dish with a border of slices of hard-boiled egg and asparagus tips.

6 helpings

Lobster salad

Section 3

Meat Dishes

Many people would eat meat at all meals if they could. They prefer it to most other foods, and only expense stops them buying more.

However, in its body-building value, meat is not really so expensive, especially if one buys wisely and learns to use the cheaper cuts. They give variety to meals as well as saving money.

A friendly and competent butcher is a great asset, and worth buying from regularly when one finds him. Today, however, many house-wives shop in stores where meat is sold pre-packed or is butchered in advance elsewhere, so they must learn to recognise the best cuts or pieces to buy in these forms. Trial and error must play its part here; but cooking experience and common sense can be a big help, especially when choosing and preparing cheaper meats. Working housewives should find the cheaper cuts particularly useful since dishes such as stews and braises can cook slowly for a whole evening (or even overnight) for use the follow-ing morning. They are simple to prepare and make less work than more costly roast and fried meals.

Meat from young animals is generally lean and tender, with unhardened bone. It may be dearer per pound, but the higher cost is offset by the minimal bone content compared with the heavy bone content of cheaper meat from more mature animals. Well-flavoured beef comes from comparatively young mature animals because the internal fat, which provides the meat's rich flavour, is laid down during growth. The tenderest beef comes from very young animals, and young lamb is particularly tender, with a fine, delicate flavour. Meat from very mature animals of any species will be coarse and suitable only for slow, moist cooking methods.

The tenderest meat from any species comes from the least-worked muscles; the toughest (and leanest) from muscles well exercised, such as those of shin and shoulder. This is particu-larly true of beef.

Long, slow cooking can do wonders for the tougher, leaner cuts. Casseroling or braising allow the flavours of other ingredients to per-meate the meat, enriching its flavour. By using various herbs and vegetables, a wide selection of excellent dishes can be made with the cheaper cuts.

COOKING MEAT

Basically, temperature and timing dictate what the cooked meat tastes like. Various kinds of heat can be used to make the meat reach a chosen temperature: radiant heat (grilling); hot air (baking or, as we call it, roasting); hot liquid (braising, stewing and boiling); contact with hot fat and metal (frying and some pot-roast-ing). Whatever kind of heat is used, the meat must be cooked for long enough to make it tender, but not so long that it becomes dry or disintegrates. The right time is dictated by:

1 the quality, weight and shape of the meat (how much cut muscle surface is exposed and how thick the piece of meat is);

2 the fierceness of the heat used.

GRILLING

Radiant heat is fierce. Whatever the source of heat (charcoal, an infra-red grill or rôtisserie, or gas) it sears and crisps the outside of the meat while leaving the inside juicy and usually undercooked. The heat should be even, and high. The meat must be of top quality, since tough meat requires longer cooking to be ten-derised. It should be about one inch thick, and should be seasoned and brushed with oil or melted fat before grilling. Steaks and chops are the most usual grilling cuts, and must be turned quickly to seal in the juices. They should not be pierced, but turned with tongs. Pork chops, unlike beef steaks, require even cooking right through. After the initial turning, reduce heat and allow 12–20 min cooking time depending on the thickness of the meat. If cooking under an infra-red grill, follow the maker's instructions on cooking times.

ROASTING AND SLOW ROASTING

Roasting, like grilling, often begins by searing the meat's surface with fierce heat, i.e. in a pre-heated oven. Hot fat and steam from the meat itself also contribute to the cooking. Roasting is the best cooking method for top-quality cuts which are too large for grilling (joints of 2–3 lb and over). The oven should be pre-heated to the recommended temperature and the full cooking time allowed. If the outside of the joint appears to be cooking too quickly, cover the meat with foil. Basting or barding (roasting with a covering of fat or bacon over the meat) helps lean joints to stay juicy and succulent.

Weigh the meat in order to calculate the cooking time. There are three well-known methods of roasting meat:

Method 1 'Sear' or brown the meat in a very hot oven (230°C, 450°F, Gas 8) for 15–20 min, then reduce heat and finish cooking in a fairly hot oven (190°C, 375°F, Gas 5); see time-table below.

Method 2 Cook the meat in a fairly hot oven (190°C, 375°F, Gas 5) for the whole time. To produce a juicy joint cover the roasting-tin with a lid or aluminium foil, although the outside will not brown so well as when the meat is cooked uncovered.

Method 3 Cook the meat in a warm to moderate oven (170°–180°C, 335°–350°F, Gas 3–4). This method, known as slow roasting, is suitable for cuts of cheaper, medium-quality meat. It is advisable to wrap them in foil to keep in the meat juices. The joint can be uncovered for the last half hour to brown the outside.

CASSEROLE ROASTING

Another method is casserole roasting. In this, a joint is baked or roasted in a sealed casserole containing hot fat. Top quality fillet of beef is sometimes cooked in butter in this way as a luxury dish, but dripping or lard is usual for less tender joints. The casserole lid is removed for the last half an hour to brown the meat. Steam, especially when vegetables are added for flavour, contributes to the cooking; and so the meat is almost braised rather than 'roasted'.

POT ROASTING AND BRAISING

A pot-roast can be cooked in the oven or on top of the stove. The meat is first seared on all sides in hot fat then placed in a casserole or tightly covered pan. A small amount of liquid ($\frac{1}{4}$ pt water, stock or wine) is poured round the meat. A layer of vegetables can be put under the joint to raise it above the level of the hot fat and liquid, so that the meat is steamed rather than simmered. Bacon rinds, mushroom stalks, bones or herbs tied in a bag (a *bouquet garni*) can be added to give a fuller flavour.

True braising is also done in the oven or on the stove. The method is used to cook large cuts of meat, but with more liquid than is used in pot-roasting. When cooked, the meat is taken out to 'rest' before being carved, and the braising liquid is used to make a variety of delicious sauces. It also makes excellent soup.

All joints should be allowed to 'rest' for a short time at room temperature before being carved, to let the juices sink into the fibres.

STEWING

The meat, cut in small pieces, is cooked slowly in liquid ($\frac{3}{4}$ pt–1 lb meat), usually on top of the stove. It is economical as all the flavour and goodness are kept in the liquid and the slow cooking tenderises tough, cheap stewing meats. The liquid is served with the meat, and often thickened with added potato or some kind of flour (rice, potato, wheat) blended with fat

Meat		Methods 1 and 2	Method 3
Beef	(without bone)	20 min per lb plus 10 min	30 min per lb plus 30 min
	(with bone)	15 min per lb plus 15 min	20 min per lb plus 20 min
Lamb	(aged)	20–25 min per lb plus 20–25 min	30–35 min per lb plus 30–35 min
	(young)	20 min per lb plus 20 min	30 min per lb plus 30 min
Pork	(thick cut)	25–30 min per lb plus 25–30 min	40 min per lb plus 40 min
Veal		25 min per lb plus 25 min	35 min per lb plus 35 min

(The above time-table is approximate and the exact time will depend on the form and thickness of the joint, and its age and condition. A square solid piece of beef will not cook as quickly as a shoulder of well-aged lamb of equal weight.)

(*beurre manié*). A stew never boils, only simmers.

BOILING AND POACHING

Actual boiling (fast-bubbling liquid) is only used for reducing meat sauces and gravies.

Ready for roasting

Frying chops

Meat is put into boiling water, to seal it somewhat, but thereafter bubbles slowly as in stewing. 'Boiling' is used for single big pieces of meat which one wants to cook slowly or cook without fat. Vegetables must be added for flavour.

Poaching is even gentler cooking in water, and is used for meat mixtures such as quenelles or meat balls. The water is kept under the boil, the meat being heated through very slowly.

STEAMING
Steaming is suited only to light, small pieces of tender meat for fatless meals. Meat can be steamed wrapped in paper or foil over a saucepan in which vegetables or pasta are being cooked, thus cooking two products at once. Some garnishes such as meat balls can be steamed on a plate over another dish like this.

FRYING AND SAUTÉING
Garnishes (e.g. small sausages) and some small pieces of meat and offal (kidneys, blanched sweetbreads, small steaks, etc) can be shallow-fried in a frying-pan by direct contact with searing hot metal and fat. Fatty meats can be 'dry-fried' or 'pan-broiled' with little or no added fat, and there are modern pans and grill-plates designed for this. The pieces of meat must be thin, to cook through quickly without burning. The fat used must be capable of heating to 200°C, 400°F, and must be heated slowly for even heat all through it. Commercial frying fats, oil, mixed oil and butter or clarified dripping can all be used. The food must be dried before being fried, dusted with seasoned flour, crumbs or oatmeal, or coated with a batter. They should be turned once, with tongs. Small pieces of meat, usually in batter, can also be deep-fried, contacting only hot fat not metal. Deep fat gets much hotter than shallow fat, and the meat must be coated first, to prevent burning, and drained on absorbent paper afterwards to avoid greasiness. As a rule, raw cutlets or meat balls in batter are plunged in hot fat (190°C, 380°F) and then allowed to fry at a reduced temperature to cook them right through.

THE MEATS WE USE

The most popular meats are beef, lamb, pork, veal and some kinds of offals, notably liver and kidneys. Mutton is said to be rare, due to the popular demand for lamb, and is often called well-aged lamb; and kid (treated like lamb in cooking) is not generally popular either. Many kinds of offals, too, suffer from prejudice almost amounting to taboo. This is a pity since they are excellent food value for money.

The cooking method for any kind of meat depends on the cut and the thickness of the piece and on its quality. So it must be pointed out that meats are cut quite differently in different places. In the New World, meat cuts are different (and are differently named) from British and European cuts. Continental cuts differ very much from British ones, and there are even differences between northern and southern English cuts. In the following pages you will find pictures of the most widely used British cuts, but they are by no means standard.

Today meat is often sold pre-cut and pre-packed as joints or tray meat (smaller pieces) and a particular piece may be hard to identify. Its label is therefore important. All packed meat should carry the name of the country of origin; 'tenderised' meat should be labelled as such, and the name of the cut should be given. The recommended names for cuts of tray meat are:

ENGLAND AND WALES

Beef	Lamb	Pork	Veal
Fillet steak	Leg chops	Leg steaks	Leg cutlets
Rump steak	Chump chops	Loin chops	Fillets (or Escalopes)
Sirloin steak	Loin chops	Spare rib chops	Loin chops
Round (or Buttock) steak	Cutlets	Shoulder steaks	Neck cutlets
Skirt	Middle neck		
Mince	Scrag	Belly (or Streaky)	Pie (or Stewing) veal
		Pork fillets (or Tenderloin)	Breast
Chuck (or Shoulder)	Breast	Feet (or Trotters)	Calves' liver
Brisket	Lambs' hearts*	Pigs' hearts	
Stewing beef†	Lambs' kidneys	Pigs' kidneys	
Shin of beef	Lambs' liver*	Pigs' liver	
Ox heart*			
Ox kidney*			
Ox liver*			

SCOTLAND

Beef	Lamb	Pork	
Fillet steak	Gigot chops	Gigot (or Leg) chops	
Pope's eye steak	Chump chops	Loin chops	
Sirloin steak	Loin chops	Shoulder	
Round (or Buttock) steak	Cutlets	Belly (or Streaky)	
Skirt	Shoulder chops	Pork fillets (or Tenderloin)	
Mince	Neck (or Scrag)	Feet (or Trotters)	
Shoulder steak	Flank	Pigs' hearts	
Brisket	Lambs' hearts*	Pigs' kidneys	
Stewing beef†	Lambs' kidneys*	Pigs' liver	
Shin of beef (or Hough)	Lambs' liver*		
Ox heart*			
Ox kidney*			
Ox liver*			

† Primarily the neck, but may include meat from the clod, lean trimmings or other meat that does not come from another named cut.
* Or cow or sheep if appropriate.

No matter where you live or how you buy, always inspect a cut carefully to make sure you have the right size, shape and quality for the cooking method you have chosen.

IMPORTED MEATS

IMPORTED MEAT
Meat imported from other countries is chilled or carcass-frozen, depending on the distance it must travel. Beef from Argentina, for example, is chilled, while New Zealand lamb is carcass-frozen. Freezing may produce ice crystals within the muscle tissue of the meat which damage the fibres and cause 'drip' or loss of juices after

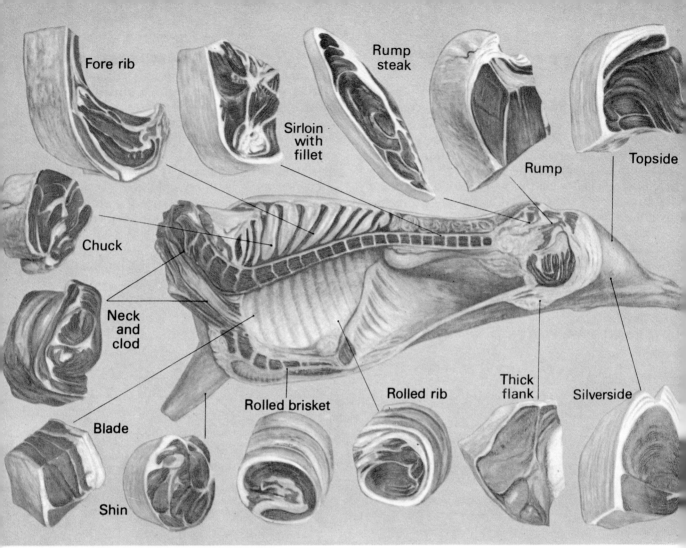

Fore rib

Rump steak

Sirloin with fillet

Rump

Topside

Chuck

Neck and clod

Thick flank

Silverside

Rolled rib

Blade

Rolled brisket

Shin

Cuts of beef

thawing. The amount of damage depends to a large extent on the rate of freezing and of thawing. For this reason, fresh or partially thawed meat should *never* be placed in the freezing compartment of a domestic refrigerator. The slow freezing which results causes excessively large ice crystals to form, and causes extensive fibre damage. Similarly, rapid thawing will increase fibre damage.

It is advisable to thaw all chilled and frozen meat before cooking. *Thaw slowly*, allowing at least 2 hr per lb at room temperature, or 5–6 hr per lb in the refrigerator.

Meat that is chilled is kept as near as possible to freezing point without actual freezing (and hence ice formation) taking place. It has a limited storage life and will deteriorate more rapidly than carcass-frozen meat. Very occasionally the fat has a slightly objectionable flavour, but this can be masked by seeing that the fat is well salted. (This also helps the outside of the joint to become crisp.)

Here is a brief description of points to look for when choosing various meats and offals, fresh or frozen.

BEEF

Most beef comes from steers and heifers between 10 and 18 months old, although a small quantity of cow beef is still sold. Cow beef, and meat from mature bulls is lean and tough, and suitable only for braising and stewing.

The lean of beef should be bright red when cut. After exposure to air it naturally becomes a duller, more muted red. The better cuts should be 'marbled' with flecks of fat between the fibres. The marbling is an aid to cooking as the melting fat bastes the lean and keeps the meat tender and succulent. Marbling is not found in the very lean cuts.

Frying and grilling cuts include *fillet* and *undercut*, *sirloin* (cut in steaks) and *rump* steak. Steaks are slices of meat cut in various sizes and thicknesses from these parts. Cutting techniques and names of cuts may vary, but the most usual names of steaks are:—Châteaubriand (for 2 people, large and very thick); tournedos (1–1½ in thick, round, small); noisettes (½–¾ in thick, round or oval); mignons or minute steaks (small, fine, thinner); porterhouse steaks (slices of loin

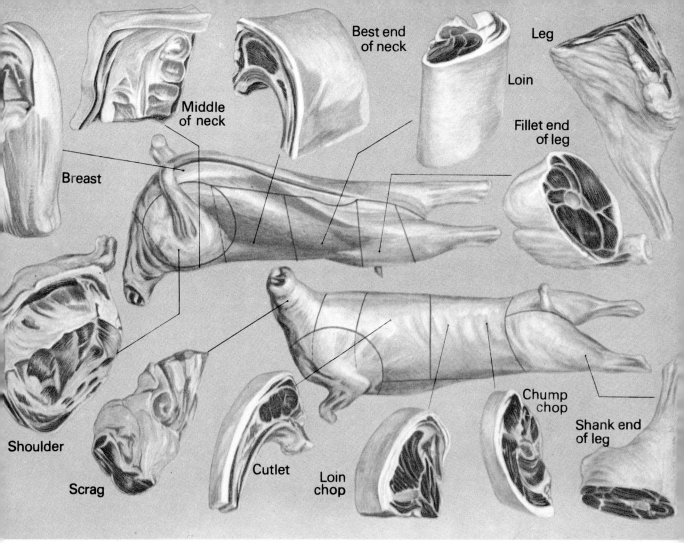

Middle of neck

Best end of neck

Leg

Loin

Fillet end of leg

Breast

Shoulder

Scrag

Cutlet

Loin chop

Chump chop

Shank end of leg

Cuts of lamb and mutton

with no fillet or undercut); fillet ($\frac{1}{2}$–$\frac{3}{4}$ in thick, from beneath blade of loin bones); T-bone (cut through sirloin, containing T-shaped bone); entrecôte (thin sirloin steak without undercut or bone).

Roasting cuts include: the sirloin; rump and topside; foreribs; back ribs; top or 'rising' ribs; good quality leg of mutton cut (shoulder). Ribs and mediocre quality topside are usually best slow roasted or pot-roasted.

Braising, stewing and boiling cuts include: silverside (roasted in Scotland); shin or hough (boiling only); skirt (diaphragm muscle); brisket; sticking and clod (neck and front chest muscles, boiling only); chuck and bladebone (sometimes called a chine or shoulder); flank and thick flank.

Salted meat is usually boiled.

LAMB AND MUTTON

Good quality lamb meat should be cherry-red with creamy white fat. Very young, early-season fresh lamb may be pinkish, and well-aged and chilled lamb is darker red with more brittle white fat. Mutton is dark red, with sometimes a tinge of yellow in the fat.

Mountain lamb and lamb from salty grass areas is darker, leaner and stronger-flavoured than valley and sweet grass pasture lamb. The joints are also smaller. There can be a lot of difference in the size, fat covering and flavour of these types of lamb. Most of the lamb we get, especially foreign chilled lamb, is 'fat' sweet pasture lamb. Although these carry more meat to the amount of bone, they must often be pared of a lot of fat before cooking.

English lamb is usually cut in the same way as beef. So is a good deal of foreign, chilled or frozen lamb.

Frying and grilling cuts include: cutlets (from the best end of the neck or the loin); chops (from loin or chump); 'fillets' (thigh slices); leg or shoulder strips cut in squares (for kebabs, etc).

Roasting cuts include: saddle; loin; best end of neck (sometimes standing upright, skewered, as a Crown Roast or Guard of Honour); shoulder; leg. Shoulder is usually moister and sweeter than leg, although cheaper (being more difficult to cook and carve well and with a higher percentage of fat).

CHOOSING PORK

Braising, stewing and boiling cuts include: leg (boiled for an alternative flavour to roast meat, not from necessity); breast; scrag end of neck; middle neck.

Unlike beef, lamb and mutton are easy to bone, and the pieces of meat can be stuffed and rolled up after boning. These joints, even very inexpensive cuts such as the breast, can then be casserole- or pot-roasted.

PORK

Modern pig-keeping and cold storage techniques mean that it is safe to eat pork at any time of the year. It is easily the most adaptable meat we have, since all parts can be roasted and all, except the loin, boiled. It can be bought fresh, salted, or cured—and sometimes smoked—as ham or bacon; and fresh, 'pickled' and cured pig meat all have pleasant but quite different flavours.

The pig can live anywhere and is a prolific breeder, and *every* part of a pig can be used in cooking. It is therefore a comparatively cheap meat.

Fresh pork flesh must be pale pink with white,

firm fat. Red-tinged or greyish meat must be rejected. Small black spots in the fat only come from the skin pigment of black and brown pigs, and do not matter, but oily or greyish fat indicates poor quality or deterioration.

Leg or gigot, and loin are the most expensive roasting cuts.

The blade bone is an economical roasting joint comparable to the blade half-shoulder in lamb. It is good boned and stuffed. So, too, is the hand and spring, or whole foreleg, comparable to a bacon forehock. The knuckle part can be removed, soaked in salt water, and then boiled to use like belly.

Belly of pork is often salted and boiled. It is an admirable 'buy' as it can be served hot as a joint, or kept for slicing (to 'stand in' for streaky bacon) or for dicing to add to other meats or to vegetable main dishes for flavour. It is also cheaper than bacon.

English spare ribs sometimes confuse Americans, being cut from the neck instead of the chest ribs. To get American spare ribs, ask for the rib end of belly of pork with bone in.

A pig's head should not be despised. It is a

Cuts of pork

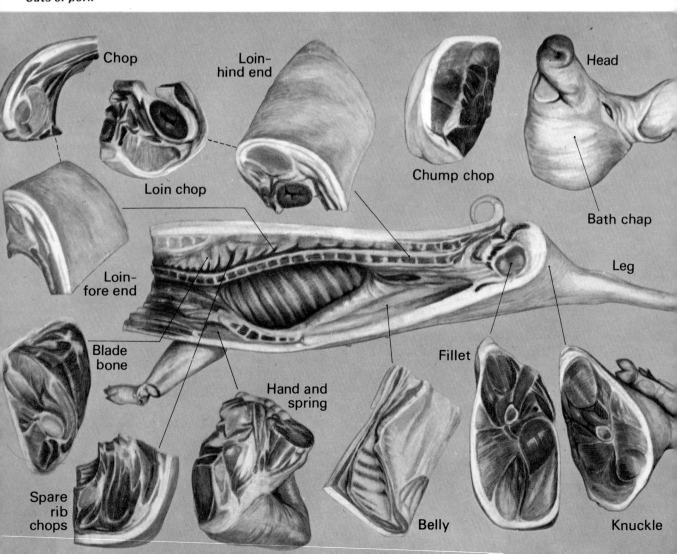

Chop

Loin-hind end

Head

Loin chop

Chump chop

Bath chap

Loin-fore end

Leg

Blade bone

Fillet

Hand and spring

Spare rib chops

Belly

Knuckle

nuisance to clean, but contains a lot of meat suitable for brawns and galantines, sausages, or stews. Cheek meat, cured and boiled, is called a Bath Chap and is excellent fried as a 'stand in' for fat ham or bacon, or for use, diced, to give body to stews.

Even a pig's skin is useful. It is the best means of greasing a pancake pan, and the layer of fat just beneath, together with scrapings, provides 'scratchings'—a fat-and-flavouring ingredient in a number of traditional recipes.

BACON AND HAM

Bacon and ham come from special types and sizes of pig, and the joints are cut differently from fresh pork. Ham and the various 'gammon' joints of bacon come from the hind leg (the gammon). The usual cuts are called gammon hock, middle gammon, corner gammon and gammon slipper. Other bacon joints suitable for cooking whole are the forehock, and its parts, called the fore slipper, small hock and butt. The remaining parts of a bacon pig's carcass give different kinds and qualities of rashers or slices. If ordering these to be cut, remember that a small number on the slicing machine gives thin rashers (3 or 5), higher numbers give thicker ones. On the whole, very thin rashers for serving with game or as bacon rolls are only practical to cut from smoked bacon. 'Green' (salted but not smoked) bacon tears too easily.

The quality and flavour of bacon rashers depend largely on the part of the animal used and whether the bacon is 'green' or is smoked as well. The smell, as well as the colour, is a good guide to flavour.

Fresh bacon rashers should have a light pink colour, in the lean, and firm white fat. A great deal of the flavour is in the fat so see that your bacon has a good layer of fat over it. You should be able to fry bacon in its own fat; added cooking fat should not be needed, and it spoils the flavour. Bacon should have a sweet or smoky smell; bacon that looks brown and dry, or smells sour, is stale and should be avoided.

Much bacon sold as rashers or joints, including the 'mild' or 'sweet' cures, is now sold pre-packed. These last should be consumed within a few days of purchase, or within the time limit on the pack, since they keep only a comparatively short time.

Hams and joints of bacon vary immensely in colour, largely according to the pig's feed and the method used to preserve the meat. Famous for their unusual appearance, as well as their flavour, are the Westphalian hams and Italian prosciutto, usually eaten raw, in paper-thin slices; the various American-style pink, peach-fed hams; English York hams and almost black-skinned Bradenham hams.

More general-use hams and bacon joints for baking, braising and boiling come to us today from many countries. Many are sold ready boned, shaped and pre-packed for economical cutting which offsets their cost compared with other meats to some extent. Each has its own flavour and cutting quality for use as steaks, and personal experience is the best guide in choosing.

VEAL

Good veal, especially continental veal, is pale pink, with bubbly tissue between the muscles, and little fat. Very young veal should have more cartilage than bone; and although often spurned, the gristly 'tendrons' or rib-ends are esteemed a great delicacy by some people. Older veal darkens in colour and texture, but should not become blueish, brown or mottled. This indicates deterioration.

Most veal needs added fat in cooking, and a stuffing or sauce. It keeps less well than other meats and should be used quickly. English veal cuts are similar to lamb and mutton cuts, and are used in much the same way. But specialist butchers often sell continental cuts.

OFFALS

Liver This is the best known and most used offal meat. Bullock or ox liver varies in flavour, but is always coarse. It is not suited to grilling or frying, but is good in pies, stews and when braised. Usually sold sliced, it is dark-coloured. Pig's liver is dark too, usually strongly flavoured, and fairly cheap. Because it is strong it is used largely for pâtés, pies, galantines and stews. Calf's liver and sheep's or lamb's liver are more delicate in flavour and texture, lighter in colour and more costly. Both are usually sold sliced for grilling or frying, but are better bought 'in the piece' and used as desired. They make a good, moist braised dish cooked in one piece; or they can be sliced, lightly grilled or fried and left pink inside.

Kidneys Ox kidney is often sold ready cubed for stews, pies and puddings. A whole kidney weighs 1–1½ lb and serves 4–6 people. It is good food value, and the fat round it makes the best suet. Pig's kidneys, like ox kidneys, are cheap and are best used in stews, pies etc., although they can be grilled or fried. Calf's and lamb's kidneys are the ones most usually grilled or fried. Both are pale-coloured and tender, and care must be taken not to overcook them, or they toughen. They should still exude a little blood and be pink inside when brought to table.

CHOOSING OFFALS

(They can be baked, if liked, in their own layer of fat or in pastry.)

Hearts These give excellent lean meat and food value. Ox-heart is often sold sliced or cubed, although whole ones can be obtained for stuffing and roasting. They need long slow roasting in foil, or pot-roasting, with a strongly-flavoured stuffing and sauce. Pigs' hearts are, by law, slashed before sale, and cannot be stuffed. Like miniature ox-hearts in colour and flavour, they are more tender; but they are fairly high-flavoured, and are probably best cubed and stewed. Calves' and lambs' hearts on the other hand are excellent stuffed and baked or braised. All hearts must have the tubes and interior connecting tissue cut out with scissors before use. This is quick and easy to do.

Tongues With liver, ox-tongue is the best-known offal meat. These tongues, 4–6 lb weight, are usually sold whole when uncooked, and may be fresh, salted or smoked. They are usually boiled, and are often eaten cold after being pressed in a round. Pigs', calves' and sheeps' tongues are used hot or cold, after boiling or braising. All tongues must be skinned before use.

Heads, and their parts Ox-cheek is economical, although it needs long, slow cooking. Pig's cheek becomes Bath Chap when boiled (see Pork). Ears are little used today. Whole calves' heads are more popular with continental people than with the English. On the continent and in the Middle East they are served hot with various sauces, whereas in England they are used mostly for brawns and pies. The same use is made of sheeps' heads. Boar's head is, however, a traditional luxury dish in England, served roasted and garlanded with similar trimmings to game.

Feet These give out a lot of gelatine, and are much used for jellied stock, aspic, etc. Cow heels are sometimes served hot, boiled, with a sauce. Calves' feet are used for 'invalid's' jelly, and for flavouring and giving body to various braises. Pigs' trotters are used cold and jellied, or hot, boned and stuffed.

Tails Ox-tail is well known, and is usually stewed. When choosing, look for a meaty tail, without excess fat or small thin joints. Cooked long and slowly, ox-tail makes an excellent thick stew. Sheep's tails are little seen today, but used to be valued for their fat; they were used in stews whole, in pies or cut up for rendered fat or soap-making.

Tripe This is usually sold ready prepared and part-cooked. But although it is more trouble, the flavour is very much better if tripe is bought unprepared and is dealt with by the cook. There are various forms of tripe, honeycomb, blanket, etc. They all need slow, careful cooking, but repay it by being delicate, easily digested meat.

Sweetbreads The pancreas and thymus glands, sweetbreads are fine food value, by no means as much work to prepare as is usually thought. They must all be soaked and then blanched, and the thicker membranes must be pulled off after soaking or blanching. They can then be braised whole, or sliced and fried in various coatings. Ox sweetbreads need slow cooking, but calf's and lamb's sweetbreads are tender and delicate.

Brains These are treated like sweetbreads, but are more delicate and need less picking over to remove membranes.

ROASTED, GRILLED AND FRIED DISHES

ROAST BEEF

Joint of beef suitable for roasting	Beef dripping (allow 1 oz per lb of meat)
Salt and pepper	

Weigh meat to be able to calculate cooking time. Wipe with a damp cloth. Place joint in a roasting-tin. season and add dripping.

Put roasting-tin into a very hot oven (230°C, 450°F, Gas 8) for 10-15 min to brown or 'sear' the meat. Then reduce heat to fairly hot (190°C, 375°F, Gas 5) and baste every 20 min for the first half of the cooking time and afterwards every 30 min. Allow 20 min per lb and another 10 min over for solid joints, i.e. joints without bone; and 15 min per lb and 15 min over for thick joints, i.e. joints with bone. Remove on to a hot dish when cooked, remove string and skewer with a metal skewer if necessary. Keep hot. Drain off fat from tin and make gravy from sediment in the tin. Yorkshire Pudding is roast beef's traditional companion, as is Horseradish Sauce.

FILLET OF BEEF DAUPHIN

1½-2 lb fillet of beef	Dripping
Salt and pepper	Meat glaze
Larding bacon	½ pt Madeira sauce
Flour	12 potato croquettes

GRILLED BEEF STEAKS

Wipe, trim and season the meat. Lard with thin strips of bacon (*see* Barded Roast Neck of Veal). Sprinkle with flour and tie into a good shape. Put into a roasting-tin with dripping. Cover with paper and put into a hot oven (220°C, 425°F, Gas 7) for 10 min, then reduce the heat to moderate (180°C, 350°F, Gas 4). Baste and cook until tender allowing 15 min per lb and 15 min over. Baste occasionally while cooking. Remove the paper 15 min before serving. Place fillet on a hot dish, remove string and brush over with glaze. Garnish with the potato croquettes. Pour away the fat from the roasting-tin and add any of the brown sediment to the sauce; heat and serve separately.

Tomato sauce can be served instead of Madeira sauce if you wish.

6 helpings

GRILLED STEAK

1½ lb rump or fillet steak for sirloin	Salt and pepper
	Maître d'hôtel butter
Oil or butter	Watercress (optional)

Wipe and cut the meat across the grain into suitable slices if required. Beat on both sides with a cutlet bat or rolling-pin if wanted thin. (*See* Beef above.) Brush the slices with oil or melted butter and sprinkle with salt and pepper. Place under a red-hot grill, and grill quickly on both sides to seal the surfaces, thus preventing the juices from escaping.

Fillet of beef dauphin

Châteaubriand steak

Wipe the steak. Remove any sinew or skin. Cover the meat with a cloth and beat lightly to flatten. Brush over with oil or melted butter and season. Place under a red-hot grill and cook both sides quickly; the steak should be well browned but slightly underdone. Serve immediately on a hot dish with potato straws. Serve also Maître d'hôtel butter and gravy, or demi-glace, tomato or Béchamel sauce.

TOURNEDOS OF BEEF À LA NELSON

1½–2 lb fillet of beef, cut as tournedos	1 glass Madeira (optional)
⅓ pt small button onions Stock	½ pt brown or Espagnole sauce
Salt and pepper	⅓ pt diced potatoes

Ask the butcher to prepare the tournedos. Parboil the onions in strong stock and then strain them. Fry the tournedos very lightly in hot fat to seal them, drain and place in individual casseroles. Season with salt and pepper and add the onions. Add the wine to the sauce, season to taste and add to the casseroles. Cook in a moderate oven (180°C, 350°F, Gas 4) for about 40 min. Fry the potato dice in hot fat until well browned. Drain well and add to the casseroles 10 min before serving.

6 helpings

TOURNEDOS OF BEEF, ROSSINI

1½ lb fillet of beef, cut as tournedos	1 tablesp brown sauce
¼ lb chickens' livers	Salt and pepper
2 oz butter or fat	1 tablesp olive oil
1 shallot	Meat glaze
1½ oz foie gras or pâté	Croûtes of fried bread
	½–¾ pt demi-glace sauce

Wipe the beef and cut into rounds 2½ in diameter and ½ in thick; that is, cut as tournedos. Wash, dry and slice the livers. Melt 1 oz of the fat in a sauté pan and fry the finely-chopped shallot slightly. Add the liver and sauté for a few minutes. Drain off the fat and pound the livers with the foie gras or pâté, brown sauce and seasoning until smooth, then pass through a wire sieve. Heat the remainder of the fat with the olive oil and fry the tournedos quickly until browned on both sides. Drain and cover one side of each with the liver farce. Brush with meat glaze, place on the fried croûtes and put in the oven to become thoroughly hot. Arrange the fillets on a hot dish and serve the demi-glace sauce separately.

6 helpings

Then grill more slowly until cooked as you wish. A 'rare' steak is sealed only, remaining red inside. A 'medium' steak is still slightly pink inside, a 'well-done' steak is fully cooked through. The heat of the grill and the thickness of the steak will determine how long to cook each type. While cooking, turn the steaks frequently, using tongs or 2 spoons. Never pierce them with a fork as this makes holes through which the meat juices escape. Serve steaks at once with a pat of Maître d'hôtel butter on top, and with watercress if available.

6 helpings

CHATEAUBRIAND STEAK

A double fillet steak not less than 1½ in thick	Olive oil or melted butter
	Salt and pepper

NOISETTES OF BEEF WITH MAÎTRE D'HÔTEL BUTTER

1½–2 lb fillet of beef	Salt and pepper
1 oz Maître d'hôtel butter	Fried potato chips or dice
Olive oil or melted butter	

Wipe and trim the meat and cut into thick round fillets. Tie with string so that they keep their shape. Knead the butter into a flat cake, and chill well to become firm. Brush the fillets with olive oil or melted butter, sprinkle with salt and pepper and grill for 8–10 min, turning 2 or 3 times. Place them in a nearly upright position down the centre of a hot dish, put a small pat of the Maître d'hôtel butter on the top of each fillet, garnish with crisply-fried potato chips or dice and serve very hot.

6 helpings

Crown roast of lamb stuffed with saffron rice

CROWN ROAST OF LAMB WITH SAFFRON RICE

A 2-section crown roast of lamb	Salt
	Pepper
Oil for brushing	

STUFFING

1 oz butter	2 oz frozen peas
1 stick celery, chopped	1 oz chopped, blanched almonds
1 onion, chopped	
5 oz long grain white rice	2 dessert apples, cored and diced
$\frac{1}{2}$ gill dry white wine	1 oz butter
1 pt chicken stock, heated with a scant $\frac{1}{4}$ teasp powdered saffron	

Ask the butcher to prepare the crown roast. Place the joint in a roasting tin. Brush with oil and season well with salt and pepper. Wrap a small piece of foil around the top of each rib to prevent it from scorching during cooking. Cook at 190°C, 375°F, Gas 5, for $1\frac{1}{4}$–$1\frac{1}{2}$ hr. Approx 30 min before the joint is due to finish cooking, prepare the saffron rice stuffing by melting the butter in a saucepan and cooking the celery and onion until soft but not browned. Stir in the raw rice and cook for 1–2 min. Pour on the wine and cook gently until the rice has absorbed it. Add $\frac{1}{2}$ pt of the saffron-flavoured chicken stock and cook, uncovered, stirring occasionally, until almost all the liquid is absorbed. Pour the remaining stock over the rice and cook until it has been completely absorbed and the rice is just tender. Remove from the heat and add the peas, chopped nuts, diced apple and butter and cover the saucepan with fitting lid.

Drain the joint and place on a warmed serving dish. Remove the foil from the rib bones. Fill the roast with the hot saffron rice. Top each rib with a cutlet frill and serve. (Any extra rice can be served separately.)

6–8 helpings

STUFFED AND ROAST LOIN OR SHOULDER OF LAMB OR MUTTON

A loin *or* shoulder of lamb *or* mutton	Salt and pepper
	2–3 oz dripping
Veal forcemeat *or* sage and onion stuffing	

Remove all the bones from the meat. Trim off any skin and surplus fat and flatten the meat with a rolling-pin. Season the meat well with salt and pepper and spread on the forcemeat or stuffing. Reform or roll up the meat to cover the stuffing neatly, and tie securely with string. Melt the dripping in a covered meat-tin, put in the meat and roast in a moderate oven (180°C, 350°F, Gas 4) until tender. Allow 25 min per lb and 25 min over. Baste occasionally. A good gravy or brown sauce should be served with the joint.

ROAST LAMB, FRENCH STYLE

A stuffed shoulder can be carved in wedges like a cake.

ROAST LEG OF LAMB, FRENCH STYLE

A small leg of lamb (boned)	1 teasp chopped parsley
1 carrot	1 clove of bruised garlic
1 onion	Salt and pepper
1 shallot	2 oz good dripping

Slice the carrot, and onion and chop the shallot finely. Mix together the parsley, shallot, garlic, salt and pepper, and then sprinkle the mixture on the inner surface of the meat. Bind into a good shape. Place in a covered baking-tin with the dripping, onion and carrot. Season well with salt and pepper. Bake for 20 min in a fairly hot oven (200°C, 400°F, Gas 6) then reduce heat to moderate (180°C, 350°F, Gas 4) for the remainder of the time, allowing 20 min per lb and 20 min over. For the last 10 min remove the covering and allow the meat to brown and become crisp. Serve on a hot dish with gravy made from the bones and the sediment in the baking tin.

6–8 helpings

LAMB OR MUTTON CUTLETS WITH CUCUMBER

8–9 cutlets	Egg and breadcrumbs
1 large cucumber	Fat for frying
3 oz butter or margarine	Mashed potatoes
Salt and pepper	¼ pt gravy

Peel and dice the cucumber, discarding the seeds. Heat the fat in a stewpan, put in the cucumber. Season with salt and pepper, cover closely and cook very gently for 15–20 min or until the pieces are tender but unbroken; drain well. Trim the cutlets into a good shape. Season both sides, dip them in beaten egg, coat with breadcrumbs and fry in hot fat in a frying-pan until lightly browned on both sides. Arrange the cutlets on a mashed potato border, serve the cucumber in the centre and pour the hot gravy round.

6–7 helpings

LAMB CUTLETS EN PAPILLOTES

6 lamb cutlets	1 dessertsp chopped parsley
A few slices cooked ham	Salt and pepper
Salad oil or butter	Grated rind of ½ lemon
1 onion	
1 dessertsp chopped mushrooms	

Prepare and trim the cutlets neatly. Cut 12 small rounds of ham just large enough to cover the round part of the cutlet. Melt a little fat in a pan and fry the finely-chopped onion until tender. Add the mushroom, parsley, salt, pepper and a little grated lemon rind. Mix well and then cool. Prepare 6 heart-shaped pieces of strong white paper large enough to hold the cutlets. Grease them well with oil or butter. Place a slice of ham on one half of each paper with a

Lamb cutlets en papillotes

little of the chopped mixture on top. Lay the cutlet on the mixture, with more of the mixture on top and place a round of ham over that. Fold over the paper and twist the edges well together. Lay the prepared cutlets in a greased baking-tin and cook for 30 min in a fairly hot oven (190°C, 375°F, Gas 5). Serve in the papers on a hot dish. A little good sauce may be served separately.

This method of cooking can be used with a number of different stuffings. Fried breadcrumbs mixed with chopped sautéed onions is good. So is a mixture of fresh white breadcrumbs, capers and a little garlic salt.

6 helpings   **Cooking time about 30 min**

NOISETTES OF LAMB

These are the neatly trimmed round or oval shaped pieces cut from the fleshy part of a loin of lamb. They are usually cooked in the same way as cutlets, but are not coated with egg and breadcrumbs.

When cooked as described they can be placed on a bed of mashed potatoes and attractively garnished with vegetables cut 'à la jardinère'. Pour a good brown gravy round the noisettes.

GRILLED LAMB OR MUTTON CUTLETS OR CHOPS

6–8 cutlets *or* chops   **Salad oil**
Salt and pepper

Trim the cutlets or chops to a neat uniform shape. Season with salt and pepper and brush all over with salad oil. Grill, turning 3 or 4 times for about 8 min for cutlets, longer for chops, according to their thickness. Cover the end of each bone with a small paper frill. Suitable accompaniments are green peas, mashed potatoes, and a good gravy or demi-glace sauce.

6–8 helpings   **Cooking time about 10 min**

ROAST LOIN OF PORK WITH APPLE SAUCE

3 lb loin of pork	**½ teasp salt**
½ teasp powdered sage	**¼ saltsp pepper**
1 saltsp dry mustard	**Apple sauce**
1 tablesp finely chopped onion	**Brown gravy**

Score the pork with narrow lines. Mix the onion with the sage, salt, mustard and pepper and rub the mixture well into the meat. Wrap the joint in greased greaseproof paper and roast in a covered tin in a hot oven (220°C, 425°F, Gas 7) for 10 min and then reduce heat to moderate (180°C, 350°F, Gas 4) for the remainder of the time. Allow 25 min per lb and 25 min over. About ½ hr before serving, remove the paper and lid and continue cooking to crisp the crackling. Serve the apple sauce and gravy separately. Roast pork is also good served cold with salad.

6 helpings

Roast loin of pork with apple sauce

PORK CUTLETS OR CHOPS

FRIED OR GRILLED PORK CUTLETS OR CHOPS

6 neck *or* loin cutlets of pork	Salt and pepper
	Breadcrumbs
1 egg	1½ oz butter *or* fat
1 teasp powdered sage	

Trim the cutlets, removing most of the fat. Beat the egg and add to it the sage, salt and pepper. Brush each cutlet with this and then coat carefully with breadcrumbs. Heat the fat and gently fry, or grill, the cutlets for about 20 min, turning frequently until golden brown.

GRILLED TENDERLOIN

6 pork chops from spare rib, tenderloin *or* neck	Stock
	1 dessert apple, cored and sliced
Salt and pepper	1 oz butter
Sage	1 8-oz packet frozen sweet corn
Marjoram	
Castor sugar	Parsley
Flour	

Prepare the chops. Sprinkle both sides of the chops with a pinch of salt, pepper, sage, marjoram and castor sugar. Grill carefully until golden brown, turning several times. Keep hot and after pouring away the fat, add flour and stock to make ½ pt fawn thick gravy.

Gentle sauté the sliced apple in the butter for 2–3 min or until tender. Cook the sweet corn according to direction on packet. Serve the chops on a bed of sweet corn garnished with cooked apple and a sprig of parsley.

Lamb or mutton chops can be served in the same way.

6 helpings

BAKED HAM

A ham	Cloves
Flour	Apple raisin sauce
Brown sugar	

Soak the ham in water for at least 12 hr. Wipe well and trim off any rusty bits. Coat with a flour and water paste crust which must be sufficiently thick all over to keep in the gravy. Place the ham in a fairly hot oven (200°C, 400°F, Gas 6) for about 15 min, then reduce heat to cool (150°C, 310°F, Gas 2) and cook for the remainder of the time allowing 30 min per lb. Remove the crust and skin, score squares in the fat and place a clove in each square, sprinkle brown sugar over the fat.

Glaze the sugar by placing the ham in a fierce oven (230°C, 450°F, Gas 8) for a few minutes or under a hot grill. Garnish the knuckle with a paper frill before serving. Serve apple raisin sauce separately.

Small joints or pieces of ham or gammon can be cooked in the same way; obviously they take less time.

FRYING AND GRILLING BACON

Cut the rind off the rashers of bacon. Heat the frying-pan for a few minutes. Place the bacon in the hot pan, reduce the heat and cook for a few minutes. Turn the rashers over and continue cooking until the fat is transparent or crisp, as preferred.

Cut the rind off the bacon rashers. Place the rashers on the grill rack below the hot grill. After a few minutes' grilling, turn and finish cooking.

SOMERSET BAKED BACON CHOPS

6 boneless bacon chops	1 large onion
1 oz melted butter	1 oz butter

SOMERSET STUFFING

1 medium-sized onion, finely chopped	4 oz white breadcrumbs
½ oz butter	1 tablesp sultanas
	Pepper
6–7 oz cooking apples	1 large egg, beaten

Cut through the bacon chops from the outside edge to within ¾ in of the inside edge with a sharp knife, to form a 'pocket'. Fry the onion in butter for 5 min. Peel, core and grate the apples. Mix onion, breadcrumbs, sultanas and pepper together. Bind with the egg. Use this mixture to stuff the 'pockets' in the chops. Place in a roasting-tin. Spoon over melted butter and bake in a moderately hot oven (190°C, 375°F, Gas 5) for 30 min, basting from time to time, until the chops are golden and tender. Garnish with fried onion rings. Cooking time—30 min.

6 helpings

GAMMON STEAKS WITH RICE

½ lb rice	2 eating apples, cored and chopped
2 tablesp chopped parsley	6 oz grated cheese
Seasoning	4 thick gammon steaks
2 oz butter	
3 oz white breadcrumbs	Parsley

Cook the rice in boiling salted water until tender. Drain, stir in the chopped parsley and seasoning, and keep warm. Grill the gammon steaks, turning them once. While they grill, sauté the breadcrumbs in butter, add the diced apple and cook for 2–3 min. Remove from the heat and stir in half the grated cheese.

Place rice in a serving dish, arrange the gammon steaks overlapping, with apple-crumb mixture between each slice, sprinkle with grated cheese and replace under the hot grill for a moment or two. Garnish with parsley.

4 helpings

Gammon steaks with rice

BARDED ROAST NECK OF VEAL

2½–3 lb neck of veal	Salt and pepper
Bacon fat for barding	6 peppercorns
2 carrots	Stock
1 onion	Fat for basting
1 small turnip (optional)	1 oz margarine or good dripping
2 sticks celery	1 oz flour

Fold the flap of the meat under if required and tie securely in a neat round. Cover with the sheet of barding fat, having first cut off decorative strips if desired. Tie the barding fat over the meat, or cover it with coarse net, sewn together. Plait strips of fat to decorate, and lay over the main sheet. Slice the vegetables, and place in a saucepan with the salt, bouquet garni, peppercorns and just enough stock to cover. Lay the meat on top, cover with greased paper and a lid, and cook gently for 2 hr, adding more stock if required. Heat a little dripping in a baking tin, put in the meat, baste well and bake in a moderate oven (180°C, 350°F, Gas 4) for ½ hr. After 15 min, remove the barding fat and trussing strings, and baste. Make a brown roux with the 1 oz fat and flour, add ¾ pt stock from the saucepan and stir until boiling. Simmer for 5 min. Season to taste. Serve the meat on a hot dish with the vegetables, and serve the sauce separately.

Veal and other meat can be larded instead of barded. Small strips of fat bacon are inserted in rows on the surface of the meat with a larding needle. Both ends of each strip are left exposed so that the meat appears to be covered with small tassels of fat.

6 helpings

ESCALOPES OF VEAL

These are thin oval or round slices of top quality veal weighing about 3 oz. They should be flattened with a wooden spoon or cutlet bat, and are usually sautéd in butter, with or without covering. Escalopes, fillets and veal cutlets and chops can all be cooked by the same method.

VEAL CUTLETS OR NOISETTES

1½ lb fillet or neck of veal	½ teasp finely grated lemon rind
2 eggs or 1 egg and milk	Salt and pepper
1 teasp finely chopped parsley	½ oz butter
¼ teasp powdered thyme	Breadcrumbs
	Butter or fat for frying

GARNISH

Parsley	Slices of lemon

Cut the meat in slices about ½ in thick and trim into neat fillets. Beat the eggs, or egg and milk, and mix with the parsley, thyme, lemon rind, seasoning and ½ oz melted butter. Brush the cutlets with this mixture and coat carefully with breadcrumbs. Fry in hot butter or fat for about 10–15 min. Fry both sides quickly first, then cook more slowly, turning as required, until golden-brown. Drain well and place on a hot dish. Garnish with parsley and slices of lemon. Serve with shallot, tomato, demi-glace or creamy Béchamel, or gravy.

6 helpings

ESCALOPES OF VEAL, VIENNESE STYLE

1¼–1½ lb fillet of veal cut in 6 slices	Egg and breadcrumbs
Salt and pepper	Oil or butter for frying
Flour	Lemon juice

Barded roast neck of veal

NOISETTE BUTTER

2 oz butter	Cayenne pepper
Salt and pepper	

GARNISH

6 stoned olives	1 tablesp chopped parsley
6 boned anchovy fillets	Slices of lemon
1 hard-boiled egg	

Wipe the meat, season, dip in flour and coat with egg and breadcrumbs. Heat the oil or butter and fry the escalopes for about 5 min until golden-brown. Make the noisette butter by heating the butter in a saucepan until golden-brown, then seasoning with salt, pepper and cayenne. Place the escalopes slightly overlapping on a hot dish. Sprinkle with lemon juice and pour over the noisette butter. Garnish with olives wrapped in anchovy fillets. Place the chopped egg white, sieved egg yolk and chopped parsley at either end of the dish. Serve with lemon slices.

6 helpings

WIENER SCHNITZEL

6 fillets of veal about ½ in thick	1 egg
Salt and pepper	¼ lb dry breadcrumbs
1 tablesp flour	3 oz butter
	1 lemon

See that each fillet is neatly trimmed, lay on a board and beat with a cutlet bat. Sprinkle the fillets with salt and pepper. Put the flour on a plate and lightly coat each fillet. Beat the egg and into it dip each fillet. Coat the fillets with breadcrumbs. Put the butter into a frying-pan and when hot fry the fillets on each side to a rich golden-brown. Drain and garnish with lemon.

6 helpings

BRAISED AND CASSEROLED DISHES

BRAISED BEEF WITH PEPPERS

2 lb topside or brisket of beef	1 oz dripping
1 large carrot	Bouquet garni
1 large turnip	6–12 peppercorns
18 button onions	Salt
	Stock

BEEF À LA MODE

2 leeks
A few sticks of celery
¼ lb fat bacon rashers

3 green *or* red peppers
Black olives (optional)

Wipe and trim the meat and tie into a good shape. Dice the carrot and turnip. Fry slightly in a stewpan with the bacon trimmings in the hot dripping. Place the meat on top and cover with slices of bacon. Add the bouquet garni and peppercorns tied in muslin, salt to taste and enough stock to nearly cover the vegetables. Cover with a well-fitting lid and cook as slowly as possible for about 3 hr, basting occasionally and adding more stock if necessary. When nearly ready, chop and cook the peppers for a few min in well-flavoured stock. Make a clear brown gravy, adding any strained stock left in the stewpan. Place the meat on a hot dish, remove string and carve in slices. Garnish with onions and peppers, and the stoned olives, if used. Pour over the gravy.

Braised beef with peppers

BEEF À LA MODE

2 lb rump of beef
1 glass claret
Juice of ½ lemon
1 small onion
2 cloves
Salt and pepper
Bouquet garni

1 oz butter *or* fat
10 button onions
1 oz flour
1½ pt stock
2 bacon rashers
2 carrots

Trim and bone the meat. Place it in a bowl with a marinade made from the claret, lemon juice, finely chopped onion, cloves, salt, pepper and bouquet garni. Leave for 2 hr, basting frequently. Melt the fat in a stewpan, drain the beef well and fry until brown. Fry the button onions at the same time. Remove both from the pan, add the flour and fry until nut-brown. Then add the stock and the marinade in which the meat was soaked and stir until boiling. Replace the meat and the onions and season to taste. Cover the meat with the bacon rashers. Add the carrots, thinly sliced, and cook gently for 2½ hr, stirring occasionally. When tender, place on a hot dish, strain the liquid in the saucepan and pour over the meat.

8 helpings

CARBONNADE OF BEEF

1½ lb good stewing
 steak
2 oz dripping
2 large onions, sliced
1 clove of garlic
½ oz flour

½ pt stock *or* water
½ pt beer
Salt and pepper
6 thin rounds of bread
Mustard and vinegar *or*
 French mustard

Wipe and trim the meat, removing all fat and cut into 1½ in squares. Heat the dripping in a stewpan and brown the meat quickly on all sides. Add the sliced onions and fry until brown. Add the crushed garlic and fry lightly. Pour off the surplus fat, sprinkle in the flour and brown slightly. Add the stock or water, beer and seasoning. Place in a casserole and cook gently in a warm oven (170°C, 335°F, Gas 3) for 1½–2 hr. When cooked, spread the rounds of bread with mustard and vinegar or French mustard, and press well down into the gravy. Return the casserole to the oven for about 15 min

Beef olives

without the lid and allow the bread to brown slightly. Serve in the casserole.

6 helpings

BEEF OLIVES

1½ lb stewing steak
2 oz fresh white
 breadcrumbs
1 rounded tablesp dried
 skim milk powder
4 level tablesp chopped
 suet
2 level tablesp chopped
 parsley
A good pinch of dried
 herbs

Grated rind of ½ lemon
Salt and pepper to taste
1 egg
1 oz plain flour
2 oz dripping
½ lb onions, peeled and
 sliced
1 pt stock
1 pt pkt dehydrated
 'instant' potato
½ teasp ground nutmeg

Remove any excess fat from the meat and cut it into 12 even-sized pieces. For the stuffing, mix together the breadcrumbs, dry milk powder, suet, parsley, herbs, lemon rind and seasoning. Stir in the egg with a little more milk powder made into liquid if necessary. Use just enough to bind the mixture lightly together. Divide the stuffing between the pieces of meat and roll into neat rolls. Wind a piece of cotton round the meat or use a wooden cock-tail skewer, to keep the stuffing in place. Add a little seasoning to the flour and roll the meat in it. Heat the dripping in a heat-proof casserole or pan and fry the meat until browned all over. Carefully lift out the meat. Fry the onions and carrots until lightly browned, then return the meat to the casserole, with any remaining flour. Pour over the stock and bring slowly to the boil. Put a lid on the pan or casserole and simmer for about 1½ hr until the meat is tender. The beef olives can also be cooked in a slow oven (150°C, 310°F, Gas 2), for about 2½ hr.

6 helpings

BEEF CREOLE

2 lb beef	2 lb onions
1 teasp salt	2 lb fresh tomatoes
1 teasp pepper	1 pepper
3 rashers fat bacon	

Season the meat. Place on the rashers of bacon in an earthenware casserole. Cover with sliced onions, tomatoes and pepper. Simmer slowly.

6 helpings   Cooking time 3½–4 hr

BRAISED BREAST OF LAMB

A breast of lamb	Salt and pepper

MIREPOIX

2 onions	2 or 3 potatoes
2 carrots	(optional)
2 sticks celery	1 or 2 sliced tomatoes
½ turnip	(optional)
½ oz dripping	Chopped spinach
1 oz fat bacon	Stock
Bouquet garni	

Braise the breast of lamb as follows: bone the meat and season well with salt and pepper. Roll tightly and secure with string. Prepare the mirepoix by cutting the onions, carrots, celery and turnip into thick pieces. Melt the dripping in a stewpan and gently fry the vegetables with the fat bacon with the lid on the pan for 10 min. Add the bouquet garni, the potatoes and tomatoes (if used) and sufficient stock to almost cover the vegetables. Bring to the boil. Place the meat on top of the mirepoix, cover with greaseproof paper and put on the lid. Cook slowly for about 2 hr until meat is tender. Baste frequently.

5–6 helpings   Cooking time about 2½ hr

BREAST OF LAMB MILANAISE

Follow the recipe for Braised Breast of Lamb but use the following garnish instead of potatoes and tomatoes.

MACARONI À LA MILANAISE

6 oz macaroni	1 glass white wine or
4 oz mushrooms	stock
2 oz butter or fat	2 tablesp tomato purée
2 oz cooked ham	or sauce
2 oz cooked tongue	1 dessertsp flour
	3 oz grated cheese

While the meat is cooking prepare the macaroni à la Milanaise as follows: break the macaroni into 2 in lengths. Cook in boiling, salted water or stock for 20 min or until tender, then drain well. Wash and peel the mushrooms and cut into fine shreds. Put the mushrooms in a saucepan with ½ the butter and cook for a few minutes. Meanwhile cut the ham and tongue into strips and add to the mushrooms

with the wine or stock and simmer for a few minutes. Now add the macaroni and tomato purée or sauce, and season carefully. Cook again until nearly dry. When ready, add the remainder of the butter mixed with the flour; this will bind the mixture together. Stir with a fork until cooked. Remove from heat and stir in the cheese. (The mixture must not boil after the cheese has been added.) Arrange the macaroni in the centre of a hot dish and place the meat very carefully on top.

5–6 helpings   Cooking time about 2½ hr

NAVARIN OF LAMB

1 large breast or boned neck of lamb	8–10 small onions
A good pinch of sugar	8–10 small potatoes
1 large tablesp flour	10 oz peas, frozen,
½ lb skinned tomatoes	dehydrated or canned
1 crushed clove of	(optional)
garlic	10 oz small whole
Salt and pepper	carrots, frozen or
Bouquet garni	canned (optional)
	Chopped parsley

Cut the lamb in neat slices, having trimmed off tag ends and excess fat. Chop the fat and heat it gently. Fry the meat pieces in some of it, then transfer them to a casserole. Pour off the fat. Sprinkle the sugar into the pan and heat until it becomes a deep gold. Work in the flour and then the chopped tomatoes (seeds discarded), then stir in enough hot water to make a sauce to cover the meat. Pour over the meat. Add the crushed garlic, a little pepper and salt and the bouquet garni. Cover, cook for 1½ hr first in a moderate oven (180°C, 350°F, Gas 4) reducing to 150°C, 310°F, Gas 2 after ½ hr. Remove bouquet garni; add the onions and potatoes, turn up the heat to 180°C, 350°F, Gas 4 and cook for a further ½–¾ hr. Add the drained, cooked peas and carrots if used, and heat through. Sprinkle with parsley and serve.

6 helpings

BRAISED LEG OR SHOULDER OF LAMB

A small leg or shoulder of lamb	Bouquet garni
2 onions	10 peppercorns
1 turnip	2 shallots
2 carrots	1½ oz butter
1 oz dripping	1½ oz flour
Stock	Salt and pepper

Thickly slice the onions, turnip and carrots. Melt the dripping in a saucepan and sweat the sliced vegetables in it with the lid on, over a gentle heat for 5–10 min. Almost cover with stock or water, add the bouquet garni and peppercorns. Place the prepared meat on top, put a piece of greased greaseproof paper on top of the pan and cover with a good-fitting lid. Cook gently for 3–3½ hr, basting occasionally with the stock and adding more stock if necessary. About ½ hr before serving, chop the shallots very finely, melt the butter and fry the shallots lightly. Then add the flour and cook until a good brown colour. Keep the meat hot, strain the stock and make up to 1 pt. Add the stock to the browned flour and butter and stir until boiling. Season to taste and pour a little over the meat. Serve the remainder in a sauce-boat. If preferred, the meat may be boned and the cavity filled with a stuffing made as follows: equal quantities of ham and trimmings from the leg finely chopped, finely chopped onion and a little garlic if liked. Allow an extra ½ hr for cooking. Either way, serve with

Lancashire hot pot

Lamb shashlik

plainly dished vegetables flavoured with a mild herb rather than with fat.

8–12 helpings

LANCASHIRE HOT POT

2 lb best end of neck of lamb	Salt and pepper Stock
2 lb potatoes	1 oz butter or
3 sheeps' kidneys	margarine
1 large onion	½ pt good gravy

Divide the meat into neat cutlets. Trim off the skin and most of the fat. Grease a fireproof baking-dish and put in a layer of sliced potatoes. Arrange the cutlets on top, slightly overlapping each other, and cover with slices of kidneys and slices of onion. Season well. Add the remainder of the potatoes. The top layer should be of small potatoes cut in halves, uniformly arranged to give a neat appearance to the dish. Pour down the side of the dish about ½ pt hot stock seasoned with salt and pepper. Brush the top layer of potatoes with warmed fat and cover with greased greaseproof paper. Bake for about 2 hr in a moderate oven (180°C, 350°F, Gas 4). Then remove the paper to allow the potatoes to become crisp and brown, cooking for a further 20 min. When ready to serve, pour some gravy down the sides of the dish and serve the rest in a gravy-boat. Serve the hot pot in the dish in which it is cooked.

6 helpings

KEBABS OR SHASHLIK

Both these consist of cubes of lamb or mutton, threaded on skewers together with a garnish, and grilled. The name and the type of garnish depend on which part of southern Europe or the Middle East the dish comes from.

Here are two of many versions, one marinaded overnight before cooking.

MUTTON OR LAMB KEBABS

6 neat pieces of lamb or mutton, cut from leg	6 small mushrooms
3 small sliced onions	6 small tomatoes
6 thick bacon rashers	Oil or melted butter
	12 bay leaves

Trim the meat into neat even-shaped cubes. Cut the bacon in squares, and slice the tomatoes. Brush all (including tomatoes) with oil or butter and thread on to 6 skewers, interleaving with bay leaves. Grill for 10–15 min, turning as required. Serve on their skewers and if liked on a bed of risotto (rice cooked in stock in a casserole until stock is absorbed).

6 helpings

LAMB SHASHLIK

1½ lb lamb from leg or shoulder	2 tablesp white wine or lime juice
1 thinly-sliced onion	6–9 small mushrooms
¾ teasp salt	or very small
Pinch of pepper	tomatoes
Juice of 1 lemon	Butter or good dripping

Cut the meat in 1½ in cubes, trimming off most of the fat. Place in a bowl with the sliced onion, seasoning, lemon juice and wine or lime juice. Mix well together and leave to stand overnight. When ready to cook, arrange the meat on skewers, alternating pieces of meat with a whole tomato or a mushroom. Brush with butter or dripping and grill for 15 min, turning frequently. Serve on the skewers with vegetables and savoury rice.

6 helpings

BRAISED CHILLED LAMB WITH PAPRIKA

2 lb middle neck chilled
  or frozen lamb,
  chopped
2 oz dripping
8 oz onions, peeled and
  chopped
1 clove garlic, crushed
1 dessertsp dried mixed
  peppers (optional)

1 dessertsp paprika
1 8-oz can tomatoes
½ pt chicken bouillon or
  stock
4 oz green beans, fresh
  or frozen
Salt and pepper

Fry the lamb cutlets in the hot fat for 3–4 min, turning to brown all sides. Drain and place in a 3–4 pt casserole. Fry the onions and garlic slowly in the remaining fat until soft but not brown; add the peppers if used, and fry for a further 2–3 min; stir in the paprika and add the tomatoes and stock. Bring this sauce to the boil and pour over the cutlets. Bake, uncovered in a moderate oven (180°C, 350°F, Gas 4) for 1¾ hr. Garnish with green beans before serving.

BRAISED PORK CHOPS IN CIDER

4 pork chops
4 tablesp cider
Bouquet garni
3 onions
2 cooking apples
Good pinch of ground
  cinnamon
Salt and pepper

2–3 large dark
  mushrooms
1 breakfastcup or 10 oz
  can garden peas
1 breakfastcup or 10 oz
  can beetroots
6–8 oz noodles

Trim off rind and excessive fat and quickly fry chops in them until golden brown. Place in a casserole, add cider and bouquet garni, cover and cook gently on the cooker or in a cool oven (150°–170°C, 310°–335°F, Gas 2–3). Meanwhile, pour off excess fat from frying-pan; peel, chop, then fry the onions and apples for a few minutes. Add the cinnamon and water to cover them, put on a lid and simmer until soft. Sieve, season to taste and turn on to the chops. Cover and cook for 1¾–2 hr in all, adding the thickly sliced mushrooms ½ hr before the end. Heat the peas and beetroots separately. Trickle the noodles into salted boiling water and boil until, on testing a piece, the centre is still slightly firm (about 8 min). Drain the noodles, peas and beetroots. Dish the noodles with the chops on top and garnish with the mushrooms, peas and beetroots.

4 helpings

BOSTON PORK CASSEROLE

1 lb dried haricot beans
2 medium onions,
  peeled and thinly
  sliced
½–¾ lb fat belly of salt
  pork cut into 1-in cubes

4 tablesp black treacle
2 level teasp dry
  mustard
1 level teasp salt
Good shake pepper

Wash the beans, cover with water and leave to soak overnight. Drain but keep ½ pt water. Fill a large heat-proof casserole (or traditional bean pot) with beans, onions and pork. Combine the reserved water with the remaining ingredients, pour into casserole, then cover with lid. Cook in the centre of a very slow oven (140°C, 290°F, Gas 1) for 5–6 hr. Stir occasionally and add a little more water if beans seem to dry slightly while cooking.

4 helpings

Braised chilled lamb with Paprika

Boston pork casserole

Loin of veal, daube style

LOIN OF VEAL, DAUBE STYLE

A small shoulder of veal	1 turnip
Salt and pepper	2 stalks celery
2 oz dripping	Bouquet garni
2 onions	Stock as required
	Piquant sauce

STUFFING

½ large onion	Parsley
1 oz butter	2 egg yolks
3 stalks celery	3–4 oz white
2 eating apples	breadcrumbs
1 oz walnuts, chopped	Stock

Bone the veal, flatten it out and season well with salt and pepper. Roll up and tie with string. Sauté in hot fat until brown on all sides and remove. Peel the onions, carrots, turnips; clean the celery, chop coarsely; fry all the vegetables in dripping until just turning colour. Make a mound of the sautéed vegetables in centre of casserole. Place veal on top, add the bouquet garni and sufficient stock to cover the vegetables and braise with lid on until meat is tender.

STUFFING

Peel and slice the onion; fry in butter until soft. Add the finely diced celery and apples, walnuts and parsley and egg yolks and sufficient breadcrumbs to make a soft stuffing. Simmer, moistening with stock when necessary, for 15 min.

Serve veal on a bed of the vegetables with the stuffing arranged at each end of the veal, and serve Piquant sauce separately.

CASSEROLE OF VEAL WITH DUMPLINGS

1½ lb lean stewing *or* pie veal	¼ pt tomato purée *or* pulp
2 onions	Salt and pepper
2 tablesp oil *or* lard	Bouquet garni
1–2 cloves of garlic	Suet crust pastry using 3–4 oz flour, etc.
½ pt white stock	Parsley

Wipe the meat, remove any skin and bone, and cut the meat into small pieces. Slice the onions, heat the oil and cook the onions and garlic until light brown. Add the meat and cook quickly until lightly browned. Pour off the surplus fat and add the stock, tomato purée or pulp, seasoning and the bouquet garni. Place in a casserole with a well fitting lid and cook in a moderate oven (180 C, 350 F, Gas 4) for 1¼ hr. When ready, remove the bouquet garni and skim off any fat. Have ready 12 small dumplings made from the suet crust pastry. Drop them into the casserole and return to the oven for ½ hr. Serve in the casserole sprinkled with parsley.

6 helpings

BOILED BEEF, FRESH OR SALTED

2½–3 lb unsalted silverside, aitchbone *or* round of beef *or* brisket	10 peppercorns A bunch of herbs Carrots
Salt	Turnips
3 cloves	Onions
	Suet dumplings

Wipe the meat with a damp cloth and tie into a

neat shape with string. Put into a pan and cover with boiling salted water. Bring to the boil again and boil for 5 min to seal the surface. Reduce to simmering point, add the cloves, peppercorns and herbs and simmer for the remainder of the time. allowing 20 min per lb and 20 min over. Skim when necessary. Add the sliced vegetables allowing enough time for them to be cooked when the meat is ready. Place the meat on a hot dish. Remove string and re-skewer meat if necessary. Arrange vegetables neatly round and serve some of the liquid separately in a sauce boat.

If suet dumplings are to be served, put them into the liquor ½ hr before serving.

In boiling meat a certain proportion of the nutritive qualities escape into the water; the liquor therefore should be utilised for soup, when it is not too salty for the purpose. With this end in view the liquor should be reduced to the smallest possible quantity by using a pan just large enough to contain the joint, with barely sufficient water to cover.

SCOTCH COLLOPS WITH ONIONS

1½ lb good stewing steak	18 small pickling onions
2 oz butter *or* fat	Salt and pepper
2 teasp finely-chopped onion *or* shallot	Gravy browning
2 teasp flour	Mushroom ketchup
½ pt stock	Sippets of fried *or* toasted bread
	Parsley

Cut the meat into small neat dice. Heat the fat in a stewpan and fry the onion or shallot lightly. Add the flour and cook for about 5 min, stirring all the time. Add the stock, seasoning, a little brown colouring, and the meat. Bring slowly up to the boil, add the mushroom ketchup and simmer very slowly for 1 hr, or until tender. Add the peeled onions ½ hr

before serving. When done, season if necessary and place on a hot dish. Arrange sippets of bread around the dish and garnish with chopped parsley.

6 helpings

EXETER STEW

1½ lb lean beef	1½ oz flour
1½ oz dripping	1 teasp vinegar
3 medium-sized onions	Salt and pepper

SAVOURY DUMPLINGS

4 oz flour	¼ teasp mixed herbs
¼ teasp baking-powder	1 teasp salt
1½ oz finely-chopped suet	¼ teasp pepper
1 tablesp finely-chopped parsley	Egg *or* milk

Wipe the meat and remove all the fat. Cut the meat into pieces about 2 in by 2½ in. Heat the fat in a stewpan until smoking hot and fry the meat until brown. Remove the meat and fry the sliced onions. Then add the flour and cook, stirring until brown. Add 1¼ pt water and bring to the boil, stirring constantly. Simmer for a few minutes. Add the vinegar and seasoning, return the meat and simmer gently for about 2 hr. Mix the ingredients for the savoury dumplings together, bind with the egg or milk into a stiff mixture and make into 12 balls. Bring the stew to boiling-point about 30 min before time for serving and drop in the dumplings. Simmer for the remainder of the time. Pile the meat in the centre of a hot dish, pour the gravy over and arrange the dumplings neatly round the base.

6 helpings

Boiled beef with carrots and dumplings

GOULASH OF BEEF

1½ lb lean beef	2 tomatoes
2 oz dripping	Salt
2 onions	Paprika
1½ oz flour	Bouquet garni
1 pt stock	6 diced potatoes
¼ pt red wine (optional)	2 tablesp sour cream (optional)

Wipe and trim the meat, removing any skin and fat. Cut into neat pieces. Heat the fat and sauté the sliced onions with the meat, until the meat is evenly browned. Add the flour and stir until brown. Then add the stock, wine, skinned and diced tomatoes, salt, paprika, and bouquet garni. Stir, bring to the boil. If liked, transfer to a casserole and cook slowly for 1½–2 hr in the oven, stirring occasionally, or continue cooking in saucepan for the same time. Add the diced potatoes about ½ hr before the goulash is ready. They should be cooked but not broken. 2 tablesp sour cream may be stirred in before serving or used to top the individual servings.

6 helpings

COOLGARDIE STEW—AUSTRALIAN

1½ lb topside steak	1 egg
2 hard-boiled eggs	½ lb bacon rashers
1 onion	Flour
1 heaped tablesp flour	1 lb tomatoes
Salt	Juice of 1 lemon
Cayenne pepper *or* curry powder	1 pt stock *or* water

Cut the steak into thin 5 in lengths. Chop the hard-boiled eggs and onion and mix them with the tablesp flour, seasoning and beaten egg. Remove rind from bacon and cut bacon into 3 in lengths. Roll a teaspoonful of egg mixture in each strip of bacon, and then in one of the pieces of steak. Secure with a wooden toothpick. Toss in flour and sear in hot fat. Transfer from pan to casserole, add the tomatoes, skinned and sliced, lemon juice and stock or water. Place in a moderate oven (180 C, 350 F, Gas 4) and allow to cook for 2 hr. Remove toothpicks. Serve with a macedoine of vegetables and mashed potatoes.

4 helpings

BOILED, STEWED, MADE-UP AND OFFAL DISHES

BOILED LEG OF LAMB OR MUTTON

A small leg of well-aged lamb *or* mutton	½ teasp mixed herbs
2 tablesp breadcrumbs	Salt and pepper
1 tablesp finely chopped suet	A little milk
1 dessertsp chopped parsley	Stock *or* water with vegetables, 10 peppercorns, and salt

Remove all bone and surplus fat; season well. Make the stuffing by mixing the breadcrumbs, suet, parsley, herbs, salt and pepper together. Moisten with milk. Spread the mixture on the meat, re-form its shape and bind securely with string. Put into the boiling stock or water and stock vegetables, and simmer for 2–3 hr, according to size. Pour caper sauce over the meat, if liked.

Leg and neck of mutton can be cooked in the same way.

6 8 helpings

HARICOT MUTTON

6 small chops from the middle neck *or* 2 lb scrag end	1 large onion
	1 oz flour
	1½ pt stock
1 oz butter *or* good dripping	Salt and pepper
	Bouquet garni

Trim off the skin and surplus fat and cut the meat into small pieces or cutlets. Put the butter or dripping into a saucepan and when smoking, fry the meat quickly and lightly. Remove the meat, chop the onion finely and fry slowly in the same fat without browning. Add the flour and fry slowly until a rich brown. Cool slightly and add the stock, seasoning and bouquet garni. Bring to the boil, put in the meat and simmer gently until tender—about 2 hr. Cut the carrots and turnip into neat dice for garnish. Add the rough trimmings to the meat Cook the diced carrot and turnip separately in boiling salted water until just tender. Arrange the meat on a hot dish. If necessary rapidly boil the liquid in the saucepan to reduce and then strain over the meat. Garnish with the diced carrot and turnip.

6 helpings

Irish stew

IRISH STEW

2 lb best end of neck of lamb	3 lb potatoes
1 lb onions	1½ pt stock *or* water
Salt and pepper	Parsley

Cut the meat into neat pieces and trim off the surplus fat. Arrange in a saucepan layers of the meat, thinly sliced onions, seasoning and ½ the potatoes cut in slices. Add stock or water just to cover and simmer gently for about 1½ hr. Add the rest of the potatoes, cut to a uniform size to improve the appearance on top. Cook gently in the steam for about ¾ hr longer. Serve the meat in the centre of a hot dish and arrange the potatoes round the edge.

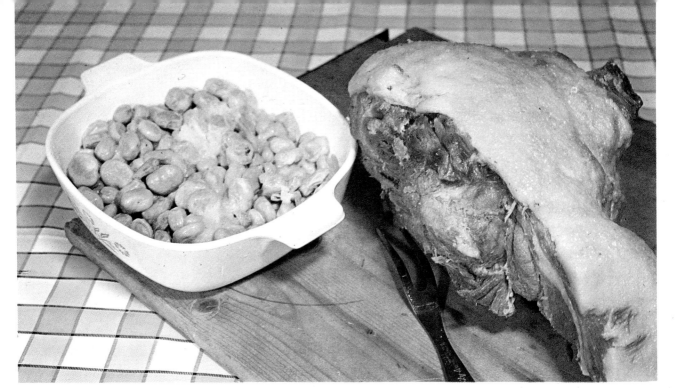
Boiled pickled pork with broad beans

Pour the liquid over the meat and sprinkle with finely-chopped parsley.

An alternative method of serving is to place the meat in the centre of a hot dish. Arrange ½ the potatoes round the edge. Then sieve the liquid (onions and remaining potatoes) or process in an electric blender. Pour over the meat. Sprinkle with chopped parsley.

6 helpings

BOILED PICKLED PORK OR BACON WITH BEANS

A joint of pickled *or* salt pork *or* bacon forehock	1 carrot
	1 onion
Broad beans *or* dried butter beans	½ turnip
	Salt
10 peppercorns	Parsley sauce

Soak the beans overnight. Soak the meat in cold water. Cover the pork with fresh cold water and simmer gently, allowing 25–30 min per lb and 25–30 min over. When the liquid is boiling, add the peppercorns, and the carrot, onion and turnip cut in thick slices. Also add the beans, if dried. About ½ hr before the pork is cooked, cook fresh beans in boiling salted water, simmer gently until tender but whole. Drain well and coat with parsley sauce. Pease pudding or peas may be served in place of the beans if liked. Serve the pork in a hot dish, garnished with the vegetables. The liquor in which the pork is cooked can be made into good pea soup.

BOILED GAMMON OR BACON WITH OLIVES

Gammon or bacon joint	Black olives
Apricot jam or treacle	Chopped parsley
	Piquant sauce

Soak the gammon or bacon for at least 2 hr, changing the water at the end of 1 hr if very salt. Scrape the underside and rind as clean as possible. Put into a pan with cold water to cover. Bring to simmering point, remove any scum, then simmer for 20–25 min per lb until tender. When done, remove from the water, strip off the skin and drain well. Spread with apricot jam or treacle, and put in a fierce oven for a few moments to glaze. Then sprinkle with chopped, stoned black olives and chopped parsley. Serve with Piquant Sauce and with boiled potatoes or pease pudding.

BOILED HAM OR BACON

1 ham *or* large smoked bacon joint such as forehock	Brown sugar (to use with raspings)
	Cumberland sauce
Meat glaze *or* raspings	

Soak the ham or bacon well for 12 hr if very salty and dry. Clean and trim off any rusty parts. Lay the soaked meat on a cloth in a big pan, cover with fresh water and simmer until cooked, allowing 20–30 min per lb. When cooked, remove from the water, strip off the skin. If to be eaten cold, replace the joint in the water until cool, to keep it moist. Before serving, sprinkle with raspings and sugar, or meat glaze. Serve hot with Cumberland Sauce or cold with fruit (*see* Bacon with Fruit below).

Boiled gammon with Cumberland sauce

BLANQUETTE OF LAMB

If you have only a small piece of ham or bacon, use this method:

1 2-lb ham *or* bacon joint	1 head celery
Vinegar	1 turnip
1 onion	1 bunch savoury herbs
	Raspings

Soak the ham or bacon as above, but soak it in vinegar and water (1 teasp vinegar per pt water). Put into cold water, bring to simmering point, add the prepared vegetables and simmer until the meat is tender, allowing 20 min per lb. Remove the skin as above, cover with raspings and put a paper frill round the knuckle.

BLANQUETTE OF LAMB OR VEAL

2 lb fleshy lamb-loin, neck *or* breast *or* veal, taken from the shoulder	Stock *or* water
	1½ oz butter
	1 oz flour
	1 egg yolk
Salt and pepper	2 tablesp cream *or* dried skim milk powder made up double strength
1 large onion	
Bouquet garni	
6 peppercorns	
Pinch of grated nutmeg	

GARNISH

Croûtes of fried bread *or* fleurons of pastry	Button mushrooms

Cut the meat into pieces about 2 in square and put into a stewpan with salt, sliced onion, herbs, peppercorns and nutmeg. Just cover with cold stock or water and simmer until tender—about 2 hr. When the meat is cooked, melt the butter in a saucepan and stir in the flour. Cook for a few minutes without browning. Strain ½ pt liquor from the meat and add to the blended flour and butter. Stir until boiling then simmer for 3 min. Beat together the egg yolk and cream or milk and add to the sauce. Stir and cook gently for a few minutes; do not allow to boil or it may curdle. Correct the seasoning. Arrange the meat on a hot dish, piling it high in the centre and strain the sauce over. Garnish with neatly shaped croûtes of fried bread or fleurons of pastry and grilled mushrooms. Serve hot.

5–6 helpings

Blanquette of veal

FRICASSÉE OF LAMB OR VEAL

2½–3 lb breast of lamb *or* veal	6 peppercorns
	Salt and pepper
1 onion	1 pt boiling stock *or* water
2 oz butter *or* fat	
2 bay leaves	1 oz flour
2 cloves	1 dessertsp roughly-chopped capers
Pinch of ground mace	

Prepare the meat and cut into 2 in squares. Slice the onion, melt the fat, add the onion, bay leaves, cloves, mace, peppercorns, salt, pepper and meat. Cover and cook very gently for about ½ hr stirring frequently. Add boiling stock or water and simmer for about 1½ hr or until tender. Mix the flour smoothly with a small quantity of cold water. Gradually add to it, stirring all the time, about ½ pt of the liquor from the saucepan. To this sauce add the meat, bring to the boil and simmer until tender. Serve on a hot dish within a border of mashed potatoes. Before serving, sprinkle the capers over the meat.

4–6 helpings, depending on the quantity of meat

STEAMED VEAL

1½–2 lb tender boneless veal	1 oz flour
	½ pt milk
Salt and pepper	1–2 egg yolks
3 sticks of celery	1–2 teasp lemon juice
1 oz butter	

Wipe, trim and season the veal and tie into a good shape. Place in a steamer with about 3 tablesp water and the celery cut into 1 in pieces. Steam for about 1½–2 hr. When the veal is nearly ready, melt the fat in a saucepan and add the flour. Cook for a few minutes, stirring well to avoid discolouring. Place the veal on a hot dish, remove string and keep hot. Add the strained liquid in which the veal was cooked, and the milk, to the roux in the pan and stir well until boiling. Stir whilst cooking for 5 min. Remove pan from heat, add the egg yolks and stir well. Add the lemon juice and more seasoning if required, and pour over veal. For a single steamed helping (for instance for an old person) take 1 veal or lamb cutlet and trim off the fat. Place the cutlet in a buttered soup plate and sprinkle lightly with salt and pepper. Cover with another plate and place on top of a saucepan of boiling water. Cook for about 45 min, turning it once or twice during the cooking. Serve with its own gravy.

6–7 helpings

CURRIED VEAL OR LAMB

1½ lb lean veal *or* lamb	½ oz grated coconut
2½ oz dripping	1 banana, sliced (optional)
½ lb onions	
1 clove garlic, minced (optional)	1 oz raisins (optional)
	6 peppercorns
½–1 tablesp curry powder	4 allspice
	Cayenne
1 oz ground rice	Salt
2 oz chutney	2 oz tomato purée
1 chopped sour apple	1¼ pt stock
½ oz plum jam	Lemon juice if required

Trim, wipe and cut meat into 1 in cubes. Melt the dripping in a saucepan and fry the meat lightly in the hot fat, then remove meat to a plate. Fry the finely sliced onions and garlic until pale golden. Add the curry powder and ground rice and fry all together for about 6 min. Add the chutney, apple,

Curried veal

QUENELLES OF VEAL

jam, coconut, banana and raisins, if used, spices, seasoning, purée and stock and bring slowly to the boil, stirring constantly. Return meat to the pan and simmer gently for about 1½ hr, stirring frequently. Lift the meat on to a hot dish. Add the lemon juice and extra seasoning to the sauce if necessary and strain over the meat. Serve in a border of long grain boiled rice or serve rice separately and a salad of fresh chopped apples with bananas or raisins, tossed in lemon juice.

Curry can be served with any of the following accompaniments: pappadums; slices of hard-boiled egg; cubes of cucumber in yogurt; green olives; Bombay duck; shredded coconut; salted almonds; sliced banana; variety of chutneys; fresh melon; chillies; silver onions; guava jelly; preserved ginger; diced pineapple.

6 helpings

QUENELLES OF VEAL

3 oz fillet of veal	1½ gills stock
½ oz butter	1 egg yolk
½ oz flour	Salt and pepper

Mince or chop meat finely. Heat butter in a saucepan; stir in flour, cook for 2–3 min. Gradually add ½ gill stock and cook until thick. Stir in egg yolk, veal and seasoning. Remove from pan and form into finger shapes. Put rest of stock in pan, bring to boil. Poach the fingers or quenelles for 10–15 min in hot stock. Serve with white sauce made partly of remaining stock.

1 helping

BEEF CREAM BORDER OR MOULDS

1½ lb best steak	½ gill cream
1½ oz butter *or* fat	Carrots
1½ oz flour	Green peas
1½ gill stock	1 doz mushrooms
2 eggs	¾ pt Espagnole sauce
Salt and pepper	*or* tomato sauce
Mushroom ketchup *or*	
Worcester sauce	

Wipe the meat and remove any fat or skin. Mince the meat well. Melt the fat in a stewpan, add the flour, stir and cook for about 3 min. Stir in the stock and cook, stirring, until thick. Add the minced meat, the beaten eggs, seasoning, ketchup or sauce, and sieve the mixture if liked. Add the cream and place mixture in a well greased ring mould. Steam gently for ¾–1 hr. Meanwhile cut pea shapes from the carrots. Cook the carrots and peas separately, toss them in butter with the mushrooms. Turn out the mould on to a hot dish, coat with Espagnole sauce. Fill the centre with a mixture of peas, carrots and mushrooms.

If you wish, use ½ the quantities given above, add the finely-chopped mushrooms to the meat and steam the mixture in 6 large well-greased dariole moulds covered with greased paper. For a baked mould, see Pork Mould below.

6 helpings   Cooking time about 1½ hr

This curry has different additions and side dishes

Fried epigrams of lamb

RÉCHAUFFÉ OF LAMB

1½ lb cold cooked lamb	1 tablesp mushroom
1 small onion	ketchup
¾ oz butter *or*	Salt and pepper
margarine	Mashed potatoes *or*
½ oz flour	boiled rice
¾ pt gravy *or* stock	Sippets of toast

Cut the meat into neat dice and boil the bones and trimmings for stock. Finely chop the onion, melt the fat in a saucepan and fry the onion lightly. Add the flour and brown. Stir in the stock, add the ketchup and season to taste. Simmer for 10 min. Put in the meat and bring to simmering point. Keep just below simmering for about ½ hr. Serve the meat surrounded by a border of mashed potatoes or boiled rice and garnished with sippets of toast.

6 helpings

BEEF, LAMB OR MUTTON HASH

1½ lb cooked beef, lamb	Gherkins
or mutton (approx)	Salt and pepper
Breadcrumbs	¾ pt brown sauce

Cut the meat into neat slices. Grease a 1 pt pie-dish and sprinkle with breadcrumbs. Arrange a layer of slices of meat slightly overlapping each other. Sprinkle with finely chopped gherkins, salt and pepper and 2–3 tablesp brown sauce. Repeat until all ingredients are used, making the top layer a rather thicker one of breadcrumbs. Cover with greaseproof paper and bake gently, for about ½ hr in a moderate oven (180°C, 350°F, Gas 4). Serve in the pie-dish.

6 helpings

EPIGRAMS OF LAMB

1 lb cooked breast lamb	Egg and breadcrumbs
Béchamel sauce, made	Deep fat
very thick	Soubise sauce
	Chopped parsley

Remove all skin and gristle from meat and cut it into neat pieces for serving. Have ready the thick, nearly cold Béchamel sauce. Season the meat well with salt and pepper then completely coat with the Béchamel sauce, repeat if necessary. When sauce is set and firm, dip the epigrams into beaten egg and coat with breadcrumbs. Fry quickly in deep fat until golden brown. Drain carefully. Arrange in a circle on a hot dish and serve the Soubise sauce in the centre, sprinkled with chopped parsley.

6 helpings

LAMB OR MUTTON AND POTATO PIE

2 lb cold cooked lean	2 onions
mutton	Salt and pepper
2 lb potatoes	¾ pt gravy

Cut the meat into neat thin pieces. Make the gravy from the meat trimmings. Parboil and slice the potatoes and onions. Line a pie-dish with slices of potato and cover with layers of meat, onions and potatoes, seasoning each layer. Repeat in layers, until all the ingredients are used, the top layer should consist of potato. Add the gravy, cover with greaseproof paper and bake in a moderate oven (180°C, 250°F, Gas 4) for 1 hr. For the last 15 min remove the greaseproof paper to allow the potatoes to brown.

6 helpings

HAM CROQUETTES

HAM OR PORK CROQUETTES

½ lb cooked ham	Salt and pepper
4 oz fresh breadcrumbs	1 egg
2 tablesp mashed	Breadcrumbs
potatoes	Deep fat
½ egg	Paprika pepper
4 tablesp white sauce	Parsley

Mince the ham and mix with the breadcrumbs and potatoes. Place in a small pan and, heating gently, bind with the beaten egg and white sauce. Season well and spread on a plate. Divide into 12 equal portions and leave until cool. Shape into croquettes, coat with egg and breadcrumbs, and fry until golden brown in deep fat. Drain, sprinkle with paprika pepper and garnish with parsley. Serve with tomato sauce.

You can use up tough dry outside bits of ham for this dish. You can also use pork mixed with a pinch each of marjoram and sage.

Rissoles are made in much the same way, but are not usually egged or breadcrumbed.

6 helpings

PORK MOULD

1 lb cold roast pork	Salt and pepper
1 teasp parboiled finely	¼ pt cream or milk
chopped onion	(approx)
2 tablesp mashed	Brown breadcrumbs
potato	½ pt gravy

Remove all the skin, fat and bone and mince or chop the pork very finely. Add the onion to the minced pork with mashed potato, seasoning and sufficient milk or cream just to bind the mixture together. Well grease a mould or pie-dish and coat it thickly with brown breadcrumbs. Put in the mixture carefully and bake for ¾ hr in a moderate oven (180°C, 350°F, Gas 4). The gravy which may be made from the bones and trimmings should be served separately.

If you like, this mixture may be shaped into small cakes, coated with egg and breadcrumbs and fried.

6 helpings

TO MAKE SAUSAGES

1 lb pork	Salt and pepper
1 lb lean veal	6 sage leaves (optional)
1 lb beef suet	⅛ teasp marjoram
½ lb breadcrumbs	(optional)
Grated rind of ½ lemon	¼ teasp savoury herbs
⅛ teasp grated	(optional)
nutmeg	Sausage skins

Remove all the skin and gristle from the pork. Chop or mince the pork, veal and suet together very finely. Add the breadcrumbs, lemon rind, nutmeg, seasoning and the herbs if desired, which must all be very finely chopped. Mix together very thoroughly and then put into skins. Alternatively, the mixture may be formed into meat cakes, floured and fried.

To boil sausages

Prick the sausages with a fork, throw them into boiling water, and cook gently for 15 min. Serve on hot buttered toast or mashed potato.

To fry sausages

Prick the sausages well with a fork, as this prevents the skins breaking. Put into a frying-pan containing a little hot fat and fry gently, turning 2 or 3 times, to brown them equally.

Serve on hot buttered toast or with mashed potatoes.

TOAD IN THE HOLE

4 oz plain flour	1 lb skinless sausages
¼ teasp salt	or sausage meat
1 egg	1 tablesp cooking fat
½ pt milk or milk and	or dripping
water	

Make a batter with the flour, salt, egg and milk, and leave to stand for ½ hr. Heat the fat in a Yorkshire pudding-tin, put the sausages or rolls of sausage meat in the hot fat, pour the batter over and bake in a hot oven (220°C, 425°F, Gas 7) for about 30 min.

BOBOTIE

2 lb cooked or raw meat	2 tablesp curry powder
2 medium-sized onions	½ teasp salt
8 almonds	1 dessertsp sugar
1 thick slice of bread	1 tablesp lemon juice
½ pt milk	or 2 tablesp vinegar
1 oz butter or fat	2 eggs

Mince the meat, slice the onions, and finely chop the almonds. Soak the bread in the milk, drain away all the milk that remains unabsorbed, and beat out the lumps with a fork. Fry the onion in the butter or fat, add the curry powder, salt, the sugar, almonds, lemon juice, meat, bread and 1 egg. Mix well and turn the whole into a buttered pie-dish or into little cups. Beat the remaining egg, add the milk strained off the bread (not less than a good ¼ pt), add a little salt and pepper, and pour over the mixture. Bake gently until the custard is set.

6–8 helpings   Cooking time 15 min when using cooked meat, otherwise about 40 min

RISSOLETTES OF VEAL

½ lb cold cooked veal	Salt and pepper
4 oz lean cooked ham	Short crust or rough
or tongue	puff pastry, using
¾ oz fat	8 oz flour, etc.
¾ oz flour	Egg and breadcrumbs
1½ gills stock	or crushed
1 teasp finely-grated	vermicelli
lemon rind	Deep fat
Pinch of mace	Parsley

Chop the veal and ham or tongue very finely. Melt the fat, add the flour and cook lightly. Add the stock and stir and cook until thick and smooth. Add the lemon rind, mace and minced meats, season well and stir over a low heat until thoroughly mixed. Then turn on to a plate and leave to cool. Roll out the pastry wafer thin and cut into rounds of 1½–2 in diameter. Place a little meat on each round, moisten the edges and fold over in half-moon shapes. Press the edges well to seal. Brush with beaten egg and toss in breadcrumbs or vermicelli. Fry in hot deep fat until golden-brown, then drain well. Garnish with sprigs of fresh or fried parsley.

6 helpings   Cooking time about 10 min

STEAK OR STEAK AND KIDNEY PIE

1½ lb lean beefsteak	Flaky, puff or short
Seasoned flour	crust pastry, using
2 onions	8 oz flour, etc.
Stock or water	Egg or milk

Wipe the meat, remove the skin and superfluous fat and cut meat into small cubes. Dip the cubes in the seasoned flour and place in a pie-dish, piling them higher in the centre. Peel and finely chop the onions; sprinkle any remaining seasoned flour between the meat. Add enough stock or water to $\frac{1}{4}$ fill the dish. Roll out the pastry $\frac{1}{4}-\frac{1}{2}$ in thick to the shape of the pie-dish, but allow an extra 2 in all round. Cut a strip about $\frac{3}{4}$ in wide from around the edge of the pastry to cover the rim of the pie-dish. Dampen the rim, place the strip of pastry around with the cut side out and allow it to overlap the rim a little. Damp the join and the rest of the pastry and cover with the pastry lid. Press the edges lightly together. Trim, make a small round hole in the centre of the pie, and decorate with pastry leaves. Brush with beaten egg or milk. Place in a hot oven (230°C, 450°F, Gas 8) until pastry is set and then reduce heat; if necessary place the pie on a lower shelf and cover with greased paper to prevent pastry becoming too brown. Heat the stock. Use the hole in the pie to pour in the hot stock before serving.

For Steak and Kidney Pie add 2 sheep or 6 oz ox kidneys. Soak the kidneys, remove the skins and cores and cut into slices or quarters. Then add to the pie meat. Prepare and cook as described above.

6 helpings   **Cooking time about 2 hr**

SHEPHERD'S PIE

1 lb cold cooked beef *or* mutton
1 small onion
$\frac{1}{2}$ pt gravy

2 lb cooked mashed potatoes
Egg *or* milk
Salt and pepper

Remove any skin, gristle or bone and cut the meat into small dice. Parboil and finely chop the onion and place in a pie-dish with the meat and the gravy. Season well. Cover with mashed potatoes and smooth and decorate the top to look like pie-crust. Glaze with beaten egg or milk if liked. Bake in a moderate oven (180°C, 350°F, Gas 4) for about $\frac{1}{2}$ hr until thoroughly warmed and the surface is well browned.

Shepherd's Pie can be made in individual dishes if you prefer.

6 helpings

LAMB PIE

2 lb loin, neck *or* breast of lamb
Salt and pepper
1–2 sheeps' kidneys

Stock *or* water
Short crust *or* puff pastry using 6 oz flour, etc.

Cumberland mutton pies

Remove the fat and bones from the meat. Boil the bones for gravy. Cut the meat into neat pieces ready for serving and put in a pie-dish, sprinkling each layer with salt and pepper, and add a few thin slices of kidney. Half-fill the dish with stock or water. Cover with pastry and bake in a moderate oven (180°C, 350°F, Gas 4) for $1\frac{1}{2}$–2 hr, until the meat is tender. Strain and season the gravy made from the bones and pour into the pie just before serving.

6 helpings

CUMBERLAND LAMB OR MUTTON PIES

12 oz minced lamb *or* mutton
Short crust pastry using 12 oz flour, etc.
1 onion
4 oz mushrooms

1 dessertsp chopped parsley
A pinch of thyme
Salt and pepper
A little good stock
Egg *or* milk

Chop and lightly fry the onion. Line 12 small round tins or small saucers with $\frac{1}{2}$ the pastry. Mix together the minced mutton, chopped onion, chopped mushrooms, parsley, thyme and seasoning. Divide the mixture between the tins. Add to each a little stock to moisten. Cover with lids made from the rest of the pastry. Brush with egg or milk and bake in a moderate oven (180°C, 350°F, Gas 4) for about 30–45 min.

6 helpings

Shepherd's pies

Corned beef pie

place the lid on top and press the edges well together. Cover with greased foil or greaseproof paper if pudding is to be steamed, or with a pudding cloth if it is to be boiled. Place in boiling water and steam for about 3½ hr—keep the water boiling, if necessary add more *boiling* water; *or* boil for 3 hr. Serve in the pudding basin, or turn out on to a hot dish.

To make a Steak and Kidney Pudding add to the meat 2 sheeps' or 6 oz of ox kidney. Soak the kidneys, remove the skins and cores and cut into slices or quarters. Dip in seasoned flour, place in the basin and proceed as described above for Beefsteak Pudding.

6 helpings

PORK AND ONION DUMPLING

1 lb lean pork	Salt and pepper
3 onions	Pinch of sage
Suet crust pastry using 12 oz flour, etc.	

Chop the pork; finely chop the onions. Roll out the suet crust pastry in a neat rectangle. On it place the pork, seasoning, sage and onion, leaving a margin all round. Roll up, securing the edges firmly. Wrap firmly in several layers of greased greaseproof paper and secure safely. Steam for 3 hr and serve with a good brown gravy.

6 helpings

CORNED BEEF PIE

Rich short crust pastry, using 8 oz flour, 4 oz lard, 1 egg yolk, etc (no sugar)	2 tablesp chopped parsley Stock Salt and pepper

FILLING

1 12-oz can corned beef	1 tablesp Worcester sauce
1 oz butter	
2 medium onions, peeled and chopped	3 oz button mushrooms, peeled and sliced

TOPPING

2 egg whites, stiffly beaten	2 oz finely grated Cheddar cheese
2 oz finely grated Parmesan cheese	

Make a flan case with the pastry, and bake it 'blind'. Mash the corned beef. Melt the butter and sauté the onions for 10 min. Stir in the meat, Worcester sauce, mushrooms and parsley. Cover and simmer for 20 min, moistening with stock when necessary. Season with salt and pepper and turn into the baked flan case. Fold the cheeses into egg whites and pile on top of the pie. Place in a hot oven (230°C, 450°F, Gas 7–8) until golden and serve hot.

POT PIE OF VEAL

1¼ lb lean veal	1 lb potatoes
½ lb pickled pork	Puff pastry using 6 oz flour, etc.
Salt and pepper	
Stock	

Cut the meat into pieces convenient for serving and cut the pork into thin small slices. Place the meat and pork in layers in a large pie-dish, seasoning each layer well with salt and pepper, and fill the dish ¾ full with stock. Cover with a lid and cook in a moderate oven (180°C, 350°F, Gas 4) for 1½ hr. Meanwhile parboil the potatoes and cut in thick slices. After cooking for 1½ hr, allow the meat to cool slightly. Add more stock if necessary, place the

STEAK OR STEAK AND KIDNEY PUDDING

1½ lb good stewing steak	Suet crust pastry, using 8 oz flour, etc.
Seasoned flour	3 tablesp stock *or* water (approx)

Wipe the meat; remove any superfluous skin and fat. Cut the meat into narrow strips or cubes and dip in the seasoned flour. Cut off ⅓ of the pastry for the lid. Roll the remainder out into a round about ¼ ins thick and line a greased pudding basin with it. Press well in to remove any creases. Half-fill the basin with the prepared meat and add the stock or water. Then add the remainder of the meat. Roll out the pastry reserved for the lid. Damp the edges, potatoes on top, cover with pastry and make a hole in the top. Bake in a very hot oven (230°C, 450°F, Gas 8) until the pastry is set, reduce heat and cook more slowly for the remainder of the time, making 40–50 min altogether. Add more hot stock through the hole in the top before serving. Garnish with parsley and serve.

6 helpings

BOILED COW HEEL

2 cow heels	1 dessertsp finely
Stock *or* water	chopped parsley
1 oz butter *or* fat	Salt and pepper
1 oz flour	

Wash and blanch the heels. Put in a saucepan and cover with cold water or stock and simmer very gently for about 3 hr. Melt the fat in a saucepan, add the flour and cook without colouring. Add 1 pt of the stock in which the cow heels were cooked, stir well until boiling, simmer for 5 min, add parsley and seasoning to taste. Remove the bones from the meat and arrange the pieces of meat on a hot dish. Pour the sauce over and serve hot.

6 helpings

CASSEROLED LAMBS' HEARTS

6 lambs' hearts	2 oz dripping
Veal forcemeat *or*	$\frac{1}{2}$ pt good stock
mixed chopped	$\frac{3}{4}$ oz flour
parsley and butter *or*	Salt and pepper
minced bacon	

Soak the hearts for about $\frac{1}{2}$ hr. Wash well in clean water. Cut the pipes from the top, leave the flaps to fasten down and cut the dividing walls of the chambers. Dry thoroughly and fill the hearts with forcemeat or parsley mixture, fold over the flaps and tie or skewer to keep it in. Heat the dripping in a casserole. Put in the hearts, baste well and bake in a cool to moderate oven (150–180°C, 310–350°F, Gas 2–4) for $1\frac{1}{2}$ hr. When cooked, place the hearts on a hot dish and keep hot. Drain off most of the fat but keep back any sediment. Blend the flour and stock and add to the sediment to make thickened gravy. Season carefully. Pour a little round the hearts and serve the rest in a gravy-boat.

Sheeps' hearts may also be stuffed with sage and onion stuffing.

6 helpings

HAGGIS

1 sheep's paunch and	2 tablesp salt
pluck	$\frac{1}{2}$ nutmeg, finely-
1 lb oatmeal	grated
1 lb beef *or* lamb suet	Juice of 1 lemon
2 Spanish onions	$1\frac{1}{2}$ pt good stock *or*
1 teasp pepper	gravy

Soak the paunch for several hours in salt and water. Then turn it inside out and wash thoroughly several times. Wash the pluck well, just cover the liver with cold water and boil for about $1\frac{1}{2}$ hr. After $\frac{3}{4}$ hr add the well-cleaned heart and lights. Chop $\frac{1}{2}$ the liver coarsely and chop the other $\frac{1}{2}$ with the heart and lights, very finely. Mix all together and add the oatmeal, finely-chopped suet, finely-chopped onions, salt, pepper, nutmeg, lemon juice and stock. Press this mixture lightly into the paunch and sew up the opening, allowing space for the oatmeal to swell. (If overfilled, the paunch is likely to burst.) Put haggis into boiling water and cook gently for about 3 hr.

Grilled and sautéed kidneys

During the first hour prick occasionally and carefully with a needle to allow the steam to escape. Usually no sauce or gravy is served with haggis. A good accompaniment is creamed potatoes and/or mashed turnips.

GRILLED KIDNEYS

6 sheeps' kidneys	Salt and pepper
Oil *or* oiled butter	Croûtes of fried bread

GARNISH

Maître d'hôtel butter *or* bacon rolls

Prepare the kidneys as directed in the preceding recipe and keep them open and flat with a skewer. Brush with oil or melted butter and season with salt and pepper. Grill quickly, cooking the cut side

SAUTÉED KIDNEYS

first and turning frequently. When ready, remove the skewer and serve on croûtes of fried bread on a hot dish. The hollow in the centre of the kidney may be filled with a small pat of Maître d'hôtel butter, or the dish can be served with rolls of bacon.

6 helpings   **Cooking time 5–8 min**

Skin and well wash the kidneys. Split open and remove the cores. Cut the kidneys into neat pieces. Melt the fat in a small pan, put in the onion and cook without browning. Then add the kidney, salt, cayenne, chutney, lemon juice, mustard and stock. Cover and stew for a short time over moderate heat

Kidneys with Italian sauce

SAUTEÉD KIDNEYS

6 sheeps' kidneys	Salt and pepper
2 shallots	Watercress
1 oz butter *or* fat	Croûtes of fried *or*
¼ pt brown sauce	toasted bread
1 tablesp sherry (optional)	

Skin the kidneys and remove the cores. Soak for 5 min in cold water. Dry and cut into ¼ in slices. Finely chop the shallots, heat the fat in a sauté pan and fry them slightly. Then put in the sliced kidney and shake and toss over the heat for about 5 min. Drain off the surplus fat and add the brown sauce, sherry (if used) and salt and pepper. Stir over a gentle heat until thoroughly hot, but take care not to let the mixture boil. Serve as hot as possible on toast or fried bread, garnished with watercress.

6 helpings   **Cooking time about 10 min**

DEVILLED SHEEP'S KIDNEYS

6 sheeps' kidneys	½ teasp mixed
1½ oz butter *or* fat	mustard
1 tablesp chopped	¼ pt stock
onion	2 egg yolks
Salt	Breadcrumbs
Cayenne pepper	Buttered toast *or*
3 teasp chutney	mashed potato
2 teasp lemon juice	border

until the kidney is cooked. Cool slightly and stir in the egg yolks. Sprinkle in enough breadcrumbs to make a soft consistency and correct the seasoning. Serve on buttered toast or in a mashed potato border.

6 helpings   **Cooking time about 20 min**

KIDNEYS WITH ITALIAN SAUCE

1½ lb calves' kidneys	1 pt Italian sauce
2 oz seasoned flour	Long grained boiled
2 oz beef dripping	rice
6–8 small onions	Parsley

Prepare the kidney cutting into ½ in slices after removing skin and core. Coat the kidney well with seasoned flour. Heat the dripping in a sauté pan and fry the kidney quickly on both sides, then slowly for 10 min with a lid on the pan. Sauté the onions at the same time, and shake the pan occasionally to turn them. Drain the kidney from the fat, place in the sauce and simmer for about ¾ hr. Serve hot garnished with long grain boiled rice and parsley.

6 helpings

LIVER AND BACON

1 lb lamb's liver	Seasoned flour
½ lb bacon rashers	¾ pt stock

Remove the rind and rust from the bacon. Wash the liver in cold water and remove any tubes or blood vessels. Dry the liver and cut in slices $\frac{1}{2}$ in–$\frac{3}{4}$ in thick. Dip each slice of liver in seasoned flour. Fry the slices of bacon and remove to a hot dish and keep hot until required. Fry the liver in the bacon fat quickly so that it is browned on both sides without hardening or overcooking. Remove to the hot dish, placing the bacon neatly on top. Drain off all but about 1 dessertsp of fat, add about $\frac{3}{4}$ oz flour and stir until browned. Add about $\frac{3}{4}$ pt stock. Boil and season to taste. Strain round the liver. Calf's liver may be used equally well.

6 helpings   **Cooking time about 10 min**

BAKED OX LIVER

1–1$\frac{1}{2}$ lb ox liver	Seasoned flour
$\frac{1}{4}$ lb fat bacon	Parsley
Stock *or* water	

Wash the liver in tepid salt water, remove any skin and tubes and cut the liver in thick slices. Place in a deep baking-tin or dish. Lay the rashers of bacon on top and add enough stock or water to $\frac{1}{2}$ cover the liver. Cover the dish with foil or grease-proof paper, greased. Bake gently for 1$\frac{1}{2}$–2 hr, basting well and dredging frequently with seasoned flour. Remove the cover some 20 min before serving, to crisp the bacon somewhat. Dish neatly and strain the gravy round. Garnish with parsley.

MARROW BONES

Marrow bones (allow	Flour
$\frac{1}{2}$ lb per person)	Dry toast

Scrape and wash the bones and saw in half across (your butcher will saw them for you). Make a stiff paste of flour and water and roll it out. Cover the ends of the bones with a piece of paste to seal in the marrow and wrap tightly in foil. Stand the bones upright in a pan of boiling salt water and simmer slowly for about 2 hr. Refill the pan with boiling water if necessary. Remove the foil and paste from each bone. Fasten a paper serviette round each one and serve with dry, crisp toast.

OXTAIL STEW

2 ox tails	Salt and pepper
2 oz fat	Bouquet garni
2 onions	Cloves to taste
1$\frac{1}{2}$ oz flour	Mace to taste
1$\frac{1}{2}$ pt stock *or* water	Juice of $\frac{1}{2}$ lemon

GARNISH

Croûtons of fried bread	Dice *or* glazed strips of carrot and turnip

Wash the tails, dry well and remove any superfluous fat. Cut into joints and divide the thick parts in half. Melt the fat in a saucepan, fry the pieces of tail until brown, then remove from the pan. Slice the onions and fry them until light brown, add the flour, mix well and fry slowly until a good brown colour. Add the stock or water, salt, pepper, bouquet garni, cloves and mace and bring to boiling point, stirring all the time. Return the pieces of tail and simmer gently for about 2$\frac{1}{2}$–3 hr. Remove the meat and arrange on a hot dish. Add the lemon juice to the sauce, correct the seasoning, strain and pour over the meat. Garnish with croûtons of fried bread and diced or thin strips of cooked carrot and turnip.

6 helpings

BOILED OX TONGUE

1 ox tongue	1 turnip
1 onion	A bunch of mixed herbs
1 carrot	Parsley

Wash the tongue thoroughly and soak for about 2 hr. If the tongue is dry and rather hard soak for 12 hr. If pickled, soak for about 3–4 hr. After soaking, put the tongue into a large pan of cold water, bring slowly to the boil, skim and add the onion, carrot, turnip and bunch of herbs. Cook gently, allowing 30 min per lb and 30 min over. When ready, lift out the tongue and remove the skin very carefully. Serve with parsley or caper sauce.

To serve cold 1.

After skin has been removed, shape tongue on a board by sticking a fork through the root and another through the top to straighten it. Leave until cold, trim and then glaze. Put a paper frill around the root and garnish with parsley.

To serve cold 2.

Alternatively put the tongue in a bowl or flat tin, curling it round tightly, cover with stock, put a saucer on top and press with a weight on top. Leave until cold, then turn out.

TRIPE AND ONIONS

1$\frac{1}{2}$ lb tripe	2 large onions
$\frac{1}{2}$ pt milk	1 oz flour
1 teasp salt	Salt and pepper

Blanch the tripe, if not bought blanched and partly cooked, and cut into 3 in squares. Put in a saucepan with the milk, $\frac{1}{2}$ pt water and the salt; bring to the boil. Peel and slice the onions finely. Add them to the tripe and simmer very slowly for 2 hr. Mix the flour to a smooth paste with a little milk and add to the pan. Stir with a wooden spoon until boiling. Simmer for another 10 min, season to taste and serve.

6 helpings

Baked ox liver

95

TRIPE À LA LYONNAISE

1½ lb cold boiled tripe as for Tripe and Onions	2 heaped teasp finely chopped parsley
1 large onion	3 teasp vinegar
3 oz butter	Salt and pepper

Cut the tripe into pieces about 2 in square and slice the onion. Heat the butter in a frying-pan and fry the onion until tender and golden-brown. Add the tripe, parsley, vinegar, salt and pepper, and toss in the pan for a few minutes until thoroughly heated. Serve immediately.

6 helpings   **Cooking time about 15 min**

FAGGOTS OR "SAVOURY DUCKS"

1 lb pig's liver *or* fry	A pinch of grated nutmeg
2 medium-sized onions	1 egg
4 oz fat pork	Breadcrumbs
A pinch of thyme	A pig's caul *or* foil
½ teasp powdered sage	Thick gravy
A pinch of basil	
Salt and pepper	

Slice the liver, onions and pork thinly. Put in a saucepan with the thyme, sage, basil, salt, pepper and nutmeg and barely cover with water. Simmer for ½ hr, then strain off the liquid and save for the gravy. Mince the contents of the stewpan finely. Add the beaten egg and sufficient breadcrumbs to make into a fairly firm mixture and mix thoroughly. Form into balls and enclose each one in a piece of caul or foil. Place in a baking-tin, and add a little gravy. Bake in a fairly hot oven (200°C, 400°F, Gas 6) until nicely browned. Remove foil if used. Serve with a good thickened gravy. If preferred, the mixture can be pressed into a well-greased baking-tin and marked into squares. Cover with caul and cut into squares after cooking.

6 helpings

BRAISED SWEETBREADS

2 oz lamb's sweetbreads	Seasoning
½ oz butter	1 bay leaf
½ oz flour	Pinch of herbs
¼ pt good brown stock	1 dessertsp sherry

Put the washed sweetbreads into a pan of water. Bring to boil and simmer for 10–15 min. Drain off liquid, skin and chop sweetbreads. Heat butter in pan; stir in flour and cook for several minutes. Add stock. Bring to boil and cook until thickened. Add the sweetbreads, seasoning, bay leaf and herbs. Simmer for 10 min. Remove bay leaf, add sherry. Serve with creamed potatoes.

1 portion   **Cooking time 25 min**

BRAISED BEEF IN ASPIC

1½ lb fillet of beef previously braised	1¼ pt aspic jelly
1 jar of meat paste	Cooked peas
French mustard	Cooked carrots

It is better to braise the beef the previous day if possible and allow it to become quite cold. Trim into an oblong shape and cut lengthwise into slices. Spread each slice alternately with meat paste and mustard, put the slices together again and press between 2 boards. Set a layer of aspic jelly at the bottom of a cake- or bread-tin and decorate with cooked peas and rings of cooked carrots. Pour on another layer of cold, liquid aspic jelly and allow it to set. Place the prepared beef on top, fill up the mould with aspic jelly and allow to set. Unmould on to an oval dish and decorate with chopped aspic. Serve with an appropriate salad or rice.

6 helpings

PRESSED BEEF

Salt brisket of beef	Bouquet garni
1 onion	10 peppercorns
1 carrot	Meat glaze
½ turnip	

Braised beef in aspic

Bacon with fruit

Weigh the meat. Wash it well, or if very salt soak for about 1 hr in cold water. Put into cold water and bring slowly to boiling point. Skim well. Cut the prepared vegetables into large pieces, add to the meat with the bouquet garni and peppercorns, and simmer gently, allowing 25 min per lb and 25 min over. Take the meat out, remove the bones and press between 2 boards or dishes or roll and tie up. Leave until cold. Then brush over with meat glaze.

BACON WITH FRUIT

1 small joint of bacon	A few cloves
Brown sugar	1 small bunch grapes
3 pears, peeled, cored and halved, dipped in lemon juice	2 small oranges, cut into wedges

Soak the bacon overnight, then boil it (*see* Boiled Ham above). Remove from water and cool. Press brown sugar around the sides. Decorate the pear halves with the cloves and place these, the grapes and the orange wedges around the ham.

PORK PIE

1 lb lean pork	$\frac{1}{2}$ gill water *or* stock
Powdered herbs	Hot water crust pastry
Salt and pepper	using 8 oz flour, etc.
1 small onion	

Cut the meat into neat small dice and season to taste with herbs, salt and pepper. Place the bones, finely-chopped onion, salt and pepper in a saucepan with the water or stock and simmer for 2 hr, so that the gravy when cold will form a firm jelly. Mould the pastry with the hands or line a pie mould. Put in the filling, add some stock and cover with pastry lid. (The remainder of the stock should be reheated and added after the pie is baked and still hot.) 3 or 4 folds of greased greaseproof paper should be fastened round the pie to preserve its shape and prevent it becoming too brown. Brush the top of the pie with egg, or milk, and make a hole in the centre. Bake in a hot oven (220°C, 425°F, Gas 7) at first and reduce heat as soon as pastry is set to moderate (180°C, 350°F, Gas 4) for about 1½ hr. Remove the grease-proof paper or mould for the last ½ hr and brush the sides with egg or milk.

If preferred, small individual pies may be made. Cook for about 1 hr.

6 helpings

VEAL AND HAM PIE

2½ lb neck *or* breast of veal	Forcemeat balls
Salt and pepper	Puff *or* rough puff pastry
1½ lb ham *or* bacon	Pinch of ground mace
2 hard-boiled eggs	Grated rind of 1 lemon

Cut the meat into 1½ in square pieces. Put into a fireproof dish or saucepan, season with salt and pepper, cover with cold water, and cook gently either in the oven or on the stove for 2 hr. Meanwhile cut the ham into narrow strips, the eggs into thin slices, make the forcemeat balls, and fry them lightly in a little hot dripping. Roll out the pastry to a suitable thickness and cut a piece to cover the top of the pie-dish. Line the edge of the dish with the trimmings. Allow the meat to cool slightly, then cover the bottom of the pie-dish with meat, add a few strips of bacon and slices of egg. Sprinkle lightly with salt, pepper, mace, lemon rind, then intersperse with forcemeat balls. Repeat until the dish is full then half-fill the dish with gravy. Put on the pastry cover, moisten and press the edges together. Make a hole in the centre of the top, decorate with pastry leaves, brush over with egg, and bake for 45–60 min in a fairly hot oven (190°C, 375°F, Gas 5). As soon as the pie is baked add a little more well-seasoned gravy through the hole in the top, and when served hot serve with gravy made from the liquor in which the meat was stewed.

A veal and ham pie can also be made in the same way as Pork Pie, for serving cold, using the same quantity of meat in all.

8–10 helpings

Section 4

Poultry and Game Dishes

No bird or any egg is known to be poisonous; but they may become unpleasant because of the food which the birds eat. Wild duck and other water birds may be rank or fishy-flavoured, for instance.

Age and flavour of chickens Young free-range cocks and hens are equally tender, but a cock becomes tough earlier in its life, and over a year old is often only fit for soup-making.

Baby chicks, often called 'spring chickens', Squabs or Poussins, are tender enough eating for babies and the aged, and they are crisp and delicious when grilled or fried. But the amount of flesh to bone is small, and they need careful cooking or they become dry.

Most households therefore prefer cockerels, roasting chickens between 2½ and 4½ lb, and capons, than boiling fowls. Any of these can be roasted if tender enough, but older birds are often braised or 'boiled' (that is, poached). The larger de-sexed birds usually grow heavier in weight than other birds and do not toughen with age so even old ones can usually be roasted. Boiling fowls are often a 'good buy' since they can be 'dressed' with many different sauces or used as 'made-up' dishes.
dishes.

Today, frozen poultry is very widely available indeed, and is one of our cheaper meats. Specially reared, the young roasting chickens between 2½ and 4 lb are the most popular, and are tender and easy to cook. Millions are sold each week. Boiling fowls can also be got, whole or ready cut into joints, and packs of chicken livers, giblets and chicken fat can also be bought.

Choosing farm-reared poultry Look for small-boned birds, plump and with some fat. The breast-bone, wing-tips and feet should be pliable, and the legs smooth. The skin should be white and soft. The signs of an old bird are stiff, horny-looking feet, long spurs, dark-coloured thighs, a stiff beak and hard bones. Size does not indicate much, since most big capons are still tender when large.

Turkeys Young turkeys have smooth dark legs and short spurs. Choose one with a broad, plump breast and white flesh, between 7 and 9 months old if free-range. The hen's flesh is more tender than the cock's. An old turkey has pale or reddish rough legs and long spurs.

Farm-reared turkeys may weigh up to 25 lb or more, and the size of the oven often indicates what size of bird one buys. But today frozen turkeys from 5 lb upward in weight are sold, and a small one may be a more economical "buy" than a chicken, since the proportion of meat to bone is often high.

Ducks and ducklings Young farm-reared ducks usually have yellow, pliable feet and bills. The webbing of the feet should be soft, and the breast should be well covered with meat. There is less meat to bone on a duck than on a chicken, but the different flavour may be worth the extra expense. Like chickens, frozen ducklings are marketed ready prepared for the oven.

All frozen poultry It cannot be emphasised too strongly that all frozen birds must be completely thawed before cooking. So they must be bought at least 48 hours before use. If a bird is not completely thawed, it is cooked with some water still in it; this means that its flavour 'evaporates' on cooking, and the flesh toughens.

Geese The signs of freshness in a goose are the same as in a duck. A fresh bird should still have some down on its legs. A gosling, or green goose, is one up to 4 months old.

Plucking If you have to pluck your own bird, tie the two feet of the bird together with strong string, and hang the bird over a hook. Draw out one wing and pull out the under feathers, taking a few at a time. Work towards the breast and then down to the tail. Repeat on the other side. Only pluck the body half of the neck; the rest is cut off. The flight feathers (large quilled feathers at the ends of the wings) are best snapped, away from the direction of growth. Small hairs may be singed away with a taper; burnt feathers, however, will give the bird an unpleasant flavour. Scoop feathers and down into a plastic bag as you pluck. They can irritate the nasal membranes, and they create an annoying clearing-up problem.

Drawing Halfway along the neck, cut a ring round the outer skin, and pull or cut off the head. Slip the knife under the skin and cut it loose towards the body without puncturing it. Holding the neck in a dry cloth, pull the skin back. At the base of the neck, cut through the meat and then, still holding the neck in a dry cloth, twist it firmly round to break it. (Keep the neck for stock.) Push one finger into the crop cavity to loosen the crop and gizzard.

With a sharp knife, cut the skin on the leg joint, place over a board or table edge and snap the bone. Grasp the foot in one hand and the thigh of the bird in the other and pull off the foot with the tendons.

To remove the viscera, make a wide slit two to three inches just above the vent, taking care not to cut into the rectal end of the gut. Insert the first two fingers of the right hand, knuckles upwards, and feel round the inner cavity wall, loosening the contents. Draw out the intestines. Try to remove all the organs at once. The crop has to be pulled with the gizzard out to the back of the bird. When they are free, trim the end of the intestines and the vent. The liver can now be separated from the gall bladder, taking care not to break the latter. The meaty outside of the crop can be skinned or cut away from the gritty contents for use as stock meat.

The lungs, which are bright red, lie close to the ribs. They are best removed by wrapping the index finger in a dry cloth and pushing in turn down from the back bone and out along each rib.

Destroy the inedible waste (head, intestines, lungs, crop, feet, container of grit from gizzard, etc) immediately. Keep the giblets—neck, gizzard, liver and heart—away from the bird so that its flesh will not be discoloured.

Wipe the inside of the bird. Do not wash it unless the bird is to be cooked immediately.

Trussing The object of trussing a bird is to make it look attractive. Poultry can be cooked just as well untrussed or semi-trussed as fully

DRESSING POULTRY

Cut the skin round neck, pull back and cut off the head

Cut the skin round leg joint, place leg over table edge and snap the bone

Cut slit above vent and draw out intestines

Separate the liver from the gall bladder

Follow trussing instructions. This picture shows the wing being secured

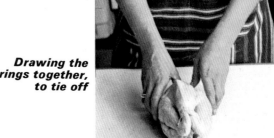

Drawing the strings together, to tie off

trussed. The easiest way to truss is with a needle, like a packing needle. Lay the bird down with the breast uppermost and away from you. Thread the needle and pass it through the left leg just above the thigh bone and near to the joint between the thigh and leg bone. (When the leg is folded down against the bird these two bones form a 'V' shape with the apex of the 'V' pointing towards the front of the bird.) Pass the needle on through the body, out the other side, and through the other leg joint. The legs should be pushed tight against the body during this operation.

The string should now be passed through the body and the leg joints. Leaving sufficient on either side, turn the bird breast downwards and carry the string through the elbow joint of the wing on each side, then twist the end of the wing under the neck of the bird to hold the neck flap of skin. Draw the two ends together not too tightly and tie off. It now only remains to tie down the legs. Loop the string over the ends of the drum sticks and draw them together, tying off round the tail end of the 'parson's nose'. When trussed the skin should be as complete as possible in order to prevent the loss of fat from the bird during cooking, so resulting in over-dryness and an unpalatable meat.

Jointing poultry This process is shown in pictures.

Accompaniments The choice of accompaniment for any particular dish is largely a personal one, but we list below the traditional accompaniments to the following dishes.

Roast Chicken Thin brown gravy, bread sauce, bacon rolls, green salad, game chips, watercress to garnish, veal forcemeat stuffing.

Roast Duck Thickened gravy, sage and onion stuffing, apple, cranberry or orange sauce, watercress to garnish.

Roast Goose Thickened gravy, sage and onion stuffing, apple sauce.

GENERAL HINTS

1 Chicken is stuffed at the neck end; duck and goose are stuffed from the vent end; turkey is stuffed with veal or chestnut stuffing in the crop and with sausage meat stuffing in the body.

2 Chickens and game birds may be roasted, for a little while at the beginning of the cooking time, on the breast, to make the breast meat more moist. It should not be done with duck or goose. All birds should be roasted on a trivet, not resting in the tin in basting fat.

3 When dishes are to be served hot, the garnish must be ready in advance and arranged quickly. If the process takes time, the serving dish may be placed in a shallow tin of hot water so that all the food is served hot.

4 Frozen chickens or chicken portions can be utilised in many of the following recipes provided they are fully thawed.

5 Aluminium foil for cooking is recommended for use under a bird being grilled, as a 'papillote' covering, etc. It can be used to ensure a tight-fitting lid when stewing or braising, or to wrap birds during roasting when a covered roaster is not available. Before cooking is completed, the foil should be turned back from the breast and legs of the bird to allow the skin to become crisp and brown.

6 If a good stock is not available it may be produced quickly by using a reliable make of consommé or a bouillon cube.

7 When cooking is done in a casserole or by stewing, dry cider or wine can be substituted for some of the stock.

TO CHOOSE GAME

Young birds are usually much better for the table than old ones, being more delicate in flavour and much more tender. The size of the spur, the smoothness of the legs, and the tenderness of the pinion are the best guides in choosing a young bird. A bird in good condition should have a thick, firm breast. Choose those which have moist supple feet, and which have not been mutilated when shot.

The most popular game birds in this country are:

Grouse A young bird has soft downy feathers on the breast and under the wings, which are pointed.

Partridge The grey partridge is considered the best of the species. In a young bird the long wing-feather is pointed, not rounded as in older birds.

Pheasant The young bird has short, not very sharp spurs, and light plumage.

Recipes for other birds are included in this chapter.

TO KEEP GAME

All water birds should be eaten as fresh as possible, as their flesh is oily and soon becomes rank. Most other game is kept or 'hung', but the length of time of keeping varies with the weather and individual taste. Game is 'hung' undrawn and unplucked, head downward, if possible in a current of air. A good sprinkling of pepper on the feathers helps to keep flies away. Unless you want it very 'high', it is ready when the tail feathers come out easily when pulled. As soon as the birds are ready, pluck them carefully so as not to break the skin. Draw them if they are to be cooked drawn, and wipe them thoroughly with a damp cloth. If the game has become too 'high', wash it with salted water containing vinegar, and then rinse.

Portions and cooking times are given in the recipes, but birds vary in size and condition, so that this information is only a guide to the cook, not a directive.

Directions for dressing poultry can be applied to any bird to be plucked, drawn and trussed for cooking. With smaller birds such as grouse and pigeons, great care must be taken in each operation as the work is rather more delicate. One-finger operation is needed for both of these.

Snipe, plover, quails and woodcock are cooked *un*drawn, merely being plucked, wiped clean, and served with the head on.

COOKING GAME

Young game birds are usually roasted. Having little fat, they must be either larded or barded before roasting. Old tough birds can be casseroled or made into pies or pâtés.

The traditional trimmings for game are watercress and/or green salad with French dressing, thin gravy, game chips, bread sauce and browned (fried) breadcrumbs.

It should be noted that game birds are protected by law and may only be shot or sold during certain months of the year. Some birds are fully protected and the penalty for shooting them can be very severe.

VENISON

The close season for most stags and buck is from May 1st to July 31st. The close season for does is from March 1st to October 31st. Roebuck are rather differently assessed.

The flesh of the deer or buck is called venison. Venison should always be well hung before cooking, and the flavour is often improved if the meat is marinaded before use. The choicest part is the haunch (leg and loin in one joint) which is usually roasted. The neck and shoulder are usually made into stews and pies. An abundance of clear creamy-white fat indicates good quality meat, that of the buck being preferred to the doe.

Venison should be hung for 10–14 days in a cool dry place, but it should be inspected carefully every day. It can be rubbed with a mixture of ground ginger and black pepper to preserve it. To test the meat, run a small sharp knife into the flesh near the haunch bone; if it has an unpleasant smell when withdrawn, the meat should be cooked at once, or washed with warm milk and water, dried thoroughly and covered with more of the preserving mixture. Wash this off before the meat is cooked.

HARES AND RABBITS

Hares may be roasted or jugged when young, and potted when old. Young ones have smooth

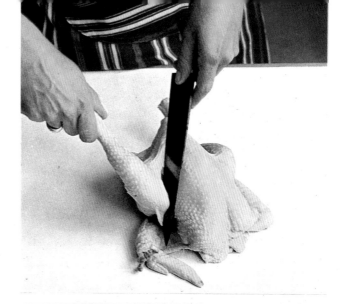

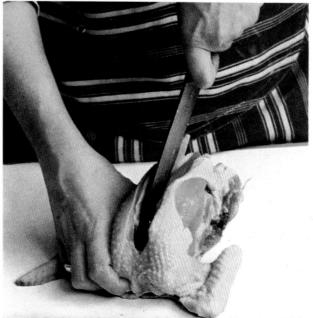

JOINTING BIRDS Top, cut legs from body, cut wing tips off. Centre, cut breast down to wing joint, remove wing. Bottom, split back

PREPARING HARES

sharp claws, a narrow cleft in the lip and soft ears which tear easily; they have short stumpy necks and long joints. A leveret is a hare up to one year old; it has a small bony knot near the foot, which is absent in a full-grown hare. A hare can be well hung, if liked, in a cool dry place. It should hang, unskinned, by the hind legs, with the head in a tin cup to catch the blood. Hares are not paunched until required for cooking.

Jointing hares

1 With a sharp knife cut off the side flaps, then the hind legs.

2 Cut off front legs at the joint.

3 Chop the back sharply once or twice (depending on size of the animal), and separate the body into fairly even parts.

Rabbits Rabbits have the same characteristics, when young, as hares. They are paunched before being hung, but should not be hung for longer than a day. Young ones can be roasted; older ones should be braised or stewed.

Rabbits are dressed like hares except that the ears and eyes are always removed. If trussed, the forelegs are jointed off and sewn back in position. Either rabbit or hare can be jointed easily with a stout-bladed knife which can be tapped through the bones.

Imported, frozen rabbit meat is now available, with and without bone. It makes excellent jugged and casseroled dishes or fricassées.

Hares and rabbits can be shot from September to March.

Skinning hares In many respects, dressing a hare is like dressing poultry. The main difference is that a furry skin has to be removed instead of feathers. First cut off the feet above the foot joint. The feet can be jointed off with a small thin-bladed knife. Next, cut through the skin straight down the belly, taking care not to cut into the meat. Then gently ease back the skin away from the flesh and work round each side until the centre of the hare is completely free from its skin. Now push forward one hind leg and work the skin free. Repeat with the other and then pull the skin away from the tail. Holding the skinned hindquarters in the left hand, gently pull the skin up the back and over the shoulders, working each foreleg through in turn. The skin must now be eased with a knife from the neck and head. Cut carefully round the base of each ear to free the fur but take care not to cut off the ears, if to be left on for cooking.

When free of skin, cut through the skin of the belly from the chest to the legs and draw out the viscera (this is known as paunching). Wipe dry with a clean cloth. The kidneys, found in the back embedded in a little fat, are left in position. The liver and heart are cooked, and care should be taken in detaching the greenish gall bladder from the liver.

Trussing hares For old-style display, a hare for roasting is sometimes trussed with a needle and string. The effect sought is of the animal crouching prone to the dish. Sew a back leg into each side and also a foreleg (shoulder). Tie a string round the neck, pass it from front to rear and tie over the rump, drawing it tight to cause a small arch in the back.

CARVING POULTRY AND GAME

The larger birds are usually jointed at the wings and legs which are served as portions or carved into slices. This is made easier if, before the bird is placed on the table, a small pointed knife is worked between each joint. The joints occur at the natural bends of the limb and are quite easy to discover. If all else fails, they are quite easily broken open, but the carving is rather more dignified if this is done out of sight in, say, the kitchen.

Duck First remove the wings, then the breast should be cut off the bone in one slice, or several slices if very plump. The legs are next removed and divided at the joints. The foot, and the bone to which it is attached, is today rarely left on the dressed bird.

Chicken and Fowl The fork should be inserted firmly in the breast of the bird and with a sharp knife a downward cut is made between the thigh and the body, after which an outward turn of the blade of the knife usually detaches the leg sufficiently to allow the joint connecting it to the body to be easily severed. Some carvers 'open' the joints with a small knife before the bird is sent to table. With the fork still inserted in the breast, the next step is to remove the wings. In doing this a good carver will contrive, by cutting widely, but not too deeply, over the adjacent part of the breast, to give the wing enough meat without depriving the breast of too much flesh. When carving a large fowl the breast can be sliced; otherwise it should be separated from the back by cutting through the rib-bones near the neck. The breast of a smaller bird should be cut across in half, thus providing two portions, to which may be added a slice of 'brown' meat off the thigh. Cut lengthwise into rather thin slices, the legs may be served as several portions or part portions. To complete the carving, the back should be turned over with the cut side to the dish, and if the knife is pressed firmly across the centre of it, and the neck raised at the same time with the fork, the back is easily dislocated about the middle. To remove the sockets of the thigh-joints (the side-bones to

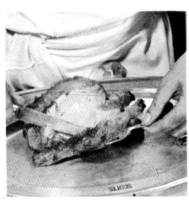

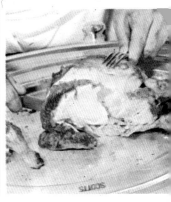

To carve bird, remove legs, cut down through the breast to detach wing and small suprême. Cut breast in slices or in two pieces

which are attached choice morsels of dark-coloured flesh), the tail part of the back must be stood on end, and held firmly with the fork, while the bones are cut off on either side. A fowl when boned and stuffed is usually cut across in slices.

Goose The breast of a goose is the best part. If the bird is large, carve only the breast and save the legs and wings for cold or re-heated dishes.

Pigeon The knife is carried entirely through the centre of the bird, cutting it into two precisely equal and similar parts. If it is necessary to serve three, a small wing should be cut off with the leg on each side. There will be sufficient meat on the breast for a third portion.

Turkey A small turkey may be carved in the same way as a large fowl. No bird is more easily carved than a large turkey, for the breast alone may, when properly carved, supply several helpings. If more meat is required than the breast provides, the upper part of the wing should be served. When it is necessary for the legs to be carved, they should be severed from the body and then cut into slices. The forcemeat in the crop of the bird should be carved across in thin slices; when the body is stuffed, serving is easiest with a spoon.

GAME

Blackcock The brains of this bird were once considered a delicacy. The head is sometimes still trussed on one side of the bird. The breast and the thigh are the best parts; the latter may be cut lengthwise into thin slices, or served whole.

Grouse Grouse may be carved in the way described for carving partridge. The backbone of the grouse, as of many game birds, is thought to have the finest flavour.

Roast Hare Place the hare on the dish with the head at the left hand. Cut along the spinal bone from about the centre of the back to the end. Then cut through the side and middle, and remove this portion. Cut off the hind leg and

afterwards the foreleg or wing. It is usual not to serve any bone and the flesh should be sliced from the legs and placed alone on the plate. Plenty of gravy should accompany each helping; otherwise this dish, which is naturally dry, will lose half its flavour.

Partridge There are several ways of carving this bird. The usual method is to carry the knife sharply along the top of the breastbone and cut it through, dividing the bird into two equal parts. When smaller portions are wanted the legs and wings may be easily severed from the body in the way described for fowl, while the breast, if removed intact, will provide a third helping. Another easy way of carving birds of this kind is to cut them through the bones lengthwise and across, thus forming four portions.

Pheasant The choice parts of a pheasant are the breast and wings. The various joints of the bird are cut in exactly the same way as a chicken's.

Rabbit In carving a boiled rabbit, the knife should be drawn along each side of the backbone, the whole length of the rabbit, thus separating the rabbit into three parts. Now divide the back into two equal parts, then cut off the leg and next the shoulder.

A roast rabbit is rather differently trussed from one that is meant to be boiled but carving is similar. The back should be divided into as many pieces as it will yield, and the legs and shoulders can then be cut off.

Teal and Widgeon see Wild Duck.

Haunch of Venison The thick end of the joint should be turned towards the carver and slices taken parallel to the dish on which the joint rests. Venison, like mutton, should be cut and served quickly.

Wild Duck The breast alone is considered by epicures worth eating, and slices are cut; if necessary, the leg and wing can be taken off as for a fowl.

Woodcock see Partridge.

ROASTED AND GRILLED POULTRY

ROAST CHICKEN

1 roasting chicken	½ pt chicken stock
Salt and pepper	Fat for basting
2–3 rashers of bacon	

GARNISH

Bunches of washed watercress	Gravy
	Bread sauce

Truss chicken for roasting, season lightly and cover with bacon. Roast on a trivet in the roasting tin, in a fairly hot oven (190–200°C, 375–400°F, Gas 5–6) for 1–1½ hr until tender. Baste frequently. The chicken may be roasted on the breast for a short while at the beginning. This will make the breast meat more moist. (Prick the thigh to test for tenderness; if there is any trace of blood the chicken is not cooked.) The bacon may be removed 10–15 min before serving, to allow the breast to brown. When the chicken is cooked, place on a hot meat dish, remove the trussing string, and keep the bird hot. Make the gravy: pour excess fat from roasting tin but retain sediment; pour in stock, boil 2–3 min. Season to taste, and strain into a hot sauceboat.

Have ready the watercress washed, drained and lightly seasoned. Garnish the chicken. Serve with the gravy and bread sauce, and with potato crisps, baked tomatoes, grilled mushrooms and bacon rolls if you wish.

To roast a chicken quickly, joint it and season the pieces. Lay them in a roasting tin with 2 rashers of streaky bacon cut into dice. Bake at 190°C, 375°F, Gas 5, for about 40 min, basting when necessary with chicken fat or butter. Cover with a buttered paper, if the chicken looks dry. When cooked, make the gravy as above.

5–6 helpings

ROAST CHICKEN, FRENCH STYLE

1 roasting chicken	2 or 3 rashers of bacon
1 oz butter	Salt and pepper
1 small onion	1½ gill chicken stock
1 carrot	

GARNISH
Watercress

Truss the chicken for roasting, and spread the breast thickly with butter. Slice the vegetables, place them in roasting tin with bacon and the washed liver and heart of the bird; fry gently. Place the bird on the mirepoix of vegetables. Roast in a hot oven (220°C, 425°F, Gas 7) for 1–1½ hr until tender. Cover the breast with buttered paper if it browns too quickly; baste if necessary. When cooked, remove trussing string. Keep the chicken hot. Drain the fat from the roasting tin, add stock, boil 2–3 min, season and strain into gravy-boat. Serve with gravy, and garnished with the watercress.

Instead of the gravy, the chicken can be served with ¾ pt Italian sauce, white or brown, and with diced carrot, turnip, leek and celery, cooked for food value.

5–6 helpings

ROAST FOWL, STUFFED

1 tender fowl	Salt and pepper
Veal forcemeat	Fat for basting

GARNISH

Bacon rolls	Onion sauce
Watercress	(optional)

Make the forcemeat rather moist, and press lightly into the bird, rounding it under the skin. Any left over can be formed into small balls, coated with egg and breadcrumbs and baked or fried. A good flavour is imparted if the bird is stuffed some hours before cooking. Truss the bird, roast it in a fairly hot oven (190–200°C, 375–400°F, Gas 5–6) for 1½–2 hr, until tender (test the thigh of the bird with a thin skewer for tenderness). Remove trussing string. Garnish the bird and serve with bacon rolls and watercress. Serve onion sauce if desired, or stuff like turkey.

5–6 helpings

ROAST DUCK WITH APPLE SAUCE OR ORANGE GARNISH

1 duck	½ pt stock
Sage and onion stuffing	Salt and pepper
½ oz flour	Apple sauce

Fill duck with sage and onion stuffing, truss for roasting. Baste well with hot fat, roast in a fairly hot oven (190–200°C, 375–400°F, Gas 5–6) for 1–1½ hr,

Roast chicken, dressed in splendour for formal serving

basting frequently. Keep the duck hot, pour fat from roasting tin, sprinkle in flour and brown it. Stir in stock, simmer 3–4 min, season and strain. Remove trussing strings from duck. Serve gravy and apple sauce separately.

For the orange garnish for roast duck, use 1 large orange and 1 tablesp brandy or red wine. Remove the yellow skin (only) from the orange with an apple or potato peeler. Stand the orange in boiling water for 1½ min, then wipe dry and remove all white pith. Divide into segments. Cut the skin into thin strips and let them stand in the boiling water for 5 min while the orange segments soak in the brandy or wine.

When you remove the trussing strings from the duck, warm the orange slightly in the brandy, add the strips of peel, and pile both in a shallow, warmed

dish as a garnish for the duck.

4–5 helpings   Cooking time 1½ hr

STUFFED DUCKLING

1 large 4–5 lb duckling	Sections of 1 large orange *or* apple
Fat for basting	and sauerkraut
¾ pt brown sauce	dressing

STUFFING

1 chicken liver	Salt and pepper
1 duckling liver	Nutmeg
½ teasp parsley	1 oz butter
¼ teasp thyme	1 egg
3 oz breadcrumbs	

Blanch chicken and duckling livers, chop them finely, add herbs, breadcrumbs, melted butter, pinch of nutmeg, salt and pepper. Bind this stuffing with

105

ROASTED AND STEWED DUCK

egg. Stuff the duckling; truss, baste well with hot fat, and roast in a hot oven (210–230 C, 425–450 F. Gas 7–8) for $\frac{1}{2}$ hr, basting frequently. Drain off all the fat, pour the hot brown sauce into the baking tin and continue cooking until the duckling is tender (about 20 min). Baste frequently with sauce. Serve on a hot dish. Strain a little sauce round, garnish with orange sections (heated in a little wine or stock, over a pan of hot water), and serve the remainder of the sauce separately.

Serve a dressing of canned sauerkraut with cored apple slices tossed in butter instead of the orange if you wish.

4 helpings   **Cooking time 1 hr**

ROASTED AND STEWED DUCK

1 duck	1½ oz flour
2 onions, sliced	1 pt brown stock
2 sage leaves	Salt and pepper
Bouquet garni	Mushrooms (optional)
1½ oz butter	

Truss the duck and roast it in a hot oven (220 230 C, 425–450 F, Gas 7–8) for 20 min. Then place in a saucepan with herbs and onions, cover tightly and cook slowly for $\frac{3}{4}$ hr. Melt the butter, add flour and brown well, stir in stock, simmer 20 min and strain. When duck is tender, remove trussing strings. Add sediment from pan to the sauce; season and serve in a sauce-boat. Some mushrooms may be added to the sauce if desired.

4–5 helpings   **Cooking time about 1¼ hr**

ROAST GOOSE

1 goose	Flour
Sage and onion stuffing	Apple sauce
Fat for basting	Gravy (see below)

Prepare the goose, make the stuffing and insert this in the body of the bird. Truss the goose, and prick the skin of the breast. Roast the bird in a fairly hot oven (190–200 C, 375–400 F, Gas 5–6) for 2½ hr or until tender. When almost cooked, dredge the breast with flour, baste with some of the hot fat and finish cooking. Remove trussing string; dish the bird. Serve with apple sauce and a gravy made with thickened beef stock. Goose giblet gravy is very rich.

8 10 helpings

ROAST TURKEY WITH CHESTNUTS

1 turkey	Cream or milk
2–3 lb chestnuts, dried or fresh	1–1½ lb sausage meat or 1 lb forcemeat
$\frac{1}{2}$ pt chicken stock	2 3 slices bacon
2 oz butter	Fat for basting
1 egg	Gravy
Salt and pepper	Cranberry sauce

If fresh, slit the chestnut skins, cook them in boiling water for 15 min, drain and remove the skins. If dried, soak overnight, then simmer 15 min in fresh water.

Stew the prepared chestnuts in stock for 1 hr; drain, and then chop or sieve them, keeping a few back for garnish. Make the stuffing with the chopped chestnuts, butter (melted), egg, seasoning and cream. Fill the crop of the bird with this stuffing and the body with sausage meat or forcemeat, well seasoned. Truss the bird for roasting. Cover it with bacon, and roast in a moderate oven (180°C, 350°F, Gas 4) until tender, basting well. Times are given in the following recipe. Towards the end of the cooking time, remove the bacon to let the breast brown. Remove the trussing string before dishing the bird. Garnish with the reserved chestnuts, and serve with gravy and cranberry sauce.

ROAST TURKEY WITH APPLE AND RICE STUFFING

One 13 lb turkey	Gravy
Apple and rice stuffing	Chipolata sausages
2–3 rashers streaky bacon	Bread sauce or Apple sauce
Fat for basting	Stuffed braised onions or apples

Stuff the crop of the bird with apple and rice stuffing, as well as the body. Truss the bird for roasting. Lay the bacon rashers over the breast. Roast in a

Roast turkey

preheated hot oven (220°C, 425°F, Gas 7) for 15–20 min; then reduce the heat to moderate (180°C, 350°F, Gas 4) and baste frequently until the bird is done. The cooking time will depend on the size and quality of the bird. As a general guide, allow 15 min per lb for a bird under 14 lb in weight, 12 min per lb for one over 14 lb. About 20 min before serving, remove the bacon to let the breast brown. Crumble it and add the crumbs to the sauce if wished.

When ready, dish the bird, having removed the trussing string. Serve with gravy, chipolata sausages and bread or apple sauce. Surround it with stuffed braised onions or apples.

A young turkey or turkey poult is cooked under buttered paper instead of bacon rashers, and takes only about an hour in a hot oven (220°C, 425°F, Gas 7). It is usually served with thin gravy and fried bacon rolls or slices of hot boiled ham.

On a large turkey, the breast meat may dry up in a small oven before the legs are cooked through. Either cover the breast with heavy duty aluminium foil for the whole cooking time; or remove the legs before cooking (or when the breast is ready) and cook them separately for another dish.

VARIATION

An attractive way of dealing with a frozen turkey is to season and baste it with fruit juice. In this case, it is best served with the stuffed, braised onions rather than the apples. For a 9–10 lb frozen turkey, use:

1 orange	Salt and freshly ground
1 large onion	black pepper
1 dessert apple	¼ teasp dried rosemary
2 tablesp olive oil	¼ teasp dried oregano

BASTING JUICE

4 oz melted butter	1 chicken stock cube
¼ pt dry white wine	Salt and freshly ground
Juice of 2 oranges	black pepper
1 clove garlic, finely chopped	

STUFFED BRAISED ONIONS

6 large onions, peeled and parboiled	1 lb full-fat soft cheese
	Salt and freshly ground
1 lb cooking apples, peeled, cored, and finely chopped	black pepper
	¼ lb frozen peas, thawed

Fully thaw the turkey before preparing any ingredients. Mix the orange segments, chopped onion and apple, olive oil, salt and pepper and herbs. Season the inside of the bird with this mixture. Prepare the basting juice by mixing all the ingredients together. Roast the turkey in the usual way, but baste with the juice instead of with fat. While the turkey is cooking, parboil the onions, stuff them with the mixed apple, cheese, seasoning and peas, and bake them in a shallow tin under the turkey until tender.

ROAST GUINEA FOWL

1 guinea fowl	Salt and pepper
2 oz butter	2 slices fat bacon

GARNISH

Fresh tarragon	Bread sauce
French dressing	Espagnole sauce
Browned breadcrumbs	

Prepare the bird, mix the butter and seasoning and place it in the body of the bird. Truss the bird, lay slices of bacon over the breast, and roast in a mode-

rately hot oven (180–190°C, 350–375°F, Gas 4–5) for 1–1½ hr, basting frequently. When the bird is almost cooked, 'froth' the breast (i.e. dredge with flour), baste and finish cooking. Wash and dry the tarragon, toss lightly in French dressing. Remove trussing strings from bird and garnish. Serve with it, browned crumbs, bread sauce, and Espagnole sauce.

4–5 helpings

GRILLED CHICKEN WITH MUSHROOM SAUCE

1 frying chicken	Croûte of fried bread
½ pt Espagnole sauce	½ lb lean raw ham
One 7–8 oz can grilling mushrooms	Salad oil or butter for frying and grilling
Salt and pepper	

GARNISH

Ham	Watercress

Make Espagnole sauce, add the canned mushrooms to it, correct seasoning, and keep the sauce hot. Divide the chicken into pieces convenient for serving, brush them with salad oil or clarified butter. Cut a slice of bread to fit the serving dish. Fry this until lightly browned. Cut the ham into short strips and fry it lightly. Grill the prepared chicken until tender (15–20 min). Pile the chicken pieces on the croûte, strain the sauce round, and garnish with the ham and with watercress.

4 helpings   Cooking time about 30 min

DEVILLED TURKEY LEGS

2 turkey legs	Mixed mustard or
Salt and pepper	French mustard
Cayenne pepper	Butter

Remove skin from turkey, criss-cross with deep cuts. Sprinkle well with seasoning and a little cayenne pepper, if you like dishes very hot. Spread with mixed mustard (or French mustard) pressing well into the cuts and leave for several hours. Grill 8–12 min until crisp and brown, spread with small pieces of butter mixed with cayenne, and serve immediately.

4 helpings

BRAISED AND CASSEROLED POULTRY

CHICKEN À LA MINUTE

3 baby chickens (poussins)	½ pt milk (approx)
	4 button onions
2 oz butter	2 egg yolks
1 oz flour	¼ pt cream
Salt and pepper	

Cut the prepared chickens into quarters. Melt the butter in a fireproof casserole, fry chicken in butter until golden brown. Sprinkle with flour, salt and pepper and stir until flour is golden brown. Just cover with boiling milk, add the blanched onions, cover tightly and cook gently until tender (20 min–½ hr). Remove onions, remove chicken and keep hot. Stir egg yolks and cream together; add to pan; heat gently until thick. Return chicken and leave over

CHICKEN 'EN CASSEROLE'

heat without boiling for a few more minutes. Correct seasoning and serve.

6 helpings   **Cooking time about ¾ hr**

CHICKEN 'EN CASSEROLE'

1 chicken	4–6 shallots *or* small
1 oz flour	onions
Salt and pepper	2 oz chopped
2 oz butter *or* dripping	mushrooms
4–6 oz bacon	1 pt stock

Joint the chicken, and dip the joints in flour and seasoning. Melt the fat in a casserole; fry the bacon, cut in strips; add chicken, mushrooms and chopped shallots or onions. Fry until golden brown, turning when necessary. Add hot stock, sufficient just to cover the chicken, simmer until tender—about 1½ hr. Correct the seasoning. Serve in casserole.

6 helpings

COQ AU VIN

One 3 lb cockerel *or*	12–16 pickling onions
frozen roasting	1 small glass brandy
chicken *or* chicken	1 carrot
joints	1 onion
Stock	1 clove garlic
¼ lb pickled belly of	Bouquet garni (2 if
pork *or* green bacon	possible)
6–8 oz button	Salt and pepper
mushrooms, fresh	3 small fried croûtes
or canned	per person, round
2 teasp tomato purée	*or* triangular, 12 in all
(optional)	Beurre manié
1½ pt red wine	

Joint the chicken if whole. Make a little stock from the giblets or a chicken stock cube, if necessary. Cut the pork into small cubes with extra fat if needed and fry slightly. Add the chicken pieces and fry until golden. Add the mushrooms and tomato purée if used, and the onions. Toss in the fat. Heat the brandy, set light to it, and pour it over the chicken. Shake the pan until the flames die down. Add the stock and wine, carrot, onion, garlic, bouquet and seasoning. Cover the pan and simmer gently for 40 min, or until the chicken pieces are tender. Remove the chicken and vegetables, etc, discard the carrot, onion and bouquet, and keep the rest hot in the oven, with the fried croûtes. Strain the wine sauce into a clean saucepan. Add the beurre manié in small pieces and stir until dissolved in the sauce. Simmer until the sauce is reduced to the consistency you want, but do not boil. Lay the croûtes in a hot casserole, with the chicken on top, pour the sauce over, and serve very hot.

CHICKEN À LA MARENGO

1 chicken	½ glass sherry
¼ pt olive oil	(optional)
1 pt Espagnole sauce	1 doz button
Salt and pepper	mushrooms
2 ripe tomatoes	6 stoned olives

GARNISH

Fleurons of pastry	Olives
or croûtes of fried	Mushrooms
bread	

Joint the chicken. Remove skin and excess fat. Fry joints in oil until golden brown, drain well, pour away oil. Heat the Espagnole sauce with the tomato pulp, add chicken, sherry (if used), whole olives and

Chicken 'en casserole'

mushrooms, and season. Simmer gently until the chicken is tender—about ¾ hr. Pile in the centre of a hot dish, strain sauce over and garnish. Place fleurons or croûtes round the dish.

6 helpings

BRAISED TURKEY OR CHICKEN

1 small frozen turkey	1 turnip, sliced
or chicken	Bouquet garni
2–4 oz butter	Salt and pepper
2 onions, sliced	Stock *or* cider and stock
2 carrots, sliced	2 slices streaky bacon

Truss the thawed bird as for roasting. Melt the butter in a large pan or roasting tin, and brown the bird in the fat. Remove it, place vegetables, bouquet garni and seasoning in pan, adding sufficient stock to almost cover the vegetables. Lay bacon slices on

Chicken à la Marengo in the making

the bird's breast, lay it on the vegetables, cover and cook gently on top of the stove or in a moderate oven (180°C, 350°F, Gas 4) until it is tender. Remove the trussing string, and dish the bird.

8 helpings

CHICKEN LEGS AS CUTLETS

2 chicken legs	8 peppercorns
Salt and pepper	½ pt stock
2 onions, sliced	2 rashers of bacon
2 carrots, sliced	½ pt Espagnole sauce
1 small turnip, sliced	Meat glaze
Bouquet garni	(optional)

Remove the thigh-bones from chicken, but leave drumsticks, season the meat. Fold the skin under, and shape as much like a cutlet as possible. Wrap each leg in foil or muslin, and fasten securely. Place vegetables, bouquet garni and peppercorns in a saucepan, add sufficient stock to barely cover the vegetables. Lay the chicken on the vegetables, covering each piece with bacon. Lay a piece of greased paper on top, and put on a tightly-fitting lid. Simmer gently until tender, about 1¼–1½ hr. Remove the covering, dish the chicken and pour the sauce over. For an alternative method of serving: remove the pan-lid about 15 min before the chicken is cooked, place the pan in a hot oven (200–220°C, 400–425°F, Gas 6–7) to brown the meat. Glaze the legs and pour the sauce round.

2 large helpings; double the quantities for 4 family helpings

CHICKEN WITH RICE AND TOMATOES

1 chicken	1½ pt chicken stock
Larding bacon	(approx)
2 onions	½ lb long grain rice
2 carrots	¼ pt tomato purée
1 turnip	3 oz grated Parmesan
Bouquet garni	cheese
10 peppercorns	

Truss the chicken, lard the breast closely or lay fat bacon on it; wrap in greased paper. Cut vegetables into thick slices, place in pan with bouquet garni, peppercorns and sufficient stock to cover vegetables, not more. Put the chicken on the bed of vegetables, cover with a tightly-fitting lid, and cook gently for about 1½ hr, until bird is tender, adding more stock if necessary. Wash and blanch the rice; cook in good stock until tender and dry, then stir in the tomato purée and cheese; season to taste. Remove paper and trussing strings from chicken; place in a hot oven (220–230°C, 425–445°F, Gas 7–8) until bacon is crisp. Serve in a border of the rice mixture.

6 helpings

CHICKEN PILAFF

1 chicken *or* fowl	6 black peppercorns
3 pt stock *or* 3 pt water	4 oz butter
and 2 lb scrag end	6 oz long grain rice
neck of mutton	Salt and pepper
2 large mild onions	1 tablesp curry paste
1 carrot	2 small onions
Pinch of ground mace	(shallots)

Joint the chicken. Put the backbone, giblets, bones and trimmings and stock (or water and the mutton cut into small pieces) into a saucepan; add outside layers of Spanish onions, carrot, mace and peppercorns. Simmer gently 2–3 hr, strain. Dice the re-

Chicken creole

mainder of the onions, fry in a saucepan until lightly browned in 2 oz of the butter, add the washed and drained rice, 1½ pt stock and seasoning. Cook gently until rice has absorbed stock. Fry chicken slowly in remaining butter until lightly brown. Mix well with curry paste and a little stock, retaining the butter. Cook gently until chicken joints are tender, adding more stock if necessary. Add the rice 10 min before the chicken is done. Cut small onions into rings, fry until golden brown in the butter in which the chicken was fried. Pile the pilaff on a hot dish, pile rings of fried onion on top. Serve very hot.

6 helpings. Cooking time about 1½ hr, excluding stock

CHICKEN CREOLE

3½–4 lb chicken *or* fowl,	One 14-oz can tomatoes
frozen *or* free-range	1 teasp dried thyme
4 oz pickled belly pork	Pinch of salt
1 onion	Pinch of ground black
1 clove of garlic	pepper
1 green pepper	½ lb okra *or* sweet corn

Thaw the chicken thoroughly. Cut the pork fat in pieces, and heat. Brown the chicken, then remove it from the pan. Fry the sliced onion, crushed garlic and sliced pepper. Add the tomatoes, thyme, salt and chicken. Cover and cook slowly. When the chicken is almost tender, stir in the okra in slices, or corn.

Chicken legs as cutlets

CURRIED CHICKEN

Continue cooking until the okra is tender.

6 helpings   Cooking time 1½–2 hr

CURRIED CHICKEN OR TURKEY

1 chicken *or* 3 lb turkey meat	1 dessertsp chutney
2 oz butter	1 tablesp lemon juice
1 chopped onion	Salt and pepper
1 dessertsp flour	1 oz sultanas
1 tablesp curry powder	1 oz blanched almonds
1 dessertsp curry paste	1 dessertsp desiccated coconut
¾ pt white stock	2 tablesp cream *or* milk (optional)
1 chopped apple	

GARNISH

Fans of lemon	Red pepper
Gherkin fans	

Divide the chicken into neat joints, remove skin, fry joints lightly in hot butter, remove from saucepan and drain. Fry the onion lightly, add flour, curry powder and paste, and fry very well, stirring occasionally. Stir in the stock, bring to the boil. Put in all other ingredients except the cream. Put in chicken joints. (Have the coconut tied in muslin, and remove after 15 min.) Simmer gently about 1¼ hr, adding a little more stock if necessary. Dish the chicken, add the cream to the sauce and pour the sauce over the chicken, after straining if liked. Garnish.

ACCOMPANIMENTS

Dry boiled rice sprinkled with paprika and pepper, mango chutney, Bombay Duck, Pappadums, fresh grated coconut, gherkins, pickled pimentoes. These are served separately, not in the dish with the curry. Bombay Duck and Pappadums are fried before serving.

6 helpings   Cooking time 1¾ hr

RAGOÛT OF FOWL

1 fowl	1½ oz flour
2½ oz butter	1¼ pt stock
1 onion	¼ lb ham *or* bacon
Salt and pepper	

Joint the fowl. Heat the butter in a saucepan, fry the joints in this until lightly browned; remove and keep them hot. Fry the sliced onion lightly, sprinkle in the flour, and brown this slowly; add the stock, stir it until boiling; season carefully. Replace the joints in the sauce, add the diced ham or bacon, cover with a tightly-fitting lid and cook gently until fowl is tender (2–2½ hr). Correct the seasoning, and serve with the sauce strained over.

5–6 helpings

BRAISED DUCK WITH CHESTNUTS OR FRUIT

1 duck	¾ pt Espagnole sauce
1 pt stock	1 glass port wine (optional)
Larding bacon (optional)	1 dessertsp redcurrant jelly
2 oz butter	

MIREPOIX

2 onions	Bouquet garni
1 small turnip	6 black peppercorns
2 carrots	2 cloves
1 stick celery	

STUFFING

1 lb chestnuts	Salt and pepper
1 large mild onion	1 egg

GARNISH

Watercress	Grapes, apple *or* orange slices
Forcemeat balls	

Chicken with suprême sauce

A boiled fowl, luxurious with oysters

Boil the chestnuts, remove the skins and chop or mince all but 6 nuts finely for stuffing. Cook the onion in water until tender, chop finely, add to chestnuts, season well and bind with egg. Stuff duck with chestnut mixture, truss, lard with bacon, if liked. Slice the vegetables for the mirepoix foundation, place in a large saucepan with butter, lay the duck on the vegetables, cover the pan; fry gently for 20 min; then add bouquet garni, spices, and enough stock to cover $\frac{3}{4}$ of the depth of the mirepoix. Cover with a buttered paper, put on lid, simmer gently until duck is tender, for about 2 hr. Add more stock if necessary to prevent burning. Heat the Espagnole sauce, add the 6 nuts, wine (if used) and jelly, re-heat and season to taste. When duck is ready, remove paper and trussing string, and place it in a hot oven (220–230 C, 425–450 F, Gas 7–8) to crisp the bacon. Serve on a hot dish, with a watercress or fruit garnish, and forcemeat balls. Serve sauce separately.

4–5 helpings

BRAISED DUCK WITH ORANGE

Cook the duck as in the recipe for Braised Duck with Chestnuts, but use a mild forcemeat stuffing instead of a chestnut one. Add 4 tablesp orange juice to the sauce, and serve it poured over the duck, with a garnish of orange slices or segments.

POACHED, BOILED AND MADE-UP DISHES

BOILED FOWL WITH OYSTERS

1 fowl	$\frac{3}{4}$ pt Béchamel sauce
2 doz canned oysters	$\frac{1}{8}$ pt cream *or* milk
Pinch of ground mace	1 egg
1 oz butter	**Salt and pepper**

Place about 1 dozen oysters inside the bird and truss it for boiling. Put the bird with mace and butter into a deep earthenware casserole with a close-fitting lid. Place this in a baking tin of boiling water, cook on the stove or in a moderate oven (180 C, 350 F, Gas 4) until the fowl is tender (about $2\frac{1}{2}$ hr). Remove trussing string from cooked fowl, dish and keep it hot. Strain the liquor from the fowl, stir it into the Béchamel sauce, heat thoroughly and stir in cream or milk blended with the egg. Continue stirring and heating, until the sauce thickens; do not allow it to boil, or it may curdle. Season. Pour some sauce over the fowl, add the oysters and their liquor to the remainder, and serve separately.

5–6 helpings

CHICKEN WITH SUPRÊME SAUCE

1 chicken	$1\frac{1}{2}$ pt white stock
$\frac{3}{4}$ pt Suprême sauce	(approx)

GARNISH

Macédoine of vegetables *or* grape garnish as below

Truss the chicken, poach it in the stock until tender, then divide into neat joints. Arrange the joints on a hot dish, pour the sauce over, and garnish with the chopped macédoine of vegetable piled at either end of the dish.

As an alternative garnish, toss 1 chopped red pepper and 1 cooked potato (sliced) in the sauce before pouring it over the chicken. Top with black and green grapes.

4–6 helpings   **Cooking time about $1\frac{1}{2}$–2 hr**

BOILED CHICKEN—TURKISH STYLE

1 chicken *or* fowl	$\frac{1}{2}$ pt tomato sauce
1 oz butter	1 teasp cornflour

STEWED FOWL WITH RICE

1 finely chopped shallot | **Salt and pepper**

GARNISH

$\frac{1}{2}$ lb boiled long grain rice

Truss and boil the chicken, cut into neat joints and remove skin. Melt the butter, fry the shallot lightly; add the tomato sauce, heat it, then add the pieces of chicken; simmer gently for 35 min. Correct the seasoning. Blend the cornflour, with a little cold water or stock, add it to the sauce and boil for 3 min. Arrange a border of boiled rice in a hot dish, put in the chicken and strain the sauce over it.

6 helpings **Cooking time 2–2$\frac{1}{2}$ hr**

STEWED FOWL WITH RICE

1 fowl
2 onions
3–4 sticks of celery
2 pt white stock
Bouquet garni
4 oz rice
Salt and pepper

Slice the vegetables and place a few pieces inside the body of the fowl. Truss the bird for boiling, place in a large saucepan or casserole, add the stock and bring to boiling point. Add the remainder of the vegetables, and bouquet garni, tied in muslin. Cover closely, and cook very gently for 1 hr, then add well-washed rice and seasoning. Continue cooking gently until fowl and rice are tender (about 2 hr). The rice should absorb nearly all the stock. Dish the fowl, removing strings. Remove vegetables and bouquet garni from the rice, correct the seasoning of this, and serve with the bird.

5–6 helpings **Cooking time about 2–2$\frac{1}{2}$ hr**

BOILED FOWL

1 fowl
1 onion
1 carrot
$\frac{1}{2}$ lemon
Salt
Bouquet garni
1$\frac{1}{2}$ oz butter
1$\frac{1}{2}$ oz flour
$\frac{3}{4}$ pt stock

GARNISH

Sprigs of parsley *or* **sieved yolk of hard-boiled egg**

Truss the fowl, inserting some pieces of vegetable in the body. Rub the breast of the bird with lemon, wrap in buttered paper and put in a pan with sufficient stock or water to cover. Add the remainder of the vegetables (sliced) salt and bouquet garni and cook gently until fowl is tender (about 2 hr). Meanwhile melt butter in a saucepan, add flour and cook without browning; gradually stir in the stock and simmer for 10 min, stirring all the time; season. Use some of the liquor from stewpan if no stock is available. Remove trussing string from fowl. Place on a hot dish, coat with sauce; garnish.

5–6 helpings

POULTRY HOT-POT

1 boiling fowl
3 rashers of bacon
Salt and pepper
Nutmeg
2 shallots
$\frac{1}{2}$ pt stock *or* **water**
$\frac{1}{2}$ oz butter
$\frac{1}{2}$ oz flour
2 teasp chopped parsley

Place the giblets from the fowl in the bottom of a casserole. Joint the fowl, remove skin and put joints into casserole, adding bacon (cut in strips), salt, pepper, nutmeg, sliced shallots and the hot stock (or water). Cover tightly, cook in a fairly hot oven (190–200°C, 375–400°F, Gas 5–6) for about 2 hr. Knead together butter and flour and add in small pieces to the hot-pot. Add parsley and cook for another $\frac{1}{2}$ hr. Correct seasoning and serve.

This may be served with plain boiled long grain rice.

6 helpings

CURRIED FOWL

Remains of 2 cold fowls
1 sliced onion
2 oz butter
1 tablesp flour
1 tablesp curry powder
$\frac{3}{4}$ pt stock
1 sliced apple
1 teasp chutney *or* **redcurrant jelly**
1 dessertsp lemon juice
Salt and pepper

Cut fowl into neat pieces (use bones and trimmings for stock). Fry sliced onion lightly in butter in a saucepan, stir in flour and curry powder, cook 3 min. Stir in stock, bring to boil. Add sliced apple, chutney, lemon juice and seasoning; simmer gently for $\frac{1}{2}$ hr. Put in fowl, keep hot but not simmering for $\frac{1}{2}$ hr. Dish fowl, pour sauce over (strain if liked). Garnish, and serve with the same accompaniments as Curried Chicken.

STEWED GIBLETS

2 sets of duck giblets *or* **1 set of goose giblets**
Stock
1 oz butter
1 oz flour
Salt and pepper

Wash the giblets. Cover with stock and water and stew until tender; Remove the liver, neck and tendons as soon as tender, leaving the gizzard until it can be pierced with a fork. Heat butter in a saucepan, stir in flour and brown slowly. Strain $\frac{3}{4}$ pt of stock from giblets, and stir into roux. Bring to boiling point, season, add giblets and re-heat thoroughly. Serve very hot.

3–4 helpings **Cooking time about 1$\frac{1}{2}$ hr**

FRICASSÉE OF COOKED CHICKEN

1 boiled *or* **one 1 lb can of chicken**
1 pt Velouté sauce
$\frac{1}{2}$ gill cream *or* **milk**
1 egg
Salt and pepper
Juice of 1 lemon

GARNISH

Chopped parsley
Sippets of fried bread *or* **creamed potato border**

Cut the chicken into joints, remove skin and excess fat. Make sauce, thoroughly heat chicken in it, add cream and egg, stir over a low heat until the sauce thickens but do not boil. Season, add lemon juice. Arrange chicken in an entrée dish, strain sauce over and garnish.

If a potato border is used, pipe or fork this into the dish, before arranging the chicken for serving.

6 helpings **Cooking time 20 min (excluding sauce)**

CHICKEN QUENELLES

12 oz raw chicken
$\frac{1}{2}$ oz butter
2 oz flour
$\frac{1}{4}$ pt stock *or* **water**
2 eggs
$\frac{1}{4}$ pt cream *or* **milk**
Salt and pepper
$\frac{3}{4}$ pt Béchamel *or* **Velouté sauce**

GARNISH

Parsley
Green peas

Chicken pie

Melt butter, stir in flour, add stock gradually, boil until cooked, stirring all the time; allow to cool. Chop or mince chicken very finely, add panada and beaten eggs gradually. Add sufficient slightly whipped cream or milk to form a moist but pliable mixture, and season well. Shape the quenelles with 2 dessertsp and place in a buttered sauté pan. Gently pour in enough boiling water to cover; cover with a sheet of greased paper, and poach very gently without boiling until firm (about 20 min). Drain, coat with sauce and decorate with chopped parsley. Garnish with peas.

6 helpings   **Cooking time about 50 min**

CHICKEN CREAM

$\frac{1}{2}$ lb raw chicken	$\frac{1}{8}$ pt double cream
1 egg	Salt and pepper
$\frac{1}{8}$ pt coating Béchamel sauce	1 pt pouring Béchamel sauce

GARNISH

Mushrooms

Brush 1 large mould (approx 5-in diameter, 3–4-in deep) with clarified butter. (Individual moulds may be used if preferred.) Chop and pound chicken until smooth, add egg and coating sauce gradually, sieve if desired very smooth. Whip cream stiffly, fold into mixture, season. Put mixture into prepared mould, cover with buttered paper, steam gently until firm, 25–30 min. Meanwhile, make 1 pt Béchamel sauce. Dish the cream, pour some sauce over. Garnish with cooked mushrooms. Serve remainder of sauce in a sauce boat.

4 helpings

CHICKEN SOUFFLÉ

$\frac{1}{4}$ lb raw chicken meat	2 tablesp cream
$1\frac{1}{2}$ oz butter	2 egg whites
1 egg yolk	$\frac{1}{2}$ pt Béchamel sauce
Salt and pepper	

GARNISH

Mushrooms, steamed *or* stewed

Mince the chicken finely, gradually add butter and egg yolk, season well, sieve if desired. Stir in half-whipped cream, fold in stiffly beaten egg whites.

Place in a well-buttered soufflé mould or straight-sided tin; cover with greased paper and steam gently and evenly for 50–60 min. (Individual moulds 25 min.) Turn out on to a hot dish, coat quickly with sauce. Garnish, and serve at once.

6 helpings

CHICKEN PIE

1 large *or* 2 small chickens	Rough puff pastry using 8 oz flour, etc
Veal forcemeat	Salt and pepper
$\frac{1}{2}$ lb ham *or* bacon	$\frac{3}{4}$ pt chicken stock
2 hard-boiled eggs	Egg for glazing

Joint the chicken; boil bones, gizzards, and trimmings for stock. Parboil the chicken liver, chop finely and mix with veal forcemeat. Cut ham into strips and eggs into sections. Make pastry. Arrange chicken and other ingredients in layers in a 1 pt pie dish, seasoning each layer carefully, then three-quarters fill the dish with stock. Cover pie dish with pastry, slit the top, decorate and glaze with beaten egg yolk. Bake $1\frac{1}{2}$–2 hr until meat is cooked. Until the pastry is set, have the oven hot (220°C, 425°F, Gas 7), then lower the heat (180–190°C, 350–375°F, Gas 4–5) until cooking is complete. Before serving, add remainder of hot stock to pie.

6–8 helpings   **Cooking time about $2\frac{1}{2}$ hr**

CHICKEN VOL-AU-VENT

6 oz cooked chicken	1 oz cooked noodles
Puff pastry, frozen *or* using 8 oz flour, etc	2–4 oz mushrooms
	Salt, pepper, nutmeg
2 oz cooked ham *or* tongue	$\frac{1}{2}$ pt Béchamel sauce
	Egg *or* milk to glaze

Prepare the pastry; roll out to $\frac{3}{4}$-in thickness. Cut into a round or oval shape and place on a wet baking sheet. Cut an inner ring through half the depth of the pastry and brush top of pastry (not sides) with beaten egg. Bake in a hot oven (220–230°C, 425–450°F, Gas 7) until well risen, firm and brown (about 25 min). Dice chicken and ham, slice mushrooms; add all these with the noodles to the Béchamel sauce, season well and heat thoroughly. Lift centre from vol-au-vent

CHICKEN JELLY

case and reserve for lid, clear any soft paste which may be inside, fill with the mixture, and replace lid.

A separate piece of pastry the size of the lid may be baked with the large case, and used as a lid for the filled case; this has a better appearance.

Alternatively make the pastry into six individual cases, and use the following filling:

FILLING

One 10½ oz can condensed Cream of Mushroom soup	2 oz cooked ham, diced
8 oz cooked chicken or turkey meat, diced	1–2 tablesp cream (optional)

Heat the chicken and ham gently in the soup, then add the cream if used. Fill the prepared cases. Put them into a preheated moderate oven (180°C, 350°F, Gas 4) to warm through and crisp. Serve hot or cold, with a crisp salad.

6 helpings

Cold chicken garnished with pimento flowers

CHICKEN JELLY

1 chicken or fowl	Salt and pepper

Joint the chicken, place the pieces in a casserole with 1 pt cold water and a little seasoning. Cover. Cook in a warm oven (170°C, 335°F, Gas 3) for 2 hr. Cut flesh from bones in thin slices, arrange the meat in a wetted mould or pie dish leaving as much space as possible at the sides and between the layers for stock. Place the bones, trimmings and stock in a pan, and boil rapidly for ½ hr. Strain this stock, season it, and pour over the chicken. Leave to set. Turn out, and serve with any suitable salad accompaniments.

6 helpings

CHICKEN LIVER PATTIES

4 chicken livers	Salt and pepper
1 oz butter	¼ pt brown sauce
Rough puff pastry using 4 oz flour, etc	Egg or milk

Remove the gall, wash and trim livers, then cut into small pieces. Toss the pieces in butter over a low heat for 5 min. Line patty tins with half the pastry, put in the livers, season well, and add a little brown sauce to each patty. Cover with pastry, brush with egg or milk, bake in a fairly hot oven (190°C, 375°F, Gas 5) for 20–30 min. Serve hot or cold.

4–6 helpings

GIBLET PIE

2 sets of duck giblets or 1 set of goose giblets	1 lb rump steak
1 onion, sliced	Puff pastry, frozen or using 6 oz flour, etc
Bouquet garni	Egg or milk for glazing
Salt and pepper	

Wash the giblets; put in a saucepan with sliced onion, bouquet garni and seasoning, cover with cold water, and simmer gently for 1½–2 hr. Slice the steak thinly, and season it. Place alternate layers of steak and giblets in a pie dish (1½ pt size) which should be filled, and strain over enough giblet stock to come three-quarters of the way up the dish. Cover the pie with puff pastry (allowing the meat to cool first, if possible), slit the top and bake in a hot oven (220–230°C, 425–450°F, Gas 7–8) until pastry is set (about 20 min), then lower heat to moderate (180–190°C, 350–375°F, Gas 4–5) and continue cooking until meat is tender (about 60 min more). Fill up the pie with the remainder of the hot stock. The pie may be glazed with egg or milk about 20 min before it is ready.

6 helpings   Cooking time 1¼–1½ hr

CHICKEN MAYONNAISE

1 cold boiled chicken or fowl	Pickled walnuts
½ pt aspic jelly	Chervil
¾ pt mayonnaise	Dressed salad, endive and cucumber

Joint chicken, remove skin and excess fat, and as much bone as possible. Trim joints to a neat shape. Melt aspic jelly; when almost cool, blend ¼ pt carefully into mayonnaise. A smooth glossy sauce will be obtained by passing it through a tammy cloth (a piece of well-washed flannel). This is most easily done by twisting the ends of the cloth containing the sauce in opposite directions. Place the pieces of chicken on a wire cooling tray, and mask them with the sauce when it cools to a good coating consistency. Use a small ladle or tablespoon. Decorate when almost set with cut shapes of pickled walnut previously drained on clean blotting-paper, and chervil, or other colourful garnish. Mask with a thin layer of the remaining aspic jelly. Arrange on a bed of dressed salad. Decorate the edge of the dish with endive, cucumber and blocks of aspic jelly, if liked.

6 helpings

COLD CHICKEN, GARNISHED

1 cold boiled chicken or fowl or 8 drumsticks	1 pt Béchamel or Suprême sauce
1 oz gelatine	½ pt aspic jelly
	6 tablesp bottled salad cream

GARNISH—selection of

Cucumber slices	Olive
Pimento, red, cut in fancy shapes	Lemon rind
Mushroom	Green leek

Roasted wild duck

Joint the chicken if required. Skin and trim the joints, then chill them. Dissolve gelatine in a little hot water, stir into the warm sauce. Add the salad cream. Tammy the sauce (i.e. pass it through a thick cloth), to get a smooth glossy result. When cool enough to be a good coating consistency, coat the chicken. Decorate with the chosen garnish, and allow to set. Coat with cold liquid aspic jelly of a coating consistency, pouring it carefully over each piece with a tablespoon. Serve with a good salad.

A cold chicken can also be attractively garnished simply with a coating of semi-liquid aspic jelly and topped with fruits such as green grapes, apricots or cherries, with tiny pieces of tomato or red pepper and walnuts or almonds.

6 helpings

CHICKEN SALAD

¾ lb cold cooked chicken	1 tablesp salad oil
3 tablesp chopped celery	1 tablesp vinegar
	Seasoning
1 hard-boiled egg	6 tablesp mayonnaise

GARNISH—selection of

Gherkins	Stoned olives
Capers	Lettuce
Anchovy fillets	

Cut chicken into neat pieces; mix with celery, the chopped egg white, salad oil, vinegar and seasoning. Allow to stand for 1 hr. Stir in the mayonnaise. Pile the mixture on a bed of lettuce, garnish with a selection of the ingredients suggested, and sprinkle the sieved egg yolk over. Chill before serving.

4 helpings

DUCK SALAD

2 slices bread, ¼-in thick	4–5 spring onions
Corn oil for frying	1-in cucumber cut in strips
6–8 oz cooked duck *or* goose	1 oz walnuts, chopped
3–4 tomatoes, skinned and quartered	4 tablesp whipped salad dressing (commercial)
	Lettuce leaves

Remove crusts from the bread, and cut into ¼-in dice. Heat the oil in a frying pan, and fry the bread cubes until golden brown on all sides. Cut up the duck, into biggish pieces or slices. Cool the fried bread cubes, and toss with the duck in the salad dressing. Line a bowl with crisp, washed lettuce leaves, and place the salad in the centre.

ROASTED, GRILLED AND FRIED GAME (BIRDS)

ROAST WILD DUCK

2 wild duck	Butter for basting
Croûtes of fried bread	Trimmings as below

Pluck and draw the birds, cut off the heads. Cut off the toes, scald and scrape the feet, truss the birds with the feet twisted underneath the body. If the fishy taste is disliked, cover a deep roasting tin to a depth of ½-in with boiling water, add 1 tablesp salt, put in the birds and bake them for 10 min, basting frequently with the salt water. Drain, sprinkle lightly with flour, baste well with hot butter and roast in a moderate oven (180°C, 350°F, Gas 4) for 20–30 min, basting frequently. The birds should always be served rather underdone, or the flavour is lost. The breast meat has much the best flavour. Serve on croûtes with Bigarade or Port Wine sauce, bacon rolls, fried croûtes cut in triangles, and orange salad.

ORANGE SALAD

Allow the oranges to stand in boiling water for a few minutes, peel them and remove all pith. Cut fruit into thin slices, removing pips. Sprinkle slices with

ROAST GROUSE

a little sugar and French dressing, to which a little brandy may be added if liked. Garnish with parsley.

3 helpings

ROAST GROUSE

A brace of grouse	**Flour**
8 oz rump steak *or*	**2 croûtes fried bread**
2 oz butter	*or* **toast**
Salt and pepper	**Trimmings as below**
2 rashers of bacon	

Prepare the birds, insert a piece of seasoned steak or butter into the body of each; truss for roasting. (If steak is used it can afterwards be used for a cold meat dish; it is inserted to flavour the birds and is not meant to be served with them.) Cover the breasts of the birds with bacon; roast in a fairly hot oven (190–200°C, 375–400°F, Gas 5–6) until tender (about 30 min). Baste if necessary. When almost cooked, remove bacon, baste, dredge with flour, baste again and return to oven. Fry the bread and place pieces in the baking-tin beneath the birds after 15 min cooking, so that they will absorb any liquid which comes from the birds. Dish the birds on the croûtes of bread, and serve with nests of potato crisps, bread sauce, fried mushrooms, and baked tomatoes.

5–6 helpings **Cooking time about 30 min**

ROAST PARTRIDGE

1 partridge	**Toasted** *or* **fried bread**
1 rasher of bacon	**croûtes**
Butter *or* **dripping**	**Trimmings as below**

Pluck, draw and truss the bird as for roasting a chicken. Cover its breast with bacon; roast in a fairly hot oven (190–200°C, 375–400°F, Gas 5–6) for about 30 min, basting frequently with butter or dripping. (A piece of seasoned butter may be put in the body of

Pigeons, duchess style

the bird if liked.) About 10 min before serving, remove bacon, baste, dredge with flour, baste and return to oven to complete cooking. Remove trussing string. Dish the bird on the croûtes. Serve with brown gravy, bread sauce and fried breadcrumbs.

2 helpings

ROAST PHEASANT

1 pheasant	Butter *or* dripping
¼ lb beef steak *or* 12	1 slice bacon *or* strips
mushrooms, chopped	of larding bacon
and seasoned (optional)	French dressing
and 2 oz butter	Trimmings as below'

GARNISH

Watercress

Pluck and draw the bird, but leave the head on. Insert the steak in the body of the bird to improve the flavour and keep the bird moist, or stuff with mushrooms and butter. The steak can be used for a cold meat dish later. Truss the pheasant as for a roasting chicken. Cover the breast with strips of bacon, or lard it with the prepared larding bacon. Roast the bird in a moderate oven (180°C, 350°F, Gas 4) until tender (40–50 min), basting when necessary. When bird is almost cooked, "froth" the breast. Remove trussing string.

Garnish with watercress tossed in French dressing, and serve with brown gravy, bread sauce and fried breadcrumbs. If preferred, the head may be removed and the bird ornamented with the best tail feathers before serving. The feathers should be washed, baked until dry in a cool oven, and stuck fanwise into the vent end of the cooked bird.

4–5 helpings　　　　　　**Cooking time 40–50 min**

ROAST PIGEON

3 pigeons	Lemon juice
3 oz butter	1 rasher fat bacon
Salt and pepper	3 croûtes of fried bread

GARNISH

Watercress	Trimmings as below
French dressing	

Wipe the birds with a damp cloth, insert in each 1 oz butter mixed with lemon juice and seasoning. Truss each and cover with a piece of bacon. Roast pigeons in a fairly hot oven (190–200°C, 375–400 F, Gas 5–6) until tender (20–30 min), basting if necessary. Remove bacon 10 min before cooking is completed to allow birds to brown. Remove trussing strings, replace bacon.

Serve each bird on a croûte of fried bread, garnish with washed watercress tossed in French dressing and serve with Espagnole, tomato or piquant sauce handed separately.

6 helpings

GRILLED PARTRIDGE

A brace of partridge	2 oz butter
Salt and cayenne pepper	

GARNISH

Grilled tomato	Sauce as below
Mushrooms	

Pluck and draw the birds, split in half, wipe the insides thoroughly with a damp cloth. Season with salt and cayenne. Grill about 20 min, turning frequently, and brush with butter just before serving. Garnish quickly, and serve with mushroom or brown sauce handed separately.

4 helpings

GRILLED PIGEONS

3 pigeons	2 oz butter *or* oil
Salt and pepper	Sauce as below

Split pigeons down the back, flatten them with a cutlet-bat (or the back of a large, wet wooden spoon) and skewer them flat.

Brush over the meat with oiled butter or salad oil; season. Grill for 20 min, turning frequently. Serve very hot. Serve with 1 pt tomato or mushroom sauce in a sauceboat.

6 helpings

Grilled pigeons

PIGEONS, DUCHESS STYLE

2 pigeons	Salt and pepper
1½ oz butter *or* salad oil	Egg and breadcrumbs
4 oz sausage meat	Frying fat
½ pt Espagnole sauce	Trimmings as below

Split the pigeons in half lengthways, remove rib and backbones and shape like cutlets. Spread one side of each cutlet with seasoned sausage meat. Coat with egg and breadcrumbs twice (the second coating will prevent the sausage meat from splitting away) and fry in hot, faintly smoking fat until well browned and cooked. Serve very hot, in a potato border; pour the sauce round the bird and garnish with a macédoine of vegetables.

4 helpings　　　　　　**Cooking time about ¾ hr**

FRIED AND GRILLED PHEASANT

1 young pheasant	Salt and cayenne
2 oz butter	pepper
	Egg and breadcrumbs

GARNISH

Grilled mushroom	Mushroom sauce *or*
Tomato	alternative
Watercress	

Joint the bird, season it, fry in butter until lightly

Salmi of pheasant with fleurons of pastry

browned, press between 2 plates until cold. Coat with egg and breadcrumbs, grill about 25 min, turning frequently, and brushing with melted butter after the coating has set. Garnish and serve immediately, piled on a hot dish, with mushroom sauce.

Alternative sauces are Madeira or piquant.

If the bird is small it may be split down the back and treated like a grilled pigeon.

4–5 helpings

GAME BIRDS IN CASSEROLES, STEWS, PIES, ETC

COMPOTE OF PIGEONS OR PARTRIDGES

3 pigeons *or* partridges	Bouquet garni
¼ lb raw ham *or* bacon	1 carrot
12 shallots *or* small	½ turnip
onions	1 oz flour
1½ oz butter	Salt and pepper
1 pt good stock	Croûtes of fried bread

Truss birds for roasting, dice ham or bacon and peel shallots or onions. Melt butter, fry birds, bacon and onions until well browned. Add stock, bring to boiling point; add the bouquet garni, diced carrot and turnip. Cover and allow to simmer steadily until birds are tender, for ¾–1 hr. Remove birds and onions; cut away trussing strings and split birds in half. Keep hot. Blend flour with a little cold water or stock, add to pan. Bring to boiling point, stirring continuously, re-cover and allow to simmer for 10 min. Season to taste, skim off any excess fat. Serve on a hot dish,

pour the sauce over, garnish with the onions and with croûtes of fried bread.

6 helpings

BLACKCOCK FILLETS À LA FINANCIÈRE

2 blackcocks	½ pt brown sauce
1 medium-sized onion	12 button mushrooms
1 small carrot	1 glass sherry *or*
½ turnip	Madeira (optional)
¼ pt game stock	Salt and freshly
3 rashers of bacon	ground black pepper

Joint the birds and cut into fillets. Slice vegetables and lay these in a sauté-pan with the bacon; put the fillets on top. Add the stock, cover with a buttered paper and close-fitting lid, and simmer gently for 30 min. Make the brown sauce, add mushrooms (if fresh, fry first in butter), and wine, if used; season to taste; keep sauce hot. Fry the bacon. When fillets are cooked, arrange on a hot dish, strain the sauce over and use the mushrooms and bacon for garnishing.

5–6 helpings

BRAISED GROUSE

Follow the recipe for Compote of Pigeons using a brace of grouse instead of 3 pigeons.

6 helpings   **Cooking time 2 hr, after the braise begins to simmer**

SALMI OF PHEASANT

1 pheasant	½ pt brown sauce
2 oz butter	1 glass Madeira

¼ teasp grated lemon rind	(optional)
	6–8 slices goose liver
2 shallots	or pâté
¼ teasp thyme	6–8 mushrooms
1 bay leaf	Salt and pepper

GARNISH

Croûtes of fried bread (triangular) or fleurons of
pastry

Pluck, draw and truss bird for roasting. Baste it
well with hot butter; roast in a hot oven (220–230°C,
425–450°F, Gas 7–8) for 30 min, basting frequently.
Pour the butter used for basting into a saucepan, add
grated lemon rind, chopped shallots, thyme and bay
leaf. Joint the bird, lay aside breast, wings and legs,
and cut remainder into neat pieces; add these to the
saucepan and fry. If any fat remains, pour it from the
saucepan, put in the brown sauce, wine (if used), and
season. Simmer for 10 min. Add remainder of pheasant, heat thoroughly. Meanwhile, reheat the butter,
fry in it the slices of goose liver if used, and the mushrooms. Correct seasoning of sauce. Serve pheasant
with pâté or liver; strain the sauce over, garnish with
the croûtes or fleurons and the mushrooms.

4–5 helpings   Cooking time about 1¼ hr in all

JUGGED PIGEONS

3 pigeons	Salt and pepper
3 oz butter	1 oz flour
1 onion	1 glass port or claret
1 carrot	(optional)
1 pt good beef stock	

GARNISH

Balls of fried forcemeat (optional)

Truss the pigeons as for roasting and fry them until
well-browned in 2 oz of the butter. Place the birds in
a casserole. Brown the sliced onion and carrot in
butter, and add to the pigeons, together with stock
and seasoning. Cover and cook in a moderate oven
(180°C, 350°F, Gas 4) for 1¾ hr. Knead together the
flour and remaining 1 oz butter and drop in small
pieces into the stock; continue cooking ½ hr, adding
wine if used, half-way through this period. Serve
pigeons with the sauce poured over, garnished with
forcemeat balls if you wish.

3 helpings

PIGEON OR GROUSE PUDDING

3 pigeons, 1 grouse or	Suet crust pastry using
any other game meat	12 oz flour, etc, and
½ lb stewing steak	add ¼ teasp mixed
1 oz flour	herbs if you wish
Salt and pepper	¼ pt stock
2 hard-boiled eggs	Gravy
(optional)	

Split the prepared pigeons in half, remove skin.
Cut the steak and any other game meat into small
pieces. Dip the pieces into seasoned flour. Cut eggs
into sections, if used. Line a basin with suet crust
pastry, put in the prepared pigeon, steak and egg,
add the stock; cover with crust. Steam the pudding
for at least 3 hr and serve with thick or thin gravy.
An excellent method of using any tough bird.

6 helpings

PIGEON PIE

2 pigeons	2 hard-boiled eggs
½ lb rump steak	Puff pastry, frozen or
¼ lb ham or bacon	using 8 oz flour, etc

Compote of pigeons

¾ pt good stock	Egg or milk to glaze
Salt and pepper	

Remove the feet from the pigeons and split each
bird in two. Cut the steak in small thin slices, cut the
bacon in strips and slice the eggs. Put all the ingredients in a pie dish in layers; season the layers well,
and season each half-bird; ¾ fill the dish with stock.
Cover pie with puff pastry, slit, glaze, and cook in a
hot oven (220–230°C, 425–450°F, Gas 7–8) until the
pastry is risen and set; then lower heat to moderate
(180–190°C, 350–375°F, Gas 4–5) and bake for 1 hr
more under buttered paper. Fill up with hot stock.

For an old-style display, cut the toes off the feet,
and scald the latter. Before serving the pie, fix the
feet in an upright position in the hole previously
made in the pastry for pouring in stock.

6 helpings

Jugged pigeons

GROUSE PIE

2 grouse	Salt and pepper
¾ lb rump steak	½ pt good stock
2–3 slices of bacon	Puff pastry, frozen *or*
2 hard-boiled eggs	using 8 oz flour, etc

Joint the birds, and discard vent-end parts of the backs, as these will impart a bitter flavour to the pie. Slice the steak thinly, slice eggs and cut the bacon into strips. Line the bottom of a pie dish with pieces of seasoned meat, cover with a layer of grouse, add some bacon, egg and seasoning. Repeat until dish is full. Add sufficient stock to ¾ fill the pie dish, cover with puff pastry as above and bake for 1½–1¾ hr. For the first 15 min of this time, have the oven hot (220–230°C, 425–450°F, Gas 7–8), then lower the heat to moderate (180–190°C, 350–375°F, Gas 4–5) and cover the pastry with greaseproof paper so that the filling may cook a further 1¼–1½ hr. Glaze the pie ½ hr before cooking is complete. Simmer the necks and trimmings of the birds in the remaining stock, strain, season and pour into the pie before serving.

Finely chopped mushrooms, parsley and shallots may be added to the pie, if liked.

6–8 helpings   Cooking time 1¾ hr

RAISED GAME PIE

1 lb well-hung game (pheasant *or* partridge)	2 hard-boiled eggs
	1 dessertsp mixed herbs
¾ lb chicken livers	6 thin rashers streaky bacon
1 small onion	
1 clove garlic	¼ oz gelatine
½ lb sausage meat	½ oz flour

HOT WATER CRUST PASTRY

10 oz plain flour	¼ pt milk and water
1 level teasp salt	3 oz lard
Pinch of black pepper	Egg for glazing
1 egg yolk	

Cut meat from birds, discarding gristle and skin. Shred finely. Mince or chop the livers, onion and garlic with a little flour to prevent sticking. Mix with the sausage meat, chopped eggs and herbs.

Warm the flour, and sift with the salt and pepper. Mix the egg yolk with 1 tablesp liquid, and boil the remaining milk and water with the lard. When the lard is melted, pour the mixture into the dry ingredients, and mix well with a wooden spoon. Add the egg mixture and knead quickly until smooth. Keep warm in a basin covered with a folded tea towel over a basin of hot water for ½ hr. To use, roll out ¾ of the pastry and line a raised pie mould or 7-in diameter cake tin with a slip-out bottom. Line the bottom and sides of the pastry with bacon, and put in a layer of the liver mixture. Then put in a layer of the game. Repeat the layers, finishing with a game one. Do not fill the pie to the top. Roll out the remaining ¼ of the pastry. Brush edges with beaten egg, and cover the pie. Trim the edges, and brush with beaten egg. Cut leaves from the trimmings, and decorate the pie with them. Brush again with beaten egg, and make a hole in the centre of the lid for steam to escape.

Bake for 1 hr at 190°C, 375°F, Gas 5; reduce heat to 180°C, 350°F, Gas 4 for a further 1–1¼ hr. While the pie is baking, boil the carcasses of the game and simmer until ½ pt liquid remains. Strain. Soften the gelatine in 2 tablesp cold water, stir into the stock and stir until dissolved.

If the pie is to be eaten hot, stir a little hot stock into the ½ oz flour, and cook over gentle heat for 1 min. Add enough hot stock to make a thick sauce, and pour this into the hot pie through the hole in the lid.

If the pie is required cold, leave it to cool, and pour in the cooled stock when it is just on the point of setting. Leave in a cool place for about 12 hr.

6–8 helpings   Cooking time 2–2¼ hr

POTTED GAME

Cooked game	Salt and pepper
Butter *or* stock *or* gravy	Cayenne pepper
	Clarified butter

Remove skin and bone from game; chop or mince meat very finely. Pound until smooth, or process in a blender, gradually adding strong game stock or gravy or oiled butter, until mixture is moist. Season well.

Press into small pots, cover with clarified butter. Use as a savoury spread, or in pastry cases.

Old hare, and hare and rabbit trimmings, poached slowly till cooked, can be used in the same way. So can cold, cooked leftover hare and rabbit.

GAME IN ASPIC JELLY

Cold cooked game	Hard-boiled eggs
Aspic jelly	Salad
Lean boiled ham	

Rinse a plain jelly mould with cold water and mask with aspic jelly. Decorate base of mould with rounds of boiled ham and hard-boiled egg; pour a little more cold liquid jelly over this and allow to set. Arrange pieces of seasoned game and more ham on the set jelly, pour more jelly on top and allow this to set. Continue in this way until the mould is full, allowing each layer to set before adding another. When jelly is quite set, dip mould quickly into warm water, dry it and turn out the jelly. Any remaining jelly can be chopped on a wet board, and used for decoration. Serve with salad.

VENISON

ROAST HAUNCH OF VENISON

A haunch of venison	Flour
Clarified butter *or* dripping	Brown sauce *or* gravy
	Redcurrant jelly

Saw off the knuckle-bone, brush joint well with clarified butter or dripping and wrap in well-greased paper. Make a stiff paste of flour and water, put it over the joint, cover with another well-greased paper and tie securely with string. Roast the joint in a moderate oven (180°C, 350°F, Gas 4) for 3–4 hr depending on size and baste frequently. After 2½ hr remove paste and papers, dredge lightly with flour, baste well with hot butter, and roast until the joint is a rich brown colour. Serve as hot as possible. Serve gravy or brown sauce and redcurrant jelly separately.

12 (or more) helpings   Cooking time 25 min per lb

CHOPS AND STEAKS OF VENISON

Venison chops are cut from the loin, and a thick slice from the leg is served as a steak. Both should be grilled and served with a sauce made from equal quantities of clarified melted butter, red wine and dissolved redcurrant jelly.

VENISON CUTLETS

6 cutlets of venison	1½ pt Cumberland
3 oz butter (approx)	sauce
	Salt and pepper

GARNISH

Mushrooms

Cut 6 cutlets from the best end of the neck of venison, trim the bones at the end, flatten and trim cutlets. Brush with melted butter; season. Heat the sauce, trim mushrooms and brush them with melted butter. Grill the cutlets, brushing with more butter if necessary. Grill the mushrooms. Place a dab of butter on each cutlet, serve very hot. Garnish with mushrooms. Serve the sauce separately.

6 helpings   Cooking time 20–25 min

STEWED VENISON

Shoulder of venison	1½ pt game stock
Thin slices of mutton	½ teasp peppercorns
fat	½ teasp allspice
1 glass port (optional)	Redcurrant jelly
Salt and pepper	

If port is used, soak the mutton fat in it for 2–3 hr. Bone the venison, flatten with a cutlet-bat, season well, cover with slices of mutton fat. Roll up lightly, tie securely with tape, place in boiling stock together with bones, peppercorns, allspice and the port in which the fat was soaked. Simmer gently for 3–3½ hr. Serve with redcurrant jelly, handed separately.

10–12 helpings

POTTED VENISON

2 lb venison	4 oz butter
½ glass port *or* a little	Salt and pepper
stock *or* gravy	Clarified butter

Put the venison into a stewing jar with a close-fitting lid. Add the wine if used, or a little stock, 4 oz butter, salt and pepper. Cover jar with 2 or 3 thick-

nesses of buttered paper or foil, press the lid down tightly, and cook in a cool oven (150–170°C, 310–335°F, Gas 2–3) for 2 hr. Drain well, mince very finely and sieve, moistening gradually with gravy, or process in an electric blender. Correct the seasoning. Press into small pots; cover with clarified butter.

HARE AND RABBIT DISHES

ROAST HARE

1 hare	Pinch of thyme
Veal forcemeat	1½ oz flour
Fat bacon	¾ pt stock

121

GRILLED HARE

Milk	1 glass port (optional)
2 oz butter	Salt and pepper
1 teasp chopped shallot	Redcurrant jelly
½ teasp chopped parsley	Watercress

Skin, draw and truss the hare, reserving the liver. After inserting the forcemeat, sew up the hare, wrap the head in foil, cover the body with bacon; bake in a fairly hot oven (190–200°C, 375–400°F, Gas 5–6) for 1½–2 hr until tender, basting frequently with milk, and a little butter if liked. Meanwhile remove the gall-bladder from the liver, wash the liver, put into cold water; bring to the boil, and boil for 5 min; chop very finely. Melt the butter, add the liver, shallot, parsley and thyme. Fry gently for 10 min. Lift the liver mixture from the butter, put in the flour, brown the roux. Stir in the stock (or milk used for basting), bring to boiling point; add the liver mixture, season, simmer for 10 min; add wine if used. Remove foil and bacon from hare, dredge with flour, baste and allow to brown. Remove trussing strings and cotton. Serve on a hot dish. Serve the liver sauce and redcurrant jelly separately, but the watercress round the hare.

5–6 helpings

GRILLED HARE

Remains of roast hare	Salt
	Cayenne pepper
Butter	Piquant sauce or gravy

Separate meat into neat pieces, brush with oiled butter and season highly. Grill under a hot grill until well browned, turning frequently and brushing with more butter if necessary. Serve very hot. Serve with the sauce or gravy.

Cooking time about 10 min

JUGGED HARE

1 hare	12 peppercorns
3 oz butter	Bouquet garni
Salt and pepper	1½ pt stock
1 onion	1 oz flour
4 cloves	Veal forcemeat
1 glass port or claret (optional)	Fat for frying
	Redcurrant jelly
1 tablesp lemon juice	

Prepare the hare and cut into neat small pieces. Heat 2 oz of the butter, and fry the pieces of hare in it until brown. Put the hare in a casserole with salt, onion stuck with cloves, half the wine (if used), lemon juice, peppercorns, bouquet garni and hot stock. Place a tight lid on the casserole, cook in a moderate oven (180°C, 350°F, Gas 4) about 3 hr. Knead the flour and remaining butter together, stir into the stock about ½ hr before serving. Add the remaining wine too, and season to taste. Form forcemeat into small balls and fry. Gently heat the blood from hare, stir into the gravy, allow to thicken. Serve hare piled on a hot dish, strain sauce over, and arrange the forcemeat balls round dish. Serve with redcurrant jelly handed separately.

5–6 helpings

HASHED HARE

Remains of cold roast hare	1 glass port or claret or cider (optional)
¾ pt brown sauce	Salt and pepper
	Trimmings as below

Trim hare into neat pieces. Make stock with bones and trimmings and use this instead of wine if liked.

Rabbit charlotte ready on a tray

Make brown sauce, add wine if used, put in pieces of hare and heat very thoroughly. Garnish with braised celery, small roast potatoes, fried bacon and croûtes of fried bread.

HARE PIE (COLD)

½–¾ lb cooked hare	Worcester sauce
½ lb streaky bacon	1 lb creamed potatoes
4 oz breadcrumbs	1 oz butter
Gravy or stock	Gravy or Cumberland sauce
Salt and pepper	

Cut the hare into small pieces; fry and cut up the bacon, mix with hare, breadcrumbs and enough gravy or stock to moisten well. Place a layer of mixture in the bottom of a greased pie dish; season well; add a little sauce. Cover with a layer of seasoned creamed potato; repeat until all mixture is used, finishing with a layer of potato. Put the butter, cut in small pieces, on the top; brown and heat thoroughly in a hot oven (220–230°C, 425–450°F, Gas 7–8). Serve with a good gravy or sauce.

4–5 helpings   Cooking time about 20 min

LARDED AND BRAISED RABBIT

1 rabbit	Salt and pepper
Larding bacon	Bouquet garni
2 oz dripping	1 oz butter
Brown stock	1 oz flour

Wash, dry, and joint the rabbit; lard each piece with strips of chilled fat bacon. Heat the dripping in a saucepan, fry the rabbit until lightly browned, pour off excess fat, cover with stock, add seasoning and bouquet garni. Cover tightly. Stew gently until rabbit is tender (1¼–1½ hr). Knead butter and flour together and add in small pieces to the stew 20 min before serving. Pile the rabbit on a hot dish; strain the sauce over.

3–4 helpings

BOILED RABBIT

1 rabbit	6 peppercorns
1 onion	1 teasp salt
1 carrot	Onion sauce

Hashed hare

½ turnip
Bouquet garni

Bacon, boiled, fried *or*
   grilled

Truss the rabbit; put it into boiling water. When the water re-boils, add the vegetables cut in pieces, the bouquet garni, peppercorns and salt. Cook gently for 45–60 min, until the rabbit is tender. Remove the skewers. Serve the rabbit, coated with onion sauce. Serve any extra sauce separately. (Fried or boiled bacon can also be served separately, or the bacon may be rolled, grilled, and used as garnish. The liquor in which the rabbit is cooked may be made into broth or soup.)

4 helpings

FRICASSÉE OF RABBIT

½ lb celery
1 tablesp cooking oil
1 small onion, chopped
2 oz margarine
2 oz flour
2 oz skim milk powder
   with water to make
   1 pt liquid

1 blade mace *or* pinch
   ground mace
Salt and pepper
1 lb cooked rabbit
   without bone
¼ lb streaky bacon
Triangles of toast

Wash and chop the celery. Heat the oil in a saucepan, add the onion and celery and cook slowly without browning. Lift out the vegetables, and reserve. Add the margarine to the pan, stir in the flour, and cook for 2 min. Remove from heat, add the liquid skim milk, then bring to the boil slowly, stirring continuously. Simmer for 3 min, add mace and season to taste. Stir in the cooked vegetables.

Cut the rabbit into bite-sized pieces, and stir into the sauce. Keep warm. Remove the rind from the bacon, flatten with a knife, cut into 3-in lengths and roll up for threading on a skewer. Cook under a hot grill until crisp, turning once or twice. Put the rabbit and sauce in the centre of a large dish. Arrange toast triangles round the edge and place bacon rolls on top. Serve immediately.

If desired, the rabbit can be prepared ahead of time, and re-heated when the bacon is grilled.

3–4 helpings

RABBIT STEW—RICH

1 rabbit
4 oz streaky bacon
18 button onions
2 oz butter
1½ oz flour

1 pt good stock
Bouquet garni
2 cloves
Salt and pepper
1 glass claret (optional)

Wash, dry and joint the rabbit, put the liver aside. Dice the bacon, peel the onions. Melt the butter in a large saucepan, fry onions and bacon until brown, then lift out. Fry rabbit lightly, sprinkle in flour and continue frying until well browned. Replace the onions and bacon, add hot stock, bouquet garni, cloves and seasoning, cover tightly and stew gently until rabbit is tender (about 1¼ hr). About 15 min before serving, add the claret if used, put in the liver (washed and cut into small pieces) and finish cooking. Pile the rabbit on a hot dish, strain the sauce over and garnish with the bacon dice and onions.

3–4 helpings   **Cooking time about 2 hr**

CREAM OF RABBIT

½ lb raw rabbit
1 small egg
¼ pt thick white sauce

Salt and pepper
½ pt brown sauce

Chop and mince the rabbit finely, and pound it until smooth or process in an electric blender. Work in the egg, add the white sauce, season well and sieve or blend if required very smooth. Press lightly into 6 well-buttered moulds, cover with greased paper, steam gently until firm. Serve with the brown sauce poured round the moulds.

6 moulds   **Cooking time 20–30 min to steam**

RABBIT CHARLOTTE

1 large slice bread and
   butter, about ¼ in thick
2–3 oz finely-chopped
   or minced cooked *or*
   raw rabbit (*or* chicken)

1 egg yolk
¼ pt milk *or* chicken
   stock
Seasoning

GARNISH

Chopped parsley   Creamed potato

Remove the crusts from the bread and butter. Put ½ the slice at the bottom of an individual pie dish with buttered side on top. Cover with rabbit meat. Place the second piece of bread and butter over rabbit, the buttered side uppermost. Beat the egg yolk well, pour over warm milk or stock. Season well. Pour into dish; stand it in a larger dish of warm water. Bake for 1¼–1½ hr in centre of a warm oven (170°C, 335°F, Gas 3). Pipe or pile creamed potato round the dish and garnish with chopped parsley.
NOTE: If using cooked rabbit, the cooking time may be shortened to 45 min, or until the custard is set.

RABBIT SOUFFLÉ

6 oz raw rabbit
2 oz butter
2 oz flour
½ pt milk

2 eggs
Salt and pepper
Brown sauce

Chop and pound the rabbit, or process in an electric blender. Melt butter in a saucepan, add the flour and cook for 3 min. Stir in the milk, simmer gently 10 min, then cool. Into the rabbit meat, work egg yolks, cooled sauce and seasoning. Fold in the stiffly beaten egg whites and half fill a well-buttered soufflé (straight-sided) tin with the mixture. Cover with greased paper. Steam gently for 40–50 min. Turn on to a hot dish and serve immediately. Serve the sauce separately.

Alternatively, the soufflé may be baked (uncovered) in a fairly hot oven (190–200°C, 375–400°F, Gas 5–6) for about 25 min—until well risen and set. Make a deep channel with the handle of a teaspoon all round the soufflé, about ½-in from the edge; the mixture will split along this line and the centre rise evenly.

6 helpings

CURRIED RABBIT

1 rabbit	Salt and pepper
2 oz butter	1 oz sultanas
1 chopped onion	1 oz blanched almonds
1 dessertsp flour	1 dessertsp desiccated
1 tablesp curry powder	coconut
1 dessertsp curry paste	1 chopped apple
¾ pt white stock	1 dessertsp chutney
1 tablesp lemon	2 tablesp cream or milk
juice	(optional)

GARNISH

Fans of lemon	Gherkin fans
Red pepper	

Wash, dry and joint the rabbit. Heat the butter in a saucepan, fry joints lightly, remove and drain. Fry onion lightly, add flour, curry powder and paste, and fry very well, stirring occasionally. Stir in stock, bring to boil. Put in all other ingredients except the cream; put in the rabbit joints. (Have the coconut tied in muslin, and remove after 15 min.) Simmer gently for about 1½ hr, adding a little more stock if necessary. Add cream or milk if used. Dish the rabbit, pour the sauce over, straining it if you wish. Garnish. For accompaniments, see Curried Chicken.

3–4 helpings

RABBIT PIE

1 rabbit	Puff pastry, frozen or
½ lb beef steak	using 8 oz flour, etc
¼ lb bacon or pickled	Egg for glazing
pork	Trimmings as below,
Salt and pepper	for cold pie
½ pt stock	

Wash, dry, and joint the rabbit, dice the beef and bacon or pork. Place these ingredients in layers in a pie dish, season well, ¾ fill dish with stock. Cover with pastry; slit and glaze it. Bake 1¾–2 hr in a hot oven (220–230°C, 425–450°F, Gas 7–8) for 15 min and in a moderate oven (180°C, 350°F, Gas 4) for the remainder of the time. Add remainder of seasoned stock; serve hot or cold. If the pie is required cold, forcemeat balls and sliced hard-boiled egg will be an improvement.

6–8 helpings **Cooking time 1¾–2 hr**

Rabbit in aspic

Rabbit pies and pasties

RABBIT PATTIES OR PIES

6 oz raw *or* cooked rabbit	Stock *or* water
2 oz raw *or* cooked ham *or* bacon	Shortcrust *or* puff pastry, frozen *or* using 8 oz flour, etc
Salt and pepper	Egg *or* milk for glazing

Cut the rabbit and ham or bacon into small dice. Mix well, add seasoning, moisten with stock or water. Line 12 patty tins with pastry, fill with the meat mixture, cover with pastry, glaze with egg or milk. Bake in a fairly hot oven (190–200°C, 375–400°F, Gas 5–6) for about 20 min, if filling is cooked, or 40 min, if meat is raw. Serve either hot or cold.

12 small patties

RABBIT IN ASPIC JELLY

| 1 cooked rabbit | 2 hard-boiled eggs |
| 1 pt aspic jelly | 2 oz shredded bacon |

Divide the rabbit into neat pieces. Rinse a mould with cold water, line it with a thin layer of cold, liquid aspic jelly (avoid air-bubbles in the jelly); allow to set. Decorate the jelly with some hard-boiled egg, cover gently with a thin layer of jelly, and allow to set. Arrange the rabbit, bacon and remaining egg in layers in the mould, interspersing the layers with jelly. Allow each layer to set before adding another. When the mould is filled, set any remaining jelly in a flat tin. When the mould is turned out, garnish it with shapes of jelly or chopped jelly.

4–5 helpings **To set the aspic 2–3 hr**

RABBIT PIE—DURHAM

½ lb cooked rabbit	2 oz cooked bacon
Short crust pastry, frozen *or* using 8 oz flour, etc	Salt and pepper
	4 eggs
	Egg *or* milk for glazing

Line a pie-plate with half the pastry. Chop the rabbit and bacon, mix together and place in 4 piles on the pastry. Between each pile of meat, drop a raw egg, keeping the yolks whole. Season the filling, cover with remainder of pastry, glaze and bake in a fairly hot oven (190–200°C, 375–400°F, Gas 5–6) for about ½ hr. Serve hot.

4 helpings

RABBIT PASTIES

1 rabbit	4 medium-sized potatoes
Short crust pastry, frozen *or* using 12 oz flour, etc	1 small onion
	Salt and pepper
	Egg *or* milk for glazing

Make the pastry and roll it into six rounds. Remove the flesh from the rabbit, cut it into small pieces, mix it with the thinly sliced onion and the potatoes, diced. Season well. Place the filling on the rounds of pastry; moisten the edges. Fold in half, seal, cut a small slit in each and glaze with egg or milk. Bake the pasties in a hot oven (220–230°C, 425–450°F, Gas 7–8) for 10 min; lower the heat (180°C, 350°F, Gas 4) and continue cooking for another 30 min. Serve hot.

The rabbit bones may be used for gravy stock.

6 pasties

Pears filled with nuts and dates, see recipe on page 146

Vegetables can, and should, be one of the most interesting and nourishing parts of a meal, yet they too often lack flavour, colour and food value. We grow good vegetables, but let them get too big and coarse; small, young peas, carrots and Brussels sprouts have a flavour quite different from fully grown ones. They can also be 'short-cooked', quickly with very little water, which makes all vegetables more flavoursome and more nourishing.

We should grow smaller crops and more varied ones, to make vegetables interesting to the cook and her 'clients'.

Simple cooking is best for good-quality vegetables. They should be 'short-cooked' to conserve their food value, and should have butter or margarine and herbs added, as well as more seasoning than is usually given to them. A well-flavoured sauce can help vegetables which are otherwise dull, and they should be cooked only just before a meal; keeping them waiting spoils them.

Vegetables are essential foods because they contain valuable amounts of the vital vitamin C, as well as other vitamins, minerals, roughage and some protein, all essential to health.

Green vegetables are particularly important for their vitamins C and F. Unfortunately, vitamin C is lost quickly when the vegetable is cut or pulled, and also in cooking; so vegetables should be cut from the garden only when they are needed, and should be cooked as quickly as possible, until just tender and no more. The cooking liquid should always be used, too, for gravies or soups. Furthermore, vegetables should be cooked in a pan with a tight-fitting lid, since vitamin C is destroyed by heat and air together; and bicarbonate of soda should never be used since it too destroys the vital vitamins. Shredding and slow cooking are also destruc-

tive, so vegetables should be cut up as little as possible, and should be plunged into fast-boiling water.

Sometimes, parboiling is useful to save one from overcooking vegetables. The food is partly boiled, but for only half the usual time or less. It is then drained quickly, and finished at once in a frying-pan or under the grill, or in sauce in the oven.

Potatoes are the most important roots and tubers, and young ones contain valuable amounts of vitamin C. They should be cooked in their skins to conserve their food value. Beetroots, carrots, swedes, and onions all have to be scraped or peeled; but there is no need to boil them in a large quantity of water, thus destroying their sugar content and flavour. They should be cooked 'for food value' (see Carrots, Cooked for Food Value), or baked.

The pulses (dried peas and beans) have comparatively little worthwhile food value, but fresh peas and beans contain vitamins, mineral salts, iron and a useful amount of second class protein, as well as sugar.

Modern dehydrated vegetables, apart from pulses, have lost little of their food value, and are a boon to busy housewives; clear instructions on cooking are given with them. Frozen vegetables, from both temperate and tropical climates, are even more popular; and, rightly used, they can be as good a source of food value as fresh ones if they are short-cooked before they have thawed out. As for canned and bottled vegetables, they too can be nourishing and flavoursome if the liquid with them is used for cooking and a sauce. Like fresh vegetables, however, all these forms of prepared vegetables lose food value quickly if they stand and wait or are kept hot where the air can reach them.

Even for people who usually prefer meat and

fish dishes, vegetables such as peas or lentils can make a pleasant main-course dish, especially with a rich savoury sauce. An attractive decoration of other vegetables or savoury stuffing can make them appealing as well as satisfying. We have given various recipes for such dishes in the second part of this section.

Colour and design play a big part in making food attractive. Vegetables should be chosen for their colour contrasts as well as their flavour, and should be attractively dressed and presented.

VEGETABLE DISHES

APPLES, APRICOTS, ETC WITH MEAT

Apples are often baked whole and served with pork instead of apple sauce. They are cored but not peeled, and the core holes are stuffed with a little herb stuffing or with raisins, so that the apples keep their shape. They are cooked just like sweet baked apples.

Apricot halves, fresh or canned, are sometimes served with ham or bacon. They are drained and sprinkled with cinnamon and sugar, then grilled briefly to glaze them. The syrup from canned apricots can be used as the basis of a sauce or as a glaze for the meat.

Prunes, soaked in boiling water or tea and simmered until tender, can be served with braised beef, or form part of some beef stews. A number of Middle Eastern lamb stews also include fruits such as dried apricots, prunes and dates.

BOILED GLOBE ARTICHOKES

6 globe artichokes	Hollandaise sauce *or*
Salt	melted butter *or*
1 tablesp lemon juice	mushroom sauce

Soak the artichokes in cold, salt water for at least 1 hr to ensure the removal of all dust and insects. Wash them well. Cut off the tails and trim the bottoms with a sharp knife. Cut off the outer leaves and trim the tops of the remaining ones with scissors. Put into a pan with just sufficient boiling water to cover them, adding salt and the lemon juice. Cook until tender, 15–45 min according to size and freshness (when cooked the leaves pull out easily). Test frequently after 15 min as they are apt to break and become discoloured if over-cooked. Remove from water and drain them well by turning them upside down.

Serve with Hollandaise sauce *or* melted butter *or* mushroom sauce.

ARTICHOKE BOTTOMS

Where economy does not matter, globe artichokes may be cooked as in the preceding recipe and only the bottoms or 'fonds' used. After cooking, the leaves are carefully pulled out of the artichokes so that the bottoms are retained, unbroken.

The bottoms may be served quite simply, tossed in hot butter or coated with a good sauce; they may be fried; or they may be stuffed with vegetable, meat or cheese fillings piled into the natural cavity in the centre of each.

ARTICHOKE BOTTOMS WITH BÉCHAMEL SAUCE

6 artichoke bottoms	½ pt Béchamel sauce
2 oz butter *or* margarine	

Trim the cooked artichoke bottoms and, if large, cut in halves. Toss in hot butter or margarine. Season and serve with hot Béchamel sauce poured

4–6 helpings   Cooking time 7 min to fry the bottoms

FRIED ARTICHOKE BOTTOMS IN BATTER

6 artichoke bottoms	Deep fat for frying
Fried parsley	

BATTER FOR COATING VEGETABLES

2 oz plain flour	4 tablesp tepid water
Pinch of salt and pepper	(approx)
1 dessertsp olive oil	1 egg white

Cut the cooked artichoke bottoms into 3 or 4 pieces according to size. Sift the flour and seasoning and mix to a smooth batter with the oil and sufficient tepid water to give a coating consistency. Leave to stand for ½ hr. Fold in the stiffly whipped egg white just before frying. Dip the pieces of artichoke into the batter on a skewer and lower each piece carefully into hot deep fat at 180°C, 340°F. Turn them during frying as they will float, and when golden-brown (5–7 min) remove from the fat. Drain well and serve garnished with fried parsley.

The bottoms will have more flavour if soaked for ½ hr before coating and frying in a marinade of olive oil, lemon juice, pepper, salt and herbs.

4–6 helpings

STUFFED ARTICHOKE BOTTOMS

Artichoke bottoms	1 tablesp of stuffing for
Butter *or* margarine	each (approx)

STUFFINGS

1 Cooked rice well seasoned and flavoured with cheese, preferably Parmesan *or*
2 Fried, finely chopped shallot, young cooked peas, mint, seasoning *or*
3 Cooked sausage meat, chopped chives, French mustard *or*
4 Finely chopped fried onion, mushroom, and a little tomato purée.

Toss the cooked artichoke bottoms in hot butter or margarine as in Artichoke bottoms with Béchamel Sauce. Pile the hot, well-flavoured stuffing on each bottom. Serve immediately. Allow 1 artichoke bottom for each person.

Cooking time 5–7 min to fry the bottoms

BOILED JERUSALEM ARTICHOKES

1½–2 lb Jerusalem	Salt
artichokes	¾ pt white sauce
White vinegar *or*	
lemon juice	

Scrub, scrape and rinse the artichokes, using 1 teasp white vinegar or lemon juice in each qt water to keep the vegetable white. Put into sufficient boiling, salted water to cover the vegetable, adding 1 teasp white vinegar or lemon juice to each quart of water. Simmer gently till just tender, about 20 min.

Fried artichoke bottoms in batter

Drain well and serve in a hot vegetable dish with the white sauce poured over. If wanted mashed, shake the pan over low heat to dry the artichokes slightly. Mash with a fork or potato-masher and beat in 1 oz butter or margarine.

5–6 helpings

BAKED JERUSALEM ARTICHOKES

2 lb Jerusalem artichokes	Salt and pepper
Lemon juice *or* white vinegar	Dripping

Prepare and parboil the artichokes 5 min. Drain them and shake the pan over heat to dry them. Put into hot dripping in a roasting tin or in the tin containing the roast joint. Roll the artichokes in the fat and cook in a fairly hot oven (190°C, 375°F, Gas 5) till brown and tender (about 1 hr), turning them during cooking. They will not be a good colour but are of excellent flavour.

4–6 helpings

FRIED JERUSALEM ARTICHOKES

Batter, double quantity, as for Fried Artichoke Bottoms in Batter	1½ lb Jerusalem artichokes
	Fried parsley

Make the batter. Prepare and parboil the artichokes (about 15 min). Cut them into slices ½ in thick and season them well. Dip the slices of artichokes in batter, and fry in hot fat, at 170°C, 340°F, until golden-brown (5–7 min), turning them once during cooking. Drain well and serve very hot with fried parsley.

6 helpings **Cooking time 15 min to parboil artichokes, 5–7 min to fry them**

ASPARAGUS 'AU NATUREL'

1 bundle of asparagus	1 oz butter
Salt	Lemon juice

Trim the hard white ends of the asparagus to suitable lengths for serving. Scrape the stalks with a sharp knife, working downwards from the head. Wash them well in cold water. Tie them into small bundles with the heads in one direction. Re-trim the stalks evenly. Keep them in cold water until ready to cook. Cook very gently, with the heads off the source of heat, in just enough salted boiling water to cover. When tender, after 15–20 min, drain and serve on a folded table napkin; buttered and lightly flavoured with lemon juice, asparagus is good with any steaks or grilled chops.

The asparagus can be cooked 'standing'. In the saucepan, place a bottling jar half-filled with boiling water. The asparagus is placed stems down in the jar and the points cook more slowly in steam only.

Asparagus 'au naturel'

ASPARAGUS POINTS

Allow 30 min for this method of cooking. Allow 6 or 8 medium-sized heads per person.

ASPARAGUS POINTS

Asparagus	Chopped shallot and
Melted butter	chopped parsley
Salt and pepper	(optional)

Cut the points and tender green parts of the asparagus into short pieces, place them in slightly salted boiling water, and cook gently 5 to 10 min, according to size and age. Drain well, put the asparagus into a saucepan containing a little melted butter, sprinkle with pepper and toss over heat for a few minutes. Serve as a garnish or a vegetable or as a filling in omelets. It is a mistake to add anything which will impair the delicate flavour of the asparagus but a little chopped shallot and parsley may be fried in the butter before adding the asparagus.

Allow 12 points per helping

Broad beans with cream sauce

FRIED AUBERGINE WITH TOMATO SAUCE

4 aubergines	1 finely chopped onion
Flour	Salad oil *or* butter
Cayenne pepper	Tomato sauce
Salt	

Slice the aubergines about ½ in thick, lay them out on a flat dish, sprinkle with salt and put on a weight (this hastens the process of removing the moisture). After ½ hr wipe them with a cloth, then coat them lightly with flour seasoned with cayenne and salt. Fry the onion in the oil or butter until lightly browned, drain and keep the onion hot. Replace the butter in the pan and fry the aubergine until both sides are lightly browned. Drain and dish. Sprinkle the onion on the aubergine; serve with tomato sauce, if liked.

6 helpings   **Cooking time, to fry the aubergine, about 15 min**

BOILED FRENCH OR RUNNER BEANS

1½ lb French *or* runner beans	1 oz butter *or* margarine Salt

Wash, top and tail and string the beans. Do not cut up French beans *or* young runner beans as they lose their flavour in cooking. For older scarlet runners, slice thinly, or, for better flavour, cut into diamonds, i.e. slice them in a slanting direction.

Have ready just enough boiling salted water to cover them and cook them with the lid on the pan. When tender (15–20 min), drain and re-heat in butter or margarine. Serve immediately.

For the French method of cooking, drain the cooked beans well, and shake in the pan until most of the water has evaporated. Add a little butter, parsley, lemon juice and seasoning and shake over heat for a few minutes. Serve immediately.

4–6 helpings

BROAD BEANS WITH CREAM SAUCE

2 lb broad beans	½ pt veal *or* chicken
A bunch of herbs	stock
(thyme, sage,	1 lump of sugar
savory, marjoram,	1 egg yolk
parsley stalks *or*	¼ pt single cream *or*
any one of these)	evaporated milk
	Salt and pepper

Shell the beans and cook them in the stock with

Haricot beans with parsley sauce

the lump of sugar and the bunch of herbs. When the beans are tender, lift out the herbs. Beat the egg yolk with the cream and stir it carefully into the saucepan. Re-heat, stirring all the time until almost simmering. Season and serve at once. If preferred, the herbs may be finely chopped and left in the sauce.

If the beans are really large strain them from the liquid when they are tender and skin them before returning them to the thickened sauce.

4–6 helpings   **Cooking time 20–40 min**

BROAD BEANS WITH PARSLEY SAUCE

2–3 lb broad beans	2–3 savory leaves (if
Salt	available)
	Parsley sauce

Wash the beans and shell them. If not to be cooked immediately, cover over with some of the washed pods as this prevents the skins of the beans from drying out and becoming slightly toughened. Cook gently in just enough boiling salted water to cover, with the savory leaves in the water. When tender, 15–35 min according to size and age, drain well. Make a good parsley sauce with ½ milk and ½ bean water and well flavoured with lemon juice. Re-heat the beans in the sauce and serve immediately.

When really young, broad beans should have heads, tails and strings removed as for runner beans, and be cooked whole in the pods. The pods are eaten after tossing them in melted butter. The pod is quite tender, with an excellent flavour, and a very economical dish can be produced by this method. When really mature, it is often necessary to skin the beans after cooking and before tossing them in the parsley sauce.

4–6 helpings (according to yield)

BOILED HARICOT BEANS

½ lb haricot beans	Salt and pepper
1 oz butter *or* margarine	Chopped parsley

Soak the beans overnight in boiling water. Drain them and well cover with cold, salted water. Bring slowly to boiling point and simmer very slowly until tender, 2–2½ hr. Drain off the water and shake them gently over the low heat to dry them. Toss them in butter and season with pepper and salt. Serve hot, sprinkled with freshly chopped parsley.

For Haricot Beans in Parsley sauce, cook the beans as above, and re-heat gently in the Parsley sauce.

6 helpings

BAKED BEETROOT

Wash the beetroots carefully. If the skin has been damaged in any way, cover the damaged part with a little flour and water paste. Put them into a baking-dish and bake in a moderate oven (180°C, 350°F, Gas 4), until tender, about 1 hr. This method is excellent for young beetroots, all the flavour and sweetness of the beetroot being retained. The beetroots may be wrapped in greased papers or covered with aluminium foil before baking.

BOILED BEETROOT

Wash the beetroots very carefully, but do not break the skins, or they will lose colour and flavour during cooking. Put them into sufficient boiling water to cover them and boil them gently until tender, 1½–2½ hr according to size and age. Unless to be served as a hot vegetable, leave them to cool in the cooking water before rubbing off the peel. If to be served hot, serve them with melted butter.

Beetroots are cooked most successfully and quickly in a pressure cooker, taking 15–40 min according to size and age, with the cooker set at 15 lb pressure.

Cooking time (in a pressure cooker)—*small* beetroots 15 min, *medium* beetroots 20 min, *large* beetroots 35–40 min.

POLISH BEETROOT

2 lb cooked, peeled beetroots	1 dessertsp finely grated horseradish *or*
1 small onion, finely chopped	1 dessertsp bottled horseradish sauce
½ oz margarine	Salt and pepper
½ oz flour	A little sugar, if necessary
½ bottle of yogurt	Chopped parsley

Grate the beetroot. Melt the fat and fry the onion in it, carefully and thoroughly. Stir in the flour, add the yogurt and bring to the boil. Add the beetroot and horseradish and heat thoroughly. Season carefully, adding a little more yogurt if the flavour is too sweet, or a little sugar if too sharp. Serve very hot and decorate with lines of parsley.

This is a very pleasant way of serving beetroot as a hot vegetable and is a very quick dish if cooked beetroots are purchased or available.

6 helpings   **Cooking time 15 min**

BROCCOLI

This vegetable is known to the cook in three different forms:

1 Most of the cauliflowers which are sold between October and June come from the broccoli plant, which is very hardy. (The cauliflower plant proper is less hardy and supplies the typical white heads during the summer and early autumn, before the frosts appear.) This form of broccoli is cooked by the methods suggested for CAULIFLOWER, see below.

2 The Calabresse, green or Italian sprouting broccoli, produces a medium-sized green central head, and is usually available in March. It is also cooked

Brussels sprouts with chestnuts

like cauliflower and served with melted butter. After the central head is cut, shoots appear from every leaf joint, each shoot having a tiny head. The shoots are cut with about 6 in of stem and provide an excellent vegetable for two or three months. The stems should be cut into short lengths and cooked, with the tiny heads, in boiling salted water as for any green vegetable; or they can be tied in bundles and cooked and served like asparagus.

3 Early purple sprouting and white sprouting broccoli come into season at the beginning of April. The tiny heads should be cut off with about 2 in of stem and adjoining leaves and cooked whole in boiling salt water like any other green vegetable. The more the heads are cut off the more prolific is the growth.

Frozen broccoli is available most of the year. It should be short-cooked in very little water until just tender, and served with melted butter and a sprinkling of ground nutmeg or thyme.

BOILED BRUSSELS SPROUTS WITH CHESTNUTS

1½ lb Brussels sprouts	12 cooked chestnuts
Salt	3 oz chopped ham
1 oz butter *or* margarine (optional)	4 tablesp cream

Choose small, close, sprouts. Remove shabby

Red cabbage with apples

outer leaves by cutting the end, then make a cross cut on the bottom of each stalk. Soak in cold water, containing 1 teasp of salt per quart, for 10 min only. Wash thoroughly under running water if possible. Choose a suitably sized pan and put in enough water to $\frac{1}{4}$ fill it only, with $\frac{1}{2}$ teasp salt to 1 pt of water. When boiling, put in half the sprouts, the largest ones if variable in size, put on lid and bring quickly to boil again. Add rest of sprouts and cook until all are just tender, with the lid on the pan all the time. Drain in a colander and serve immediately in a hot vegetable dish or toss in melted butter before serving. Sprouts should be served quickly as they soon cool.

To serve with chestnuts put the sprouts, chopped chestnuts, ham and cream into a casserole, cover and re-heat gently in the oven at 180°C, 350°F, Gas 4.

6 helpings   **Cooking time 15 min**

BOILED CABBAGE

1 large, fresh cabbage   Salt
  (about 2 lb)

Cut across the end and remove only the very thick, coarse piece of stalk and shrivelled or discoloured outer leaves. Pull off the green leaves and put to soak, with the heart cut into 4 pieces, in cold water with 1 teasp of salt per quart of water. Soak for 10 min only. Choose a suitably sized pan and put in enough water to $\frac{1}{4}$ fill it only, with $\frac{1}{2}$ teasp of salt to 1 pt of water. Cut out the stalk from the green leaves and heart of the cabbage, shred it and put on to cook with the lid on the pan. Shred the green outer leaves and add these to the pan. Replace lid and bring to boil again quickly, while shredding the cabbage heart. Add the heart to the pan a handful at a time so that the water barely goes off the boil. Cook with lid on pan only until the cabbage is just tender. Drain well in a colander but do not press out

liquid. Serve in a hot dish and send to table immediately.

6 helpings

RED CABBAGE WITH APPLES

1 small red cabbage	1 tablesp golden syrup
1 oz margarine	Juice of $\frac{1}{2}$ lemon
1 onion chopped very fine	2 tablesp vinegar
2 cooking apples	Salt

Melt the fat. Add the onion and fry gently until light brown. Add cabbage finely shredded, peeled and sliced apples, and syrup. Cook over very gentle heat for 10 min, shaking pan frequently. Add lemon juice, vinegar and salt and simmer covered, 1–1$\frac{1}{2}$ hr Stir occasionally. Season and serve.

6 helpings

Carrots cooked for food value

CARROTS—COOKED FOR FOOD VALUE

1½ lb carrots	½ teasp salt
1 oz butter *or*	½–1 gill boiling water
margarine	Chopped parsley

Cut off the green tops, scrub and scrape the carrots. Slice them thinly if old carrots (or leave whole if really young). Fat steam the carrots for 10 min, i.e. shake them in the melted fat, well below frying temperature, with the lid on the pan until the fat is absorbed. Add the liquid (less for young carrots) and the salt, and simmer gently until the carrots are tender—15–30 min according to age of carrots. Serve hot, with the small amount of liquid remaining, and garnished with parsley.

This method should be employed for cooking most root vegetables. Both flavour and food value are conserved.

6 helpings

GLAZED CARROTS

1½ lb young carrots	¼ teasp salt
2 oz butter	Good stock
3 lumps sugar	Chopped parsley

Melt the butter in a saucepan. Add the scraped, whole carrots, sugar, salt and enough stock to come half-way up the carrots. Cook gently, without a lid, shaking the pan occasionally until tender. Remove the carrots and keep them hot. Boil the stock rapidly until reduced to rich glaze. Replace the carrots 2 or 3 at a time, turn them until both sides are well coated with glaze. Dish, sprinkle with chopped parsley and serve.

6 helpings   **Cooking time about ¾ hr**

BOILED CAULIFLOWER WITH WHITE SAUCE

1 large cauliflower	Salt
½ pt white sauce made with ½ milk and ½ cauliflower water	

Trim off the stem and all the leaves, except the very young ones. Soak in cold water, head down, with 1 teasp salt per qt of water, for not more than 10 min. Wash well. Choose a suitable sized pan and put in enough water to ¼ fill it, with ½ teasp salt to 1 pt water. Put in cauliflower, stalk down, and cook with lid on pan until stalk and flower are tender. Lift out carefully and drain. Keep hot. Coat the cauliflower with the sauce and serve immediately. To reduce cooking time, the cauliflower may be quartered before cooking or broken into large sprigs.

6 helpings

CELERIAC WITH CREAM SAUCE

3 roots of celeriac	Lemon juice
¾ pt good white sauce	2 tablesp cream (or more)
Salt	

Scrub the root well, then peel thickly. (If the roots are spongy discard them as useless.) Cut into ½ in slices and stew them slowly in boiling, salted vegetable stock or water till tender—about 45 min. Drain. Make a good white sauce with ½ pt milk and cooking liquid. Season and add a little lemon juice. Coat the celeriac, add the cream and serve immediately. The vegetable stock can be water in which onions, etc., have been cooked.

6 helpings

Cauliflower with white sauce

BRAISED CELERY

4 heads of celery	Meat glaze (if
Stock, meat *or* vegetable	available)

MIREPOIX

½ oz dripping	Bouquet garni (thyme,
½ oz bacon	marjoram, sage,
2 large carrots	parsley)
1 small turnip	1 bay leaf
2 onions	Watercress to garnish
A pinch of mace	Salt
6 white peppercorns	

Trim the celery but leave the heads whole. Wash them well and tie each securely. Prepare the mirepoix. Fry the bacon in the dripping in a large saucepan, then fry all the vegetables cut in pieces ¾ in thick, until lightly browned. Add herbs, spices and ½ teasp of salt and enough stock to come ¾ of the way up the vegetables. Bring to boiling-point. Lay the celery on top. Baste well with the stock in the pan and cover closely with greased paper or metal foil. Put on lid and cook until the celery is soft (about 1½ hr). Baste several times during cooking. Dish the celery and keep hot. Strain the liquor, put it back in the pan. Reduce by boiling quickly until of glazing consistency or use meat glaze. Pour over the celery. If you wish, place the dish under a hot grill for a moment until it begins to brown. Garnish with watercress.

Braised celery

CELERY WITH WHITE SAUCE

Use the coarse outer stems of the celery for soups. A few pieces may be cut up and fried for the mirepoix. The cooked mirepoix can be served sprinkled with parsley as a separate vegetable dish or if sieved and thinned down with stock it makes an excellent soup.

4–8 helpings, according to the size of the celery heads

CELERY WITH WHITE SAUCE

2 large heads of celery	Salt
½ pt good white sauce	Lemon juice

Trim off the green tops of the celery, reserving a few pale green ones. Remove the very tough outer stalks. Separate the other stalks and wash or, if necessary, scrub in cold water. Rinse and reserve the tender hearts for eating raw. Scrape the stalks to be cooked, cut into suitable lengths for cooking and tie in bundles. Stew in barely sufficient boiling water, slightly salted, to cover the celery. If possible, cook in vegetable water from cooked artichokes, onions etc. When tender (in about 1 hr), drain. Make a good white sauce with ½ milk and ½ cooking liquid. Season and add a little lemon juice. Coat the celery with the sauce, garnish with some of the pale green leaves and serve immediately.

4–6 helpings　　　　　**Cooking time 1 hr**

CHESTNUTS AU JUS

2 lb chestnuts	1 pt good brown stock
2 cloves	Cayenne pepper
1 small onion	Salt
1 outside stick of celery	1 dessertsp meat glaze
1 bay leaf	(if available)
A pinch of mace	Fleurons of pastry

Take a sharp knife and make an incision in each chestnut, in the shell only. Put into a saucepan and cover with cold water. Bring to the boil and cook for 2 min. Drain and peel and skin them while very hot. Stick the cloves into the onion and put chestnuts, onion, celery, bay leaf and mace into the boiling stock. Season. Simmer about 1 hr until the chestnuts are tender. Strain and keep the chestnuts hot. Return stock to pan, add the meat glaze if available and reduce to a glazing consistency. Pile the chestnuts in a hot vegetable dish, pour the glaze over and decorate with fleurons of pastry.

For a purée, sieve the cooked chestnuts and add a little butter and cream to taste.

6 helpings

CHICORY AND WHITE SAUCE

6 large heads of chicory	Salt
¾ pt good white sauce	Lemon juice

Cut off the end of the chicory and the outer leaves. Split each head to within ½ in of the end and wash well between the leaves. Blanch, by bringing to the boil in just enough water to cover and boiling 5 min. Drain, then tie the heads together in bundles of 2 and cook in boiling salted water until just tender. Finish and serve the dish as for Celery with White Sauce.

6 helpings　　　　　**Cooking time 30–40 min**

CORN FRITTERS

One 7 or 8 oz can sweet corn	1 egg
1 apple chopped small	2 tablesp apple sauce or cider
1 oz flour	Milk to mix
1 level teasp baking powder	Salt and pepper

Drain the liquid from the corn. Chop the corn, if necessary. Mix with the apple. Make a batter with the flour, baking powder, egg yolk, and 2 tablesp liquid from the corn made up with milk. Stir in the corn. Whip the egg white very stiffly and fold into the mixture. Season. Fry in spoonfuls in a little hot fat in a frying-pan, turning them when golden-brown on the underside. Drain and serve at once.

They may be served with fried chicken, fried bacon or sausages and are fried in the same fat after chicken, etc, is fried, and drained.

4–6 helpings　　　　　**Cooking time 5–7 min**

STEAMED CUCUMBER WITH WHITE SAUCE

2 large cucumbers	¾ pt white sauce
1 oz butter or margarine	1 egg
1 teasp finely chopped shallot	1 teasp finely chopped parsley
	Salt and pepper

Peel the cucumber and steam it until tender (about 20 min). Drain well and cut into 1 in slices. Melt the butter in a saucepan, put in the shallot and cook it without browning. Add the sliced cucumber, toss over heat for a few minutes, then stir in the white sauce. Just before boiling point is reached, add the well-beaten egg and parsley, stir and cook gently until the egg thickens. Season and serve hot.

6 helpings

BRAISED ENDIVE

6 heads of endive	Mirepoix (see Braised Celery)
Stock	
Meat glaze (if available)	

Cut off the stumps of the endive and discard any outer leaves that are discoloured or tough. Wash in several waters, then parboil in salted water 10 min to remove bitter flavour. Drain well; pressing out water with the fingers. Braise and serve as for Braised Celery, see above.

6 helpings

BOILED OR BRAISED LEEKS

12 leeks	2 tablesp cream (or more)
Salt	
¾ pt white sauce	

Trim off the roots and outer leaves and as much of the tops as necessary. Split from the top to within 1 in of the bottom. Wash very thoroughly under running water, separating each leaf with the fingers to ensure that no grit is left between the leaves. Drain and tie in bundles. Boil in as little water as possible (barely enough to cover), with 1 teasp salt to 1 pt water. Cook until tender—30–40 min. Drain well and coat with white sauce made with ½ milk and ½ leek water. Add the cream just before serving.

To braise leeks, follow the same method as for Braised Celery.

6 helpings

BOILED LENTILS

¾ lb lentils	1 onion
Bouquet garni	1 clove
1 ham bone (if available) or bacon rinds	Salt and pepper
	½ oz butter or margarine

Corn fritters

Put the lentils into cold water with the herbs, ham bone, onion stuck with the clove, and a little salt. Bring to boiling point and cook until the lentils are soft—about 1 hr. Strain the lentils, toss in a little melted butter *or* margarine; season and serve. If preferred, sieve the lentils before tossing in butter.

6 helpings

BRAISED LETTUCES

6 heads of lettuce	Mirepoix (*see* Braised
Stock	Celery)
Glaze (if available)	

Boiled lentils and braised leeks

Follow the method for Braised Celery above.

VEGETABLE MARROW—COOKED FOR FOOD VALUE

2 small marrows	$\frac{3}{4}$ pt white sauce
1 oz butter *or* margarine	$\frac{1}{2}$–1 gill boiling water
$\frac{1}{2}$ teasp salt	

Peel the marrows. Cut into halves length-wise and scrape out the seeds and pith with a tablespoon. Cut into pieces, about 2 ins square. Fat steam the pieces for 10 min, i.e. shake them in the melted fat, well below frying temperature with the lid on the pan until the fat is absorbed. Add the liquid and the salt, and simmer gently until the marrow is tender, about 15 min. Drain well, retaining the cooking liquor for use in making the white sauce. Dish the marrow in a hot dish and coat with the sauce. Serve immediately.

6 helpings

GRILLED MUSHROOMS

12 flat mushrooms	Buttered toast
Salt and pepper	Chopped parsley
Butter *or* bacon fat	Lemon juice

Wash, peel and trim the stalks. Season and brush with melted butter *or* bacon fat. Cook under a hot grill, turning them once. Serve in a hot dish or on rounds of buttered toast, with a sprinkling of chopped parsley and a squeeze of lemon juice. A pinch of very finely chopped marjoram, sprinkled on each mushroom prior to grilling, imparts an excellent flavour.

6 helpings

CANNED OKRAS (to serve as a vegetable)

1 can okras	Salt and pepper
$\frac{1}{2}$ oz butter *or* margarine	

Turn the contents of the can into a saucepan and heat. Drain. Toss in melted butter *or* margarine. Season and serve.

Baked onions

BAKED ONIONS

6 large onions	A little margarine *or*
Salt and pepper	butter
	A little milk

1 Peel the onions and cook in boiling, salted water 20 min. Drain and place in a fireproof dish. Sprinkle with salt and pepper. Put a small pat of margarine *or* butter on the top of each and pour enough milk in the dish to come ⅓ of the way up the onions. Cover with a greased paper. Bake in a moderate oven (180°C, 350°F, Gas 4) until tender (about 1½ hr), basting frequently with the milk. Serve with any milk and onion liquor in the dish.

2 Boil the onions till tender, in their skins. Drain and dry in a cloth and wrap each onion in well-greased paper or in foil. Bake in a moderate oven (180°C, 350°F, Gas 4) for an hour. Unwrap and serve in their skins with butter or margarine.

3 Trim off the roots of the onions, wipe, but do not skin. Put a little margarine, butter *or* dripping in a fireproof dish, or roasting-tin. Place the onions in it and bake until tender in a fairly hot oven (180°C, 375°F, Gas 5). Take out the onions and peel them. Put them back in the dish, season with salt and pepper, and baste well, using a little extra fat if necessary. Re-heat for 10 min.

6 helpings

FRIED ONIONS (1)

6 large onions	Salt and pepper
Frying fat	

Peel and slice the onions. Heat enough frying fat in a frying-pan to cover the bottom of the pan. Fry the onions slowly until golden-brown and quite soft, stirring them occasionally during frying. Drain well, season and serve hot.

6 helpings

FRIED ONIONS (2)

6 large onions	A little flour
A little milk	Salt and pepper

Peel the onions and cut into slices ¼ in. thick. Separate into rings. Dip in milk, then toss in seasoned flour. Fry them in deep fat, adding the rings gradually to the fat, at 170°C, 340°F, until golden-brown. Drain well, season and serve at once.

6 helpings

STUFFED ONIONS

6 large onions	½ stuffing as for Stuffed
	Peppers (*see* below)

Peel and steam the onions for about 1 hr until almost soft. While they are cooking, prepare the stuffing suggested for Stuffed Peppers below, but make only half the quantity. When the onions are almost cooked, lift out their centres with a teaspoon handle. Chop the centres, add them to the stuffing and season well. Press stuffing firmly into each onion shell and pile neatly on top. Sprinkle the top of each onion with a little melted butter or margarine. Pin a stiff band of paper round each onion to prevent splitting. Put into a greased fireproof dish, and bake for 20–30 min at about 180°C, 350°F, Gas 4.

6 helpings

PARSNIPS COOKED FOR FOOD VALUE

2 lb parsnips	½ teasp salt
1 oz butter *or*	1 gill boiling water
margarine	Chopped parsley

Scrub and scrape the parsnips and slice them thinly. Fat steam the parsnips for 10 min, i.e. shake them in the melted fat, well below frying temperature with the lid on the pan until the fat is absorbed. Add the boiling water and the salt, and simmer gently until the parsnips are tender, about 30 min. Serve hot with the small amount of liquid remaining, and garnish with chopped parsley.

6 helpings

GREEN PEAS

2 lb peas	A little sugar
Salt	½ oz butter *or*
Sprig of mint	margarine

Shell the peas. Have sufficient boiling, salted water to cover the peas. Add the peas, mint and sugar. Simmer gently until soft, from 10–20 min. Drain well. Re-heat with butter *or* margarine and serve in a hot vegetable dish.

If the peas must be shelled some time before cooking, put them in a basin and cover them closely with washed pea-pods.

4–6 helpings (according to yield)

GREEN PEAS, FRENCH STYLE

2 lb green peas	2 oz butter *or*
(1½ pt shelled peas)	margarine
4 very small onions *or*	2 teasp sugar
spring onions	Salt and pepper
1 lettuce	Egg yolk (optional)

Shell the peas. Peel the onions. Remove the outer leaves of the lettuce, wash the heart, leaving it whole. Put the peas into a thick saucepan, add the lettuce heart, onions and the butter cut into small pieces. Stir in the sugar and a little salt. Cover with the lid and cook over a very low heat, about 1 hr, shaking the pan occasionally. Re-season and serve. The liquid in the pan may be thickened with an egg yolk before serving.

6 helpings

PEASE PUDDING

1½ pt split peas	2 oz butter *or* margarine
1 small onion	2 eggs
Small bunch of herbs	Salt and pepper

Soak the peas overnight, remove any discoloured ones. Rinse and cover with cold, salted water. Bring slowly to boiling point in the water, to which has been added the onion (whole) and the bunch of herbs. Simmer very slowly until tender—2–2½ hr. Drain well and rub through a sieve. Add the butter, cut in small pieces, the beaten eggs, pepper and salt. Beat well until the ingredients are well incorporated. Tie tightly in a floured cloth and simmer in water for an hour. Turn out and serve very hot. Pease pudding is served with hot pickled pork.

6 helpings

FRIED PEPPERS

4 green peppers	Egg and breadcrumbs
Butter *or* margarine *or* deep fat	(if to be fried in deep fat)

Wash the peppers. Parboil in salted water for 5 min. Drain and cut into strips or rings. Remove seeds and inner partitions. Toss in hot butter or margarine in a frying-pan for 5–10 min *or* dip in egg and breadcrumbs and fry in deep fat (180°C, 360°F) 5–7 min. Drain well and serve hot.

4–6 helpings

ANNA POTATOES

2 lb even-sized waxy potatoes	Melted clarified butter *or* margarine
Salt and pepper	

Grease a thick cake-tin and line the bottom with greased paper. Peel and trim the potatoes so that they will give equal sized slices. Slice them very finely and arrange a layer of slightly overlapping slices. Sprinkle with clarified fat and seasoning. Make a second layer of potato and repeat. Continue until the tin is full, pressing each layer well into the tin. Cover with greased paper and a lid and bake in a fairly hot oven (190°C, 375°F, Gas 5) for about 1 hr. Look at the potatoes from time to time and add more clarified butter if they become dry. Turn out on to a hot dish and serve at once.

6 helpings

POTATOES BAKED IN THEIR JACKETS

6 large potatoes	Butter *or* margarine *or* bacon fat

Scrub the potatoes, rinse and dry them. Brush with melted butter, or margarine or bacon fat or rub with a greasy butter paper. Prick with a fork. Bake on the shelves of a fairly hot oven (190°C, 375°F, Gas 5) until soft—about 1½ hr. Turn once whilst they are cooking. Make a cut in the top of each, insert a pat of butter or margarine. Serve in a hot vegetable dish.

New potatoes can be cooked in the same way.

6 helpings

BOILED, MASHED OR CREAMED POTATOES

2 lb even-sized potatoes, old *or* new	Salt
	Chopped parsley

Scrub the potatoes. Peel or scrape thinly, if desired. Rinse and put in a saucepan with enough *boiling* water to cover, and 1 teasp salt per qt water. Boil gently for 15–40 min according to age and size. Test with a fine skewer. When cooked, drain, steam-dry for a moment over low heat, and serve hot, sprinkled with chopped parsley.

For mashed potatoes, use:

Potatoes baked in their jackets

Potato chips

Sautéed potatoes

Boiled new potatoes

Parisian potato balls and croquettes

138

2 lb potatoes	A little milk
1 oz butter *or* margarine	Salt and pepper
Chopped parsley	Grated nutmeg

Prepare and cook peeled potatoes as for Boiled Potatoes, pass them through a sieve, or through a potato masher, or mash with a fork. Melt the fat (in one corner of the pan if the potatoes have been mashed in the pan itself) and beat in the potatoes. Add milk gradually and beat well until the mixture is thoroughly hot, and smooth. Season well and add a little grated nutmeg. Serve in a hot dish. Sprinkle with chopped parsley.

Successful mashed potato depends upon the use of a floury type of potato, thorough drying of the potatoes after the water has been strained off them, and the thorough mashing of the potatoes before the fat and milk are added.

For creamed potatoes, add 1 tablesp cream (single or double) to mashed potatoes.

For potato balls or croquettes, mix 1 lb mashed potatoes with 1 oz butter and 1 beaten egg. Season well with salt and pepper. Form into small balls or rolls. Coat twice with egg and crumbs and fry in deep fat at 190°C, 375°F, for 4–5 min. Drain well and serve at once. If wanted for a garnish, re-heat briefly, in the oven or by plunging into deep hot fat.

6 helpings

POTATO CHIPS AND POTATO STRAWS

6 medium-sized potatoes	Deep fat
	Salt

Scrub and rinse the potatoes. Peel them thinly. For chips—cut into sticks about 2 ins long and ½ in wide and thick. For straws—cut into strips the size of a wooden match. Drop them into cold water as they are cut. Rinse and drain and dry in a clean cloth. Put them into the frying-basket and lower them gently into hot deep fat at 180°C, 360°F. (Keep the heat fairly high as the potatoes will have cooled the fat.) When the potatoes are soft but *not* brown—about 3 min for chips and 1 min for straws—lift out the basket and heat the fat to 190°C, 375°F. Put back the basket and leave in the fat until the potatoes are crisp and golden brown—about 3 min for chips and 2 min for straws. Drain on absorbent paper, sprinkle with salt and serve immediately.

If potato chips or straws are to be served with any other fried dish, the second frying of the potatoes to brown and crisp them should be done after the other is fried. In this way the potatoes will be sent to table in their best condition.

6 helpings   Cooking time for chips, about 6 min for straws, about 3 min

SAUTÉED OR TOSSED POTATOES

6 medium-sized potatoes (waxy ones)	1–2 oz butter *or* margarine
	Seasoning

Cook the potatoes, preferably in their skins, until only just soft. Let them dry thoroughly then peel and slice them ¼ in thick. Heat the fat in a frying-pan and put in the potatoes. Season them with salt and pepper. Toss in the fat until they are light brown and have absorbed all the fat. Serve at once.

4–6 helpings

LYONNAISE POTATOES

2 lb potatoes	Chopped parsley

½ lb onions	Salt and pepper
3 oz butter *or* margarine	

Cook the potatoes in their skins until nearly soft. Peel and slice thinly. Slice the onions thinly across and cook them slowly in the butter in a frying-pan until just golden coloured. Remove the onions and keep them hot. Toss the potatoes in the fat as for Sautéed Potatoes. Add the onions to them and mix. Season well with salt and pepper. Serve in a hot dish and sprinkle with chopped parsley.

6 helpings   Cooking time, to fry, 15 min

ROAST POTATOES

2 lb even-sized potatoes	Salt and pepper
	Dripping

Peel the potatoes and cut in halves or even in quarters if very large. Parboil and strain off the water and dry the potatoes over a low heat. Put into hot dripping in a roasting-tin, or in the tin containing the roast joint. Roll the potatoes in the fat and cook till tender and brown.

Cooking time, to parboil, 10 min; to bake, 1 hr (approx)

BOILED LONG-GRAIN RICE

8 oz long-grain rice	1 teasp salt
Water to cover	

Put rice, water and salt into a saucepan, bring to the boil and stir once. Lower heat so that the water only simmers. Cover and cook for about 15 min, or until the water is absorbed.

To serve hot, rinse the rice under hot water and top with a few flakes of butter if desired. If wanted for a salad, rinse under cold water, cool, cover and chill.

BOILED SPINACH

3 lb spinach	2 tablesp cream (optional)
1 oz butter *or* margarine	Salt and pepper

Pick over the spinach carefully and wash it in at least 3 waters. Break off the stalks and at the same time pull off the central ribs if coarse. (Young, summer spinach need not be stripped of the central ribs.) Put the wet leaves into a saucepan, without additional water. Cook slowly until tender, about 15 min, stirring the spinach in the pan occasionally. The pan should have a tightly fitting lid. Drain well, pressing out the water. Re-heat in the butter. Add the cream, if used, and mix it well with the spinach. Season and serve hot.

For spinach purée, drain the cooked spinach well and sieve it or purée in an electric blender before adding the cream.

5–6 helpings

BAKED TOMATOES

6 tomatoes	Finely chopped tarragon (optional)
A little butter *or* margarine	Browned breadcrumbs (optional)
Salt and pepper	
Castor sugar	

Wash the tomatoes and cut them in halves. Put them in a greased, deep fireproof dish. Season and sprinkle each with a pinch of sugar and a pinch of chopped tarragon, if used. Put a tiny piece of butter on each or cover with a well greased paper. Bake in a moderate oven (180°C, 350°F, Gas 4) until soft—

139

FRIED TOMATOES

about 20 min.

Alternatively, cut the tomatoes in half horizontally or make crossways cuts in the top of each. Press the cut portion into browned breadcrumbs before baking and top with the butter or margarine.

6 helpings

FRIED OR GRILLED TOMATOES

6 large tomatoes	Salt and pepper
Butter *or* margarine *or*	
bacon fat for frying	

Wash the tomatoes and cut in halves. Fry in hot fat, turning them once during frying. Season. Serve hot.

To grill tomatoes prepare as for fried tomatoes. Season and brush with melted fat. Cook under a fairly hot grill, turning them once. Serve hot with bacon, sausages, fish dishes and all grilled meats.

6 helpings

Cooked mixed vegetables

TURNIPS COOKED FOR FOOD VALUE

2 lb turnips	½ teasp salt
1 oz butter *or*	½–1 gill boiling water
margarine	Chopped parsley

Scrub and peel the turnips thickly. If large, cut into quarters, then slice thinly (if young turnips, slice the whole turnip). Fat steam the turnips for 10 min, i.e. shake them in the melted fat, well below frying temperature with the lid on the pan until the fat is absorbed. Add the liquid and the salt, and simmer gently until the turnips are tender, 15–30 min according to age of turnips. Serve hot with the small amount of liquid remaining, and garnished with chopped parsley.

6 helpings

GLAZED TURNIPS

1½ lb young turnips	¼ teasp salt
2 oz butter	Strong vegetable stock
3 lumps sugar	Parsley

Melt the butter in a saucepan. Add the scraped, whole turnips, sugar, salt and enough stock to come halfway up the turnips. Cook gently, without a lid, shaking the pan occasionally, until tender. Remove the turnips and keep them hot. Boil the stock rapidly

until reduced to a rich glaze. Replace the turnips 2–3 at a time, turn them until both sides are well coated with glaze. Dish, sprinkle with chopped parsley and serve.

6 helpings   Cooking time about ¾ hr

COOKED MIXED VEGETABLES

1½ lb mixed vegetables:
In winter: parsnip, turnip, carrot, leek, cauliflower
In summer: new carrots, new turnips, broad beans, peas, spring onions, tomato

1 oz butter *or* margarine	Salt and pepper
½–1 gill boiling water	Chopped parsley

Prepare all the vegetables. Cut the winter vegetables into thin slices, cutting the slices in halves or quarters when large. Break the cauliflower into sprigs. Leave most of the summer vegetables whole, cutting the carrots in thick slices, if not really small, trimming the spring onions rather short and cutting the tomatoes into wedges. Melt the fat in a saucepan.

Aubergines with poached eggs

Add the vegetables to it at intervals, starting with the ones which take the longest time to cook. Put the lid on the pan after each addition and toss the vegetables in the fat. (Do not add the tomatoes to the summer vegetables until 5 min before serving.) Add the liquid and the salt (use very little water with the summer vegetables), and simmer gently until the vegetables are tender. Serve hot, sprinkled with chopped parsley.

MAIN-COURSE VEGETABLE DISHES

STUFFED GLOBE ARTICHOKES

6 globe artichokes	½ oz butter *or* margarine
(cooked)	3 tablesp chopped ham
1 teasp finely chopped	1 tablesp breadcrumbs
onion	Brown sauce *or* egg to
2 tablesp finely chopped	bind
mushrooms	Salt and pepper

Remove the inner leaves and the 'chokes' from the artichokes. Fry the onion and mushrooms in the butter, add the other ingredients and sufficient brown sauce or egg to bind. Season the mixture carefully and fill the artichokes with it. Put them into a greased, fireproof dish, cover with greased paper and bake for 10–15 min in a fairly hot oven (190°C, 375°F, Gas 5) to ensure they are served hot.

6 helpings

OTHER STUFFINGS

1 Cooked, chopped chicken liver, mushrooms, onion, chicken stock.
2 Hard-boiled egg, lemon juice, spinach purée (see Boiled Spinach).

ASPARAGUS ROLLS—HOT

50 heads of asparagus	1 egg
6 small baton rolls	Salt and pepper
½ pt white sauce	Lemon juice

Cut off the tops of the rolls and scoop out the inside. Heat the shells of crust in the oven till they are very crisp. Cook the asparagus in the usual way, cut off the points and keep them hot and rub the stalks through a fine sieve (stainless metal or nylon). Stir the asparagus purée and the beaten egg into the white sauce. Cook until the mixture thickens (without boiling or the egg will curdle). Season well and use a little lemon juice or additional flavour. Fill the crisp rolls, piling the mixture high, garnish the top of each with asparagus points. Put the tops of the rolls on again like lids, and serve very quickly.

This dish may be served as a vegetable luncheon dish or as a vegetarian main course.

6 helpings Cooking time about 40 min

AUBERGINES WITH POACHED EGGS

3 aubergines	1 tablesp breadcrumbs
½ oz butter	Salt and pepper
¼ pt tomato pulp	6 small poached eggs
2 tablesp chopped ham	Chopped parsley

Boil the aubergines in slightly salted water until tender, or steam them. Halve them lengthwise, and remove seeds if necessary. Heat the butter, add the tomato pulp, ham, breadcrumbs and stir over heat. Season well, then fill the cavities of the aubergines with the mixture. Put into a greased dish in a moderate oven (180°C, 350°F, Gas 4) and heat thoroughly. Place a neatly trimmed poached egg on each half; garnish with parsley and serve.

6 helpings Cooking time about 1 hr altogether

HARICOT BEANS WITH CHEESE

½ lb haricot beans	Cayenne pepper and
1 oz butter or	salt
margarine	1 tablesp cream or
1 egg yolk	evaporated milk
2 oz grated cheese	1 tablesp chopped
(preferably	parsley
Parmesan)	Sippets of fried bread

Cook the beans. Melt the fat, add all the other ingredients except 1 dessertsp of the cheese. Shake over the heat till thoroughly hot. Put into a hot, greased fireproof dish, sprinkle with the rest of the cheese and brown quickly under a hot grill.

4 helpings

STUFFED CABBAGE

6 large leaves of cabbage	Powdered mace
4 oz cooked rice	Pepper and salt
2 teasp very finely	Worcester sauce
chopped onion	Stock

4 oz fresh minced meat	Arrowroot

Wash and boil the cabbage leaves for 5 min in salt water. Drain. Mix the filling, moistening it with stock and flavouring it carefully. Form into rolls. Remove a little of the coarse vein of the cabbage leaves. Wrap each roll of filling in a cabbage leaf and tie with cotton or secure with a cocktail stick. Place in a saucepan, barely cover with stock, put on lid and simmer very gently 45 min. Lift on to a hot dish and thicken stock by boiling it with blended arrowroot (1 teasp to ¼ pt of stock). Season carefully. Pour sauce over cabbage rolls and serve immediately.

6 helpings

CAULIFLOWER WITH CHEESE

1 large cauliflower	1 heaped tablesp grated
¾ pt cheese sauce	cheese (dry Cheddar)
Salt	or 1 dessertsp grated
	Cheddar cheese and
	1 dessertsp grated
	Parmesan cheese

Stuffed cabbage

Cook the cauliflower as in the recipe for boiled cauliflower; drain well and dish up in a fireproof dish. Coat with thick cheese sauce. Sprinkle with grated cheese and immediately brown under a hot grill or in the top of a hot oven (220°C, 425°F, Gas 7). Serve at once before the cheese becomes 'tacky'.

Other vegetables can be cooked in the same way. Celery, leeks and onions are particularly good as main-course dishes when cooked with cheese.

BOILED OR BAKED CORN ON THE COB

6 ears or cobs of corn	Seasoning
freshly picked	Butter

Remove the outer husks of the corn. Open the tender, pale green inner husks and take away all the silk surrounding the corn. Replace the inner husk and tie securely; place the ears in a saucepan with sufficient boiling water to cover them. Simmer gently 15–20 min. Drain and remove strings and husks. Serve with melted, seasoned butter. The flavour is best if the corn is nibbled from the cob with the teeth, each guest being supplied with melted butter in which to dip the corn.

For baked corn, remove husks and silk of the corn. Place in a roasting dish, cover with milk and bake

Boiled corn on the cob

at 190°C, 375°F, Gas 5 for about 45 min. Toss in 2 oz melted butter and place under a hot grill for a few minutes before serving.

6 helpings

VEGETABLE MARROW STUFFED WITH NUTS

1 vegetable marrow	Salt and pepper
1 oz butter	1 oz chopped pine
3–4 tablesp coarsely	kernels
chopped mushrooms	Brown sauce
2 tablesp breadcrumbs	

Peel the marrow, cut off the ends and remove the seeds with a teaspoon. Heat the butter, fry the mushrooms lightly, add the other ingredients and season to taste. Put this stuffing inside the marrow, wrap it up in well-greased paper, place it in a baking-dish with some butter and bake slowly for ½ hr. Remove the paper, place the marrow on a hot dish and pour over some brown sauce.

3 helpings

STUFFED PEPPERS

6 small *or* 3 large peppers	A little melted butter
1 tablesp breadcrumbs	*or* margarine
(optional)	(optional)

STUFFING

1 oz butter	1 green pepper,
1 oz flour	de-seeded and
¼ pt milk, warmed	finely chopped
Salt and freshly ground	1 large cooking apple,
black pepper	peeled, cored and
	chopped
	¼ lb grated Gruyère
	cheese

Wash and parboil the peppers. Drain, cut in half lengthways and remove seeds. Prepare the stuffing. Melt the butter, and add the flour. Cook gently for a few minutes. Add the milk slowly, and season to taste. Cook for a further 2–3 min until sauce thickens slightly. Add the apple, chopped pepper and cheese, and re-season if required. Fill the halved peppers with the stuffing, sprinkle with a few breadcrumbs and a little melted fat if desired. Put the stuffed peppers in a greased baking-dish or on a baking sheet, and bake for 30 min at 150°C, 300°F, Gas 1–2.

6 helpings

BAKED, STUFFED POTATOES

6 large potatoes

STUFFING

1 **3 oz grated cheese; 1 oz butter *or* margarine; a little milk; seasoning; nutmeg**
2 **3 oz chopped, fried bacon; a little milk; seasoning**
3 **3 oz mashed, cooked smoked haddock; chopped parsley; lemon juice; a little milk; nutmeg**
4 **2 boned kippers, cooked and mashed; a little milk**
5 **2 oz grated cheese; 1 oz butter; chopped parsley; a little milk; seasoning; 2 egg yolks stirred into the filling; 2 egg whites folded in at the end**

Scrub, rinse and dry the potatoes and grease as in preceding recipe. With a small sharp knife, cut through the skin of the potatoes to give the appearance of a lid. Bake in jackets. Lift off lids carefully, scoop out cooked potato from skins, including lids, taking care not to split the skins. Mash the potato in a basin and add the ingredients of any one of the stuffings listed above. Mix well and season thoroughly. Fill the potato skins with the mixture, piling it high. Fork the tops and brush with a little

Stuffed peppers

egg, or sprinkle with a little grated cheese (if an ingredient of the stuffing). Put back in the oven and bake till thoroughly hot and golden brown. Serve in a hot dish garnished with parsley and with the skin 'lids' replaced, if liked.

A stuffing consisting of cooked minced meat in a sauce or gravy, *or* of cooked mixed vegetables *or* flaked fish in a sauce may replace the floury meal of the potato entirely. The latter should then be mashed and served separately *or* mashed and piped round the opening of the potato after it has been stuffed and before returning it to the oven.

6 helpings   Cooking time about 2 hr

PUMPKIN PIE

½ pt pumpkin (cooked and sieved)	2 tablesp brandy
¼ teasp ground ginger	¼ pt milk (approx)
¼ teasp nutmeg	4 oz castor sugar (approx)
Good pinch of cinnamon	
3 eggs	Short crust pastry using 8 oz flour, etc.

Put the pumpkin in a mixing-bowl. Stir in the spices, the well beaten eggs, the brandy and sufficient milk to give a consistency of thick batter. Sweeten to taste. Turn into a deep 9-ins pie plate lined with pastry. Cover with pastry. Bake in a fairly hot oven (190°C, 375°F, Gas 5) about 45 min. Serve hot.

Pumpkins should be peeled, sliced and the seeds removed before boiling in slightly salted water until tender.

5–6 helpings

SPINACH WITH POACHED EGGS

Spinach purée (*see* Boiled Spinach)	Fleurons of pastry *or* crescents of fried bread
6 poached eggs	

Poach the eggs in as plump a form as possible. Trim the edges and put the trimmings on the bottom of a hot dish. Serve the spinach on top, flattening the surface. Arrange the poached eggs on it; garnish the base with fleurons of pastry *or* crescents of fried bread.

STUFFED TOMATOES

6 large firm tomatoes	1 tablesp fresh breadcrumbs
1 teasp finely chopped onion	½ teasp chopped parsley
1 teasp finely chopped mushrooms	Salt and pepper
½ oz butter *or* margarine	1 teasp dry grated cheese
1 heaped tablesp finely chopped cooked ham	6 croûtes of fried *or* toasted bread

Wash and dry the tomatoes. Cut a small round from each tomato at the end opposite the stalk. Scoop out the centre with the handle of a teaspoon. Fry the onion and the mushroom in the butter or margarine until cooked. Add the ham, crumbs, parsley and sufficient tomato pulp to bind the mixture. Season well. Fill the tomatoes with the mixture, piling some on top. Bake in a moderate oven (180°C, 350°F, Gas 4) until the tomatoes are soft—about 20 min. Sprinkle the tops with cheese, replace the lids and serve on the fried or toasted bread. Garnish with parsley.

VEGETABLE PIE

For a vegetarian filling replace the ham and cheese in the above recipe with chopped mushrooms *or* chopped nut meats.

6 helpings

VEGETABLE PIE
SHORT CRUST PASTRY, USING

6 oz plain flour	**Water to mix**
3 oz lard *or* vegetable fat	

FILLING

¾ lb mushrooms	**1 lb leeks**
1 lb tomatoes	**Salt and pepper**

Make the pastry and set it aside to rest while preparing the filling.

Wash and slice the mushrooms. Skin the tomatoes, quarter and remove seeds. Clean and slice the white ends of the leeks. Arrange the vegetables in layers, seasoning well with salt and pepper. (Sliced peeled potatoes may also be added.) Cover with pastry, seal edges and cut vents to allow steam to escape. Cook in the centre of the oven at 190°C, 375°F, Gas 5 until crust is brown. The tomatoes and mushrooms will provide their own juice.

4 helpings

WALNUT ROAST

½ lb milled walnuts	**2 oz vegetable**
½ lb fresh, wholemeal	** margarine**
** breadcrumbs**	**¼ teasp powdered sage**
Salt and pepper	**6 tablesp thick**
1 large onion	** vegetable gravy**

FILLING

4 oz fresh, wholemeal	**2 tablesp chopped**
** breadcrumbs**	** parsley**
2 oz melted margarine	**Rind of ½ lemon (grated)**
½ teasp thyme	**Salt and pepper**

Mix the nuts, breadcrumbs and seasoning together. Chop the onion finely and fry until golden-brown in the margarine, mix in the powdered sage. Place the onion on top of the nut mixture and pour over the gravy. Mix to a stiff dough and form into a roll. Cut through the centre of the roll lengthwise. Mix together all the ingredients for the filling and spread over one half of the roll, sandwich the two halves together and smooth with a knife. Place on a greased baking-sheet and bake for 30 min.

COLD VEGETABLES AND SALADS

Cold vegetables, properly used, are both health-giving and flavoursome. They must be used rapidly after being cut, to avoid loss of vitamins and salts. If cooked, they must be short-cooked, for food value, in as little water as possible; and any liquid or fat used in cooking should be used afterwards for a sauce or dressing.

Cold vegetables and salads, properly presented, can add glamour to many hot main courses as well as cold ones, and they can even aid digestion by being attractive and colourful. It is becoming recognised, therefore, that some hot dishes are better supplemented by a salad than by hot accompaniments. This is particularly true when salads are served with fat-rich or strongly flavoured meat and fish dishes.

Some substantial salads can serve as main-course dishes in their own right.

APPLE AND CUCUMBER SALAD

1 cucumber	**Cream *or* evaporated**
3 dessert apples	** milk**
Salt and pepper	**Finely chopped mint**
Lemon juice	** (optional)**

Slice the cucumber thinly; quarter, core and slice the apples. Season lightly and sprinkle with lemon juice. Stir in a little cream *or* evaporated milk. Pile in a salad bowl. Sprinkle with a little mint, if liked.

6 helpings

APPLES FILLED WITH BANANA AND NUT SALAD

6 small rosy apples	**2 bananas**
4 lettuce leaves	**Salad dressing**
1 tablesp coarsely	**Watercress *or* fine**
** chopped nuts**	** cress**

Wash and dry the apples; cut a small piece off the top of each, and carefully scoop out most of the inside with a teaspoon. Shred the lettuce leaves and mix very lightly with nuts, sliced banana, a little of the apple pulp (chopped), and salad dressing. Fill the polished apple cases with the mixture. Serve on individual plates, decorating each with watercress

Vegetable pie

Apples filled with banana and nut salad

or tiny bunches of fine cress.

6 helpings

BANANA SALAD

6 bananas	Chopped parsley
Lemon juice	Watercress
Mayonnaise sauce *or* salad dressing	French dressing

Cut the bananas into rounds $\frac{1}{8}$ in thick and put them into a salad bowl containing about 1 tablesp lemon juice. Mix lightly, and pile in the dish. Coat with salad dressing or mayonnaise, sprinkle with parsley. Arrange watercress around the dish and sprinkle it with French dressing. Coarsely chopped walnuts may be added to this salad. Alternatively, add one shredded celery heart or 1 oz seedless raisins and 2 carrots, peeled and shredded.

6 helpings

BEETROOT SALAD

2 cooked beetroots	Grated horseradish
French dressing	

Slice or dice the beetroot and arrange neatly. Baste with French dressing, after sprinkling with freshly grated horseradish. Dry mustard may be added to the French dressing and the horseradish omitted.

For a more elaborate salad, add 2 peeled, cored and diced dessert apples, 2 oz shelled walnuts and 1 large celery heart, diced. Garnish with watercress.

6 helpings

COOKED CABBAGE SALAD

1 medium-sized cabbage	A few stoned raisins
Salt	Tartare sauce *or* mayonnaise
1 small cooking apple	Salt and pepper to taste

Cut across the end and remove the coarse stub of stalk and outer coarse leaves of the cabbage. With a sharp-pointed knife, cut a deep cross down from the top of cabbage into the centre. Do not separate or take off any leaves. Wash the cabbage well under cold water, to remove any grit and dirt. Plunge the cabbage into fast-boiling salted water, and boil until just tender but no more. Let the cabbage cool slightly. Make a deep circular cut in the top of the cabbage, and scoop out most of the inside, leaving a shell of leaves $\frac{1}{2}$–$\frac{3}{4}$ in thick. Shred the scooped-out inner leaves finely. Peel, core and chop the apple and add with the raisins to the shredded leaves. Put the mixture into a basin, and mix with enough Tartare Sauce or mayonnaise to moisten. Season to taste. Make sure the cabbage shell will stand level and upright. Fill the shell with the seasoned mixture. Cover with damp paper or cloth and chill slightly before serving.

CARROT SALAD

3 large carrots	French dressing
1 lettuce	Finely chopped parsley

Grate the carrots finely and serve on a bed of lettuce leaves. Sprinkle with the French dressing. Garnish with chopped parsley.

Grated, raw carrot can be used with success in many salads. It should be grated very finely to be digestible, and sprinkled with lemon juice or French dressing as soon as grated to retain its bright colour.

6 helpings

COOKED CAULIFLOWER SALAD

1 large cauliflower	Vinaigrette sauce

Steam the cauliflower then divide carefully into small sprigs. Arrange the sprigs neatly in a salad bowl and pour the sauce over while the cauliflower is still warm. Serve when quite cold.

6 helpings

Beetroot salad

CUCUMBER SALAD

1 large cucumber	Chopped parsley
Salt	Chopped tarragon
French dressing	

Slice the cucumber. Put on a plate and sprinkle with salt. Tilt the plate slightly so that the water may drain off easily and leave for ½ hr. Rinse quickly in a colander and drain. Dish and pour over the French dressing. Sprinkle with parsley and tarragon.

6 helpings

CHUNKY CUCUMBER AND YOGURT SALAD

¼ pt plain yogurt	2 cucumbers
1 tablesp vinegar	Paprika
Sugar	

Mix the yogurt with the vinegar and a little sugar. Cut the cucumbers into 2 in lengths and stand upright on a dish. Pour the yogurt dressing over, and sprinkle with paprika.

GRAPEFRUIT AND CHICORY SALAD

3 grapefruits	French dressing made
3 small heads chicory	with grapefruit juice
2 oz seedless raisins	Fine cress

Halve the grapefruits and remove the pulp in sections. Remove the partitions from the halved shells. Shred the chicory, reserving some neat rounds for garnish. Mix the grapefruit pulp, raisins and chicory lightly with the dressing. Fill the grapefruit shells with the mixture. Decorate with tiny bunches of cress and rounds of chicory.

6 helpings

LETTUCE SALAD

Lettuce, of the cabbage or cos variety, prepared correctly and dressed with a French dressing *or* Vinaigrette Sauce, provides the finest of all salads.

To prepare lettuce, cut off the stump of the lettuce and discard the coarse outer leaves only. Separate all leaves and wash them leaf by leaf under running water if possible, otherwise in several waters in a basin. Put into a salad shaker or a clean tea-towel and swing them to shake out the water. Leave to drain. If possible put into a covered box *or* into a casserole with a lid in the refrigerator for at least ½ hr before dressing them for table.

The salads in which lettuce is used as a foundation are so numerous that it is unnecessary to name them all here.

MIXED VEGETABLE SALAD

IN SUMMER, USE

3 large new potatoes	1 tablesp chopped
3 new turnips	parsley
½ pt shelled peas	1 teasp chopped mint
½ bunch new carrots	Salad dressing

Cook the vegetables and slice the carrots, potatoes and young turnips. Save some of each vegetable for garnish and toss the rest in the salad dressing with the herbs. Put the mixture in a suitable dish and garnish with the remainder. Baste with a little French dressing.

IN WINTER, USE

1 cauliflower	1 small can of peas
2 large carrots	Salad dressing
1 parsnip *or* 2 turnips	Watercress *or* fine cress
1 cooked beetroot	A little French dressing

Steam the cauliflower, carrots, parsnip or turnips. Divide the cauliflower into sprigs. Dice the carrots, parsnip or turnip, and beetroot, or cut into neat rounds with a cutter. Rinse and drain the peas. Mix all trimmings and uneven pieces of vegetable lightly with salad dressing—include some of the peas. Put this mixture into a dish, preferably oblong in shape. Cover with lines of each vegetable, very neatly arranged and with suitable colours adjoining. Garnish the edges with watercress or fine cress. Baste the surface with French dressing.

For Russian Salad, mix the prepared vegetables with mayonnaise instead of salad dressing.

4–6 helpings

ORANGE SALAD

4 sweet oranges	Chopped tarragon and
½ teasp castor sugar	chervil *or* chopped
1 tablesp French dressing	mint

Peel the oranges thickly with a saw-edged knife, so that all pith is removed. Cut out the natural orange sections. Place in a salad bowl, sprinkle with sugar. Pour the dressing over and sprinkle with tarragon and chervil, or with chopped mint.

4–6 helpings

PEARS FILLED WITH NUT AND DATE SALAD

3 ripe dessert *or* canned	2 oz chopped walnuts
pears	Chopped parsley
1 small crisp lettuce	French dressing *or*
4 oz chopped dates	salad dressing

Peel and halve the pears. Remove the cores with a sharp teaspoon, then scoop out a little of the pulp of the pears to leave a hollow for the filling. Shred a few lettuce leaves very finely and mix with dates, walnuts, chopped parsley and finely diced pear pulp and French dressing *or* salad dressing. Place the halved pears on small crisp lettuce leaves on individual plates. Pile the mixture on each piece of pear. If fresh pears are used, squeeze lemon juice over them to prevent discoloration.

6 helpings

POTATO SALAD

6 large new potatoes *or*	1 teasp chopped mint
waxy old potatoes	1 teasp chopped chives
French dressing *or*	*or* spring onion
Vinaigrette sauce	Salt and pepper
2 heaped tablesp	
chopped parsley	

Cook the potatoes until just soft, in their skins. Peel and cut into dice while still hot. Mix while hot with the dressing and the herbs and a little seasoning. Serve cold.

6 helpings

TOMATO SALAD

6 large firm tomatoes	French dressing *or*
Salt and pepper	cream salad dressing
	Finely chopped parsley

Skin and slice the tomatoes. Season lightly. Pour the dressing over the tomatoes. Sprinkle with chopped parsley.

6 helpings

The British probably eat more cooked sweet dishes than any other people in Europe. They have specialised for centuries in dishes made up of several sweet ingredients 'translated' by processing into a new guise. Other peoples rely much more on cheeses and fresh fruits to end their meals, and keep made-up sweet dishes, pastries and ice creams for café snacks and feast days. But the British made such dishes daily meal-time fare long ago, and so their recipes for them are widely known and are used by many people elsewhere.

Here is a selection of all the various kinds of dishes which the British 'sweet tooth' demands. They comprise: hot and cold milk puddings, custards, batter dishes both baked and fried as pancakes or fritters; soufflés; boiled, steamed and baked 'starchy' puddings, and other pastry dishes including open pies, tarts and flans; grain- and gelatine-set moulds, and jellies; creams and half-creams or bavarois; meringue dishes and gâteaux; fruit purées and fools; and, finally, all kinds of ices and ice creams.

Some are simple. Others are rich, luscious confections. But all are 'classics', whether made by traditional means, or using the new products which modern technology has provided. They should all have a place in any civilised cookery repertoire.

MILK PUDDINGS

All milk puddings are made from a starchy product, sugar and milk. Some, but not all, contain beaten eggs and various suitable flavourings. A description of these and ways to use them will be found in the section on Trimmings, Sauces and Flavourings. But, briefly, the ones used most for milk puddings are either plant flavourings such as bay leaf or lemon peel, infused in the milk and then removed, powdered flavourings such as cinnamon or liquid flavouring such as vanilla essence. A pinch of salt improves the flavour of all puddings.

Dried skim milk can be used in most milk puddings, and ¼–1 oz butter or suet can be used per pint, to make up the fat if you wish. Evaporated or sweetened, condensed milk can be used likewise, made up with water to the fluid content of fresh milk; but obviously the sugar in a recipe must be reduced if you use sweetened milk in any form.

By adding eggs, a milk pudding is made richer; by whisking the whites before adding them, it is made lighter. Always cool a pudding a little before adding eggs; and never add them until any grain in the pudding is fully cooked. The extra cooking will curdle the egg. In baked puddings, eggs need only 30 min in a warm oven to set a one-pint pudding and to brown the top.

All milk puddings must be cooked very slowly so that they stay moist and creamy. Most people prefer their hot milk puddings just liquid enough to flow over the plate.

Most milk puddings are boiled (or rather simmered) or are baked. But they can also be steamed and unmoulded, provided they contain at least 2 eggs per pint of liquid as well as the starchy ingredient.

In puddings which include eggs, cool the mixture slightly before adding the egg yolks.

Boiling and steaming Puddings cooked directly in a saucepan, not in a mould, must only be allowed to simmer. The saucepan must be thick, and it should be rinsed with cold water or greased before putting in the pudding mixture. Stir the mixture well, from the bottom of the pan, as it cooks.

A pudding cooked in the top of a double boiler needs no stirring but does take longer to cook.

For moulded puddings, prepare the mould or basin, and a cover of greased paper or foil, first.

Grease them well with unsalted butter, margarine or cooking fat. Cover the pudding, and steam very gently until set. (*See* the comments about Steamed Puddings.)

Baking The dish in which a baked pudding is cooked must be well greased and ready for use before making the pudding. It should stand in a shallow tray of water, so that it cooks evenly and slowly. It should also stand on a baking sheet, for easy removal from the oven. Wipe round the rim of the dish after filling it, to remove any drops of spilt pudding.

Finely shredded suet or flaked butter or margarine dotted over the top of a baked milk pudding improves its flavour, texture and food value.

HOT MILK PUDDINGS AND EGG DESSERTS

ALL LARGE GRAIN MILK PUDDINGS
(Sago, whole rice, flaked tapioca or rice)

4 oz grain, any type above	$\frac{1}{2}$ oz finely shredded suet *or* butter
2 pt milk	Grated nutmeg *or*
2–3 oz sugar	similar flavouring

Grease a pie dish. Wash the grain in cold water if required, and put it into the dish with the milk. Leave to stand for $\frac{1}{2}$ hr. Add the sugar, flake on the fat if used, and sprinkle on the flavouring. Bake very slowly (150°C, 310°F, Gas 2) until the pudding is thick and creamy, and brown on top, a minimum of 2–2$\frac{1}{2}$ hr. (The pudding is better if it cooks even more slowly, for 4–5 hr.)

NOTE 1. If a flavouring essence is used, it is mixed into the milk before cooking. 2. If dried or canned milk is used, reduce the amount of rice to 3 oz, use the amount of milk product which makes up to 1$\frac{3}{4}$ pt, and cook at 140°C, 275°F, Gas $\frac{1}{2}$, for at least 3$\frac{1}{2}$–4 hr.

4–6 helpings

RICE CREAM

$\frac{1}{2}$ pt milk	Sugar to taste (1 dessertsp approx)
Flavouring: a piece of lemon rind *or* few drops of vanilla essence	1 oz long-grain rice
	1 tablesp cream

Heat the milk in a double saucepan or basin over hot water. Add lemon rind if used, sugar and rice, and cook slowly until rice is very tender. Remove lemon rind. Beat well, add cream, and a few drops of vanilla essence if used. Pour into small dishes and serve hot or cold with redcurrant jelly or fruit purée (*see* Fruit Purée below).

Cooking time 1 hr (approx)

ALL LARGE GRAIN MILK PUDDINGS WITH EGGS

4 oz large grain, any type	2–3 oz sugar
2 pt milk	Flavouring
2–4 eggs	

Wash the grain in cold water if necessary. Put the grain and milk into a strong or double saucepan, and cook slowly until the grain is tender. Remove from the heat, and allow to cool slightly. Separate the eggs and whisk the whites stiffly. Stir into the pudding the slightly beaten egg yolks, sugar and flavouring, and, lastly, fold in the whisked whites. Pour into a well-buttered pie dish and bake in a warm oven (170°C, 335°F, Gas 3) for about 40 min, until the top is brown.

6 helpings

CARAMEL RICE PUDDING

3 oz loaf sugar	2 eggs
$\frac{1}{2}$ gill water	1$\frac{1}{2}$ oz castor sugar
4$\frac{1}{2}$ oz rice	Pinch of salt
1$\frac{1}{2}$ pt milk	

Heat a charlotte mould and have ready a thickly

folded band of newspaper so that the hot mould can be encircled with it and held firmly in one hand. Prepare the caramel by heating the loaf sugar and water together; stir until it boils; then remove the spoon and allow to boil without stirring until golden-brown. Immediately pour the caramel into the warmed charlotte mould and twist it round until the sides and base are well coated.

Wash the rice, and simmer it in the milk with the salt until the rice is soft and all the milk has been absorbed. Cool slightly, and stir in the beaten eggs and sugar. Turn into the caramel-lined mould, cover closely with greased paper and steam for 1 hr, until firm. Serve either hot or cold.

6 helpings

ALL MEDIUM AND SMALL GRAIN MILK PUDDINGS
(Semolina, ground rice, small sago, crushed tapioca)

2 pt milk	2–3 oz sugar
Flavouring	
3 oz grain, any type above	

Heat the milk and infuse a stick or peel flavouring if used for about 10 min. Remove the flavouring.

Sprinkle the grain into the milk, stirring quickly to prevent lumps forming. Place over heat, and continue stirring while the milk simmers, until the grain is transparent and cooked through; this takes about 15 min. Add the sugar and any flavouring essence used.

The pudding can then be served as it is, hot or cold, or can be poured into a well-buttered pie dish and baked in a moderate oven (180°C, 350°F, Gas 4) for 20–30 min until the top has browned.

6 helpings

ALL MEDIUM AND SMALL GRAIN MILK PUDDINGS WITH EGGS

2 pt milk	2–4 eggs
Flavouring	2–3 oz sugar
3 oz grain, any type in previous recipe	

Heat the milk, and infuse any stick flavouring used for about 10 min. Then remove it. Sprinkle the grain into the flavoured milk, stirring quickly to prevent lumps forming. Continue stirring for about 15 min, until the grain has become transparent and cooked through. Leave to cool slightly. Stir in the slightly beaten egg yolks. Add the sugar and flavouring essence if used, and, lastly, fold in the egg whites whisked until stiff. Pour the mixture into a well-buttered pie dish and bake in a warm oven (170°C, 335°F, Gas 3) until the top is brown. This takes 30–40 min.

6 helpings

TIMBALE OF SEMOLINA

1 pt milk	6–7 apricot halves
3 oz semolina	½ pt apricot syrup (approx)
2 oz sugar	Maraschino (optional)
A few drops of vanilla essence	
2 tablesp cream or top of the milk	

DECORATION

Glacé cherries	Angelica
Almonds	

Heat the milk, sprinkle in the semolina, stirring briskly, and simmer until it is cooked through. Cool slightly; then add the sugar and vanilla essence. Separate the eggs and stir the beaten yolks into the milk mixture. Beat until the mixture is nearly cold. Add the cream, and fold in lightly the stiffly-whisked

Caramel rice pudding

egg whites. Three quarters fill a well-greased timbale or 6 small dariole moulds with the mixture. Cover with greased paper. Steam small moulds for about $\frac{1}{2}$ hr until set, a large mould for about $\frac{3}{4}$ hr.

Meanwhile, heat the apricots between 2 plates. Boil the apricot syrup until well reduced and flavour with a little maraschino if you wish.

When the pudding is cooked and set, unmould on to a hot dish. Place half an apricot on top of each small mould, and decorate with a glacé cherry, chopped almonds and angelica. Treat a large mould in a similar way. Pour the syrup round, and serve.

For a cold timbale, use

1½ pt milk	2 tablesp powdered
4 oz finely ground	gelatine
semolina	½ pt double cream
4 tablesp water	

FILLING

2 dessert apples	5 tablesp apricot jam
2 ripe dessert pears	Lemon juice to taste

Heat the milk until boiling, then sprinkle on the semolina and stir in quickly. Heat gently, covered, for 10 min, stirring occasionally. Add the water to the powdered gelatine and dissolve over boiling water until it is liquid and clear.

Add the gelatine to the semolina. Remove from the heat, and cool.

Whip the cream until it holds its shape, and fold into the cooled semolina. Turn the mixture into a 2 pt ring mould, and allow to set in a cool place.

To make the filling, thinly slice the apples and pears in wedge shapes, after peeling and coring. Heat gently in the apricot jam with lemon juice to taste until soft. Cool.

When ready to serve, unmould the timbale carefully. Spoon the filling into the centre of the ring. Serve with whipped cream if you wish.

6–7 helpings

ALL POWDERED GRAIN PUDDINGS
(Arrowroot, cornflour, custard powder, finely ground rice, powdered barley, fine oatmeal)

2½ oz grain, any type	2–3 oz sugar
above	Flavouring
2 pt milk	

Mix the grain to a smooth paste with a little of the milk and put the rest of the milk on to boil. Pour the boiling milk on to the blended paste, stirring briskly to prevent lumps forming. Return the mixture to the saucepan, heat until it thickens, then simmer for 2–3 min to cook the grain completely, stirring continuously. Add the sugar. The pudding can then be served as it is, or poured into a well-buttered pie dish and baked for 20–30 min in a moderate oven (180°C, 350°F, Gas 4) until the top is browned.

6 helpings

ALL POWDERED GRAIN PUDDINGS WITH EGGS

2½ oz powdered grain,	2–3 oz sugar
any type	Flavouring
2 pt milk	
2–4 eggs	

Cook the grain completely as in the previous recipe. Let the mixture cool.

Separate the eggs and whisk the whites until stiff.

Beat the yolks slightly and stir them into the pudding with the sugar and any flavouring essence used. Lastly fold in the whisked whites. Pour the mixture gently into a well-buttered pie dish, and bake in a warm oven (170°C, 335°F, Gas 3) for about 30 min until the top has browned. Sprinkle with brown Demerara sugar and/or butter flakes before baking if you wish.

CUSTARDS AND CUSTARD MIXTURES

Basically these are made from a mixture of eggs, milk and sugar, cooked very slowly until the mixture is just set. Custards can be cooked by 'boiling' (that is, by poaching) or by baking or steaming; but they must always be cooked very carefully and slowly since overcooking will make the mixture curdle. A custard which is to be unmoulded needs at least four eggs to one pt liquid or it is liable to break.

Pouring custards These are made by heating the mixture, and keeping it at a temperature *below* boiling point until the eggs are cooked evenly throughout. Doing this in a double boiler lessens the risk of curdling.

Baked custards The dish to contain the custard should be well greased. When filled, it should be placed in a tray of warm water. Bake slowly at about 170°C, 325°F, Gas 3 until the custard is set. Take it out of the water at once to prevent further cooking.

Steamed custards The basin must be well greased, and the custard covered with greased paper to prevent dripping condensed steam falling into it. Only a very gentle flow of steam should be allowed.

Flavourings Any of the flavourings suggested for milk puddings can be used.

BAKED OR STEAMED CUSTARD

1½ pt milk	1–1½ oz castor sugar
Flavouring	3–4 eggs for a baked
Wine sauce	custard, plus 1 more
	for a steamed custard

Beat the eggs with the sugar. Warm the milk and flavouring, and add gradually to the egg mixture, stirring well. Pour the mixture into a greased pie dish for a baked custard or a buttered mould for a steamed one. Stand the pie dish in a tray of warm water and bake in a warm oven (170°C, 325–335°F, Gas 3) for about 50 min. For a steamed custard, cover the mould with greased paper, secure it firmly, and steam gently for about 40 min until the custard is set in the centre. Turn out and serve with wine sauce.

5–6 helpings

CUP CUSTARD

½ pt milk	1 oz castor sugar
Flavouring: lemon rind	2 tablesp double cream
or vanilla essence	(optional)
1 egg and 1 yolk *or*	
3 egg yolks	

Warm the milk, with the lemon rind if used. Mix

Timbale of semolina

the eggs and sugar together until liquid. Pour the warmed milk over the eggs and strain the custard into a pan previously rinsed with cold water. Cook the custard gently until the eggs have thickened the milk. To ensure a smooth, creamy texture, stir briskly all the time. If cooking the custard in a saucepan, use a wooden spoon as it works smoothly over the bottom of the pan and clears it. If cooking the custard in a double boiler over hot water, a whisk is better since thickening takes place at the sides as well as on the base. Do not let the custard boil. When the custard coats the spoon, pour it into a cool bowl, and add the vanilla if used. Add the cream if you want it, and stir in lightly. Stir the custard often during cooling to prevent a skin forming.

Makes $\frac{3}{4}$ pt

BREAD AND BUTTER PUDDING

6 thin slices of bread and butter	3 eggs
2 oz sultanas *or* currants *or* stoned raisins *or* chopped candied peel	$1\frac{1}{2}$ oz sugar
	$1\frac{1}{2}$ pt milk

Grease a 2-pt pie dish. Remove the bread crusts if you wish. Then cut the bread into squares or triangles, and lay them neatly in the dish. Sprinkle fruit over each layer. Beat the eggs with the sugar, add the milk and pour the mixture over the bread. It should only half fill the dish. Leave to soak for at least 30 min. Then bake for about 1 hr in a moderate oven (180°C, 350°F, Gas 4) until the custard is set.

5–6 helpings

CARAMEL CUSTARD

3 oz loaf sugar	$\frac{3}{4}$ pt milk
$\frac{1}{2}$ gill cold water	A few drops of vanilla essence
4 eggs	
1 oz castor sugar	

Have ready a warm charlotte or plain mould.

Prepare caramel with loaf sugar and water, and line the mould as for Caramel Rice Pudding above.

Work together the eggs and sugar without beating them, and pour the warmed milk on to them. Add the vanilla essence. Strain the custard into the mould, and cover with greased paper. Steam very slowly for about $\frac{3}{4}$ hr until the custard is set in the centre; or stand the custard uncovered in a tray of warm water and bake in a warm oven (170°C, 335°F, Gas 3) until the centre is set. This takes about 40 min. Turn the custard out carefully so that the caramel runs off and serves as a sauce.

Small caramel custards can be made in dariole moulds. Cook for about 20 min.

6 helpings

QUEEN OF PUDDINGS

1 pt milk	2 oz granulated sugar
$\frac{1}{2}$ pt breadcrumbs	2 eggs
2 oz butter *or* margarine	3 tablesp jam
Grated rind of 2 lemons	2–4 oz castor sugar

Heat the milk and add the breadcrumbs, fat, lemon rind and granulated sugar. Leave to soak for 30 min. Separate the eggs, and stir the yolks into the milk mixture. Pour the mixture into a buttered pie dish, and bake for about $\frac{3}{4}$ hr in a moderate oven (180°C, 350°F, Gas 4) until set. Now spread the jam on the pudding. Whip the egg whites very stiffly, sprinkle with 1 oz castor sugar and whip again until stiff. Then fold in lightly the rest of the sugar. Spread the meringue over the pudding, and put into a very cool oven (130°C, 265°F, Gas $\frac{1}{2}$) until the top is set and golden-brown.

5–6 helpings

QUEEN'S PUDDING

$\frac{1}{4}$ lb biscuit or cake crumbs	6–9 apricot halves, canned *or* bottled
1 pt milk	Glacé cherries for

HOT SOUFFLÉS

2 oz sugar   decoration
2 eggs
Vanilla essence

APRICOT SAUCE

½ pt apricot syrup   1 tablesp kirsch *or*
Sugar to taste   rum

Rub the crumbs through a fine sieve. Heat the milk, add the crumbs, leave to stand for 10–15 min until soft, then beat until smooth. Beat in the sugar and eggs. Flavour with the essence. Grease a plain mould or basin with butter, line the base with a round of greased paper and sprinkle with castor sugar. Pour in the mixture and cover with paper. Stand the mould in a tin of hot water, and bake in a warm oven (170°C, 335°F, Gas 3) until the mixture is firm; this takes about 1 hr.

While the pudding cooks, make the sauce by boiling the apricot syrup with sugar added to taste until it is slightly reduced. Use the syrup from the can or bottle for this. Add the kirsch or rum after reducing it.

When the pudding is set in the middle, leave it to stand for a few minutes, then carefully unmould on to a dish. Tear off the paper, arrange the apricot halves round the dish, decorate the pudding with the cherries and pour the apricot sauce round it.

6 helpings

HOT SOUFFLÉS

Soufflés are flavoured starchy or fruit purées. They depend for their lightness on the air whisked into the egg whites which they contain. They must not get wet, or be jolted to knock the air out, and they should be served immediately they are removed from the cooking heat, as they fall as soon as they are cooled.

General hints

1 Before making a soufflé, prepare the tin or mould (see below) and see that the steamer or oven is on.

Equipment for making desserts

2 When making, whisk the egg whites very stiff, incorporating as much bulk of air as possible by lifting the fork or whisk in a rotating movement. Fold them into the soufflé very carefully. Cook straight away.

3 Time the preparation and cooking so that the soufflé *can* be served as soon as it is cooked.

To prepare the tin or mould Grease with clarified butter or tasteless cooking fat. Tie a double band of greaseproof paper or aluminium foil round the container, which rises 3 in above the top. (The cut edge of paper should be at the top.) For a steamed soufflé, cut a circle of greaseproof paper for the top of the tin to prevent water dripping on to the soufflé.

Steamed soufflés These are cooked in a steamer or saucepan containing enough boiling water to come half-way up the sides of the pan. Stand the soufflé tin on an upturned saucer or plate so that it does not touch the bottom of the pan itself. Only half fill the mould. Steam gently but steadily, avoiding jolting the pan. The soufflé is cooked when it is just risen and firm to the touch. Turn out on to a hot dish, and serve at once.

Baked soufflés These are served in the cooking dish, usually a large charlotte or soufflé mould, or in individual ovenproof dishes. The greased dish should not be more than ¾ full. Avoid opening the oven door during cooking, so that no cold draught or jolting can make the soufflé sink. When cooked, it should be well risen and firm.

CHOCOLATE SOUFFLÉ

2 oz finely-grated plain   4 egg yolks
    chocolate   3 oz castor sugar
⅜ pt milk   ½ teasp vanilla essence
1 oz butter   5 egg whites
1½ oz plain flour

Prepare a soufflé tin or mould. Dissolve the chocolate in the milk. Melt the butter, add the flour and let it cook for a few minutes without colouring. Add the milk and beat well until smooth. Reheat until the mixture thickens and comes away from the sides of the pan. Allow to cool slightly. Beat in the egg yolks well, one at a time, add the sugar and vanilla essence. Whisk the egg whites stiffly and fold them lightly into the mixture. Turn into the mould; cover, and steam very gently for about 1 hr.

6 helpings

LEMON OR ORANGE SOUFFLÉ

1½ oz butter   1½ oz castor sugar
1½ oz plain flour   2 teasp lemon juice *or*
⅜ pt milk   juice of ¼ orange
5 egg yolks   6 egg whites
Finely grated rind of 1½
    lemons *or* oranges

Grease and prepare a soufflé mould. Melt 1½ oz butter, stir in the flour and cook for a few minutes. Add the milk gradually, beating well, and continue cooking until the mixture thickens. Leave it to cool. Beat in the yolks one at a time. Stir in the lemon rind, sugar and lemon juice. Whisk the egg whites stiffly, and fold them into the mixture. Pour into the mould, cover with a buttered paper. Steam for 50–60 min until firm on top.

6 helpings

VANILLA SOUFFLÉ

1½ oz butter	1½ oz castor sugar
1½ oz plain flour	½ teasp vanilla essence
⅜ pt milk	5 egg whites
4 egg yolks	

Prepare the soufflé mould according to the cooking method to be used, as described under Hot Soufflés. Melt the butter, stir in the flour and cook gently for a few minutes without colouring. Add the milk, stir well until smooth. Reheat, stirring continuously, until the mixture thickens and leaves the sides of the pan. Leave to cool. Beat in the egg yolks, sugar and vanilla essence. Whisk the egg whites stiffly and fold them in lightly. Pour the mixture into the mould and cover it. Steam for ¾–1 hr, or bake in a fairly hot oven (190°C, 375°F, Gas 5) for 30–35 min.

6 helpings

SWEET OMELETS

1 Sweet omelets can be flat, or puffed like a soufflé by whisking the egg whites separately and folding them into the rest of the mixture.

2 The pan should be the right size for the number of eggs; a two-egg omelet needs a 6-in diameter pan. Ideally, the pan should be kept only for omelets, and should only be cleaned with a dry cloth and a little salt.

3 A palette knife or fish slice is useful for folding omelets.

4 Take care not to overcook an omelet and make it tough; cook it only until the top is just set. A puffed or soufflé omelet may need finishing under the grill. All omelets should be served as soon as they are made.

SWEET OMELET AND FILLINGS

2 eggs	½ oz castor sugar
Pinch of salt	½ oz unsalted butter
1 tablesp cream or top of the milk	

Beat the eggs thoroughly with the salt, cream and castor sugar. Heat the butter in an omelet pan and remove any scum. When the butter is really hot, pour in the omelet mixture and stir until it begins to set. Lift the edge nearest the pan handle. Fold it over to rest on the edge furthest from the handle. Tip the folded omelet out on to a hot dish. Dredge with castor sugar and serve at once.

Any sweet filling can be added, such as warmed jam, fruit purée or diced soft fruit. It should be spread evenly in the centre of the omelet just before folding it.

For a rum omelet, add 1 tablesp rum to the egg mixture. Pour 1 tablesp warmed rum round the completed omelet and light it.

2 helpings

Chocolate soufflé omelet

CHOCOLATE SOUFFLÉ OMELET
FOR THE SAUCE AND FILLING

1 oz cocoa	2 tablesp apricot jam
1½ oz soft brown sugar	1 oz butter
¼ pt milk	

FOR THE OMELET

2 large eggs	1 tablesp rum
1 oz castor sugar	½ oz butter

Make the sauce. Place all the sauce ingredients in a saucepan; dissolve the sugar over gentle heat, then bring the mixture to the boil, stirring continuously. Cook for about 5 mins until smooth and shiny. Keep warm over hot water until required.

To make the omelet, separate the yolks and whites. Whisk the yolks with the sugar until light, trickle in the rum and whisk until pale and light. Whisk the egg whites stiffly and fold them into the mixture. Melt the butter in a heavy frying-pan about 7-in in diameter. Do not allow it to brown. Pour the egg mixture into the pan, and cook over gentle heat, stirring occasionally, until the underside is brown. Brown the top for a few min under a hot grill.

Pour some of the chocolate sauce into the centre of the omelet, fold it over carefully and turn it on to a hot plate. Serve immediately, with the extra sauce separately.

2–3 helpings

JAM OMELET

Make the omelet like the Chocolate Soufflé Omelet above, but use vanilla or another essence to flavour it instead of rum. Fill with 1 tablesp warmed jam, fold and dredge with sugar.

BATTER PUDDINGS, PANCAKES AND FRITTERS
SWEET BATTER MIXTURES

Sweet batters, baked, steamed or fried, are made from flour, milk and eggs, with a pinch each of sugar and salt for flavouring. They are beaten together, using only half the liquid at first, until well blended and smooth.

153

BATTER PUDDING

The lightness of any batter depends on steam forming quickly within the mixture and on the flour cooking quickly. Bake a batter in a hot oven (220°C, 425°F, Gas 7) at first; reduce the heat to 190°C, 375°F, Gas 5 to finish cooking.

To steam a batter, prepare a mould in the same way as for a steamed pudding, and use the same method (*see* Steamed and Boiled Puddings).

Batters are most often fried to make pancakes or as a coating for fritters.

BATTER PUDDING, BAKED OR STEAMED

½ lb plain flour	1 pt milk
¼ teasp each sugar and salt	1 tablesp cooking fat or lard
2 eggs	Wine, syrup *or* jam sauce

Sift the flour, sugar and salt into a basin. Make a well in the centre of the flour and break the eggs into this. Add about a gill of the milk. Stir, gradually working the flour down from the sides and adding more milk, as required, to make a stiff batter consistency. Beat well for about 5 min. Add the rest of the milk. Cover and leave to stand for 30 min if desired.

Put the fat into a Yorkshire pudding tin and heat in the oven until hot. The fat should just be beginning to smoke. Quickly pour in the batter and leave to cook in a hot oven (220°C, 425°F, Gas 7) at the top of the oven until nicely browned. Reduce the heat to 190°C, 375°F, Gas 5, and finish cooking through for 10–15 min. Serve with wine, syrup or jam sauce.

For a steamed Batter Pudding, prepare the same mixture. Pour it into a well-greased pudding basin. Cover with greased paper and steam for 2 hr.

6 helpings

BATTER PUDDING WITH APPLES

½ lb plain flour	2 oz granulated sugar
¼ teasp each sugar and salt	¼ teasp ground cinnamon *or* grated lemon rind
2 eggs	½ oz butter
1 pt milk	
1 lb apples	

Prepare the batter as for Batter Pudding. Cover and leave to stand for 30 min. Core, peel and slice the apples thinly. Sprinkle them with the sugar and cinnamon or lemon rind. Spread them over a well-greased basin or pudding tin. Pour the batter over, flake the butter on top, and bake in a hot oven (220°C, 425°F, Gas 7) until brown, 20–25 min. Reduce the heat to 190°C, 375°F, Gas 5, and finish cooking. Dredge with sugar before serving.

For Batter Pudding with Dried Fruit, substitute 4 oz mixed dried fruit for the apples.

6 helpings   **Cooking time 30-40 min**

PANCAKES

Batter as for Batter Pudding above	1 lemon
A little cooking fat	Castor sugar

Put about ¼ oz of cooking fat into a cleaned frying pan and heat until it is just beginning to smoke.

Apple pancakes

Batter pudding with apples

Quickly pour in enough batter to coat thinly the bottom of the pan, tilting the pan to make sure that the batter runs over evenly. Move the frying pan over a quick heat until the pancake is set and browned underneath. Make sure that the pancake is loose at the sides, then toss, or turn with a broad bladed knife or fish slice. Brown on the other side and turn on to a sugared paper. Sprinkle with sugar and lemon juice, roll up and keep hot while cooking the rest. Serve dredged with castor sugar and pieces of cut lemon.

Other flavourings such as apple, jam, orange, tangerine or brandy may be used, as follows:

Apple pancakes Add grated lemon rind to the batter. Fill with apple purée mixed with seedless raisins and a little lemon juice.

Jam pancakes Spread with jam before rolling up.

Orange pancakes Make the pancakes but sprinkle with orange juice and serve with pieces of cut orange.

Tangerine pancakes Add grated tangerine rind to the batter. Sprinkle with tangerine juice before rolling up.

Brandy filling for pancakes Cream together 2 oz butter and 1 oz castor sugar until soft. Work in 1 tablesp brandy and 1 teasp lemon juice. Spread the pancakes with this mixture. Roll up and put immediately into the serving dish.

CREPES SUZETTE

½ pt batter as for Batter Pudding above	Icing sugar Brandy *or* rum

FILLING

2 oz butter	2 teasp orange juice
3 oz castor sugar	1 teasp lemon juice
Grated rind of ½ orange	1 tablesp Kirsch *or* Curaçao

Make the batter, and leave it to stand. Cream together the butter and sugar for the filling until very soft. Then work in the orange juice, rind lemon juice and liqueur. Make a very thin pancake, spread with some filling, roll up and dredge with icing sugar. Put into a warm place while making the rest of the pancakes, and filling them. Just before serving, pour the warmed brandy or rum over the pancakes and light it. Serve immediately.

If you prefer, warm the filling with the brandy until liquid, and pour it over the unfilled pancakes folded over twice. Light and serve.

SWEET FRITTERS

1 Most fritters are made with batter, used as a coating or to make a mixture stick together. Some batters contain whisked egg whites, others yeast or beer or brandy. Some are sweetened or flavoured with liqueurs or spices.

2 The fritters can be deep-fried, or shallow-fried in fat at least 1-in deep. The fat must be hot enough to seal the batter instantly; it should show signs of 'hazing'. At the correct temperature, a drop of batter will sink, rise to the surface at once and then begin to colour.

3 Lower fritters gently into the hot fat, using a perforated spoon if you can. Turn them and withdraw them in the same way. Place a frying basket, if used, in the fat *before* putting in the fritters, so that they are sealed by the hot fat before touching it.

4 Only fry a few fritters at a time, and let the undersides brown before turning them. Turn once only. Let the fat reheat when you take out

155

FRITTERS

the fritters, while you drain them on absorbent paper. Keep warm until all the fritters are made. Do not dust with sugar until dryish.

SWEET FRITTER COATING BATTERS

1 LIGHT

2 oz plain flour	½ gill warm water
Pinch each of sugar and salt	1 egg white
1 dessertsp salad oil or oiled butter	

Sift together the flour and salt. Mix to a smooth consistency with the oil and water. Beat well, and leave to stand for 30 min. Just before using, whisk the egg white stiffly and fold it into the batter.

2 RICH

4 oz plain flour	1 egg
Pinch each of sugar and of salt	1 gill milk

Sift together the flour and salt. Make a well in the centre of the flour and add the egg and some of the milk. Mix to a stiff consistency, using more milk if required. Beat well. Add the rest of the milk. Leave to stand for about 30 min.
For a batter for loose mixtures, see Indian Fritters.

3 WITH YEAST

¼ oz yeast	6 oz plain flour
¼ teasp castor sugar	Pinch of salt
1½ gills warm milk (approx)	1 oz melted butter

Cream the yeast and sugar, and add a little milk. Sift together 2 oz of the flour and the salt into a warm bowl. Mix to a batter consistency with the yeast mixture, adding more milk if required. Leave to rise until doubled in bulk. Add the rest of the flour and warm milk, work in and add the melted butter. Leave to rise again, in a warm place for quick rising or low down in the fridge overnight. After coating, fritters made with yeast batter should stand for 30 min on buttered paper before being fried.

VARIOUS FRITTERS

Sweet fritters can be divided into those made with fruit or other solid ingredients, such as stale cake or bread, and those made with loose or near-liquid foods such as raisins, rice or jam. Fruit can be fresh, frozen or canned; it may be plain, or soaked in a syrup or liqueur before coating. Stones (e.g. prune stones) *must* be removed from fruit before coating.

Fritters should be dredged with castor sugar just before serving.

Apple Fritters 2 apples, cored and sliced; coating batter; castor sugar for dredging; lemon wedges and lemon hard sauce as accompaniments.

Apricot Fritters 2 canned apricot halves, drained; coating batter; castor sugar mixed with ground cinnamon for dredging.

Banana Fritters 4 firm bananas, cut lengthwise and across; coating batter; castor sugar for dredging.

Bread and Butter Fritters 6 thin jam sandwiches without crusts; coating batter; castor sugar mixed with ground cinnamon for dredging.

Orange Fritters 4 oranges, peeled and without pith, in pieces of 3–4 segments; coating batter; castor sugar for dredging.

Pineapple Fritters 8–10 canned pineapple rings, drained; coating batter; castor sugar for dredging.

Use the syrup from the can for a sauce.

INDIAN FRITTERS

3 oz plain flour	2 egg yolks
Pinch of salt	Frying-fat
Boiling water	Jam or jelly
2 eggs	

Sift the flour into a basin with a pinch of salt. Stir in a good ½ gill of boiling water and beat to form a very stiff smooth paste. Leave to cool slightly. Beat in the eggs and egg yolks gradually and thoroughly. Have ready a deep fat, just beginning to haze. Half fill a tablespoon with the mixture and put a teaspoon of jam or jelly in the centre and cover with some more of the batter mixture and drop this into the hot fat. Cook until golden-brown, about 3 min. Drain well. Dredge with castor sugar or serve with a sauce made from the same jam or jelly as the filling.

5–6 helpings   Cooking time 15–20 min

WAFFLES

8 oz plain flour	1 pt milk
¼ teasp salt	2 oz margarine
¾ oz yeast	2–3 eggs
½ teasp sugar	Maple or golden syrup

Sift flour and salt into a bowl. Cream the yeast with the sugar and add to it the warm milk and margarine; beat the eggs. Add the yeast, milk and egg to the flour, using more milk if required to make a pouring batter. Set aside to rise for 30–45 min. Heat and grease the waffle iron and pour in enough batter to fill the iron sections – the lid must press on the batter. The waffles are ready when nicely browned. Serve hot with maple or golden syrup.

30–40 waffles

STEAMED, BOILED AND BAKED PUDDINGS

ALL FLOUR-BASED, HOT PUDDINGS

1 Almost all the 'flour and fat' hot puddings are made with flour, breadcrumbs or cake crumbs and a raising agent such as baking powder, mixed with sugar and eggs. You get a lighter pudding by using some breadcrumbs or cake crumbs instead of all flour in any suet mixture. Always add a good pinch of salt for every ½ lb flour. If you want to use self-raising flour, use a mixture which contains 1 teasp baking powder per ½ lb plain flour.

2 The fat can be worked into the pudding mixture in various ways.

a Chopped-in method (suet) Either beef or lamb suet can be used although some cooks avoid lamb suet in case it gives its own definite flavour to the pudding. Many use shredded packet suet which is ready for use without further chopping.

To prepare your own suet, remove the skin, gristle and fibres in it. Sprinkle it with some of your measured flour. Then slice it into flakes, and chop finely. Use a sharp kitchen knife. Hold the handle in your right hand and raise and

Apple fritters

lower the knife quickly while holding the point on the chopping board with the other hand. Add more measured flour while chopping if the suet becomes sticky. When the suet is chopped, mix in all the remaining dry ingredients.

b Rubbed-in method (all fats) Sift the flour, salt and raising agent into a mixing bowl. Cut the fat into small pieces. Rub the fat into the flour with the tips of the fingers only, lifting it so that it becomes aerated as it falls back. Continue until the mixture is like breadcrumbs, without any big lumps.

c Creaming method (all fats) This method is used for puddings with too much fat to rub in, or which contain no flour. Use castor sugar because the small crystals dissolve easily.

Work the fat with a wooden spoon and, as it becomes soft, work in the sugar bit by bit. Work the mixture until it is pale and as soft as very thick cream. You can use a warmed bowl in cold weather but take care not to let the butter oil. Beat the eggs and add a little at a time, beating briskly. The mixture may curdle if the egg is straight from the refrigerator or is added too quickly.

3 To finish the mixtures above, use these methods:

a Mix liquid flavouring, beaten eggs and milk together, and add last to chopped-in and rubbed-in mixtures.

b Mix dry flavourings, flour, salt and raising agent, and sift them together into a creamed mixture, followed by any other ingredients (e.g. dried fruit).

Note that a 'dropping consistency' in a recipe means that the mixture should just drop from the spoon when it is shaken lightly. A 'soft dropping consistency' means that the mixture drops from the spoon easily. A 'slack

Waffles with fruit and jam

MAKING PUDDINGS

consistency' means that it falls off almost of its own accord.

4a Always prepare the container and a greased paper foil or lid cover, if needed, before making the pudding. They should be well greased with unsalted or clarified butter, or with margarine or cooking fat. The edges must be wiped clean, to prevent marks on a dish in which a pudding will be served, and to stop the cover slipping off.

b Our picture of various containers and tools

c For the method of lining a basin with pastry before boiling or steaming, *see* Fruit Pudding with Suet Crust.

d Cover the pudding basin with greased paper or with foil, to prevent steam getting in. Put the cover on greased side down. Twist the edges under the rim of the basin, or tie them.

e After taking the pudding out of the steamer, give it a few moments to shrink before turning it out on to a dish.

6a **For a boiled pudding,** have rapidly-boil-

Nursery castle puddings

for desserts shows several commonly used for boiled, steamed and baked puddings. For instance, a charlotte mould or tin can be used for any of them, a pie dish is often used for a baked pudding and, for individual puddings, the small dariole moulds are popular.

5a **For a steamed pudding,** have the pan of boiling water ready. If you have no steamer, stand the pudding in a saucepan on an old saucer or plate, with water coming half-way up it. Put a close lid on the pan, and simmer gently. This is 'half-steaming'.

b When a recipe calls for gentle steaming, only let the water simmer. Always 'top up' with boiling water however. For a steamed pudding, only $\frac{3}{4}$ fill the basin.

ing water ready, enough to cover the whole pudding. Cover the pudding securely as above.

b If you wish, you can boil a pudding in a basin covered with a floured cloth or in a well-floured cloth only. Roly-poly puddings can be rolled in a floured cloth, forming a sausage shape; tie loosely at each end, leaving room for the pudding to swell.

c If you use a basin, fill it completely.

d Put the pudding into fast-boiling water. Then only let the water simmer; but always 'top up' with boiling water.

e Let the pudding 'stand' for a few moments after removing it from the water, to let it shrink.

Note that Christmas Puddings should be

given a clean, dry cloth on top after boiling, and should then be stored in greaseproof paper. They must be boiled for at least $1\frac{1}{2}$ hr longer before serving.

7 **For baked puddings,** use a well-greased basin or pie dish, with a really clean edge. They are easier to handle if placed on a flat baking sheet in the oven.

In the following recipes, boiled and steamed puddings are put first, and baked puddings afterwards.

APRICOT PUDDING

6 halves canned apricots	**2 eggs**
3 oz butter *or* margarine	**Rind of $\frac{1}{2}$ lemon**
3 oz castor sugar	**3 oz plain flour**
	$\frac{1}{4}$ teasp baking-powder

Grease a $1\frac{1}{2}$ pt basin. Drain the apricots well and cut them into small pieces.

Cream together the fat and sugar and when really soft beat in the eggs gradually. Stir in the grated lemon rind, apricots and the sifted flour and baking-powder. Turn the mixture into the basin, cover and steam steadily for $1\frac{1}{4}$–$1\frac{1}{2}$ hr. Serve with apricot sauce (*see* Queen's Pudding).

4 helpings

BROWN BREAD PUDDING

3 oz raisins	**8 oz brown breadcrumbs**
3 oz sultanas	**3 oz castor sugar**
4 oz finely-chopped suet	**2 eggs**
	A little milk

Grease a basin; clean the fruit; prepare the suet if shredded suet is not used.

Mix together the breadcrumbs, sugar, fruit and suet. Add the beaten eggs and some of the milk, and mix to a dropping consistency. Leave to stand for $\frac{1}{2}$ hr. Add more milk if needed, to make a soft dropping consistency. Put into the basin; cover. Steam or boil for $2\frac{1}{2}$–3 hr. Serve with custard sauce.

6–7 helpings

STEAMED NURSERY CASTLE PUDDINGS

4 oz butter	**4 oz self-raising flour**
5 oz castor sugar	**1 tablesp milk**
2 eggs, well beaten	**3 tablesp apple purée (*see* below)**
$\frac{1}{2}$ teasp vanilla essence	**2 oz raisins**

STRAWBERRY GLAZE

$\frac{1}{4}$ pt water	**2 teasp arrowroot**
$\frac{1}{2}$ oz castor sugar	**1 tablesp sieved strawberry jam**
Few drops of red colouring	

Cream butter and sugar together until light and fluffy. Gradually beat in the eggs, one by one. Stir in vanilla essence. Fold in sieved flour, milk, apple purée and washed raisins. Turn into 8 or 9 greased and floured individual moulds, and cover with buttered greaseproof paper. Steam in $\frac{3}{4}$ in boiling water for 30–40 min or until sponge is springy. Turn out on to a warmed serving dish, and serve immediately.

FOR THE APPLE PURÉE

2 apples, peeled, cored and sliced	**1 oz castor sugar**
Juice of $\frac{1}{2}$ lemon	**2 tablesp water**

Gently cook the apple slices with the lemon juice, castor sugar and water for 4–5 min or until soft and tender. Drain, sieve and cool.

STRAWBERRY GLAZE

Prepare the glaze while the puddings are steaming. Mix 1 tablesp of water with the arrowroot. Add to the remaining water and bring to the boil, stirring constantly. Stir in castor sugar and strawberry jam. Tint red. Cook for 3 min and serve poured over the steamed puddings.

CHRISTMAS PUDDING (Rich, boiled)

10 oz sultanas	**1 level teasp mixed spice**
10 oz currants	**1 level teasp grated nutmeg**
$\frac{1}{2}$ lb raisins	**$\frac{1}{2}$ lb breadcrumbs**
2 oz sweet almonds (skinned and chopped)	**10 oz finely-chopped *or* shredded suet**
1 level teasp ground ginger	**6 eggs**
$\frac{1}{2}$ lb plain flour	**$\frac{1}{2}$ gill stout**
Pinch of salt	**Juice of 1 orange**
1 lb soft brown sugar	**1 wineglass brandy**
$\frac{1}{2}$ lb mixed finely-chopped candied peel	**$\frac{1}{2}$ pt milk (approx)**

Grease three 1 pt pudding basins. Prepare the dried fruit; stone and chop the raisins; chop the nuts.

Sift the flour, salt, spice, ginger and nutmeg into a mixing bowl. Add the sugar, breadcrumbs, suet, fruit, nuts and candied peel. Beat the eggs well and add to them the stout, orange juice and brandy, and stir this into the dry ingredients adding enough milk to make the mixture of a soft dropping consistency. Put the mixture into prepared basins. Cover and boil steadily for 6–7 hr. Take the puddings out of the water and cover them with a clean dry cloth and, when cold, store in a cool place until required.

When required, boil the puddings for $1\frac{1}{2}$ hr before serving. Serve with brandy butter.

3 puddings (each to give 6 medium helpings)

CHRISTMAS PUDDING (Economical, boiled or steamed)

1 apple	**6 oz mixed chopped candied peel**
1 lb mixed dried fruit (sultanas, currants, raisins)	**Juice and rind of 1 lemon**
4 oz plain flour	**2 eggs**
1 oz self-raising flour	**Milk to mix**
Pinch of salt	**A little caramel *or* gravy browning**
4 oz breadcrumbs	**A few drops of almond essence**
4 oz soft brown sugar	
$\frac{1}{2}$ lb shredded suet	

Grease two small basins or one large basin; peel, core and chop the apple; prepare the dried fruit. Sift together the plain flour, self-raising flour and salt into a mixing bowl. Add the breadcrumbs, dried fruit, sugar, suet, candied peel and grated lemon rind. Beat the eggs and milk together and stir them into the dry ingredients with the lemon juice, adding more milk to make the mixture of a soft dropping consistency. Add a little caramel *or* gravy browning to darken the mixture slightly (about a level teasp), and the almond essence. Mix well in. Turn into the basin, cover and boil for 4 hr or steam for 5 hr.

12 helpings

LEMON PUDDING

FRUIT PUDDING WITH SUET CRUST

1–1½ lb fresh fruit	2–3 oz granulated sugar

SUET CRUST PASTRY

½ lb plain flour	Pinch of salt
1 teasp baking-powder	3 oz finely-chopped suet

FILLINGS

Apples	Damsons
Blackberries and apples	Gooseberries
Blackcurrants	Plums

Sift the flour and baking-powder, add the suet and salt. Mix with sufficient water to make a soft, but firm, dough. Grease and line a basin (*see below*). Fill to the top with the fruit and sugar and add ¼ gill of cold water. Put on the top crust.

To boil   Cover over with a well-floured cloth and boil for 2½–3 hr.

To steam   Cover with greased paper and steam for 2½–3 hr.

To line the basin   Cut off one quarter of the pastry for the top. Roll the remaining pastry ½ in larger than the top of the basin, drop the pastry into the greased basin, and with the fingers work the pastry evenly up the sides to the top. Roll out the lid to the size of the top of the basin, wet the edges and secure it firmly round the inside of the pastry.

6 helpings

LEMON PUDDING (Using butter or magarine)

6 oz flour	2 oz sugar
Pinch of salt	Juice and rind of 1
1 rounded teasp baking-	lemon
powder	1 egg
2 oz butter *or* margarine	Milk to mix

Grease a 1½ pt pudding basin. Sift together the flour, salt and baking powder. Rub in the fat and add the sugar and grated lemon rind. Mix to a soft drop-

ping consistency with the beaten egg, lemon juice and milk. Put the pudding into the greased basin and cover with a piece of greased paper. Steam for 1½–2 hr.

For a steamed jam pudding, substitute vanilla essence for lemon juice. Put 1 tablesp red jam in the basin before the mixture, and serve a hot jam sauce with the pudding.

4–6 helpings

ROLY POLY OR SPOTTED DICK

12 oz plain flour	Pinch of salt
2 rounded teasp baking-	Water to mix
powder	Jam
6 oz finely-chopped suet	

Sift the flour and baking-powder, add the suet and salt. Mix with sufficient water to make a soft, but firm, dough. Roll it into a rectangle about ¼ in thick. Spread with jam almost to the edge. Damp the edges and roll up lightly. Seal the edges. Wrap the pudding in a scalded well-floured cloth; tie up the ends. Put into fast boiling water. Simmer for 2–2½ hr.

For Spotted Dick, mix 6 oz castor sugar and 6 oz currants into the dry ingredients instead of spreading the pastry with jam. Use milk to mix instead of water.

SYRUP SPONGE PUDDING

6 oz plain flour	Pinch of salt
6 oz breadcrumbs	1 egg
4 oz finely-chopped suet	2 tablesp golden syrup
2 oz castor sugar	1 tablesp treacle
1 teasp ground ginger	Milk to mix
1 level teasp bicarbonate	
of soda	

Grease a basin and, if liked, put a tablesp of golden syrup in the bottom. Mix together the flour, bread-

Christmas pudding

Apple charlotte

crumbs, suet, sugar, ginger, bicarbonate of soda and salt. Beat the egg with the golden syrup, treacle and a little of the milk. Stir this into the other ingredients, using more milk if required, to mix to a very soft dropping consistency. Put the mixture into the basin; cover with greased paper. Steam for $1\frac{1}{2}$–2 hr.

6–7 helpings

TREACLE LAYER PUDDING

2 oz breadcrumbs	$\frac{1}{2}$ lb treacle *or* golden
Rind of 1 lemon	syrup (approx)

SUET CRUST PASTRY, RICH

4–6 oz finely-chopped	2 rounded teasp baking
or shredded suet	powder
12 oz plain flour	Water to mix
Pinch of salt	

Sift flour, salt and baking-powder and mix with suet and sufficient water to make a soft, but firm, dough. Divide the dough into two equal portions, using one portion to line a 2 pt basin. From the other portion cut off enough to make the lid; roll out the remainder thinly.

Mix the breadcrumbs and grated lemon rind. Put a layer of treacle in the basin; sprinkle well with the breadcrumbs. Cover with a round of the thinly-rolled pastry. Moisten the edge of it with water and join securely to the pastry at the side of the basin. Add another layer of treacle, crumbs and pastry; then more treacle and crumbs. Finally cover with the rolled-out top as the last layer of pastry. Cover with greased paper. Steam for $2\frac{1}{2}$ hr.

6–7 helpings

APPLE CHARLOTTE

2 lb cooking apples	8 thinly cut slices of
4 oz brown sugar	bread and butter
Grated rind and juice of	Castor sugar
1 lemon	

Grease a 2 pt charlotte mould with butter. Peel, core and slice the apples. Place a layer in the bottom of the mould and sprinkle with sugar, grated lemon rind and lemon juice. Cover with thin slices of bread and butter. Repeat until the dish is full, finishing with a layer of bread and butter. Cover with greased paper. Bake in a moderate oven (180°C, 350°F, Gas 4) for $\frac{3}{4}$–1 hr. Turn out of the dish, if desired, and dredge well with castor sugar before serving.

Alternatively, cut the bread $\frac{1}{4}$-in thick before buttering it; line the mould with it, buttered side outward, so that the pieces fit tightly together. Fill with the remaining ingredients packed tightly, and bake as above.

5–6 helpings

APPLE OR OTHER FRUIT CRUMBLE

$1\frac{1}{2}$ lb apples	3 oz butter *or*
4 oz brown sugar	margarine
A little grated lemon	6 oz plain flour
rind	3 oz castor sugar
$\frac{1}{2}$ gill water (approx)	$\frac{1}{4}$ teasp ground ginger

Peel, core and slice the apples into a pan. Add $\frac{1}{2}$ gill water, 4 oz brown sugar and lemon rind. Cook gently with lid on the pan until soft. Place in a greased 2 pt pie dish. Rub the fat into the flour until of the consistency of fine breadcrumbs. Add the castor sugar, ground ginger and mix well. Sprinkle the crumble over the apple; press down lightly. Bake in a moderate oven (180°C, 350°F, Gas 4) until the crumble is golden-brown, and the apples are cooked; this takes about 30–40 min, depending on the cooking quality of the apples. Dredge with castor sugar and serve with custard *or* cream.

For apples the same weight of the following may be substituted: damsons, gooseberries, pears, plums, raspberries *or* rhubarb, and the crumble named accordingly.

6 helpings

BAKED APPLES

BAKED APPLES OR APPLE DUMPLINGS

| 6 cooking apples | ½ gill water |
| 2 oz demerara sugar | Pastry (optional) |

FILLINGS

| 1 | 2 oz moist sugar and 2 oz butter | 3 | 3 oz stoned dates *or* sultanas *or* currants *or* raisins, 2 oz soft brown sugar and 1 teasp ground cinnamon |
| 2 | Blackcurrant *or* raspberry *or* strawberry *or* apricot jam | | |

Prepare the filling. Wash and core the apples. Cut round the skin of the apple with the tip of a sharp knife, ⅔ of the way up from the base. Put the apples into a fireproof dish and fill the centres with the chosen filling. Sprinkle with the demerara sugar. Add the water. Bake in a moderate oven (180°C, 350°F, Gas 4) until the apples are soft in the centre —about ¾–1 hr depending on the cooking quality of the apples.

To make baked apple dumplings Stuff the apples after peeling and coring them. Use 12 oz short crust pastry if they are big apples, 8 oz if they are small. Cut the pastry into 6 pieces, and roll out in rounds. Work a piece of pastry round each apple, and seal with a little water. Place the dumplings, join side down, on a greased baking sheet. Brush with milk, dredge with castor sugar and bake at 200°C, 400°F, Gas 6 for about 30 min.

6 helpings

BAKED JAM ROLL

12 oz plain flour	6 oz finely-chopped suet
1 teasp baking-powder	Jam
Pinch of salt	

Mix the flour, baking-powder, salt and suet with sufficient water to make a soft, but firm dough. Roll the dough into a rectangle about ¼ in thick. Spread with jam almost to the edges, damp the edges and roll up lightly. Seal the edges. Put on to a well-greased baking sheet. Cook in a fairly hot oven (200°C, 400°F, Gas 6) for about 1 hr until cooked through.

6 helpings

PASTRY MAKING

The aim in making pastry for puddings, sweet pies etc, is to make a crust which is as light as possible. As with all pastry, the lightness depends on the amount of cold air trapped in the mixture when making it. In puff or flaky pastry, this air is trapped between thin layers of dough.

Baked jam roll

But in short crust, suet crust and similar pastry, the air is in a myriad tiny spaces right through the pastry.

You can only use self-raising flour for *plain* short crust pastry and suet crust pastry. Use plain flour for all sweetened or rich pastry.

Butter, or butter mixed with lard or white cooking fat, should be used for pastry-making if possible. However, you can use margarine in the following recipes if you wish.

When the amount of fat is less than half the amount of flour, add a little baking-powder (1 level teasp to ½ lb flour).

General hints on pastry-making and the basic recipes for most kinds of pastry are given in the section on Trimmings, Sauces and Flavourings. But recipes for Suet and Crumb Crust, Choux Pastry, Pâté Sucrée, Puff Pastry, Short and Rich Short Crust, designed for use in sweet dishes, are given below.

SPECIAL HINTS ON MAKING PASTRY FOR PUDDINGS

1 Always sift the flour and any sugar used.

MAKING A FLAN CASE Read from left. 1, Lifting the pastry on a rolling pin. 2, Tucking pastry into flan case. 3, Filling the flan case with beans. 4, Lifting the flan case off the baked pastry shell

STAGES IN MAKING SHORT CRUST PASTRY

Sifting the flour into a bowl

Rubbing in the fat

Gathering the dough into shape

2 Use only your fingertips when rubbing fat into flour. Lift your hands high, so that air is caught up as the flour falls back into the bowl.

3 Use chilled water for mixing if you can, and mix with a round-bladed knife. Do not use more water than you need; it will make the pastry hard.

5 Handle the pastry little and lightly. Let puff and flaky pastry 'stand' for 15 min between every two rollings. *All* pastry should 'stand' in a cool place after being made for 15 min at least.

6 Roll pastry lightly and evenly, with short strokes, travelling one way only. Lift the rolling-pin just short of the edge so as not to squeeze air out.

7 Use only very little flour for rolling out. Remove any extra with a pastry brush. Occasionally, pastry is rolled on sugar, or sugar is rolled into the surface before baking. Keep the board cool and your hands dry, and sweep off any surplus with a pastry brush.

8 The richer the pastry, the hotter the oven you need. If it is not hot enough, the melted fat runs out and leaves the pastry hard and tough. It also wastes fat. (Choux pastry and Genoese pastry are exceptions to this rule.)

TO GLAZE PASTRY FOR SWEET DISHES

Fruit tarts, puffs, etc, can be brushed lightly with cold water and dredged with castor sugar before being baked. If a thin coating of icing is wanted, they can be brushed over with well-beaten egg white and dredged with castor sugar when nearly baked.

BOUGHT PASTRY

Frozen short crust or puff pastry, in a block or already shaped, is quite satisfactory for most of the dishes below. So is a pastry mix in a packet, with the added advantage that flavourings or egg yolk can be added to make the pastry spicier or richer than usual.

1 Pastry trimmings, especially of puff pastry, can be well used for fritters and for small decorative biscuits to accompany desserts such as ice creams. They can also be used for jam tartlets.

2 For Suet Crust pastry, *see* Fruit Pudding with Suet Crust, and for a richer Suet Crust pastry, *see* Treacle Layer Pudding.

TO MAKE A FRUIT PIE OR TART

A 1½ pt pie dish will require about 6 oz pastry (i.e. 6 oz flour plus the other ingredients made into pastry) and 1½–2 lb fruit.

Place ½ the amount of fruit in the dish, sprinkle over the sugar and flavouring, if used, and pile the remaining fruit on top, piling it high in the centre. The sugar should not be sprinkled on top as it would go into the pastry and make it soggy. If the fruit is likely to shrink during cooking, or if there is insufficient fruit to fill the dish, place a pie funnel or inverted egg-cup in the centre.

Roll out the pastry a little larger than the pie dish. Cut off a strip of pastry the width and length of the rim of the dish, wet the edge of the pie dish with cold water and place the strip on the pie dish cut edge inwards, without stretching it. Join the strip by wetting the cut ends and pressing them firmly together.

Wet the strip of pastry; lift the remaining pastry with the rolling-pin and place it gently over the dish, taking care not to stretch it. Press the strip and the cover together and trim off the surplus with a sharp knife. Knock up the edge of the pastry with the back of a knife and decorate to your fancy.

To allow the steam to escape, either cut a slit in the centre of the crust before placing pie in the oven (if a pie funnel has been used the slit should come over it); *or* leave a few gaps under the pastry cover at the edge; *or* raise the pastry slightly at one corner immediately after cooking.

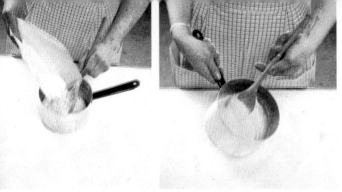

STAGES IN MAKING CHOUX — Tipping flour into hot mixture. Blended mixture with eggs

STAGES IN MAKING CHOUX **Tipping flour into hot mixture. Blended mixture with eggs**

Filling a forcing bag with choux pastry. Piping small choux on a baking sheet

DOUBLE CRUST PIES OR TARTS

Double crust pies or tarts can be made in fireproof glass or enamel plates or dishes.

About 8 oz pastry (i.e. 8 oz flour plus the other ingredients made up into pastry) will be required for an 8–9-in plate.

Divide the dough into 2 portions, form each into a round shape and roll one portion into a round about ⅛-in thick and a little larger than the plate. Fold over the rolling-pin and lift on to the plate; smooth to fit the plate without stretching the pastry. Cut off the surplus pastry with a sharp knife or scissors. Put in a layer of filling, sprinkle with sugar if you wish and cover with another layer of filling. This prevents the sugar getting into the pastry and making it soggy.

Roll the remaining piece of pastry into a round and a little larger than the plate; lift on the cover and ease into position without stretching; if stretched it will only shrink back later. Press the 2 edges together firmly, knock up the edge and decorate.

Bake according to the type of pastry, and to ensure that the bottom crust cooks through, stand the plate on a baking sheet.

OPEN TARTS

Open tarts are usually baked on fire-proof glass or enamel plates. The tarts can be filled with jam, syrup, treacle, custard, fruit etc. For a 7-in plate, about 4 oz of pastry will be needed.

Knead the dough into a round shape then roll into a circle about ⅛-in thick and a little larger than the plate. Fold the pastry over the rolling-pin and gently lift it on to the plate. Smooth it over carefully with the fingers so that no air is trapped between the pastry and the plate – but take care that the pastry is not stretched in the process, as it will only shrink back later.

If the tart is being baked with a filling, prick the base well or bake it 'blind' (*see* below), as the recipe tells you. Stand the plate on a baking-sheet in the oven.

The tart may be given a lattice top or the edge may be decorated with fancy shapes.

To line a flan ring To line a 7-in flan ring, you will need about 4 oz pastry (i.e. 4 oz flour plus the other ingredients made into pastry). Grease a baking-sheet and the flan ring; place the flan ring on the baking-sheet. Roll the pastry into a circle about 1 in larger than the flan ring and ⅛-in thick. Lift the pastry with the rolling-pin to prevent stretching and line the ring carefully with the pastry. Press to fit the bottom and sides so that no air bubbles form underneath the crust. Trim off the surplus pastry with a sharp knife or roll across the top of the ring with the rolling-pin.

Baking blind If a flan is to be cooked without filling, it must be baked 'blind'. Prick the bottom of the flan, cover it with a piece of greaseproof paper and fill with rice or beans (this prevents the flan from losing its shape during cooking). Bake according to the kind of pastry. When the pastry is cooked, remove the paper and rice or beans, and replace the flan case in the oven for 5 min to dry the bottom. The rice or beans can be used over and over again. Cool, store in a tin and keep them for this purpose.

OTHER PASTRY PUDDINGS

While pies, tarts and flans are the best-known desserts using pastry, many boiled and steamed puddings such as Treacle Layer Pudding are made with pastry. So are baked puddings such as the baked apple dumplings above, and some gâteaux used as desserts. (Other gâteaux and desserts are made with cake or meringue, with custard or fruit.)

PUDDINGS USING YEAST DOUGH

Some puddings, such as savarins, are made with a yeast mixture. In making these, remember that yeast is a plant, and needs gentle heat, moisture and food to make it grow and raise a dough. As a rule, the growth is started by creaming the yeast with a little sugar. Once it has started and the dough is rising, cover the basin containing the dough with a damp cloth to prevent surface evaporation. Do not raise the dough for too long, or it will become overstretched and collapse. But always give it a chance to rise again or 'prove' a second time to replace the air knocked out when kneading it. Most yeast doughs need to be baked in a hot oven, to kill the yeast cells.

CHOUX PASTRY (For soufflé fritters, cream puffs, profiteroles, etc)

4 oz plain flour	½ teasp vanilla essence
½ pt water	1 egg yolk
⅛ teasp salt	2 eggs
2 oz butter *or* margarine	

Sift and warm the flour. Place water, salt and fat in a pan, and bring to boiling-point. Remove from heat, add flour all at once and beat well over the heat again, until it becomes a smooth soft paste and leaves the sides of the pan clean. Remove from the heat, add vanilla and egg yolk immediately and beat well. Add the other two eggs one at a time, beating thoroughly between each addition. (It is important to get the first of the egg in while the mixture is hot enough to cook it slightly, otherwise it becomes too soft.) Add any flavouring last. Use while tepid. Bake in a fairly hot oven (200°C, 400°F, Gas 6–7). Do not underbake.

CRUMB PASTRY

Crumb pastry can provide a useful short cut to making a tart shell or pie crust. It is made with breadcrumbs, toast or biscuit crumbs or cornflakes. The materials are crushed by hand, wrapped in a cloth and rolled with a rolling-pin, or are processed in an electric blender. As a rule, 6 oz crumbs combined with 3 oz melted butter is used, with sugar and spice flavouring to your taste. This should make a shell for an 8-in plate tart. Mix the crumbs together with the butter well, and press firmly into the bottom and sides of the plate. Either chill, and then fill with a custard or firm fruit purée; or chill and then bake 'blind' at 180°C, 350°F, Gas 4, for 15 min.

Fatty crumbs may need less butter, wholemeal stale breadcrumbs may need a little more. A luxury crust can be obtained by using ginger-snaps for the crumbs, or the following mixture:

1½ cups digestive biscuit crumbs	¼ cup thin cream
	¼ cup melted butter
6 tablesp unblanched ground almonds	⅓ teasp cinnamon

PÂTÉ SUCRÉE

8 oz plain flour	2 oz sugar
Pinch of salt	1 egg yolk
5 oz butter	Cold water to mix

Sift together the flour and salt. Cut the butter into small pieces and rub it lightly into the flour using the finger tips. Add the sugar and mix with egg yolk and sufficient cold water to make a stiff paste. Use as required.

In warm weather only a very small quantity of water will be required.

PUFF PASTRY (For pies, tarts, tartlets, etc)

1 lb plain flour	1 teasp lemon juice
Pinch of salt	⅓ pt cold water (approx)
1 lb butter	

Sift the flour and salt and rub in about 2 oz of butter. Press the remaining butter firmly in a floured cloth to remove the moisture, and shape into a flat

cake. Add the lemon juice to the flour and mix to a smooth dough with cold water. The consistency of the dough must be the same as that of the butter. Knead the dough well and roll it out into a strip a little wider than the butter and rather more than twice its length. Place the butter on one half of the pastry, fold the other half over and press the edges together with the rolling-pin to form a neat parcel. Leave in a cool place for 15 min to allow the butter to harden.

Roll out into a long strip 3 times the original length but the original width, keeping the corners square and the sides straight to ensure an even thickness when the pastry is folded. Do not let the butter break through the dough. Fold the bottom third up and the top third down, press the edges together with a rolling-pin and half turn the pastry so that the folded edges are on the right and left. Roll and fold again and lay aside in a cool place for 15 min. Repeat this process until the pastry has been rolled out 6 times. The rolling should be done as evenly as possible and the pastry kept in a long narrow shape which, when folded, forms a square. Roll out as required and leave in a cool place before cooking.

Bake in a very hot oven (230°C, 450°F, Gas 8). The oven door should not be opened until the pastry has risen and become partly baked, as a current of cold air may cause the pastry to collapse.

SHORT AND RICH SHORT CRUST PASTRY FOR PIES, TARTS, ETC

FOR STANDARD SHORT CRUST PASTRY

½ lb plain flour	2 oz lard
Pinch each of sugar and salt	Cold water to mix
2 oz butter *or* margarine	

Sift the flour, sugar and salt together. Rub the fats into the flour, using only the finger tips. Mix to a stiff paste with cold water.

FOR RICH SHORT CRUST PASTRY

½ lb plain flour	1 teasp castor sugar
4–6 oz butter (sweet cream type, if possible)	1 egg yolk
	Cold water to mix (about 1 tablesp)

Make as above, on a flat surface rather than in a bowl. Before adding water, make a well in the dry ingredients, and put in the egg yolk. Sprinkle with the sugar, and mix with the finger tips or a knife. Add the water as required, and mix.

PIES, TARTS AND FLANS
APPLE-RAISIN LATTICE TART

Short crust pastry, frozen *or* using 8 oz flour, etc	4–6 oz sugar, brown *or* white
¼ lb tart dessert apples	½ oz flour
½ lb seedless raisins	Pinch of salt
1 tablesp lemon juice	1 oz butter

Line a 9-in pie plate with ⅔ pastry, reserving the rest for lattice strips. Peel, core and chop apples, and toss in lemon juice to coat. Mix the fruits, and then mix in any dry ingredients. Turn into the pastry-lined plate. Dot with butter and arrange a lattice of pastry strips over the top. Bake in a very hot oven (230°C, 450°F, Gas 8) for 7–8 min, then reduce heat to moderate (180°C, 350°F, Gas 4) for 30–40 min.

APPLE PIE

Short crust pastry, frozen or using 6 oz flour, etc.	4 oz moist sugar
	6 cloves or ½ teasp grated lemon rind
1½–2 lb apples	

Peel, quarter and core the apples and cut in thick slices. Place half the apples in a 1½ pt pie dish, add the sugar and flavouring and pile the remaining fruit on top, piling it high in the centre. Line the edge of the pie dish and cover. Knock up the edges of the pastry with the back of a knife. Bake for 40 min, first in a fairly hot oven (200°C, 400°F, Gas 6), reducing the heat to moderate (180°C, 350°F, Gas 4) when the pastry is set. Dredge with castor sugar and serve hot or cold.

If you wish, brush the pastry with egg white and sprinkle with sugar before cooking.

6 helpings

BAKEWELL TART

Short crust pastry, frozen or using 4 oz flour, etc.	1 egg
	2 oz ground almonds
Raspberry jam	2 oz cake crumbs
2 oz butter	Almond essence
2 oz sugar	Icing sugar

Line a 7-in flan ring or a pie plate with the pastry. Place a good layer of raspberry jam on the bottom. Cream together the butter and sugar till thick and white. Beat in the egg and add the ground almonds and cake crumbs and a few drops of almond essence. Spread the mixture on top of the jam and bake in a fairly hot oven (200°C, 400°F, Gas 6) for about ½ hr. Sprinkle icing sugar on top and serve hot or cold.

5–6 helpings

CREAM PUFFS OR CHOUX

Choux pastry, using 4 oz flour, etc	Icing sugar

FILLING

½ pt sweetened double cream flavoured with vanilla essence or confectioner's custard.

Put the pastry into a forcing bag and pipe balls on to a greased baking-sheet, or shape the mixture with a spoon into piles. Bake in a fairly hot oven (220°C, 425°F, Gas 7–6) for 30 min (do not open the door), then move to a cooler part of the oven for about 10 min until dried inside. Split the puffs and remove any damp mixture. When cold fill with whipped cream and dust with icing sugar.

24 puffs	Cooking time 40 min

FRUIT FLAN OR TART

Rich shortcrust pastry, using 4 oz flour, etc

FILLING

1 medium sized can of fruit *or* ¾ lb fresh fruit, e.g. apples, strawberries, pears, pineapple, cherries, apricots, peaches, plums, etc or dried fruit such as apple slices, apricots and prunes, well soaked

COATING GLAZE

¼ pt syrup from canned fruit, or fruit juice, or water	Sugar (if necessary)
	1 teasp arrowroot
	Lemon juice to taste

DECORATION (OPTIONAL)

Whipped sweetened cream

Line a 7-in flan ring or tart plate with the pastry. Prick the bottom and bake it 'blind' as described above. Bake for about 20 min first in a fairly hot oven (200°C, 400°F, Gas 6), then reducing the heat as the pastry sets to moderate (180°C, 350°F, Gas 4). When the pastry is cooked, remove the paper and filling used for 'blind' baking and replace the case in the oven for 5 min to dry the bottom. Allow to cool.

If fresh or dried fruit is used, stew gently till tender, if necessary. Drain the fruit. Place the sugar if used and the liquid in a pan and boil for 10 min. Blend the arrowroot with some lemon juice and add it to the syrup, stirring all the time. Continue stirring, cook for 3 min then cool slightly. Arrange the fruit attractively in the flan case and coat it with fruit syrup.

If liked, a flan can be decorated with piped whipped, sweetened cream.

Apple pie

Meringue pie with apple filling

For a quick flan or tart case, a crumb crust or cake mixture from a packet can be used satisfactorily.

In some areas, apple flans or tarts are given a crumbled cheese topping instead of fruit syrup.

JAM TART

Trimmings of puff pastry   Any kind of jam

Grease a fireproof plate or tart pan. Roll out the pastry to a thickness of $\frac{1}{8}$-in and line the plate with it. Spread with jam and decorate the edges. Bake the tart in a hot oven (220°C, 425°F, Gas 7) for 10–15 min.

LEMON MERINGUE PIE

**Rich shortcrust pastry,
   using 8 oz flour, etc**

FILLING

2 eggs	2 level teasp cream of
8 oz can sweetened	tartar
condensed milk	1 lemon
2 oz castor sugar	

Make the pastry and line an 8 or 9-in pie plate. Bake it 'blind'.

To make the filling Separate the egg yolks from the whites. Beat the yolks until thick and lemon coloured. Fold in the condensed milk, lemon rind, juice and cream of tartar. Pour into the baked pie shell. Spread with meringue made from the egg whites and the sugar. Decorate lightly with cherries and angelica. Bake in a cool oven (100°C, 200°F, Gas $\frac{1}{2}$) for $\frac{1}{2}$–1 hr.

MERINGUE FLAN WITH APPLE OR PEAR FILLING

Short crust pastry, frozen or using 4 oz flour, etc	2 oz butter or margarine
	3 oz brown sugar
$1\frac{1}{2}$ lb cooking apples or pears	2 eggs
	2–3 oz castor sugar for the meringue
2 tablesp water	
Rind of $\frac{1}{2}$ lemon	Marzipan apples or
1 pinch each ground cinnamon and cloves	glacé cherries

Peel, core and slice the apples or pears; put them in a saucepan and stew with the water and the finely-grated lemon rind. When soft, sieve or process in an electric blender. Return the pulp to the pan and re-heat slightly, add the butter, brown sugar and egg yolks. Meanwhile line a 7-in flan ring with the pastry. Put the fruit mixture into the uncooked lined flan ring and bake gently in a moderate oven (180°C, 350°F, Gas 4) for about 30 min, until the fruit mixture is set. Stiffly whisk the egg whites and fold in 2–3 oz castor sugar. Pile on top of the fruit mixture, dredge lightly with castor sugar and decorate, if you wish, with pieces of angelica and glacé cherry. Bake in a very cool oven (140°C, 290°F, Gas 1) until the meringue is golden-brown, about 30–40 min. Top with marzipan apples or glacé cherries before serving.

This recipe can also be used for tartlets, if the cooking time is reduced.

6–7 helpings

TREACLE TART

TREACLE TART

Short crust pastry, using 6 oz flour, etc	3 tablesp golden syrup
	Lemon juice *or* ginger
	3 oz fresh breadcrumbs

Slightly warm the syrup, flavour with a pinch of ginger or a little lemon juice, then stir in the breadcrumbs. Line an 8-in fireproof plate with the pastry, trim and decorate the edge. Spread over the syrup mixture, decorate with cross strips of pastry, and bake in a fairly hot oven (200°C, 400°F, Gas 6) for about 30 min.

If preferred the tart may be baked as a double crust tart. Increase the amount of pastry and bake for 50 min. Crushed cornflakes can be substituted for the breadcrumbs.

6 helpings

BABAS WITH RUM SYRUP

½ lb plain flour	1 gill milk
Pinch of salt	4 eggs
½ oz yeast	4 oz butter
1 oz castor sugar	2 oz currants

RUM SYRUP

3 oz granulated sugar	1 wineglass rum
1 gill water	1 wineglass sherry
Rind of ½ lemon	

Grease 9 dariole or baba moulds. Sift the flour and salt into a warm basin. Cream the yeast with a pinch of castor sugar, and add to it the gill of warm milk. Mix this into the flour to form a soft dough. Beat well until the dough leaves the sides of the basin clean. Cover the basin with a damp cloth and leave the dough to rise in a warm (but not hot) place until about twice its size. When the dough has risen sufficiently add 2 eggs, the melted butter and castor sugar; beat well in. Then add the rest of the eggs and the currants and beat again for 5–10 min, until the dough is smooth and glossy. Half-fill the moulds with the mixture. Put them in a warm place until the mixture has risen to the top of the moulds. Bake in a fairly hot oven (220°C, 425°F, Gas 7) for about 20–25 min until brown and firm.

TO MAKE THE SYRUP

Put the granulated sugar and water into a pan with the thinly peeled lemon rind. Boil for 10 min, add the rum and sherry, then strain. Re-heat the syrup. Soak the babas in it for a minute; lift them out and serve immediately, with syrup poured round them.

9 babas

SAVARIN

4 oz plain flour	1 egg
Pinch of salt	¼ oz sugar
¼ oz yeast	1½ oz butter
¼ gill warm water	

KIRSCH SAUCE

| 3 oz loaf sugar | 1–2 tablesp kirsch |
| ¼ pt water | Juice of ½ lemon |

DECORATION

| Apricot jam | Blanched almonds, browned |

Sift the flour and salt into a basin and put it to warm. Cream the yeast with the tepid water. Make a well in the centre of the flour and pour in the yeast mixture. Sprinkle over the top with a little of the flour from the side of the bowl. Leave to prove for 10–15 min in a warm place. Add the egg gradually, beating well to a smooth elastic dough, using a little more tepid water if necessary. Knead well. Put the dough back into the basin and press down, sprinkle the sugar on the top and put on the butter in small pieces. Cover with a damp cloth and leave in a warm place to double its size. Beat well again until all the sugar and butter is absorbed. Grease a border or ring mould and fill it ⅓ of the way up with the mixture. Leave to prove in a warm place until the mixture just reaches the top of the mould. Then bake in a fairly hot oven (200°C, 400°F, Gas 6) for about 20 min.

Make the sauce Boil the water and sugar steadily for about 10 min. Add the kirsch and the lemon juice.

Turn the savarin out on to a hot dish, prick with a needle or hat pin and soak well in the sauce. Coat with hot sieved apricot jam and decorate with spikes of almonds, etc. Serve with the rest of the sauce poured round.

A savarin can be served with a rum sauce. Use rum instead of kirsch. It can also be served, hot or cold, with stewed cherries and stiffly-whipped sweetened cream in the centre. In this case, make the syrup with cherry brandy. Stiffly whipped sweetened cream mixed with crushed macaroons is another classic filling.

4 helpings

COLD, MOULDED AND SET PUDDINGS

ALL COLD CEREAL MOULDS

These puddings are made of whole or ground cereals, milk and sugar, flavouring and sometimes a little gelatine. In cooking them, take care not to let too much liquid evaporate so that they are rubbery. A knob of butter gives them a better flavour and texture.

Simmer whole grain cereals such as rice in the top of a double saucepan. Sprinkle small grain cereals into boiling milk and cook until soft and clear. Blend powdered grain with a little cold milk, pour on the rest of the milk heated almost to boiling point and return the whole mixture to the saucepan to boil gently. Stir carefully, and take great care that the mixture does not burn on the bottom of the pan.

When ready for moulding, any cereal mixture should be thick, so that a spoonful dropped back on the hot mixture only merges when shaken.

Choose china or glass moulds as the cold surface 'sets' the starch mixture at once and gives the mould a clean glossy surface when turned out. Pour in quickly from above the mould so that the mixture's own weight drives out all the air and it fills the mould entirely. A border mould should be brushed with sweet almond or pure olive oil, to make turning out easier.

To unmould, loosen the mixture from the edge

of the mould with your finger, place the moistened serving dish over the mould, invert both together and tap the mould sharply to dislodge it. The mould should be movable on the dish if it is moistened.

cocoa with a little of the warm milk. If chocolate is used, chop roughly and add to the mixture ½ hr before moulding.

OTHER FLAVOURINGS

Lemon *or* **Orange** Wash fruit, dry well and grate

Peach Condé

WHOLE RICE MOULD

6 oz rice   **Flavouring** (*see* **below**)
1 qt milk   **½–1 oz fresh butter**
3 oz castor sugar   **(optional)**

Wash the rice and put it with the milk into a double saucepan, or a thick pan standing over a very low heat. Simmer very gently, with the lid on the pan to prevent undue evaporation. Stir occasionally to prevent the rice from settling on the bottom of the pan, and cook until the rice is quite tender and the milk almost absorbed. Sweeten to taste, add the flavouring you wish, stir in the butter if used. Pour quickly into a cold, wet basin or mould. Turn out when set and serve with stewed, canned, or fresh fruit, jam, jelly, etc.

FOR CHOCOLATE RICE MOULD

6 oz rice   **Vanilla** *or* **coffee**
2 oz cocoa *or*   **essence** *or* **1 teasp**
   3 oz chocolate   **brandy** *or* **rum**
1 qt milk   **1 oz fresh butter**
4 oz castor sugar

Make like the Whole Rice Mould, blending the

rind finely; stir into the cooked mixture just before moulding. Alternatively, peel rind in thin strips, omitting white pith, and infuse in mixture during cooking; remove before adding sugar and butter.

Coffee Add coffee essence to taste, with the sugar.

6 helpings   **Cooking time 2–3 hr**   **Setting time 2 hr**

PEACH OR PEAR CONDÉ

1 pt cold rice mould   **1 small can peaches** *or*
⅛ pt double cream   **pears**
Whipped cream   **1 level teasp arrowroot**

Stir the cream into the rice. Pour into serving dishes. Drain the fruit and arrange it prettily on top.

Make the juice up to ¼ pt with water. Blend in the arrowroot, and boil until clean. Cool, then pour over the fruit. Decorate with whipped cream.

4 helpings

RICE A L'IMPÉRATRICE

Make like a cold Timbale of Semolina, using ground or whole long grain rice. Set it in a border

Coffee mousse and junket

mould. Either: (*a*) fill the central hollow with fruit salad and piped whipped cream (*see* Fruit Salad) *or* (*b*) place selected fruit, e.g. apricot halves, on the top of the border, glaze with apricot juice thickened with arrowroot (1 level teasp to ½ pt juice) and decorate with piped whipped cream and angelica.

JUNKET

2 pt fresh milk	**2 teasp rennet**
2 teasp castor sugar	**Flavouring (*see* below)**

Warm the milk to blood heat and stir in the sugar until dissolved. Add the rennet, stir and pour at once into serving dishes. Put in a warm place to set.

Serve with cream, if liked.

Coffee Add to milk, coffee essence to flavour, and decorate finished junket with chopped nuts.

Chocolate Add 2–3 oz plain chocolate, grated and dissolved in a little of the measured milk.

Rum Add rum to taste.

Vanilla, almond, raspberry, etc Add a few drops of essence.

Note: When using rennet in liquid or powder form, the manufacturer's instructions should always be followed carefully.

6 helpings

ALL JELLIES

Jellies may be strained, cleared or whipped.

They are made from fruit juice or purée, milk flavoured with an essence, or water and wine, set with gelatine. They must not be rubbery, so using the right amount of gelatine is important. Manufacturers give very clear directions on powdered gelatine packets. Unmarked gelatine should be used in the proportion of ¾ oz–1 pt liquid, or more (1 oz–1 pt) in hot weather or if the jelly contains pieces of fruit. It must also be firm for use chopped as a garnish, or for lining a mould, or if it is to be whipped.

Use jelly moulds of glass, glazed china or metal. A metal mould gives the jelly the clearest, sharpest outline. Make sure the mould is clean and cold before use, and rinse with cold water just before using.

Unmould jellies by one very quick dip to the rim in *very* hot water, or by holding a hot cloth round the mould when already inverted on the serving dish.

CLEARED JELLIES

Cleared jelly is filtered through a foam of set egg whites and crushed egg-shells. The pan, whisk and metal jelly mould must first be scalded. The egg whites are lightly whisked until liquid, then added with the washed and crushed egg-shells to the liquid jelly. The mixture is heated steadily and whisked constantly until a good head of foam is produced, and the contents of the pan are hot, but not quite boiling. As the hardened particles of egg white rise to the surface they carry with them all the insoluble substances, forming a thick 'crust' of foam. The correct temperature is reached when the foam begins to set, so take care not to break up, by whisking too long, a completely set foam. Remove the whisk, and heat to allow the foam crust to rise to the top of the pan. Then let the contents of the pan settle in a warm place covered with a lid, for 5–10 minutes.

The jelly is then poured through a scalded jelly cloth, while the cloth is still hot, into a scalded bowl below. The bowl of strained jelly is replaced with another scalded bowl, and the jelly re-strained very carefully by pouring through the foam 'crust' which covers the bottom of the cloth and acts as a filter.

Filtering is most easily carried out using a

TO DECORATE A MOULD

Put 2 tablespoons cold liquid jelly in mould and rotate to coat. Fix garnish in place with pins. Pour in a little more jelly to hold garnish. Fill mould when set. To unmould invert and jerk to loosen.

jelly bag and stand made for the purpose, but if these are not available the 4 corners of a clean cloth can be tied to the legs of an upturned stool, and a bowl placed below the cloth.

Careful filtering produces a jelly of clear brilliance. This is needed for lining moulds and setting decorations and fruit. Otherwise the colour of these would be obscured.

For instructions on lining and garnishing a mould, see the caption to the picture series, *To Decorate a Mould.*

WHIPPED JELLIES

If jelly is whipped or whisked just before setting, tiny bubbles of air are enclosed. These give a light texture both stimulating and refreshing. The addition of egg white, slightly whisked and then whipped with the cold liquid jelly increases the volume of the jellied foam and also adds to its food value without unduly diluting the flavour, although a strongly-flavoured jelly is needed if more than 1 egg white is used.

BANANA JELLY WITH CREAM

1 pt lemon *or* orange jelly	6 bananas
½ oz peeled pistachio nuts	¼ pt double cream

Make the jelly and allow to cool. Chop green pistachio nuts finely and stir into 2 tablesp jelly. Set the nut jelly in the bottom of a mould. Beat the bananas to a purée and half-whip the cream. Stir the banana purée into the remaining jelly; add cream and fold together lightly. Fill up the mould and turn out when set.

6 helpings   Cooking time 5 min
                              Setting time 2 hr

BLACKCURRANT OR OTHER FRUIT WHIP

¼ pt blackcurrant purée (see Fruit Purée) and ½ pt water *or* ¾ pt blackcurrant juice	½ oz gelatine Sugar to taste

Heat the gelatine slowly in the juice *or* purée and water until dissolved. Add sugar if necessary. Cool, then whisk briskly until a thick foam is produced. When the whisk leaves a trail in the foam, pile quickly into a glass dish.

Damson Whip Use ¾ pt damson juice, ½ oz gelatine and sugar to taste.
Lemon Whip Use 1 pt lemon jelly tablet, sugar, ¾ pt water and 1 tablesp lemon juice.
Pineapple Whip Like Damson Whip.
Orange Whip Like Lemon Whip, using orange instead of lemon juice.

6 helpings   Time ½ hr

LEMON JELLY

4 lemons	1 in cinnamon stick
Sherry (optional)	1¾–2 oz gelatine
1½ pt water	Shells and whites of 2
6 oz sugar	eggs
4 cloves	

Scald a large pan, whisk and metal jelly mould. Wash the lemons and cut thin strips of rind, omitting the white pith. Extract juice and measure. Make up to ½ pt with water *or* sherry, but do not add sherry until just before clearing the jelly. Put the 1½ pt water, ½ pt juice, rinds, sugar, flavourings and gelatine into the scalded pan and infuse, with a lid on, over very gentle heat until sugar and gelatine are dissolved. Do not let the infusion become hot. Wash egg-shells and crush. Lightly whisk the whites until liquid and add, with shells, to the infusion. Heat steadily, whisking constantly, until a good head of foam is produced, and the contents of the pan become hot, but not quite boiling. Strain through the crust as described above, and add the sherry, if used, as the jelly goes through the filter.

6 helpings   Time 1–1½ hr

ORANGE FLUMMERY

1st layer

6 oz canned orange juice	3 oz castor sugar
1½ level teasp gelatine	2 eggs, separated
1 oz castor sugar	Orange segments

2nd layer

1 13½ oz can orange juice	2 level tablesp cornflour
2 level teasp gelatine	Angelica

Make the first layer, by dissolving the gelatine in the orange juice, warmed. Add the sugar and dissolve without boiling. Pour this jelly into the base of a 2 pt mould. Chill to set it.

Make the second layer. Dissolve the gelatine in 4 oz of the juice, warmed. Leave to cool. Blend the cornflour with a little juice, dissolve the sugar by warming it in the rest of the juice, and pour it on the blended cornflour. When the mixture has cooled slightly, beat in the egg yolks. Stir in the dissolved gelatine, trickling it in from a height, and chill the mixture. When it begins to thicken, whisk the egg whites and fold them carefully into the mixture with a wooden spoon. Pour into the mould and leave to set. When the whole is set, turn out carefully, and decorate with orange segments and angelica.

CREAMS AND HALF-CREAMS

A full cream is made wholly of cream flavoured with an essence or liqueur, set with gelatine. A half-cream, also called a Bavarois or Bavarian Cream, is made of custard and cream, flavoured with a fruit purée, essence or liqueur.

No substitute tastes like pure fresh cream but cheaper substitutes can be used in some strongly flavoured half-creams without spoiling them. *Evaporated unsweetened milk* can be used if you boil the can, unopened, for 20 min, then refrigerate for 24 hr. (It will keep for several weeks there if not opened.) Tinned cream is less satisfactory as a rule. Packeted cream toppings and 'whips' can be used to supplement real cream.

You need less gelatine in creams than in jellies because the mixture to be set is thicker. The dissolved gelatine must be added when tepid; if hot, it spoils the mixture's lightness, if cold it 'sets' in tiny hard lumps before being fully blended into the mixture.

The smoothness of any cream depends on careful blending. This is an art. Mixtures, e.g. cream and custard, must be the same consistency when mixed, and the same temperature. Custard must be cooled until it is the same temperature and consistency as a fruit purée before being mixed with it. Ice cream must be slightly warmed, if adding cream (for instance, to improve bought ice cream). Fresh whipped cream must only be *folded* into other mixtures, and added just before they set; this gives them a spongy lightness instead of an oily texture.

Apart from the whipped cream, most of the mixtures can be made extremely well in an electric blender. Do not overblend, or the flavour will be lost.

A mould for a cream should be of metal. If the cream is to be decorated, the mould should first be lined with jelly which holds the garnish. (It gets 'lost' in a cream, and looks smeared and dull.) It is in fact usually easier to decorate a cream after it is turned out by sticking the garnish to it with dabs of jam or cream.

CHARTREUSE OF BANANAS
(A fancy full cream)

2 pt clear lemon *or* claret jelly (*see* above)	½ pt double cream
	Vanilla essence
1 oz pistachio nuts	Castor sugar to taste
4 bananas	

Line a 1 qt border or ring mould with jelly. Blanch, skin, chop and dry the pistachio nuts, mix with 2 tablesp jelly and run smoothly over the base of the mould. When set, cover with a ½ in layer of clear jelly. Slice a banana evenly, dip each slice in jelly and arrange them, slightly overlapping, in an even layer on the jelly when set. Cover with another ½ in layer of clear jelly and allow to set. Repeat with fruit and jelly until the mould is full, the last layer being jelly. When set, turn out and pipe the whipped cream, sweetened, and flavoured with vanilla, into the centre. Surround with chopped jelly.

Strawberries or tangerines may be substituted for bananas and the chartreuse named accordingly.

6 helpings
Setting time (without ice) 2–3 hr:
(with ice) ¾ hr

FRUIT BAVAROIS OR CREAM

½ pt fruit purée (*see* Fruit Purée)	½ oz gelatine
	4 tablesp water *or* thin
½ pt. thick, rich custard	fruit juice
Castor sugar to sweeten	Colouring (optional)
Lemon juice (optional)	½ pt double cream

Purée the fruit. You can use an electric blender after sieving out any pips or stones. Blend the purée with the cool custard, sweeten, and flavour with lemon juice if required. Soak the gelatine in the water *or* juice for a few minutes and heat to dissolve. Pour into the custard and fruit mixture, and stir to keep well blended until the mixture begins to feel heavy and drags on the spoon. Colour if necessary. Fold in the whipped cream very lightly with a metal spoon and pour into a prepared mould.

Apricots, blackcurrants, damsons, gooseberries, greengages, peaches, raspberries *or* strawberries can be used for the purée and the cream named accordingly.

6 helpings   Setting time 1–2 hr

GARIBALDI CREAM

½ pt strawberry cream	½ pt pistachio cream
½ pt vanilla cream	(*see* Velvet Cream)

Place the strawberry cream at the bottom of a prepared mould. Allow to set. Add the vanilla cream and set. Put the pistachio cream on the top. Turn out and surround with chopped jelly.

6 helpings   Setting time (with ice) 45 min
(without ice) 2–3 hr

ITALIAN BAVAROIS OR CREAM

1 lemon	2–3 oz castor sugar
½ pt milk	½ oz gelatine
3 egg yolks *or* 1 whole egg and 1 yolk	½ gill water
	½ pt double cream

Infuse thin strips of lemon rind in the milk. Beat eggs and sugar until liquid and make a thick pouring custard with the flavoured milk, straining back into the pan to cook and thicken. Allow to cool. Soak gelatine in the water for 5 min, then heat to dissolve. Stir juice of lemon gently into the cooled custard, and add the dissolved gelatine, stirring again as it cools. Whip the cream and fold lightly into the custard mixture just before setting.

Pour into a prepared mould and leave to set. If you like, the cream can be poured into individual glass dishes, and decorated according to your own taste For vanilla cream, use vanilla essence instead of lemon.

6 helpings   Setting time 1–2 hr

VELVET CREAM

¼ oz gelatine	Sherry *or* vanilla
4 tablesp water	essence
1½–2 oz castor sugar	1 pt double cream

Soak the gelatine in the cold water for 5 min. Heat gently until quite dissolved and clear. Stir in the sugar until dissolved. Add the sherry or vanilla. Whip the cream until thick and fold into it the flavoured liquid gelatine. Pour into a prepared mould and leave to set.

For *Pistachio Cream*, substitute 4 oz pistachio nuts, skinned and finely chopped, for the sherry or essence, and add a few drops of green colouring.

6 helpings   Setting time 1 hr

COLD CHARLOTTES

Most cold charlottes are half-creams surrounded by sponge fingers or similar biscuits. You can line the charlotte mould with these before pouring in the cream mixture. But for a perfect, unsmeared 'fit', it is usually easier to stick them on the outside of the cream after unmoulding it. The great Carême invented these cold desserts.

CHARLOTTE RUSSE

20 savoy fingers	1½ pt Italian cream

Coat the bottom of a mould with jelly. When the jelly has set, line the sides of the mould with savoy fingers, having trimmed the ends so that they fit closely on to the jelly. Remove any crumbs from the surface of the jelly with the tip of a dry pastry brush. Pour the cream mixture into the lined mould and leave to set. Trim the fingers level with the rim. Turn out and decorate with piped cream.

If you prefer, line the base of the mould with sponge fingers.

6 helpings

COLD SOUFFLÉS AND MOUSSES

These are light, frothy desserts, usually of egg and cream whipped to hold air, and 'set' with gelatine or by freezing. The egg yolks and sugar are whisked together, either over warm (not hot) water or with an electric or rotary whisk, the warmth of which dissolves the sugar. The mixture is then cooled and so (as a rule) is the gelatine dissolved by mild heating. When cool but not yet set, they are blended together with care so as not to beat out any of the air in the yolks.

The cream is then half-whipped and the egg whites are whisked until stiff but not yet 'dry'. These are folded in when the mixture is on the point of setting.

A band of greaseproof paper or foil is often tied round the soufflé mould, rising 3 in above its rim. The soufflé mixture is poured in to 'more than fill' the mould. When fully set, the paper is carefully peeled off and the soufflé looks as if it has risen above the mould.

BASIC MILANAISE SOUFFLÉ

2 lemons	½ oz gelatine
3–4 eggs, according to size	¼ pt water
5 oz castor sugar	½ pt double cream

DECORATION

Chopped pistachio nuts

Wash lemons dry, and grate rind finely. Whisk the egg yolks, sugar, rind and lemon juice over hot water until thick and creamy, then remove bowl from the hot water and continue whisking until cool. Soften the gelatine in the ¼ pt water, and heat to dissolve. Half-whip the cream. Whisk the egg whites very stiffly. Add the gelatine, still hot, in a thin stream, to the egg mixture, and stir in as you do it. Fold in the cream and the stiffly-whipped whites. Fold the mixture very lightly until setting is imminent, when the mixture pulls against the spoon. Pour into the soufflé dish and leave to set. Remove the paper band by coaxing it away from the mixture with a knife dipped in hot water. Decorate the sides with chopped, blanched pistachio nuts, and the top with whipped cream, if liked.

This is a good 'basic' soufflé recipe. It can be flavoured and decorated with almost any flavouring and garnish, such as coffee, chocolate, fruit or a liqueur, with appropriate small sweets or nuts as decoration.

6 helpings   **Setting time 2 hr**

DESSERTS WITH COLD CUSTARD, CAKE, MERINGUE AND FRUIT

COLD CUSTARDS

Cold custard desserts are often made in the

Garibaldi cream

same way as hot ones, or cooled custards may be used with various other ingredients such as cake (e.g. trifles). Confectioners' custard or Pastry Cream, which is an egg custard with some form of flour in it, is a common filling for many cake-based desserts and pastries. With whipped egg whites included, it becomes St Honoré cream.

CONFECTIONERS' CUSTARD

½ pt milk	1 oz sugar
¾ oz cornflour	½ teasp vanilla essence
2 yolks *or* 1 whole egg	

Blend the cornflour with the milk, stir in the egg yolks and sugar, and cook over a gentle heat until thick. Beat in the vanilla. Allow to cool.

Milanaise soufflé

TRADITIONAL TRIFLE
TRIFLE (TRADITIONAL)

4 individual sponge cakes	1 oz almonds (blanched and shredded)
Raspberry *or* strawberry jam	½ pt custard using ½ pt milk, 1 egg and 1 egg yolk
6 macaroons	
12 miniature macaroons	¼ pt double cream
¼ pt sherry	1 egg white
Grated rind of ½ lemon	1–2 oz castor sugar

DECORATION

Glacé cherries	Angelica

Split the sponge cakes into two and spread the lower halves with jam. Replace tops. Arrange in a glass dish and cover with macaroons and miniatures. Soak with sherry, and sprinkle with lemon rind and almonds. Cover with the custard and leave to cool. Whisk the cream, egg white and sugar together until stiff and pile on top of the trifle. Decorate with glacé cherries and angelica.

Fruit trifles, such as Apricot or Gooseberry, are made by substituting layers of puréed or chopped fruit for the jam.

6 helpings

Traditional trifle

PEAR SHORTCAKE

4 oz butter	2–4 pears, fresh *or* canned
4 oz castor sugar	
2 eggs, beaten	1–2 pieces crystallised ginger
4 oz plain flour	
2 oz cornflour	Whipped cream
2 level teasp baking powder	Icing sugar (optional)

Cream the butter and sugar until soft, gradually beat in the eggs. Sift flour, cornflour and baking powder together, and work this into the creamed mixture. Make the dough dryer than a sponge but softer than scone dough.

Grease two 7-in sponge tins, and put half the mixture in each. Press in with finger-tips. Bake in a hot oven (230°C, 450°F, Gas 8) for about 15 min. Turn out and cool. Arrange slices of pear and ginger on one surface. Cover with whipped cream and place the other shortbread round on top. Dust with icing sugar for interest, and decorate with ginger.

MERINGUE TOPPING AND SHELLS

4 eggs	½ lb castor sugar

Meringue for topping fruit dishes may be required less sweet than the recipe below. If so, only half the sugar is whisked into the stiff foam. The mixture is then piled on the dessert, dusted lightly with castor sugar and baked in a cool oven (140°C, 290°F, Gas 1) for about 30–40 min.

Make sure that the egg whites are fresh and contain no trace of yolk or grease. Break down with a whisk to an even-textured liquid by tapping lightly for a few moments. Then whisk evenly and continuously until a firm, stiff, close-textured foam is obtained. Whisk in 1 tablesp of the sugar. Add the rest of the sugar, a little at a time, by folding it in lightly with a metal spoon.

For a single large meringue shell, make a circle in pencil on greaseproof paper. Cover the pencil line with a layer of meringue. Pipe a 'wall' of meringue round the edge with a forcing bag. (For small meringue shells, force through a ⅜-in pipe into small rounds, *or* form into egg-shapes with two spoons, dipped in cold water, and place on strips of oiled kitchen paper on baking sheets.) Dredge well with castor sugar and dry in a cool oven (140°C, 290°F, Gas 1), placed low to avoid discolouring and reduce to 130°C, 265°F, Gas ½ after 1 hr. If a pure white meringue is required, *very* slow drying is essential, by leaving the meringue in a barely warm oven overnight.

MERINGUE GÂTEAU

1½ lb strawberries, hulled	¼–½ pt double *or* whipping cream
Juice of 1 lemon	
6 egg whites	12 oz castor sugar

Sprinkle the strawberries with lemon juice and a little castor sugar, and allow to stand until the meringue case is ready. Keep in the fridge if necessary.

Make a meringue mixture, as described in the previous recipe. Mark a 6-in circle with pencil on a sheet of oiled greaseproof paper. With a plain ½-in forcing pipe, make a 'plate' of meringue by working from the centre of the circle outward. Build up the edge to a height of 1½ in. Pipe the rest of the meringue into small shell shapes. Bake as directed in the previous recipe. Reserve a few choice strawberries for decoration. Whip the cream stiffly. Mix the rest of the strawberries with the cream, and pile into the meringue shell. Decorate the top with the small shells and the reserved strawberries.

The meringue shell will not stay crisp for long after the fruit is put in. Fill the case only a few minutes before serving, and do not refrigerate once filled.

PAVLOVA CAKE

3 egg whites	½ teasp cornflour
6 oz castor sugar	½ teasp vinegar
½ teasp vanilla essence	Filling as below

Beat the egg whites until stiff. Continue beating, gradually adding the sugar. Beat until sugar is dissolved. At this stage the mixture should be very stiff and standing well in peaks. Fold in the vanilla, cornflour and vinegar. Spread the mixture in a 6–8 inch circle on greaseproof paper on a baking sheet, making the sides higher than the centre to form a shell. Place in a cool oven (150°C, 310°F, Gas 2) for 1–1¼ hr.

The pavlova should be crisp and very lightly tinted on the surface yet remain soft and of the consistency of marshmallow in the centre. Cool and remove very carefully on to a flat cake-tray or board. Fill and serve cut in wedges.

NOTE: You can also decorate the shell in various ways. Use a fancy forcing pipe to make small rosettes on the sides, for instance.

FRUIT PUREÉS (for all desserts)

Fruit purées for all sweet dishes including creams, ice creams and sauces are made by rubbing fresh, frozen or canned fruit through a fine sieve, or by using an electric blender. Fruit containing pips or

Meringue tartlets with pear filling

FILLINGS

1 Pile ½ pt whipped and flavoured cream into the pavlova shell and on top of this arrange a selection of fruit: use pineapple, apricots, mandarins, passion fruit, grapes, fresh or canned peaches, etc, according to taste and season. Finally decorate with angelica, maraschino cherries or almonds as desired.

2 Mash or slice 4–6 bananas. Mix a few tablespoonfuls of sherry or brandy into the mashed bananas, or place the slices in a basin and cover with sherry or brandy. Allow to stand for 1 hr.

Strain off liquid if bananas are sliced, then fold fruit into ½ pt whipped and sweetened cream, with a cupful of halved fresh or maraschino cherries. Pile into the pavlova shell and sprinkle the surface generously with shredded chocolate and chopped nuts or toasted coconut.

3 There are many other pavlova filling mixtures. Try blackcurrants with a little cassis liqueur, or pear slices and raspberries with lemon juice. Canned peaches or apricots are also good.

stones must be sieved before blending. A nylon sieve should always be used as fruit is acid.

FRUIT SALAD

3 oz granulated sugar	6 oz green grapes
½ pt water	1 small can pineapple
3 oranges	segments
Rind and juice of	3 red-skinned dessert
1 lemon	apples
3 ripe dessert pears	

Bring the sugar and water to the boil, together with strips of rind taken from 1 orange and the lemon. Cool. Sieve to remove the rind.

Cut up the oranges, removing the skin and white pith, and section out the flesh, removing the pips. Halve the grapes removing the pips. Place these in the cooled sugar and water. Empty the pineapple pieces and juice into the fruit salad. Refrigerate if possible.

Just before serving, quarter, core and slice the apples thinly and toss in the lemon juice. Dice the pears and also toss in lemon juice. Add these to the fruit salad. Arrange attractively in a suitable serving dish. Chill and serve.

Fresh pineapple and canned mandarin segments are attractively coloured fruit to use. Try piling the salad in a shell or half shell of pineapple.

STEWED FRUIT AND FRUIT FOOL

Fresh or dried fruit, as below	Flavouring of lemon *or* orange rind, claret,
Sugar, as below	sherry *or* 1 *or* 2 cloves

The amount of sugar needed will depend on the sweetness of the fruit. Dried fruit usually needs only 1–2 oz per lb; tart gooseberries may need 2–4 oz. The amount of water varies likewise. Forced rhubarb needs little or none, but apples and pears should be covered to keep them white. Flavourings should be added to the water before cooking, and rind removed before reducing the juice (see below). Soak dried fruit in water (1 pt–1 lb) before cooking.

Leave small fresh apples and pears whole, cut large ones into quarters. Place immediately in syrup (see below) to prevent them going brown. Cloves flavour apples well.

Forced rhubarb is cut into 1–2-in lengths and brown sugar gives it the best flavour. Cook gently without water in a fireproof or ovenproof dish. Strip the skin off old unforced rhubarb before cooking.

Gooseberries, plums and any tart stone fruit should be de-stalked; take out the stones or not as you wish. Cook very slowly until the skins crack.

To stew any fruit, make a syrup by dissolving the chosen amount of sugar in water. Add the flavouring and fruit. Cook either on top of the stove, just under the boil, or in a warm oven. When the fruit is cooked, drain it, and pile it in a serving dish. Boil the syrup to make it thick, cool it and pour it over the fruit.

To make a classic fruit fool, sieve the drained fruit or process it in an electric blender after removing the stones if necessary. Make 1 pt thick pouring custard per 1½ lb fruit *or* use 1 pt whipped double cream (or ½ pt cream and ½ pt custard). Make the fruit purée the same consistency as the cream, by adding a little fruit syrup if necessary. Blend the two mixtures gently with a metal spoon or spatula, and decorate the fool with miniature macaroons.

ICES

Ices can be divided into two classes: water ices and ice creams.

WATER ICES, SHERBETS AND SORBETS

Water ices are made from the juice of fresh fruit or fruit purée mixed with syrup or fruit syrup. Sherbets and Sorbets are half-frozen water ices containing egg white or gelatine.

ICE CREAMS

These are sometimes composed almost entirely of cream, sweetened, flavoured, and decorated in many ways; but more often the so-called 'ice cream' consists principally of custard, of varying degrees of richness, with the addition of fruit pulp, almonds, chocolate, coffee, liqueurs or other flavourings. The cream, when used, should be double cream; evaporated milk can be substituted for part of the cream but the can should first be boiled, unopened, for 20 min, then cooled quickly and if possible chilled for 24 hr in a fridge.

MAKING ICE CREAM IN A FRIDGE

To obtain a smooth, evenly-textured ice cream in a fridge, the mixture must be frozen quickly and whisked well. The quicker the freezing, the less likelihood there is of 'grainy' ice crystals forming, so set the fridge to the coldest point ½ hr before putting the mixture to freeze, unless instructed otherwise in the recipe. Chill all ingredients and utensils before use.

Prepare the mixture, place it in the ice tray or drawer, and replace the tray in the freezing compartment.

Air acts as a deterrent to crystal formation, so remove the mixture after ½ hr and whisk well in a chilled bowl. Replace in the tray and put back into the freezing compartment.

MOULDING ICES

If the mixture is to be moulded it should be removed from the freezer or fridge in a semi-solid condition, and then packed into a dry mould, well shaken, and pressed down into the shape of the mould. The mould should have a tightly fitting lid. It should be wrapped in greaseproof paper and buried in broken ice and freezing salt for 1½–2 hr.

To unmould, remove the paper, wipe the mould carefully, dip it into cold water, and turn the ice on to a dish in the same way as a jelly or cream.

SYRUP FOR WATER ICES

2 lb loaf sugar	1 pt water

Place the sugar and water in a strong saucepan. Allow the sugar to dissolve over gentle heat. Do not stir. When the sugar has dissolved, gently boil the mixture for 10 min, or, if a saccharometer is available, until it registers about 100°C, 220°F. Remove scum as it rises. Strain cool and store. 1 pt syrup.

LEMON WATER ICE

6 lemons	1½ pt syrup, as above
2 oranges	

Peel the fruit thinly and place the rind in a basin. Add the hot syrup, cover and cool. Add the juice of the lemons and oranges. Strain, chill and freeze.

6 helpings

LEMON OR ORANGE SORBET

1 pt water	½ pt lemon *or* orange
8 oz loaf sugar	juice
2 egg whites	

Dissolve the sugar in the water. Boil for 10 min,

Coffee ice cream

strain and cool. Add the juice and stiffly whisked egg whites. Freeze and serve at once.

6 helpings

BASIC ICE CREAM CUSTARDS

1 ECONOMICAL

1 oz custard powder	**4 oz castor sugar**
1 pt milk	

Blend the custard powder with a little of the milk. Boil remaining milk and pour on to the blended mixture. Return to pan and simmer, stirring continuously. Add sugar; cover, and allow to cool.

2 WITH EGGS

1 pt milk	**4 oz castor sugar**
3 eggs	

Heat the milk. Beat together the eggs and sugar. Add the hot milk slowly, stirring continuously. Return to the pan and cook without boiling until custard coats the back of a wooden spoon. Strain, cover and cool.

3 RICH

1 pt milk	**2 eggs**
8 egg yolks	**4 oz castor sugar**

Heat the milk. Beat together eggs and sugar until thick and white; add the milk. Cook, without boiling until it thickens. Strain, cover and cool.

BASIC (VANILLA) ICE CREAM

1 ECONOMICAL

¼ pt cream or prepared evaporated milk *(see above)*	**1 pt cold ice cream custard**
	1 teasp vanilla essence

Half whip the cream or evaporated milk. Add the custard and vanilla. Chill and freeze.

6 helpings   **Time 2½ hr**

2

¼ pt cream	**½ oz castor sugar**
½ pt cold ice cream custard	**1 teasp vanilla essence**

Half whip the cream. Add the custard, sugar and vanilla. Chill and freeze.

3 RICH

½ pt cream	**1 teasp vanilla**
½ pt cold ice cream custard (2) *or* **(3)**	**2 oz castor sugar**

Half whip the cream. Add the custard, vanilla and sugar. Chill and freeze.

4 REFRIGERATOR

2 level teasp icing sugar	**2 egg whites**
1 gill cream	**Vanilla essence**

Sieve the icing sugar. Whip the cream, and add one tablesp of the sugar. Stiffly whip the egg whites and fold in the other tablesp of sugar. Mix together carefully the cream, egg whites and vanilla. Turn into a tray and freeze in the ice-making compartment of the fridge for ½ hr. Remove the tray and whisk the mixture till mushy. Return it to the tray, and finish freezing it.

Other essences and flavourings can be used instead of vanilla in all the recipes above.

BURNT ALMOND ICE CREAM

2 oz loaf sugar	**¾ gill cream**
2 oz almonds	**1 tablesp kirsch**
1½ pt ice cream custard (3)	**(optional)**

Blanch, shred and bake the almonds until brown. Put the sugar and a few drops of water in a saucepan and boil until it acquires a deep golden colour. Add the cream, boil up and stir into the custard. Chill, add almonds and kirsch, if used, and then freeze the mixture.

BANANA SPLIT

For Caramel Ice cream, omit the almonds and substitute brandy for the kirsch.

6–7 helpings

BANANA SPLIT

6 bananas	¼ pt sweetened whipped
1 pt vanilla ice cream	cream
or 1 bought brick	2 oz chopped walnuts
½ pt Melba sauce	8 maraschino cherries

Peel the bananas, split in half lengthways and place in small oval dishes. Place two small scoops or slices of ice cream between the halves of bananas. Coat the ice cream with melba sauce; sprinkle with whipped cream and cherries.

HAWAIIAN DREAMS

1 large can crushed	2 oz chopped browned
pineapple	almonds
½ oz gelatine	¼ pt sweetened whipped
2 teasp lemon juice	cream
1 pt vanilla *or* chocolate	6–8 maraschino
ice cream	cherries

Measure the crushed pineapple and make it up to 1 pt with water. Dissolve the gelatine in a little of the liquid but do not allow to boil. Add it to the crushed pineapple with the lemon juice. Pour into individual glasses to set. Just before serving, place a scoop of ice cream on top of the set mixture. Sprinkle with nuts. Decorate with a rose of cream and place a cherry on top.

6 individual glasses

KNICKERBOCKER GLORY

1 pt red jelly	1 pt Melba sauce
1 pt yellow jelly	2 oz chopped walnuts
1 small can chopped	¼ pt sweetened whipped
peaches	cream
1 small can pineapple	8 maraschino cherries
2 pt vanilla ice cream *or*	
2 large bought bricks	

Make the jellies, allow to set, then whip with a fork. Place portions of chopped fruit in tall sundae glasses. Cover these with 1 tablesp of whipped jelly. Place a scoop or slice of ice cream on top of the jelly.

Hawaiian dreams

Knickerbocker glory

Coat the ice cream with melba sauce. Repeat again with fruit, jelly, ice cream and sauce. Sprinkle with chopped nuts. Pipe with sweetened whipped cream. Place a cherry on top of each.

6 helpings

PEACH MELBA

4–5 firm, ripe peaches	4 oz sugar
½ gill Melba sauce	½ pt vanilla ice cream,
Vanilla essence	home-made *or* bought

Halve and peel the peaches. Add the vanilla to the syrup and dissolve in it the sugar. Poach the peaches in the syrup until tender but not broken. Lift out the peaches, drain them on a sieve, and allow to get thoroughly cold. Serve them piled around a mound of vanilla ice cream in a silver dish. Set this dish in another dish containing shaved ice. Pour over a rich raspberry syrup, which must be previously iced. Serve at once.

This is the original recipe created in honour of Dame Nellie Melba. It is now often made as follows:

1 pt vanilla ice cream	½ pt Melba sauce
6 canned peach	¼ pt sweetened whipped
halves	cream

Place a scoop or slice of ice cream in 6 sundae glasses. Cover with a peach half. Coat with Melba sauce. Pipe a large rose of cream on top of each.

Other fruits are also used. Pears dipped in lemon juice team well with raspberries, for instance.

6 individual glasses

Afternoon and high tea are British institutions. Other nations eat pastries and gateaux as desserts or at social meetings between meal-times. But the British have invented two 'real meals' and created a whole calendar of plain and fancy 'baked goods' for them. Many, such as some of the gingerbreads, are very old, local specialities, and even many of the national cakes and breads are still quite different from any made elsewhere.

This section, then, contains a major British contribution to Western cookery, and one in which traditional and local recipes are still used by housewives with love and care, and justified pride. Home baking has always been treated as an honoured and a skilled craft in Britain, whereas the continental housewife 'handed over' to the professional pastrycook centuries ago.

Plain cakes and buns form a large part of this range of 'baked goods' (which people overseas enjoy and copy, finding in some of them symbols of their own history). These come first, therefore, followed by the so-called 'rich' cakes, butter sponges and sponges, and then meringue, pastry and other mixtures. Biscuits, both of the 'cookie' and 'wafer' types, come after these, and then icings or frostings and fillings. The section ends with the gingerbreads, scones, quick breads and yeast breads, which are still the chief pride of many housewives.

CAKES, BUNS AND BISCUITS

Cakes and buns can be classified as:

Plain cakes and buns They contain little fat, and it is 'rubbed in' or melted before being added, as in (a) rock cakes (b) gingerbreads.

Rich cakes and 'butter sponges' They contain more fat, and it is usually creamed with the sugar before the dry ingredients are added.

They usually contain more sugar, eggs and fruit or flavouring per lb of flour, too. Examples are Queen cakes, layer cakes and Dundee cake.

Sponge cakes These are leavened with eggs, and contain little or no fat.

Cakes made with egg whites, pastry, etc Examples are meringues, brandy-snaps and tartlets.

BAKING TINS AND SHEETS

These can be round or square. If you want to use a square tin instead of a round one for a particular recipe, the size of the tin matters. A 7-in square tin holds the same amount as an 8-in diameter round tin of the same depth; that is to say, one side of the square tin must only be 1-in shorter than the diameter of the round tin.

If you want to use a different sized tin from the one stated, you must adjust the cooking time, and, occasionally, the oven heat. A mixture in a small deep tin needs longer cooking than the same amount of mixture in a shallow, wider tin; sometimes the temperature must be reduced for the extra cooking time, or the outside of the cake overcooks. Small deep tins may also need extra lining, especially in gas ovens.

If you have an oblong tin, calculate its size as a square and a half or a square and a quarter, according to the length of its sides. A tin 12 in × 8 in is an 8 in square plus a half. Alternatively, line an oblong tin with heavy-duty aluminium foil, making it a square inside by blocking off one end.

PREPARING TINS AND SHEETS

Most cake and bun tins, and baking sheets for biscuits, must be greased; or they can be lined with silicone-treated non-stick paper, or with greaseproof paper or aluminium foil which is then greased.

For small cakes and sponges, brush the tins

well with clarified fat. For most sponge cakes, dust the greased tins lightly with flour or a mixture of equal quantities of castor sugar and flour, to give the cake a crisp outside. All sandwich type and large cakes should be baked in tins lined with paper or foil. The richer the mixture and the longer the cooking time, the thicker the lining should be to prevent the cake being overcooked outside before the heat has completed its work in the centre.

A cake tin can be surrounded by a 'jacket' of aluminium foil and stand on an asbestos mat as an extra 'lining'.

All linings should be brushed well with clarified fat inside, or have an innermost lining of silicone-treated paper. This paper is a blessing to cake-makers, and is less expensive than it seems, since it can be used over and over again. Housewives who do a lot of baking can keep a stock of circles and squares of this paper to fit their usual bases; it can save a lot of labour and mess, since no fat need be used.

To line a tin—round or square

1 Cut a single or double piece of greaseproof paper to fit the bottom. Be careful that it is not bigger than the bottom or it will spoil the shape of the cake.

2 Measure the circumference of the tin and cut a strip, single or double, long enough to line the sides of the tin, allowing for an overwrap. Make the strip 2 in deeper than the height of the tin.

3 Fold up 1 in along the bottom of the strip and cut this 1 in fold with diagonal cuts so that it will 'give' and shape well into the roundness of the tin. Paper for a square tin need not be snipped; but it should be mitred at the corners—two pieces are easier to fit than one.

4 Place the strip round the sides of the tin with the cut edge on the bottom of the tin. Fit in the bottom piece. Grease the lined tin with clarified fat if necessary.

To line a swiss roll tin

Cut a piece of greaseproof paper just large enough to fit the tin, base and sides. If the paper is made higher than the sides of the tin it may prevent the heat from browning the top of the roll. Bisect each corner by cutting down 1½-in. Fit the paper into the tin and grease it carefully.

INGREDIENTS USED IN CAKE-MAKING

Flour In cake-making, use a 'weaker' flour than that needed for bread. For large, solid rich cakes with a close texture, use plain flour plus baking powder or bicarbonate of soda rather than self-raising flour. Self-raising flour can be used for some smaller cakes, sandwich cakes and sponges where the texture is more open.

Rice flour is occasionally used, e.g. in shortbread, macaroons, etc. Cornflour, sometimes called cornstarch, is another type of flour sometimes used with plain flour. It tends to produce a cake which is rather short and dry, which crumbles easily and 'melts' in the mouth.

For cake-making, flour must always be sifted.

Fats Butter gives the best flavour, particularly in large rich cakes and shortbreads. However, margarine is cheaper and gives a better volume when creamed. Lard is flavourless and 100 per cent fat, and does not hold air well when creamed. But it is good for solid cakes, spiced cakes and pastry, especially if combined with margarine.

Homogenated or 'all purpose' fats have air finely dispersed through them, which helps to give a quick start when creaming. The 'fork mixing' method is the quickest and most economical way to distribute the fat and mix to the required consistency. Because both butter and margarine contain water, it is claimed that 'all purpose' fats are more economical, e.g. when 4 oz margarine or butter is given in a recipe, 3–3½ oz shortening is enough. Butter or margarine has been suggested for most recipes in this book, but you can substitute other fats if you adjust the proportions, i.e. the fat in the recipe when replaced by 'all purpose' fat should be reduced by about one fifth.

Sugar Castor sugar is best for most cakes. Granulated sugar is apt to give a speckled appearance. Soft brown sugar is suitable for gingerbread and cakes where a dark brown colour is wanted. Loaf sugar, crushed into small pieces, is effective when sprinkled on the top of bath buns, etc.

Icing sugar, being very fine, is used mostly for icings, but it can be used successfully in short crust pastry and some specialised mixtures.

Golden syrup, treacle and honey are also used as sweetening in some cakes and 'bread' mixtures, such as gingerbreads.

Eggs All eggs should be fresh. New-laid eggs are best for sponge cakes and meringues. Eggs can be whisked with a fork, rotary whisk or electric beater. It is usually enough to whisk till the liquid flows freely and is well frothed.

In making large cakes, eggs are usually added whole to the creamed fat and sugar, one at a time, each being beaten in.

Dried fruits It is best to buy dried fruits when the grocer gets in a fresh stock. Much purchased fruit is already cleaned for use. But a methodical housewife washes uncleaned fruit as soon as possible, and after drying it slowly in a warm place, stores it in suitable jars. Dry-cleaning of fruit with flour is not wise. You can

A table set for the 'traditional' English tea

wash the fruit immediately before use, provided you dry it thoroughly on a clean cloth. Wet fruit alters the consistency of the cake, and it sinks.

Take out raisin stones and scrape sugar from peel before shredding and chopping. Use citron peel for the top of a madeira cake. Glacé cherries are very heavy; cut them into pieces. Angelica is used mostly as decoration but it can be chopped as peel and used in the cake. Caraway seeds should be used with care; they are not universally popular.

AIDS TO SUCCESS IN CAKE-MAKING

1 Collect your tools and ingredients before beginning to make the cake. Measure the ingredients with care.

2 Line tins as described above.

3 Pre-heat the oven to the temperature you will want.

4 To cream fat and sugar: cream the fat first, then scatter on the sugar while still beating. Use an electric beater, rotary whisk or a fork, and beat until mixture is white and fluffy. You can warm the fat slightly to make creaming easier, but do not melt it, since melted fat does not hold air.

5 If a creamed mixture shows signs of curdling when eggs are added, add a spoonful or two of the measured flour.

6 Do not over-whisk whites; they should be stiff but not too dry.

7 Test your oven with a thermometer from time to time. As a rule bake cakes in the centre of the oven, having pre-heated it accordingly.

8 Plain cakes are cooked in a hotter oven than rich mixtures.

9 Try not to open the oven door once the cake has been put in. If you must open it, shut it again very gently.

10 Test a cake for readiness by inserting a poultry skewer in the centre. If the cake is done, it will come out clean. The cake will also be springy when touched, and may have begun to shrink very slightly from the sides of the tin.

11 Follow cooling directions carefully. Most cakes are best cooled on a rack. Some, however, must be cooled in the tin before being turned out. Never turn out a cake and cool it on a hard board or table; it will become soggy.

PLAIN BUNS AND CAKES

BASIC PLAIN BUNS

1 lb flour
½ teasp salt
4–6 oz fat (butter, margarine *or* all purpose fat, alone *or* mixed
3 rounded teasp baking powder *or* 1 teasp bicarbonate of soda plus 2 teasp cream of tartar (*or* vinegar)

4 oz sugar
2 eggs
1–1½ gills milk, to make a stiffish mixture
Flavouring or additions as in variations below

Basic buns

Sift the flour, salt and baking powder into a bowl, cut in the fat with a round-bladed knife, then rub in with the finger-tips only, raising the hands to let the mixture fall back into the bowl. Then add sugar and stir in lightly with a fork. Add any powdered flavouring.

Mix the eggs and a little milk in a bowl or jug. Make a hole in the centre of the dry ingredients and pour in the liquid. Mix well with the fork. Add more milk if needed, but the fork should still stand upright in the mixture without being held. Use a dessertsp to place the mixture in small heaps on a greased or lined baking sheet. Bake in a hot oven (220°C, 425°F, Gas 7) for 10–15 min until springy and browned.

24–32 buns

NOTES
1 You can use self-raising flour for buns if you omit the raising agent (baking powder, etc).

2 You can use dripping as the fat for plain buns, nut buns, oaten buns, rock buns, seed buns, or spiced buns. Use 6 oz.

3 You can sprinkle the buns with crushed loaf sugar before baking if you wish.

VARIATIONS
Cinnamon Buns Add 2 level teasp ground cinnamon with the flour.

Chocolate Buns Add 1–1½ oz cocoa with the flour and 1 teasp vanilla essence with the milk.

Coconut Buns Mix in 4 oz desiccated coconut with the sugar.

Coffee Buns Add 2 level teasp powdered 'instant' coffee to the milk and whisk in well before adding to the mixture.

Fruit Buns Add 2 oz chopped glacé cherries, currants or sultanas (or a mixture of them) with the sugar.

Ginger Buns Add 2 small teasp ground ginger to the flour and add 4 oz chopped or grated crystallized ginger with the sugar.

Jam or Marmalade Buns Form the basic mixture into 24 balls. Make a 'thimble' or finger hole in

each, and place a little jam or marmalade in the hole. Close the opening, brush with glaze and sprinkle with crushed loaf sugar. Apricot or raspberry jam or coarse-cut marmalade have the best flavours. (If the hole is left open, these buns are called Thimble Buns or cookies.)

Lemon or Orange Buns Add 1 teasp grated lemon or orange rind to the flour. Replace 1 tablesp milk with lemon or orange juice; or add ¼ teasp lemon or orange essence to the milk before adding it to the mixture. If you wish, turn the mixture on to a floured board, form it into a roll, and cut it into 24 slices. Roll each slice lightly into a ball, and place on the baking tray. Brush with egg yolk, cream or milk glaze, and/or sprinkle with crushed loaf sugar.

London Buns (sometimes called Johnny Cakes) Add 2 oz chopped peel and 2 teasp grated lemon rind when adding the sugar, and form the mixture into balls as for lemon buns. Glaze and sprinkle with crushed loaf sugar. Place 2 pieces of candied lemon or orange peel on each bun.

Nut Buns Add 4 oz chopped nuts when adding the sugar.

Oaten Buns Use rolled oats instead of half the flour, and add 1½ tablesp chopped, stoned raisins with the sugar.

Rock Buns Add 4–6 oz currants and 2 oz chopped peel when adding the sugar. Make the mixture a little stiffer than usual.

Seed Buns Add 2 dessertsp caraway seeds with the sugar.

Spiced Buns Add 2 teasp mixed ground cinnamon and nutmeg or 2 teasp mixed spice when sifting the flour. You can add a pinch of ground coriander, ginger or mace as well if you like.

VICTORIA BUNS

10 oz plain flour	2 teasp golden syrup
¼ teasp salt	2 teasp treacle
3–4 oz sugar	4 oz butter *or*
2 small teasp ground	margarine
cinnamon	2 eggs
⅛ teasp grated nutmeg	Enough warm milk to
1 level teasp	make a pouring
bicarbonate of soda	consistency

DECORATION
Blanched almonds

Grease queen cake or deep patty tins and place a half blanched almond in the bottom of each. Mix all dry ingredients in a bowl, heat the fat, syrup and treacle and add to dry ingredients with the beaten eggs. Add enough warm milk to make a pouring consistency. Half-fill the prepared tins and bake in a moderate oven (180°C, 350°F, Gas 4).

26–30 buns   Cooking time 20–30 min

BASIC PLAIN CAKE

Average proportions of basic ingredients are:

1 lb plain flour
½ teasp salt
4–8 oz fat (*see* **Ingredients used in Cake Making**)
4–8 oz sugar or other sweetening (*see* **Ingredients used in Cake Making**)
2–4 teasp raising agent, e.g.
   3 teasp baking powder, *or*
   1 teasp bicarbonate of soda plus 2 teasp cream of tartar or vinegar, *or*
   1–2 teasp bicarbonate of soda without cream of tartar for brown cakes and gingerbreads
2–4 eggs

Flavouring and decoration are described in the Trimmings, Sauces and Flavourings section.

PLAIN APPLE CAKE

½ lb plain flour	¼ teasp ground
2 teasp baking powder	cinnamon
¼ teasp salt	¼ teasp nutmeg
2 tablesp sugar	1 lb cooking apples,
1½ oz margarine	peeled, cored and
1 egg, beaten with about	sliced thinly
¼ pt milk	**Sugar glaze**
1 oz butter	**Chopped nuts**
3 tablesp soft brown	
sugar	

Sift together the flour, baking powder, salt and sugar. Rub in the margarine. Beat the egg and milk together, and stir into the flour mixture. Stir quickly, to make a soft dough. Mix the 1 oz butter, sugar and spices. Spread this mixture over the base of an oblong tin about 11 × 7 in and 1 in deep. Cover the mixture with apple slices. Cover the apple slices with dough, and pat down flat. Bake at 180°C, 350°F, Gas 4 for about 45 min or until cake is brown and springy. Brush with the sugar glaze and follow with the nuts. Serve cold as a cake, although you can also serve it hot for high tea with whipped cream.

6–8 helpings

LUNCH CAKE

8 oz plain flour	¾ teasp ground
⅛ teasp salt	cinnamon
3 oz butter *or* lard	¾ teasp mixed spice
and margarine	3 oz currants
4 oz sugar	2 oz raisins
½ level teasp cream	1½ oz shredded peel
of tartar	2 eggs
Small ¼ teasp ground	Milk to mix
cloves	1 level teasp
	bicarbonate of soda

Sift flour and salt; rub the fat into the flour. Add other dry ingredients to flour. Beat eggs and add with milk to make a dropping consistency. Place in a greased 7 in tin and bake in the middle of a fairly

Plain orange cake

hot oven (190°C, 375°F, Gas 5) for 15 min, then reduce heat to moderate (180°C, 350°F, Gas 4).

Cooking time 1½ hr

PLAIN ORANGE OR SPICE CAKE

8 oz plain flour	1 egg
¼ teasp salt	1–1½ gills milk *or*
3 oz margarine	1 dessertsp fresh
1 teasp mixed spice *or*	orange juice with
1 dessertsp grated	enough milk to make
orange peel (orange	a soft dropping
cake)	consistency (orange
3 oz castor sugar	cake)
1½ teasp baking powder	

Grease the sides of a 6 in cake tin with a dusting of flour and castor sugar. Line the bottom of the tin with silicone-treated paper or with greaseproof paper well greased.

Apple cake

LARGE RICH CAKE

Sift the flour, salt and spice if used into a bowl. Cut in the fat with a round-bladed knife, then rub in lightly with the finger-tips until it is fine and crumblike. Add the sugar and baking powder, and the grated orange peel if used. Mix about half the milk or the orange juice and ½ milk with the egg. Pour this mixture into the dry ingredients, and add more milk as required to make a soft dropping consistency. Put into the cake tin, and bake in a fairly hot oven (190°C, 375°F, Gas 5) until risen, brown and springy. This will take between 45 min and 1 hr.

You can make this cake with self-raising flour and no baking powder if you prefer.

RICH CAKES

BASIC LARGE RICH CAKE

Average proportions of basic ingredients are:

½–1 lb fat of a type suited to recipe (see Ingredients for Cake Making above)
½–1 lb sugar or other sweetener (see Ingredients for Cake Making above)
4–12 eggs as recipe requires
1 lb plain flour
½ teasp salt
2–4 teasp baking powder or other raising agent, depending on the number of eggs used
Flavouring (see flavourings in the Trimmings, Sauces and Flavourings section)
½–1 lb fruit, if used, as recipe requires
Milk, water, buttermilk, fruit juice or purée, etc to mix, as recipe requires

The more 'melting' ingredients (e.g. fat, sugar) there are, the stiffer the mixture should be.

FOR A 7-in CAKE

6 oz butter *or* margarine   ⅛ teasp salt
6 oz castor sugar   2 level teasp baking
3 eggs   powder or other
8 oz plain flour   raising agents
Milk to mix

Line a 7-in cake tin with greaseproof paper or foil, greased, or with silicone-treated paper. Cream the fat, add the sugar gradually and beat until white and fluffy. Beat in the eggs, one at a time, making sure each is blended in thoroughly before adding the

Birthday cake

next. Sift in a little of the flour if the mixture shows any signs of curdling. Sift in the flour, salt and baking powder gradually, and stir in lightly with a spoon. Add enough milk to make a fairly soft batter. Turn into the cake tin, and bake at 180°C, 350°F, Gas 4 for 1–1½ hr or until the cake is springy and brown on top.

If you want to use any of the variations below containing dried fruit, add the eggs to the creamed mixture alternately with the flour divided into 3 parts. Probably no other liquid will be needed, and the cake will be close-textured enough to hold the fruit.

VARIATIONS OF BASIC RECIPE
CHOCOLATE CAKE, LIGHT

Use 2 oz cocoa instead of 2 oz flour, or add 1 oz melted chocolate after the eggs.

FRUIT CAKE

Add 6–8 oz sultanas, currants, raisins or dates to basic mixture. Add eggs and flour alternately. Stir in fruit mixed with some of the flour *after* eggs have been added

GINGER CAKE

Sift ½ teasp ground ginger with the flour, add 2–4 oz coarsely chopped crystallized ginger with the flour.

LEMON CAKE

Add the grated rind of 2 lemons with the flour. The cake can be iced when cold with lemon glacé icing.

MADEIRA CAKE

Add the grated rind of 1 lemon with the flour. Place 2 strips of candied citron peel on top of the cake when mixture has begun to set (after about 30 min)

SEED CAKE

Add 2 teasp caraway seeds with the flour.

BIRTHDAY CAKE
(1 FRUIT and 2 BUTTER SPONGE)

Ingredients for (1)
4 oz butter *or* margarine   1 level teasp mixed
4 oz soft brown sugar   spice
1½ oz golden syrup   11 oz mixed fruit—
2 eggs   sultanas, currants,
6 oz plain flour   glacé cherries
⅛ teasp salt   2 oz candied peel *or*
1 level teasp baking   marmalade
    powder   ½ gill milk (approx)

For the older child, a birthday cake should be a fruit cake.

Line a 6–7 in cake tin. Cream fat, sugar and syrup thoroughly. Whisk eggs and add alternately with the sifted flour, salt and baking powder, beating well with each addition. Add remaining ingredients and fruit, which has been mixed with a little of the flour. Mix to a fairly soft consistency with milk and place in the cake tin. Bake for ½ hr in a moderate oven (180°C, 350°F, Gas 4) and a further 2–2½ hr in a cool oven (150–140°C, 310–290°F, Gas 2–1).

For a younger child, a 'butter sponge' birthday cake is more suitable than a fruit cake. A most attractive cake can be made from enough of the basic Butter Sponge Cake (2) mixture to fill 3 7-in sandwich tins. One third of the mixture should be coloured with a few drops of food colouring before being put in its tin; and, after baking, it should be 'sandwiched' between the other two layers, to make a coloured layer between them.

A birthday cake is usually coated with almond paste and decorated with royal icing. But it can also be decorated most successfully with a butter icing (*see* Icings and Fillings).

Cooking time about 3 hr (fruit cake) 40 min (butter sponge)

CHRISTMAS CAKE

8 oz butter *or* margarine	5–6 eggs
8 oz castor sugar	1 lb currants
½ teasp gravy browning	8 oz raisins
8 oz plain flour	4 oz glacé cherries
⅛ teasp salt	2 oz chopped peel
1 level teasp mixed spice	4 oz blanched, chopped almonds
½ level teasp baking powder	Milk, if necessary
	4–5 tablesp brandy (optional)

Line an 8 in cake tin with greaseproof paper.

Cream the fat and sugar until white; add gravy browning. Sift together flour, salt, mixed spice and baking powder. Add egg and flour alternately to the creamed fat, beating well between each addition. Stir in the prepared fruit, almonds and (if necessary) add a little milk to make a heavy dropping consistency. Place the mixture in the cake tin and tie a piece of paper round the outside of the tin. Smooth the mixture and make a depression in the centre. Bake in a warm oven (170°C, 335°F, Gas 3) for ½ hr, then reduce heat to 150°C, 290°F, Gas 1 for a further 3–3½ hr. Allow to firm before removing from tin and when cold remove paper. Prick bottom of cake well and sprinkle brandy over it. Leave for a few days before icing (*see* Icings).

Cooking time 4 hr

COFFEE WALNUT CAKE

4 oz margarine	4 oz self-raising flour
4 oz castor sugar	2 oz chopped walnuts
2 eggs	Coffee glacé icing
1 tablesp coffee essence	

Coffee walnut cake

Cream together the margarine and castor sugar until light and fluffy. Gradually add the beaten eggs, beating well between additions. Stir in coffee essence and fold in sifted flour, together with chopped walnuts. Turn mixture into a deep 7 in sandwich tin, well greased, and bake at 190°C, 375°F, Gas 5 for 25–30 min. Cool on a rack. Decorate with Coffee Glacé Icing and walnut halves.

DUNDEE CAKE

7 oz butter *or* margarine	3–4 eggs
7 oz castor sugar	1 level teasp baking powder

(*continued on Page 186 at top of Column 1.*)

Christmas cake

DUNDEE CAKE

¾ lb plain flour	Milk *or* water as
¼ teasp salt	required
12–16 oz mixed fruit—	Blanched almonds
currants, raisins,	
sultanas	

Line a 7–8 in cake tin with greaseproof paper (oiled). Cream the fat and sugar till light. Sift together flour and salt and mix the fruit with a small amount of the flour. Add the eggs and flour alternately to the creamed fat, beating well between each addition. Mix the baking powder in with the last batch of flour, stir in the fruit and if necessary add a little milk *or* water to make a heavy dropping consistency. Put into the tin, make a slight depression in the centre and spread some split blanched almonds over the surface. Bake in a moderate oven (180°C, 350°F, Gas 4); reduce heat after ¾ hr from warm to cool (170–150°C, 335–310°F, Gas 3–2).

Cooking time 2½ hr

HAZLENUT CAKE

3 oz butter *or*	12 oz self-raising flour
margarine	¼ teasp salt
5 oz sugar	4 oz hazelnuts
2 eggs	Milk as required

Line a 7 in cake tin with greaseproof paper. Cream the fat, add the sugar and beat well till light and white. Beat in each egg very thoroughly. Sift together the flour and salt; pass the nuts through a nut mill. Add to the mixture the flour, nuts and enough milk to make a fairly soft dough. Put the mixture into the cake tin and bake in a fairly hot oven (190°C, 375°F, Gas 5), reduce heat to warm (170°C, 335°F, Gas 3) after 30 min.

Cooking time 1¼–1½ hr

SAND CAKE

4 oz butter *or*	Pinch of salt
margarine	½ level teasp baking
Grated rind of 1 lemon	powder
4 oz castor sugar	Ratafia *or* macaroon
2 large eggs	crumbs (optional)
4 oz cornflour	
½ oz ground rice	

Grease a border mould or 6 in cake tin and if liked, coat with ratafia or macaroon biscuit crumbs *or* with equal quantities of castor sugar and flour.

Cream the fat with the lemon rind; add the sugar and cream again. Beat the eggs and add them gradually, beating well between each addition. Sift together the cornflower, ground rice, salt and baking powder. Add the flour lightly to the creamed fat, ⅓ at a time, and put the mixture into the mould. Bake in a moderate oven (180–170°C, 350–335°F, Gas 4–3).

Cooking time about 1 hr

SIMNEL CAKE

Mixture: as for Birthday Cake or any other fruit cake
Almond paste: 6 oz ground almonds, etc
Glacé icing: 2 oz icing sugar, etc

Line a 6–7 in cake tin thickly. Cut off about ⅓ of the almond paste and roll out into a round slightly less than the diameter of the tin to be used. Place ½ the cake mixture in the tin, cover with a round of almond paste and place the remaining cake mixture on top. Bake in a moderate oven (180°C, 350°F, Gas 4) for ½ hr, reduce heat to cool (150–140°C, 310–290°F, Gas 2–1) for 2–2½ hr. Leave for 24 hr. Using about ½

the remaining almond paste, cover the top of the cake. With the remainder, make small balls and place these at even intervals round top edge of the cake. Brush them over with egg wash. Tie a band of greaseproof paper tightly round the top of the cake. Place in a hot oven until the balls are nicely browned. When cool, pour glacé icing into the centre of the cake and decoarate as required with almond paste eggs, small chicks, etc.

This cake used to be served on Mother's Day but is now usually served on Easter Sunday.

Cooking time about 3 hr

SPICED FRUIT UPSIDE-DOWN CAKE

4 oz butter	1 lb self-raising flour
12 oz brown sugar	1 teasp cinnamon
1 large can pineapple	1 teasp nutmeg
slices	2 eggs
10 maraschino cherries	½ cup milk

Melt half the butter in the baking tin; add half the sugar; stir until dissolved. Drain the pineapple slices and arrange in a neat pattern on this caramel coating. Place a cherry in the centre hole of each pineapple slice. Sift together the flour and spices. Beat the eggs with the remaining brown sugar and add milk and remaining butter, melted; stir into the spiced flour. Pour this mixture over pineapple in tin. Bake in a moderate oven (180°C, 350°F, Gas 4) for 45–50 min. Remove the tin from the oven and invert on to a serving plate; leave the tin on for a few min so that the caramel will run down over the cake and not stick to the tin.

Remove the tin and serve the cake warm with cream.

APRICOT OR PEACH UPSIDE-DOWN CAKE

Use drained, canned apricot or peach halves instead of pineapple slices, flavour with vanilla essence and omit spices.

PEAR AND GINGER UPSIDE-DOWN CAKE

Flavour the cake with ½ teasp ground ginger instead of cinnamon and nutmeg.

Use drained, canned pear halves instead of pineapple slices. Place them cut side down in the tin with ½ a maraschino cherry in each core hollow. Sprinkle chopped crystallized ginger over the caramel before pouring in the cake mixture.

WEDDING CAKE

NOTE. These quantities are sufficient for a 3-tier cake.

3–3¼ lb flour	24 large eggs
¼ teasp salt	5½ lb currants
3 level teasp ground	2 lb sultanas
cinnamon	1–1½ lb glacé cherries
3 level teasp ground	1–1¼ lb mixed
mace	chopped peel
1 nutmeg (grated)	Rind and juice of 1
1½ teasp baking	lemon
powder	½–1 lb blanched
3 lb butter	chopped almonds
3 lb castor sugar	1½ gills rum *or* brandy
1½ teasp gravy	*or* rum and brandy
browning	

Prepare and line 3 cake tins, one 12 in diameter, one 8 in, and one 4 in diameter.

Sift together the flour, salt, spices and baking powder. Mix together all the fruit with a little of the measured flour. Cream the butter and the sugar very well; add the browning. Add egg and flour altern-

*Three-tier
Wedding cake*

ately to the creamed fat beating well between each addition. Stir in the prepared fruit, almonds and brandy. Divide $\frac{1}{2}$ of the mixture between the 2 smaller tins, and put the remaining $\frac{1}{2}$ of the mixture in the biggest tin. Tie a thick band of brown paper round the outside of each tin. Smooth the mixture and make a depression in the centre of each cake. Bake the 4 in cake for 2–3 hr, the 8 in cake for $3\frac{1}{2}$–4 hr, and the 12 in cake for 5–6 hr. Put in a cool oven (150°C, 310°F, Gas 2) for the first $\frac{1}{2}$ hr, then reduce heat to very cool (140–130°C, 290–240°F, Gas 1–$\frac{1}{2}$) for the remainder of the time.

To cover the 4 in cake with almond paste about 1 lb ground almonds etc will be required; 2 lb ground almonds etc for the 8 in cake and 3 lb ground almonds, etc for the 12 in cake.

For the royal icing use 1 lb sifted icing sugar, etc, for the 4 in cake, 2 lb for the 8 in cake and 3 lb sugar, etc, for the 12 in cake.

Transparent icing cooled may be poured over as a last layer, if liked. For the 4 in cake use 1–1$\frac{1}{2}$ lb loaf sugar, etc, for the 8 in cake use 3 lb sugar, etc, and for the 12 in cake 4 lb sugar, etc.

The decoration of each cake is then completed upon silver boards (of correct size) each covered with a lace d'oyley. The cake is then assembled by placing one cake on top of the other with pillars supporting them. The pillars for the bottom tier should be 3 in in height and for the top the pillars should be 4 in high. Place a silver vase containing white flowers on top.

BUTTER SPONGE AND SPONGE CAKES

True sponges contain little or no fat. This type of cake containing butter is the one most used for sandwich cakes, e.g. Victoria Sandwich cake. It can be baked as one cake and then split across through the centre, or in two sandwich tins. In either case, each tin must be lined on the bottom and greased; it is then usually dusted with flour or castor sugar (*see* Preparing Tins and Sheets, under All Cakes and Buns).

BASIC "BUTTER SPONGE" CAKE
(1 With self-raising flour)

2 oz butter *or* margarine	Pinch of salt
3 oz castor sugar	$\frac{1}{2}$ level teasp baking powder
2 eggs	1–2 dessertsp cold
3 oz self-raising flour	water to mix

Make like the Victoria Sandwich cake below, using a 6 in tin.

This is quite a close-textured mixture. A double quantity, baked in an 8 or 9 in square tin, can be cut into small squares, diamonds, etc, which can be iced in different colours as petits fours or children's party cakes.

BASIC "BUTTER SPONGE" CAKE
(2 With plain flour)

3 oz butter *or* margarine	4$\frac{1}{2}$ oz plain flour
	Pinch of salt

VICTORIA SANDWICH CAKE

4½ oz castor sugar	2 level teasp baking
3 eggs	powder

Make like the Victoria Sandwich cake below using an 8-in sandwich tin. Cook for 50–60 min.

This is a little looser in texture than the cake above.

BASIC VICTORIA SANDWICH CAKE

4 oz butter *or*	4 oz plain flour
margarine	Pinch of salt
4 oz castor sugar	1½ level teasp baking
2 eggs	powder

Cream fat and sugar very thoroughly. Add well-whisked eggs gradually beating well between each addition. If the mixture shows any signs of curdling, add some flour. Sift flour, salt and baking powder and fold lightly into the creamed mixture. Mix to a soft dropping consistency, by adding a little warm water if necessary. Place the mixture in a prepared 7-in sandwich tin and bake in a moderate oven (180°C, 350°F, Gas 4).

Cooking time 40–45 min

BATTENBURG CAKE

2 Victoria sandwich cakes made in oblong tins, one white and the other coloured pink (see 'All Cakes and Buns' above)
1 tablesp apricot glaze
Almond paste, using 3 oz ground almonds, etc

Coffee walnut layer cake

DECORATION

Glacé cherries	Angelica

Cut the cake into strips 8–9 in long and 1½ in square; 2 pink and 2 white pieces will be needed. Join these together with apricot glaze to make a block 9 × 3 × 3 in, with a pink and a white strip side by side, topped with a white strip and a pink one respectively. Roll the almond paste into an oblong, wide enough and long enough to wrap round the cake leaving the ends open. Trim the edges of the almond paste. Spread the top of the cake with apricot glaze and invert on to almond paste. Spread the remaining three sides with glaze, roll up firmly and join almond paste neatly. To decorate, pinch the two top edges between thumb and forefinger. Mark the top of the cake lattice fashion with a knife and decorate with cherries and angelica.

COFFEE WALNUT LAYER CAKE

4 oz butter *or* margarine	3 tablesp milk
4 oz castor sugar	American frosting *or*
2 eggs	fondant icing, half of
8 oz plain flour	it flavoured with
1 teasp baking powder	coffee
2 teasp "instant" coffee powder	Walnut halves

Cream the fat and sugar until very light. Add the eggs one at a time with a dessertsp of the flour, and beat well. Sift the flour, baking powder and coffee powder, and fold lightly into the mixture alternately with the milk. Pour into two greased or lined sandwich tins, and spread evenly. Bake in a fairly hot oven (190°C, 375°F, Gas 5) for 35–40 min, until firm. Cool.

Scrape the bottom and top of the two cakes if very brown, and sandwich them together with the coffee-flavoured icing. Spread the rest of the icing on the top and sides, and decorate with walnut halves.

LEMON OR ORANGE SANDWICH CAKE

1 basic 'butter sponge' cake (2)	Crystallised lemon *or* orange slices
Lemon *or* orange-flavoured butter icing	

Cut cake through the centre and spread with flavoured butter icing. Sandwich together again. Spread the top of the cake with icing, smooth with a knife and finally decorate with slices of crystallised fruit.

A more pronounced flavour may be obtained by adding the finely grated rind of 1 lemon or orange when mixing the cake.

BASIC LARGE SPONGE CAKE

4 oz plain flour	4½ oz castor sugar
Pinch of salt	Grated lemon rind
3 eggs	

Grease and dust a 6 in tin with 1 teasp flour and 1 teasp castor sugar mixed together. Sift the flour and salt. Beat the eggs and sugar over a pan of hot water till thick and creamy. Fold flour, salt and lemon lightly into the egg and turn the mixture into the tin. Bake in a warm oven (170°C, 335°F, Gas 3). When cold, split the sponge and spread with jam. Dust with icing sugar.

This may be cooked in a border mould or tube pan if to be used as the base of a sweet.

Cooking time 45 min

ANGEL CAKE

2 oz flour	$\frac{1}{2}$ teasp cream of
4$\frac{1}{2}$ oz castor sugar	tartar
$\frac{1}{4}$ pt egg whites	$\frac{1}{2}$ teasp vanilla essence
Pinch of salt	

Use a 6 in sandwich cake tin or a tube pan, *not* greased. Sift the flour and sugar separately three times, then sift the flour with $\frac{1}{4}$ of the sugar. Put the egg white and salt in a large, clean, dry bowl and whisk until frothy. Sprinkle on the cream of tartar and continue whisking till the white stands up in peaks. Avoid overwhisking so that the white loses its glossiness. Lightly beat in the sugar and flavouring, then using a tablespoon fold in the sifted flour and sugar carefully and gradually. Pour into the tin and gently cut through mixture with a knife to release air bubbles. Bake for 40–45 min in a very cool oven (140°C, 290°F, Gas 1) increasing the heat to (170°C, 335°F, Gas 3) for the last 10–15 min. Allow the cake to stand in the inverted tin for 30 min then turn out on to a cooling tray.

SWISS ROLL

3 oz plain flour	3 oz castor sugar
Pinch of salt	$\frac{1}{4}$ teasp vanilla essence
1 level teasp baking	2 tablesp raspberry
powder	jam
3 fresh eggs	

Line and grease a Swiss roll tin.

Sift flour, salt and baking powder. Beat eggs and sugar in a bowl over a pan of hot water till very thick and pale in colour. Use an electric beater if possible. Do not let the bottom of the bowl touch the water. Lightly fold in the flour, etc and add the vanilla essence. Spread on the tin and bake in a hot oven (220°C, 425°F, Gas 7). Quick cooking is essential to keep the roll moist. Sprinkle castor sugar on a sheet of kitchen paper, turn the roll on to this and cut halfway through the roll about 1 in from the bottom end. Spread the roll with warm jam to within $\frac{1}{2}$ in of edge. Turn in the 1 in at the bottom to make the initial roll and continue to roll up firmly with the aid of the kitchen paper. Press gently to keep in place. Remove paper and dust with castor sugar. (A very *lightly* damped clean tea cloth may be used instead of paper.)

If the edges are crisp it is advisable to trim them

Jam Swiss roll

before rolling or the roll may crack.

Cooking time 7 min

CHOCOLATE SWISS ROLL

As for Swiss roll, with the addition of 2–3 teasp cocoa sifted with the flour.

When the roll is cooked, turn on to sugared paper, place a piece of greaseproof paper on top and roll up. When the roll has cooled, unroll it gently and spread with vanilla butter icing. Roll up again. Dust with castor sugar.

MISCELLANEOUS LARGE CAKES AND GÂTEAUX

APRICOT GÂTEAU

1 round of Genoese pastry (*see* Genoese pastry below) 6 in diameter and 1 in thick	2 tablesp sieved apricot jam
2 tablesp sherry *or* fruit juice	A length of 1 in wide pale coloured ribbon to tie round the sponge fingers (about 12 in)
2 doz soft textured sponge finger biscuits	

FILLING

1 large can apricots	$\frac{3}{4}$ pt double cream
$\frac{1}{2}$ pt lemon jelly tablet	Castor sugar to taste

DECORATION
Angelica

Place the round of cake on a serving plate and sprinkle with the sherry or juice. Trim the sponge

Orange sandwich

LINZERTORTE

fingers so that the sides are quite straight and all are equal in length, with one end trimmed straight across. Melt the $\frac{1}{2}$ pt jelly tablet in $\frac{1}{4}$ pt of apricot juice and allow to cool, but not set. Brush inside of trimmed end of each sponge finger to 1-in in depth with sieved apricot jam; dip one edge only in cool jelly, and press firmly against the side of the round of cake. As each finger is so treated, the jellied edge will be in contact with the dry edge of the adjacent finger, and a firm case will be made without the fingers becoming sodden and crumbling. The rounded, sugary surface of the finger faces outwards. Tie the ribbon round the finished case so that the sponge fingers are held firmly upright, and leave to set.

FILLING Drain the apricots well, and reserve halves for decoration. Cut the remainder into quarters. Whip the cream until the fork leaves a trail; sweeten to taste with castor sugar. Put $\frac{1}{4}$ of the cream into a forcing bag with rose pipe, for decorating (optional). Stir the quartered apricots into the remainder of the cream. Lastly trickle in $\frac{1}{8}$ pt of the hot liquid jelly, stirring all the time. Pour immediately into the sponge-finger case. Arrange the 6 apricot halves (either whole or cut as liked) on the top, and pipe cream roses between and around to cover the surface of the cream. Decorate with leaves of angelica.

VARIATIONS Use fresh or canned strawberries, or chopped pineapple, or fruit-flavoured ice cream, or confectioners' custard filling.

LINZERTORTE

5 oz butter	Juice and rind of $\frac{1}{2}$
2 eggs	lemon
5 oz castor sugar	5 oz sifted flour
Pinch of powdered cloves	6 oz raspberries or redcurrants, well
Pinch of ground cinnamon	sugared or raspberry jam
$\frac{1}{4}$ lb finely chopped almonds	

Beat the butter until white and creamy. Beat together one egg and one egg white and add slowly to the butter together with the sugar, cloves, cinnamon, almonds, lemon juice and grated lemon rind. Sift in the flour and work into a dough. Grease a 9 in tart or flan tin and put the dough in, about $\frac{1}{4}$ in thick, without raising the edge. Form the rest of the dough into long strips or into a number of small leaf shapes cut out with a knife. Paint the edge of the tart with the remaining egg yolk and stick a piece of pastry round it to form an edge, or using the leaves, stick them overlapping all round the edge of the tart. Spread the sugared raspberries or jam in the centre of the tart and cover them with a lattice of the long strips of pastry, sticking them at the edges with egg yolk; or, if leaves are being used, form a lattice by putting 4 leaves together at right-angles in groups over the pastry. Paint the lattice and edge of the tart with egg yolk and bake about 45 min in a hot oven (220°C, 425°F, Gas 7). Cover with greaseproof paper if the tart gets too brown.

6 helpings

MOCHA GÂTEAU

4 oz butter (preferably unsalted)	4 oz melted plain chocolate
10 oz castor sugar	$\frac{1}{4}$ pt cold strong black coffee
4 eggs	

10 oz self-raising flour	$\frac{1}{2}$ pt double cream
1 small teasp salt	American frosting Chocolate glaze

Combine butter, sugar and yolks of eggs and cream thoroughly. Sift flour and salt together and add gradually to the mixture, together with the coffee and melted chocolate. Lastly fold in the stiffly-beaten egg whites. Pour the mixture into a well greased and lined round 9 in cake tin. Bake in a moderate oven, at 180°C, 350°F, Gas 4 until cooked. This takes about 1 hr. When cold, cover all over with American frosting and drizzle with chocolate glaze.

SCOTTISH SHORTBREAD

8 oz flour	4 oz butter
2 oz castor sugar	

Put the flour and sugar in a pile on a pastryboard. Gradually knead the sugared flour into the butter with your hand without breaking up the butter. When a firm dough is formed, roll out and shape into a cake about 1-in high. Decorate the edges by marking with a fork or fluting with finger and thumb, or make in a shortbread mould, and prick a pattern on top with a fork or skewer. Fasten a narrow band of paper round to keep the cake in shape. Bake in a warm to cool oven (170–150°C, 335–310°F, Gas 3–2). Dredge with castor sugar when cooked.

Cooking time about 1 hr

STRAWBERRY SHORTCAKE

8 oz plain flour	$4\frac{1}{2}$ oz margarine
$\frac{1}{8}$ teasp salt	2 oz sugar
Pinch of baking powder	1 egg yolk
$\frac{1}{2}$ oz ground almonds	

FILLING
1 pt strawberries	1–2 gills whipped
Sugar to taste	cream

Sift flour, salt and baking powder and mix with the ground almonds. Cream the fat and sugar and add egg yolk. Work in the flour mixture as for a cake of shortbread. Divide into three pieces and roll into rounds a good $\frac{1}{4}$-in thick. Bake in a moderate oven (180°C, 350°F, Gas 4) until golden-brown, then allow to become cold. Crush strawberries slightly with sugar to taste and add a little whipped cream. Spread this on to the first round of shortcake, cover with the second round and so on, finishing with a layer of strawberries. Pipe whipped cream on top and round the edges. Decorate as desired.

1 Self-raising flour can be used, without the baking powder.
2 Pears make a good addition to the strawberries. Slice the peeled pears, poach them and drain well before using.

Cooking time 30–40 min

SMALL CAKES

For small plain cakes, see the variations suggested under Basic Plain Buns. Small 'butter sponge' cakes can be cut from the Basic 'Butter Sponge' Cake (1) mixture, baked in a square or oblong tin, as described in All Cakes and Buns. Small sponge cakes, rich cakes, meringue-style cakes, and cakes and tartlets made with short crust and other kinds of pastry are mentioned below. Flavourings for these are described in Section Nine, and the illustrations show ways of decorating cakes.

Pear and strawberry shortcake

BASIC SMALL SPONGE CAKES

3 oz plain flour	1 level teasp baking
Pinch of salt	powder
3 eggs	½ teasp vanilla essence
3 oz sugar	

Make like the Basic Large Sponge Cake. Put the mixture into oblong sponge cake tins prepared by greasing and dusting with equal quantities of flour and castor sugar. Half-fill the tins and dredge the tops with castor sugar. Bake in a moderate oven (180–170°C, 350–335°F, Gas 4–3) until well risen, firm and a pale fawn colour.

10–12 cakes   **Cooking time 20 min**

BASIC SMALL 'RICH' CAKES

The following is a suitable mixture for all these small cakes and can be varied in many ways.

BASIC RECIPE

2 oz butter *or* margarine	Pinch of salt
2 oz castor sugar	Water *or* milk as
1 egg	required
3 oz self-raising flour *or*	
3 oz plain flour and	
1 level teasp baking	
powder	

Beat the fat and sugar until creamy and white. Whisk the egg and add gradually; beat well between each addition. Sift together the flour, salt and baking powder. Gently stir the flour, etc, into the creamed fat; add milk or water to make a soft dropping consistency. Half-fill greased bun tins with the mixture and bake in a fairly hot to moderate oven (190–180°C, 375–350°F, Gas 5–4).

NOTE. This mixture can be baked in paper cases and

191

decorated with glacé icing or cherries.

10–12 cakes   Cooking time 15–20 min

VARIATIONS OF BASIC RECIPE
Cherry Cakes
Add 1–2 oz coarsely chopped glacé cherries with the flour.

Chocolate Cakes
Sift $\frac{1}{2}$ oz cocoa with the flour, and add a few drops of vanilla essence with the water or milk. The cakes can be iced with chocolate glacé icing.

Coconut Cakes
Add $\frac{1}{2}$ oz coconut with the flour and add $\frac{1}{4}$ teasp vanilla essence with the milk or water.

Lemon or Orange Cakes
Add the grated rind of 1 lemon or orange with the flour, and ice with lemon or orange glacé icing.

Madeleines
Bake the basic mixture in greased dariole or castle pudding moulds. Turn out when baked; cool. Spread all round, top and side, with warmed apricot jam. Roll in desiccated coconut and decorate with $\frac{1}{2}$ glacé cherry.

Nut Cakes
Add 1–2 oz coarsely chopped walnuts, almonds or hazelnuts, with the flour.

Queen Cakes
Add 1–2 oz currants *or* sultanas with the flour, or a few currants may be placed in the bottom of each queen cake tin and the mixture placed on top.

BUTTERFLY ORANGE CAKES
The basic mixture for small rich cakes, flavoured with orange, and cooked in greased bouchée tins
1 gill sweetened cream, flavoured with orange liqueur *or* essence
A little apricot jam

Cut a thin slice from the top of each cake. Cut each slice in two, to make two wings. Dredge with icing sugar. Spread the cut top of each cake with a little jam, pipe a rosette of whipped cream on this, and place the wings in position.

10–12 cakes

MERINGUES
2 egg whites	$\frac{1}{4}$ pt sweetened,
Pinch of salt	whipped cream *or*
4 oz castor sugar	fruit as below

Put the egg whites and salt in a mixer bowl which must be clean, dry and free of grease. Using an electric or rotary whisk, beat until stiff but not dry. Whisk in half the sugar until just incorporated, then fold in the remainder by hand. Put the mixture in spoonfuls on a baking tray lined with greaseproof paper, brushed lightly with cooking oil. Dust the meringues with castor sugar. Cook at the lowest possible oven setting for 4 to 5 hr until firm and crisp but still white. Cool and store. Do not fill with cream until serving time.

The egg whites or the cream, or both, can be coloured with a drop or two of food colouring.

For fruit meringues, pipe circular bases with a forcing bag. Then pipe around the edge of each to build a wall of meringue. Bake as above. When cold, fill these meringue shells with a mixture of the following fruits: 2 ripe pears, peeled, cored and sliced; 1 small tin mandarin oranges, drained; ⅓ small ripe melon, with seeds removed and flesh scooped out with baller; a few maraschino cherries and fresh strawberries.

The fruit can be glazed with a mixture of 2 tablesp golden syrup and 1 tablesp castor sugar, heated gently together until the sugar is dissolved, then cooled. Serve meringues as soon as possible after filling. They do not stay crisp for long.

COCONUT PYRAMIDS

3 egg whites	8 oz desiccated coconut
1½ oz rice flour	½ teasp vanilla essence
4–5 oz castor sugar	Rice paper

Whisk the egg whites very stiffly, stir in lightly the rice flour, castor sugar, coconut and essence. Put the mixture in small close heaps on rice paper; bake in a cool oven (150°C, 310°F, Gas 2) till they are light brown.

18 pyramids

MACAROONS

2 egg whites	Rice paper *or* grease-
4 oz castor sugar	proof paper
3 oz ground almonds	Whole blanched
1 teasp rice flour	almonds for top
½ teasp vanilla essence	

Beat the egg whites stiffly in a large bowl. Mix the sugar, almonds and rice flour together and fold into the beaten whites; add the vanilla essence. Place the rice paper or greaseproof paper on a baking sheet. Put the mixture into a large bag with a ½–1 in plain pipe and pipe on to the rice paper in rounds about 1½-in diameter. Place an almond in the centre of each round and bake in a moderate oven (180°C, 350°F, Gas 4).

20 macaroons   Cooking time 20–30 min

GENOESE PASTRY

This pastry is used as a base for desserts, and also as a basic mixture for small iced cakes and gâteaux of various kinds.

BASIC GENOESE PASTRY

4 oz flour	4 oz castor sugar
Pinch of salt	3 oz butter *or*
4 eggs	margarine

Sift flour and salt. Beat eggs and sugar in a basin over a pan of hot water till thick. Clarify the fat and fold lightly into egg mixture, then fold in salted flour. Pour into lined Swiss roll tin and bake in a moderate oven (180°C, 350°F, Gas 4). When cold (after 24 hr) cut and use as desired for small iced cakes, etc.

Cooking time 30–40 min

SMALL ICED OR FRENCH CAKES

One oblong Genoese	Cake decorations:
pastry cake, 1–1½ in	chopped nuts,
thick	crystallised violets,
Filling of your choice:	rose petals, silver
jam, lemon curd	balls, glacé fruits,
confectioners' custard	angelica, etc
or butter icing	Glacé icing

Cut the cake through the centre, spread it thinly

with filling and join together again. If necessary, trim off the brown top of the cake, and brush off any loose crumbs. Cut the cake into rounds, triangles, squares, etc. Brush off loose crumbs carefully, and put the pieces of cake on an icing rack over a large flat dish.

Make the icing so that it will flow easily over the cakes but will not run right off. Pierce each cake in turn with a skewer, spear it, and dip it into the icing. Return it to the rack, and dislodge the skewer with a fork, so that you do not leave finger marks on the cake. Once or twice, you can change the colour of the icing, say from white to pale pink to darker pink. Before the icing sets, arrange a little decoration on the top of each cake. When firm, serve the cakes in decorative paper cases.

About 24 cakes

PETITS FOURS (1)

2 egg whites	Rice paper
4 oz ground almonds	Glacé cherries
2 oz castor sugar	Angelica
A few drops almond	
essence	

Whisk the egg whites very stiffly, and fold in gradually the mixed almonds and sugar. Drip in the almond essence as you work. Place the mixture in a forcing bag with a large decorative pipe and force it on to rice paper in rosettes or oblongs. Decorate with tiny pieces of glacé cherry or angelica and bake in a moderate oven (180°C, 350°F, Gas 4) until golden-brown. They take about 20 min.

20–30 small petits fours

PETITS FOURS (2)

1 square *or* oblong	Butter icing and cake
Genoese pastry cake,	crumbs
1–1½ in thick	Almond paste
Apricot marmalade *or*	Glacé *or* royal icing
glaze	

Cut neat shapes from the pastry: make squares, rings, triangles and so on. Using apricot marmalade, fasten a small piece of almond paste *or* butter icing mixed with cake crumbs on top of each piece of Genoese. Coat with icing, and decorate with fine piping in scrolls etc, as you fancy.

Petits four are usually smaller than French cakes. They are often served in sweetmeat cases.

TARTLETS AND PASTRIES

In the following recipes, use home-made, frozen or packet short crust and puff pastry, as you prefer.

Recipes for these, and for other kinds of pastry for sweet dishes are given in the section on Puddings, Desserts and Icings.

ALMOND CHEESECAKES

Short crust pastry,	2 oz ground almonds
using 6 oz flour, etc	¼ teasp almond essence
1–2 dessertsp jam	2 egg whites
4 oz castor sugar	1 dessertsp water

Roll the pastry out thinly, cut into rounds and line patty or bouchée tins.

For almond cheesecakes, put a little jam in the bottom of each pastry shell. Mix the castor sugar and ground almonds; add the essence to the egg whites and whisk stiffly. Fold the sugar-almond mixture into the egg whites, and add the water. Half fill the

BANBURY CAKES

pastry cases with the mixture. If you wish, put small pastry crosses on top. Bake in a fairly hot to moderate oven (190–180°C, 375–350°F, Gas 5–4) for about 15 min until firm.

For lemon cheesecakes, ¾ fill the patty cases with good lemon curd (home-made if possible; see the section on Preserved Foods). Top with candied peel and bake in a fairly hot oven (200°C, 400°F, Gas 6) for about 20 min.

BANBURY CAKES

Rough puff pastry using 8 oz flour, etc, or puff or flaky pastry

FILLING

Small 1 oz butter or margarine	4 oz currants
½ oz plain flour	½ oz chopped candied peel
¼ nutmeg (grated) or ¼ teasp ground cinnamon	2 oz brown sugar
	2 tablesp rum

GLAZE

Egg white	Castor sugar

To make the filling melt the fat, stir in the flour and spice, and cook for a minute or two. Remove from the heat, add the fruit, sugar and rum.

Roll the pastry out ¼ in thick and cut into 3-in rounds. Place a spoonful of filling in the centre of each, damp the edges and gather them together to form a ball; turn over so that the smooth side is uppermost. Roll each out and shape into an oval shape 4-in by 2½-in; make 3 cuts in the centre. Put the cakes on a greased tin and bake in a hot oven (220°C, 425°F, Gas 7). Brush with the egg white and dust immediately with castor sugar. Return to the oven for a few minutes, to frost the glaze.

14 cakes   **Cooking time 20 min**

CREAM BUNS AND CHOUX

Choux pastry, using 4 oz flour, etc
Icing sugar or glacé icing
Filling
½ pt sweetened double cream flavoured with a liqueur or essence or confectioners' custard or mock cream, fruit or jam

Put the pastry into a forcing bag and pipe balls on to a greased baking sheet using a 1-in pipe; or shape the mixture with a spoon into piles. Bake in a fairly

hot oven (220–200°C, 425–400°F, Gas 7–6) for 30 min (do not open the door), then reduce the heat to 170°C, 325°F, Gas 3 for about 10 min until the buns are dried inside. Cover with greaseproof paper if they are becoming too brown. Split the buns and remove any damp mixture. Dry in the turned off oven for a few moments if very damp. When cold, fill with whipped cream, and fruit or jam if you wish, and dust with icing sugar or top with a little glacé icing.

For baby cream buns or choux, sometimes called profiteroles, use a teasp or small forcing pipe to shape the pastry into walnut-sized piles. Bake for 10 to 12 min at the higher heat, and a further 5–8 min at the reduced heat. Split, and dry out like cream buns if required. Do not underbake.

These baby choux are attractive among a selection of petits fours.

12 big buns, about 28 small ones Cooking time 40 min

CREAM HORNS

Puff or flaky pastry using 4 oz flour, etc	1 gill sweetened and flavoured cream
Raspberry jam	Chopped pistachio nuts

Roll pastry out ⅛-in thick and cut into strips ½-in wide and 12–14 in long. Moisten strip with water and wind round the cornet mould from the point upwards keeping moist surface on the outside. Finish final overlap on underside of tin and trim neatly. Allow to stand for 1 hr. Place horns on baking sheet, brush over with egg and milk and place in a hot oven (220°C, 425°F, Gas 7) until nicely browned and cooked through. Remove tins and return horns to oven to dry for a few minutes. When cool, place a little jam in each horn, pipe a rosette of cream on top and sprinkle with nuts.

7–8 horns   **Cooking time 15–20 min**

ECCLES CAKES

Flaky or rough puff pastry, using 6 oz flour, etc (trimmings can be used)	¼ oz sugar
	2 oz currants
	¾ oz chopped peel
	¼ teasp mixed spice
½ oz butter or margarine	A little grated nutmeg
	Granulated sugar

Roll out pastry ¼-in thick, cut into 4 in rounds. Cream fat and sugar, add currants, peel and spice

Cream buns

Filling and decorating tartlets, see recipe below

and place a good teasp of the mixture in the centre of each round of pastry. Gather the edges together, pinch firmly, and form into a flat cake; reverse the cake and pat gently till the fruit begins to show through. Make two cuts on top of each, brush with water and dust with granulated sugar. Bake in a hot oven (220°C, 425°F, Gas 7).

12–14 cakes   **Cooking time 20 min**

FLUTED ROLLS

Puff pastry trimmings   **Castor sugar**

Roll out the trimmings of pastry, dredge well with castor sugar and fold in three. Repeat this twice and then roll out to $\frac{1}{4}$-in thickness. Cut into rounds with a 2-in fluted cutter. Roll up, brush with water and sprinkle with castor sugar. Bake in a fairly hot oven (200°C, 400°F, Gas 6) till crisp and lightly browned.

This recipe is a practical one for using up pieces of frozen puff pastry, after making a slightly smaller tart than the packet supplies.

Cooking time 10 min

FRUIT TARTLETS

Short crust pastry, using 3–4 oz flour, etc

FILLING
Fresh fruit, e.g. apples, blackcurrants, pears (poached), grapes, raspberries, redcurrants, etc, *or* canned fruit, e.g. cherries, pears, peaches, mandarin oranges, etc, *or* preserved ginger in syrup

COATING GLAZE

1 teasp arrowroot	$\frac{1}{4}$ pt fruit syrup *or*
Colouring	ginger syrup

If no fruit syrup is available, use:

$\frac{1}{2}$–1 oz sugar	A few drops of
1 teasp arrowroot	colouring
$\frac{1}{4}$ pt water	Lemon juice to taste

DECORATION
1 gill whipped, sweetened and flavoured cream (optional)

Roll out the pastry thinly. Cut out with a fluted cutter and line small tartlet tins. Bake them "blind" in a fairly hot oven (220–200°C, 425–400°F, Gas 7–6) for 15 min. Remove weighted paper and return cases to oven for 2–3 min or till dry. When cool, arrange

Fruit tartlets

FRUIT TURNOVERS

the fruit attractively in the cases. Blend the arrowroot with a little syrup, boil remainder of syrup and pour on to blended mixture, stirring gently. Return to pan and bring to boil again, stirring very gently, otherwise the mixture loses its clear colour because of bubbles of air introduced in stirring or boiling syrup. Pour the glaze gently over the fruit and allow to cool. Pipe the cream neatly around the edge, if wished.

8–10 tartlets

FRUIT or JAM TURNOVERS

Short crust, flaky, rough puff *or* puff pastry	Stewed fruit *or* jam Castor sugar

Roll the pastry thinly and cut into rounds of about 4 in diameter. Place some jam *or* fruit in the centre of each round and moisten the edges with cold water. Fold the pastry over and press the edges together. Knock up the edges with the back of a knife and place on a baking sheet. Brush the top with water, sprinkle with sugar and bake in a fairly hot or hot oven (200–220°C, 400–425°F, Gas 6–7), depending on the type of pastry. Bake for about 20 min.

MINCE PIES

Short crust, rich short crust, flaky, rough puff *or* puff pastry using 6 oz flour, etc	10–12 oz mincemeat Castor *or* icing sugar

Roll the pastry out to about $\frac{1}{8}$-in thickness. Cut half of it into rounds of about $2\frac{1}{2}$-in diameter and reserve these for lids. (Use a plain cutter for flaky, rough puff or puff pastry.) Cut the remaining pastry into rounds of about 3-in diameter and line some patty tins. Place some mincemeat in the tins, brush the edge of the pastry with water and place a lid on top of each. Press the edges well together; if a plain cutter has been used knock up the edges. Brush the tops with water and sprinkle with sugar. Make a hole or 2 small cuts in the top of each. Bake in a hot oven (230–220°C, 450–425°F, Gas 8–7) depending on the type of pastry, for 25–30 min. Dredge tops with castor sugar *or* icing sugar. Serve hot or cold.

8–10 pies

POLISH TARTLETS

Puff pastry trimmings *or* 1 x 7$\frac{1}{2}$-oz pkt frozen puff pastry Raspberry jam	Apricot jam Chopped pistachio nuts Desiccated coconut

Roll the pastry out thinly and cut into 3$\frac{1}{2}$-in squares. Moisten each corner, fold them over to meet in the centre and cover the join with a small round of pastry. Bake in a fairly hot oven (200°C, 400°F, Gas 6) for about 15 min. When cool, place a little jam at each corner. Sprinkle coconut on the raspberry jam and finely chopped pistachio nuts on the apricot jam.

This recipe is excellent for using a frozen puff pastry.

VANILLA SLICES

1 x 7$\frac{1}{2}$-oz pkt frozen puff pastry *or* puff pastry using 3 oz flour, etc	A little glacé icing

FILLING

$\frac{1}{2}$ pt milk	1 oz sugar
$\frac{3}{4}$ oz cornflour	$\frac{1}{2}$ teasp vanilla
2 egg yolks *or* 1 whole egg	essence

Roll pastry $\frac{1}{2}$-in thick and cut into fingers 4-in by 1-in. Bake in a fairly hot oven (220°C, 425°F, Gas 7) until pastry is well risen. Allow to cool. Blend the cornflour with the milk, beat in the egg yolks and sugar, and cook over a gentle heat until thick. Beat in the vanilla. Allow to cool. Slit carefully through the centre of the pastry fingers, spread the custard over one half and sandwich the halves together again. Spread tops thinly with glacé icing.

8 slices   Cooking time 20 min

BISCUITS

BASIC BISCUIT RECIPE (Shrewsbury Biscuits)

4 oz butter *or* margarine	$\frac{1}{2}$ level teasp ground cinnamon *or* 1 teasp grated lemon rind
4 oz castor sugar	
1 small egg	Milk as required
8 oz plain flour	

Cream the fat and sugar and beat in the egg. Sift flour with cinnamon, *or* add grated rind, and add to the creamed fat mixture. Mix to a stiff consistency, using milk if required. Roll out fairly thinly and cut out with a 2$\frac{1}{2}$-in cutter. Place on a greased baking sheet and bake in a moderate oven (180°C, 350°F, Gas 4) till light fawn colour.

30–32 biscuits   Cooking time 15–20 min

EASTERTIDE BISCUITS

Add $\frac{1}{2}$ level teasp mixed spice and 2 oz currants to the basic recipe for Shrewsbury Biscuits. Roll out mixture to $\frac{1}{4}$-in thickness and cut into 4-in rounds. If desired, brush with egg white and dredge with sugar. Bake in a moderate oven (180°C, 350°F, Gas 4) until golden-brown.

12–16 biscuits   Cooking time 20–30 min

BRANDY SNAPS

2$\frac{1}{2}$ oz sugar	1 oz plain flour
1 oz butter *or* margarine	1 level teasp ground ginger
1 oz golden syrup	

Brandy snaps

196

Mocha biscuits

Cream sugar, fat and syrup, and stir in the sifted flour and ginger. Make into 12–16 small balls and place really well apart on greased baking sheets. These biscuits spread. Bake in a cool oven (150°C, 310°F, Gas 2) until rich brown colour. Allow to cool slightly, remove from sheet with a knife and, while soft enough, roll round the handle of a wooden spoon, remove when set. The snaps can be filled with sweetened and flavoured cream just before serving.

12–16 brandy snaps   **Cooking time 10–15 min**

CRUNCHIES

4 oz butter *or* margarine	1 tablesp golden syrup
2½ oz sugar	5 oz rolled oats

Melt fat, sugar and syrup in a saucepan and stir in the oats. Spread on a greased baking sheet with a raised edge, 7-in by 13 in to within ½-in of the edge. Place in a moderate oven (180°C, 350°F, Gas 4) and bake until a good brown colour and firm. Cut into fingers before completely cold.

16 crunchies   **Cooking time 20–30 min**

GINGER SNAPS

6 oz self-raising flour	3–4 oz sugar
Pinch of salt	2 oz lard *or* hydro-
1 level teasp bicarbonate of soda	genated shortening
	1½ oz golden syrup
2 level teasp ground ginger	1 egg

Take small measure of bicarbonate and ginger. Sift flour, salt, soda and ginger; add sugar. Melt lard and syrup, cool slightly, then add to dry ingredients; add the egg. Divide into 24 pieces and make into balls, place well apart on greased baking sheets. Bake in a fairly hot to moderate oven (190–180°C, 375–350°F, Gas 5–4) till a good rich brown colour.

24 Ginger Snaps   **Cooking time 20 min**

MARGUERITES

BISCUIT BASE

2 oz butter	1 tablesp coffee essence
1 oz castor sugar	4 oz plain flour

TOPPING

1 egg white	3 oz ground almonds
1 tablesp strong liquid coffee	10 blanched almonds, whole
2 oz castor sugar	

Cream the butter and sugar well, then beat in the liquid coffee essence. Work in the flour until a smooth dough is obtained. Roll out to just over an 8-in circle; then cut out, using an 8-in fluted flan ring as cutter. Alternatively, crimp with your fingers to decorate the edge.

To make the topping whisk the egg white until very stiff, then whisk in the liquid coffee. Fold in the sugar and ground almonds. Spread this mixture over the biscuit base to within 1-in of the edge. Decorate with almonds evenly spaced. Bake at 190°C, 375°F, Gas 5 for about 35 min. Cool slightly and cut into 10 wedges while still warm.

MELTING MOMENTS

2 oz lard *or* hydrogenated shortening	½ egg
	½ teasp vanilla essence
2 oz margarine	5 oz self-raising flour
3 oz sugar	Cornflakes

MOCHA BISCUITS

Cream fat and sugar and beat in egg. Add flavouring, stir in the sifted flour and with wet hands make into balls the size of marbles and roll in crushed cornflakes. Bake in a fairly hot to moderate oven (190–180°C, 375–350°F, Gas 5–4).

24 biscuits   Cooking time 15 min

MOCHA BISCUITS

5 oz butter	1 tablesp liquid coffee
2 oz castor sugar	essence
7 oz self-raising flour	Beaten egg
½ level teasp powdered cinnamon	

Cream the butter and castor sugar together until light and fluffy. Sift the flour and cinnamon and add to the butter and sugar together with the coffee essence. Work together. Using a forcing bag and rosette pipe, press out round and finger shapes on a greased baking sheet. Brush with beaten egg. Bake in a moderate oven, (180°C, 350°F, Gas 4) for 25 min or until golden-brown.

PARKIN BISCUITS

2 oz plain flour	1 oz lard or
2 oz oatmeal	hydrogenated
1½ oz sugar	shortening
½ level teasp ground ginger	1 level teasp bicarbonate of soda
½ level teasp powdered cinnamon	1½ oz golden syrup
¼ level teasp mixed spice	¼ egg

DECORATION

Blanched almonds

Sift and mix flour, oatmeal, sugar and spices, and rub in the fat. Add soda, syrup and egg. Mix well to a fairly stiff consistency. Form into balls and place a little apart on greased baking sheets; put ½ a blanched almond on top of each. Bake in a moderate to warm oven (180–170°C, 350–335°F, Gas 4–3). Allow to cool slightly before removing from sheet.

12–14 biscuits   Cooking time 15–20 min

RICH OATCAKES

3 oz plain flour	1 lb oatmeal
½ teasp salt	1 oz sugar
2 level teasp bicarbonate of soda	4 oz butter and lard or margarine and lard
2 level teasp cream of tartar	Milk

Sift the flour, salt, soda and cream of tartar; add the oatmeal and sugar and rub in the fat. Add the milk, and mix to a stiff but not hard dough. Dust the baking-board with a mixture of flour and oatmeal, and roll out thinly. Rub the surface with oatmeal and cut out with a 3½–4-in cutter or cut into triangles. Place on a baking-sheet and cook in a warm to cool oven (170–150°C, 335–310°F, Gas 3–2).

About 40 oatcakes—depending on size
Cooking time 20–30 min

ICINGS AND FILLINGS

ALMOND PASTE (ICING)

Almond paste—often called almond icing or marzipan—is used to cover rich cakes before applying royal or glacé icing. (It is also used alone to decorate cakes such as Simnel Cake and Battenburg Cake.) It is often coloured and flavoured and then moulded into various shapes to be used for cake decoration.

6 oz icing sugar and 6 oz castor sugar or 12 oz icing sugar	¾ teasp orange flower water (optional)
12 oz ground almonds	¾ teasp vanilla
Juice of ½ lemon	essence
1–2 egg yolks	

Sieve the icing sugar into a bowl and mix with the ground almonds and castor sugar. Add the lemon juice, essences and enough egg yolk to bind the ingredients into a pliable but dry paste. Knead thoroughly with the hand until smooth.

A whole egg or egg whites may be used instead of egg yolks. Egg yolk gives a richer and yellower paste, whilst egg white gives a whiter, more brittle paste. (Economically the yolks can be used for almond paste and the whites used for royal icing.) This quantity of paste is sufficient to cover the top and sides of an 8-in cake.

To apply almond paste

To cover the top and sides of a rich fruit cake, the cake top should be fairly level and the surface free from loose crumbs.

Brush the top and sides with warm apricot glaze, using a pastry brush. Dredge a little castor sugar on to a clean board and roll out the almond paste to a round which is 4-in wider than the diameter of the cake. Place the cake in the centre of this with its glazed top downwards and work the paste upwards round the sides of the cake with the hands until it is within ¼-in of the top edge, i.e. the cake bottom. Using a straight-sided jar or thick tumbler, roll firmly round the sides, pressing slightly with the other hand on the upturned bottom of the cake and turning the cake round on the sugared board when necessary. Continue rolling and turning until the sides are straight and smoothly covered and the top edges of the cake are sharp and smooth, when the process is completed and the cake is turned upright.

Allow a few days for the almond paste to dry, before putting on the royal icing, or the oil from the almond paste will discolour it. Cover with a clean cloth to protect from dust whilst drying.

For coloured almond paste, use a few drops of food colouring and egg white rather than yolks.

AMERICAN FROSTING

8 oz granulated sugar	1 egg white, beaten
4 tablesp water	with flavouring

Put the sugar and water into a pan. Dissolve the sugar slowly in the water, then bring to boiling point. Boil to 130°C, 240°F without stirring. Brush down the sides of the pan with a brush dipped in cold water, and remove scum as it rises. Pour on to the beaten egg white and flavouring, beating all the time. Continue beating until the icing begins to thicken and coats the back of a spoon thickly. Pour quickly over the cake. Spread with a palette knife, and work up the icing in swirls. You can also use the icing as a filling. ½ teasp vanilla essence or lemon juice and a pinch of cream of tartar are the most usual additions. For other flavourings, see Butter Icings.

APRICOT GLAZE

2 tablesp apricot jam	1 tablesp water

*Birthday cake
with butter icing*

Sieve the jam and water into a saucepan. Place over heat and bring to boiling point. Remove and cool. Use to glaze the tops of small cakes, to stick almond paste to Christmas cakes, etc.

APRICOT MARMALADE FOR COATINGS, FILLINGS, ETC.

8 tablesp apricot jam	1 teasp lemon juice, or
1 gill water	to taste

Warm the jam and water. Boil gently for about 5 min. Add the lemon juice. Strain, then boil again, briefly, if too thin. The marmalade should drop slowly from the hot spoon.

BUTTER ICING OR BUTTER CREAM FILLING (1) (quick)

2 oz butter *or*	Flavouring
margarine	Pinch of salt
3 oz icing sugar	Colouring

Cream the butter or margarine. Add the sugar and salt gradually and cream together. Beat until smooth, creamy and pale. Add flavouring and colouring to taste.

FLAVOURINGS

Almond Beat in $\frac{1}{4}$ teasp almond essence.
Chocolate Dissolve 1 oz chocolate in 1 tablesp water and beat in, *or* beat in 1 dessertsp cocoa and a few drops of vanilla essence.
Coffee Beat in 1 dessertsp coffee essence.

Jam Add 1 tablesp strong flavoured jam, e.g. plum, raspberry.
Lemon Beat in 1 teasp strained lemon juice.
Orange Beat in 1 dessertsp strained orange juice.
Vanilla Beat in $\frac{1}{2}$ teasp vanilla essence.
Walnut Add 2 oz chopped walnuts and 1–2 teasp coffee essence.

In cold weather, you may warm the butter slightly, but do not let it oil. This butter icing always has a slight taste of raw sugar. A better but more costly one is made thus:

BUTTER ICING OR BUTTER CREAM (2)

4–6 oz castor sugar	4 oz unsalted butter
4 egg yolks	(for filling) *or* 8 oz
$\frac{1}{4}$ pt milk	unsalted butter (for
	icing)
	Flavouring as above

Beat the egg yolks until fluffy, and then beat in the sugar gradually until the mixture is thick and very pale. Heat the milk and when at boiling point, trickle it into the egg yolk mixture beating all the time. Return the mixture to the milk saucepan and heat it gently until it thickens. Place the saucepan in a pan of cold water to cool, cover, and beat often enough to prevent a skin forming. When the custard is tepid, beat in the flavouring and butter alternately. Chill if required very stiff.

TO COLOUR BUTTER ICING

Use a few drops of food colouring. These are very

199

Pouring glacé icing

concentrated, so it is wise to add less than you think you need at first. Wear a rubber glove to handle the colouring, if possible, as it stains the skin. Put a teasp white icing aside; then pour a drop or two of colouring into the lid of its bottle. Do not try to shake drops from the bottle directly into the icing. Drip the colouring into the icing from the lid. Mix the colouring in thoroughly. Test the colour you have obtained by holding the test teasp of white icing beside it.

CHOCOLATE GLAZE

2 oz plain chocolate	½–2 oz unsalted butter
1 tablesp water, coffee *or* rum	

Stir the chocolate and liquid in a bowl set over a pan of very hot water until the chocolate dissolves. Remove from the heat and beat in the butter a tablesp at a time. Stand the bowl on ice or in a pan of cold water until cooled. Beat again. When it reaches the consistency you want, spread or drizzle the glaze on your cake.

FONDANT OR TRANSPARENT ICING

1 lb loaf *or* granu-lated sugar	1½ teasp glucose *or* a good pinch of cream of tartar
¼ pt water	

Dissolve the sugar in the water over a low heat, add the glucose or cream of tartar, bring to the boil quickly, and boil to a temperature of 110°C, 237°F. Pour on to an oiled or wetted slab, let it cool slightly (if worked when too hot it will grain), and work well with a palette knife, keeping the mass together as much as possible. When the paste is sufficiently cool, knead well with the hands. Wrap in paper and store in an airtight tin.

When required put into a basin over a saucepan containing sufficient hot water to come half-way up

the sides of the basin. Stir over a very low heat until icing has the consistency of thick cream. Flavour and colour as required. Allow to cool slightly before using. Flavour Transparent Icing with lemon.

FLAVOURINGS

Chocolate Add 3 dessertsp grated chocolate, *or* 2 dessertsp cocoa, or to taste.
Coffee Stir in 2 dessertsp coffee essence or to taste.

GLACÉ ICING

Glacé icing or water icing (soft icing) is made from sifted icing sugar moistened with warm water to make a thin coating consistency. It is used for icing sponges, sandwich and layer cakes, small cakes, biscuits and petit fours.

BASIC RECIPE

4 oz icing sugar	Flavouring
1 tablesp warm water	Colouring

If the sugar is lumpy, break up the lumps by rolling the sugar with a rolling-pin before sieving. Sieve the icing sugar and put into a small bowl over hot water. Add the 1 tablesp warm water gradually. Stir until all the sugar is dissolved and the icing is smooth and warm. Do not allow to get too hot or the icing will lose its gloss. Add the flavouring and the colouring a drop at a time until the required shade is obtained. The icing should be thick enough to coat the back of the spoon; if too thin add more sugar, if too thick add more water. When of the correct consistency, cool slightly, then use at once. This quantity will coat the top of a 6–8-in cake.

CHOCOLATE ICING

3 oz chocolate (preferably couverture *or* plain chocolate)	8 oz icing sugar
	½ gill water

Break the chocolate into small pieces, put into a small bowl over a bowl of warm water and allow to dissolve. Add the sieved icing sugar and water, stir until well mixed and smooth. Use as required.

Coffee icing Add ½ teasp coffee essence to the basic recipe, omitting ½ teasp of the water.
Lemon icing Substitute strained lemon juice for all or part of the water in the basic recipe. Add a few drops of colouring.
Orange icing Substitute strained orange juice for all or part of the water in the basic recipe. Add a few drops of colouring.

TO APPLY GLACÉ ICING

Place cakes on a wire cooling tray over a large flat dish or clean table-top. Petits fours and other small cakes that have to be coated all over are best dipped into the icing on a fork or skewer, then drained. For large cakes the cake top should be fairly level. Brush off any loose crumbs. When the icing is the desired consistency pour quickly into the centre of the cake and allow to run down the sides. Avoid using a knife if possible, but if this is necessary use a palette knife dipped in hot water and dried.

If the top only is to be iced, a smooth flat surface can be easily obtained by pinning a double thickness of greaseproof paper round the sides of the cake so that the paper stands 1 in higher than the cake. Pour on the icing which will find its own level, and allow to set. When the icing has set remove the paper with

Stages in making a piped decoration in royal icing, as described below

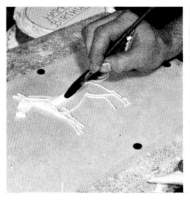

the aid of a knife dipped in hot water. ·

Put any ready-made decorations on to the icing while it is still soft, but piped icing should be added after the surface is dry and firm.

ROYAL ICING

1 lb icing sugar	2 egg whites
(approx)	1 teasp lemon juice

If the sugar is lumpy, roll with a rolling-pin before sieving. Put the egg whites into a bowl, beat slightly with a wooden spoon. Add 2 tablesp sieved sugar and beat again. Gradually add the remainder of the sugar, beating well until a thick, smooth consistency and a good white colour are obtained. Add the lemon juice and beat again.

If a softer icing is required 1 teasp glycerine may be stirred in after the sugar; this prevents the icing becoming brittle and facilitates cutting.

If the icing is not wanted at once, cover the bowl with a damp cloth to keep it soft.

TO ICE A CAKE WITH ROYAL ICING

These quantities are sufficient to coat a cake of 8-in diameter.

Place the cake, already covered with almond paste, on a cake-board or inverted plate. Place the cake-board on a turntable if available.

AMOUNTS REQUIRED

First coating Royal icing, using 1¼ lb icing sugar, etc, mixed to a stiff consistency.
Second coating ¾–1 lb icing sugar, etc, consistency to coat the back of a spoon.

Decorative piping ½ lb icing sugar, etc, mixed to a stiff consistency, i.e. that will stand up in points when the back of the spoon is drawn away from the side of the bowl.

TO APPLY FIRST COATING

With a tablesp take enough icing to cover the top, and place it in the centre of the cake. Spread evenly over top, smoothing the surface with a hot, wet palette knife (shake or dry the knife after dipping it in hot water as too much water softens the icing). Take up small portions of the icing with the end of the palette knife blade, spread it smoothly round the side until the cake is completely covered and the surface smooth.

Allow to set for a few days before applying the second coat. Whilst the icing is drying and as soon as it is hard enough, place a thin sheet of paper lightly over the top to protect it from dust.

TO APPLY SECOND COATING

Mix icing to a thin coating consistency and pour over the cake. Prick any bubbles with a fine skewer or pin; allow to firm before decorating.

TO DECORATE THE CAKE WITH PIPED ICING

Cut pieces of greaseproof paper the same sizes as the top and sides of the cake. Sketch on to these the patterns to be used for the decoration. Pin papers firmly into position on cake and prick pattern through. Mix icing to a stiff consistency and pipe design on to cake, starting at centre and working outwards, and finishing with the sides and the base.
Using a forcing bag Decorative icing can be piped from a forcing bag and pipe. Plastic forcing bags are available. Alternatively, fold an oblong of grease-proof paper in half diagonally and cut along the fold. Form one half into a cone-shaped bag. Cut off the pointed end of the cone and slip a forcing pipe into the bag so that it protrudes halfway through the cut point. Make a bag for each pipe to be used. Fill the bags ⅔ full with icing and fold over the top edges. Holding the pipe between the first and second fingers force the icing through the pipe by exerting pressure with the thumbs on the top of the bag.
Icing syringes are made of metal or plastic and can be bought in sets complete with decorative pipes. Excellent plastic turntables are also available. If coloured icings are being used the syringe must be washed before filling with another colour.

All pipes must be kept clean. Always keep the bowl containing the icing covered with a damp cloth whilst decorating, to prevent the icing drying out.

The beginner should practise on an upturned cake tin or plate before starting on the cake, and the icing may be removed if scraped off immediately and returned to the covered bowl.

For Christmas cakes other decorations may be made with coloured marzipan, e.g. holly, marzipan, apples, etc, and the smooth icing surface roughened into points with a palette knife to form 'snow drifts'. For this one coat only is needed.

BASIC FILLINGS FOR CAKES

Butter icings, confectioners' custard and sieved jam are the most usual fillings for cakes. Cream is also used for some cakes, but does not 'keep' long. Cream can also be used to make custard-based or jam fillings richer.

Any of these fillings can be flavoured with a liqueur or essence to suit your choice, or with a little very strong 'instant' coffee or melted chocolate. Chopped glacé or candied fruit, chopped or ground nuts, cake crumbs or desiccated coconut can be added to any basic filling for an alternative flavouring or as thickening.

CREAM AS FILLING

Good combination flavourings for cake fillings are made by mixing: coffee and chopped walnuts; coffee and vanilla essence; rum and chocolate or coffee; cherry jam and Kirsch or brandy.

CREAM AS FILLING AND TOPPING FOR CAKES, GATEAUX, MERINGUES, ETC.

Cream tends to sink into the fabric of a cake or pastry. It should only be added, therefore, shortly before serving.

Whipped cream for cake, meringue or tart fillings should be stiff. It is best to use double cream, undiluted by milk, egg white or single cream.

To sweeten whipped cream for fillings Whip the cream until almost stiff. Then sift in a little icing sugar with a pinch of salt. Whip again. Repeat this process until the cream is as sweet as you want it. If you add all the sugar at once, the cream will liquify, and may be difficult to whip stiffly again. Add any flavouring *before* sweetening. Adjust flavouring after sweetening.

MOCK CREAM

$\frac{1}{2}$ oz cornflour	1 oz sugar
$\frac{1}{4}$ pt milk	A few drops of vanilla
1 oz margarine	essence

Blend the cornflour with a little of the milk, and put the rest of the milk on to boil. Pour the boiling milk on to the blended cornflour, stirring well. Return mixture to pan and cook for 2–3 min. Cool. Cream together the margarine and sugar. Gradually beat the cornflour mixture into the creamed fat a little at a time, beat well. Stir in the vanilla essence.

BREAD MAKING

The bread we eat every day as a staple food is 'leavened' or raised, usually with yeast, to make it light and porous. Some breads, called 'quick breads' are raised with baking powder, eggs or similar ingredients, and others, such as crispbreads, are not leavened at all.

We eat mostly white bread, made from wheat without its husk. Wholemeal bread is made from wheat flour made from the whole of the wheat grain endosperm.

White flour is 'enriched' however, with iron, calcium and two B vitamins. For bread-making, a 'strong' flour with a lot of gluten (protein) is needed to make it cohesive and elastic and to give a good volume. Cakes are best made with a 'softer' flour with less gluten.

Wheat contains more gluten than any other grain, so when other grains are used for bread flour, they are mixed with wheat. Maize, potato and rye flours are the most commonly used ones today.

Raising bread dough with yeast is not as difficult as many people think. You can either use fresh yeast, bought in a small cake, or dried yeast in powder form. Dried yeast lasts a long time, but fresh yeast must be used while fresh. This yeast should have a slightly beery smell, and be a fresh putty colour. Both forms are used in the same way, but you need only half as much dried as fresh yeast to raise a given amount of flour, and dried yeast must be reconstituted in some warm liquid first.

Yeast raises dough by producing carbon dioxide gas. It is a plant, and therefore requires food, warmth and moisture to do this. Sugar is a food for yeast and a little sugar is often added to the yeast liquid. Since cold slows down the working of the yeast, its raising action can be retarded by chilling it in a fridge, and can be speeded up by gentle warmth. Too much warmth makes it smell 'beery' in the finished bread, however, and great heat kills it (which is why we bake bread at a high temperature).

One ounce of fresh yeast will raise up to $3\frac{1}{2}$ lb flour in one hour in a warm room (at about 21°C, 70°F).

HINTS ON USING YEAST

1 See that the liquid used with the yeast is 'just warm'.

2 Add enough liquid to form a soft but not sticky dough. A stiff dough will not rise well.

3 Always add all the prepared yeast liquid to a bread flour before adding any other liquid.

4 Either mix the flour and liquid to a dough at once or 'set the sponge' as in the recipe for White Bread below. (This only means 'let a little flour-yeast mixture stand awhile before making the whole amount of dough'.)

5 The less dough you make, the more yeast you will need proportionately. You will need $\frac{1}{2}$ oz fresh yeast to raise 1 lb dough, although 1 oz will raise 3 lb. Also, the longer you let the dough rise, the less yeast you will need.

6 Always let dough rise twice. The second raising or 'proving' takes place when the dough is ready to be baked, in its tin. This raising 'proves' that added ingredients have not harmed the yeast, and it replaces air knocked out of the dough when kneading it.

7 When the dough is rising, cover it with a slightly damp clean towel or greased polythene bag to prevent the surface hardening and cracking.

8 Add any fruit, etc, after the first 'raising'.

9 Do not raise dough too long. It may get overstretched and will collapse, giving a heavy bread, like dough which is not 'proved' a second time. It is risen when it has doubled in size and springs back when pressed lightly with a floured finger.

10 The finished loaf should be evenly shaped, well risen, with a browned crust. It should be smooth on the bottom, and should sound hollow when tapped.

OTHER RAISING AGENTS

Baking powder is used for a good many 'quick breads' and scones. The usual proportion is 1–3 teaspoonfuls to 1 lb of flour. Usually the plainer the mixture (e.g. fewer eggs, less fat) the more baking powder will be needed.

Eggs are sometimes used as raising agents because when beaten they hold air which expends on heating.

Bicarbonate of soda and cream of tartar are used for scones, etc. Use 1 teasp bicarbonate of soda with 3¼ teasp cream of tartar per lb of flour. Be careful not to overdo the cream of tartar which will affect the taste and colour of the finished product. Use equal quantities of bicarbonate of soda and cream of tartar if you are using sour milk as liquid. Use bicarbonate of soda alone for a brown bread, such as some gingerbreads.

Because gingerbreads are more like cakes than breads (although often eaten with butter and cheese or jam), they come first among the recipes below. They are followed by scones and other 'quick breads'. The classic yeast breads and buns come last.

LIGHT GINGERBREAD (ANDREW'S)

¾ lb plain flour	2 oz sugar
¼ teasp salt	3 oz golden syrup
1 small dessertsp ground ginger	1½–2 eggs
3 oz butter *or* margarine	

Sift the flour, salt and ginger. Cream the fat, sugar and syrup, and beat in the eggs, one at a time. Add the flour to make a mixture which will roll out on the board. Roll out ⅛–¼-in thick and cut into squares or rounds, using a plain 2½–3-in cutter. Bake on greased baking-sheets in a moderate oven (180–170°C, 350–335°F, Gas 4–3).

Cooking time 20–25 min

Ginger cake

RICH DARK GINGERBREAD

8 oz plain flour	2–4 oz crystallised ginger
⅛ teasp salt	
1–2 level teasp ground cinnamon	2 oz blanched and chopped almonds
1–2 level teasp mixed spice	4 oz butter *or* margarine
2 level teasp ground ginger	4 oz sugar
2 oz dates *or* raisins, *or* sultanas	4 oz treacle
	2 eggs
1 level teasp bicarbonate of soda	A little warm milk, if required

Grease a 7-in tin and line the bottom with grease-proof paper, well greased, or silicone-treated paper.

Mix flour and salt and other dry ingredients with the prepared fruit, crystallised ginger cut into pieces, and almonds chopped roughly. Melt the fat, sugar and treacle, add to the dry ingredients with the beaten eggs. If the mixture seems stiff, add a little warm milk but do not make it too soft. Pour into the tin, and bake in a warm to cool oven (170–150°C, 335–310°F, Gas 3–2).

Cooking time 1¾–2 hr

BASIC PLAIN SCONES

1 lb plain flour	2–3 oz lard *or* margarine
½ teasp salt	

and

2 level teasp bicarbonate of soda and 4½ level teasp cream of tartar with ½ pt fresh milk

or

2 level teasp bicarbonate of soda and 2 level teasp cream of tartar with ½ pt sour *or* butter milk

or

4–6 level teasp baking powder with ½ pt fresh milk

Sift flour and salt and lightly rub in the fat; sift in the raising agents and mix well. Add *all the milk at once* and mix *lightly* to a *spongy* dough. Knead very lightly to make the dough smooth and roll out ½–¾ in thick. Cut out with a 2-in cutter, brush with egg *or* milk, if desired, and bake in a hot oven (220–230°C, 425–450°F, Gas 7–8). If you prefer, the dough can be divided into 4 and each piece formed into a round cake and marked into 6 with a knife.

24–30 scones   **Cooking time about 10 min**

VARIATIONS OF BASIC RECIPE

Cheese scones

Add 4–6 oz grated cheese to the dry ingredients above. Cut out in finger shapes or squares.

Cheese whirls

Add 4–6 oz grated cheese to the basic recipe. Roll out dough into oblong shape. Spread with cheese and roll up like a Swiss Roll. Cut into slices and lay on greased baking sheets with the cut side uppermost. Brush with milk or egg. If any cheese is left over, sprinkle it on and bake the whirls in a hot oven (220–230°C, 425–450°F, Gas 7–8).

20–24 scones   **Cooking time 10–15 min**

Fruit scones

Add 2 oz sugar and 2–4 oz fruit (currants, sultanas, etc) to the basic recipe.

DOUGHNUTS WITHOUT YEAST

Griddle scones

Add 2–3 oz currants; roll out $\frac{1}{4}$-in thick, cut into 2$\frac{1}{2}$-in rounds or triangles; cook on both sides on a moderately hot griddle about 5 min till nicely brown and edges dry. Cool in a towel.

Nut scones

Add 2–4 oz chopped nuts to the basic or to the wholemeal recipe.

Sweet scones

Add 2 oz sugar and, if liked, 1 egg.

Treacle scones

Add 1 oz sugar, 1 teasp ground cinnamon, 1 teasp mixed spice, 2 tablesp black treacle. Put the treacle in with $\frac{2}{3}$ of the milk, then add the rest as required.

Wholemeal scones

Use half wholemeal flour and half plain flour.

DOUGHNUTS WITHOUT YEAST

2 oz lard
2 oz sugar
1 egg
1 gill skim milk powder, made up as liquid

8 oz plain flour
Pinch of salt
2 level teasp baking powder
$\frac{1}{2}$ level teasp cinnamon
$\frac{3}{4}$ level teasp nutmeg

Cream the lard and sugar. Add the eggs and beat well. Add the milk, then the flour which has been sifted together with the baking powder and spices. Chill mixture for a short time in a cool larder or a fridge. Put on a lightly floured surface and roll out to $\frac{3}{8}$ of an inch thickness. Cut with a floured doughnut cutter and allow to stand for 15 min. Fry in deep hot lard (190°C, 375°F, Gas 4) until lightly browned. Turn once during the cooking process. Drain on absorbent paper. Dust lightly with granulated or icing sugar before serving.

12–16 doughnuts

Doughnuts made without yeast

FARM HOUSE SCONES

1 lb self-raising flour
$\frac{1}{2}$ teasp salt
2 level teasp bicarbonate of soda

2 level teasp cream of tartar
1–2 eggs
$\frac{3}{4}$–1 pt milk

Sift flour, salt and raising agents into a bowl. Mix to a very thick batter with the milk and egg; do not

Scotch pancakes

make the scones so soft that they cannot be lifted. Place a tablesp of the batter on a thickly floured board and dust the top with more flour. Lift the scone in the hands and drop on to a well-floured fairly hot griddle or electric hot-plate. Pat into a round shape. Cook on one side till well risen; turn over and cook the other side. When ready they should be slightly coloured, very floury and the edges should be cooked. Cool on a towel.

When the flour on the griddle becomes brown, remove and reflour.

16–20 scones

SCOTCH PANCAKES OR GRIDDLE SCONES

4 oz self-raising flour	1 egg
Pinch of salt	$\frac{1}{4}$ pt milk
1 oz sugar	1 oz margarine, melted

MARMALADE

$\frac{1}{2}$ lb cooking apples	1 tablesp lemon juice
1 oz sugar	1 tablesp marmalade

Sift together the flour, salt and sugar. Add the beaten egg, and then milk. Mix well. Stir in the melted margarine.

Drop the mixture in spoonfuls on a hot griddle, electric hot-plate or frying pan, and cook for 2 min on each side. Keep warm in a folded tea towel while preparing the marmalade.

Peel, core and slice the apples. Simmer gently with the sugar and lemon juice until tender. Stir in the marmalade. Serve hot with the warm pancakes.

TEA SCONES

8 oz plain flour	1 level teasp
$\frac{1}{4}$ teasp salt	bicarbonate of soda
2 oz margarine	2 eggs
2 oz castor sugar	Water or milk to make
2 level teasp cream of	a light spongy
tartar	mixture (average
	$\frac{1}{2}$–$\frac{3}{4}$ gill)

Sift the flour and salt and lightly rub in the fat. Add the other dry ingredients and mix with the beaten eggs and water to make a light spongy dough. Roll out $\frac{1}{4}$-in thick and cut into rounds. Bake on a greased, fairly hot griddle or in a hot oven (230–220°C 450–425°F, Gas 8–7). If the scones are baked in the oven, roll the dough $\frac{1}{2}$-in thick.

12–15 scones   **Cooking time 10 min**

QUICK BREADS

APPLE LOAF

1 lb plain flour, sifted	1 cooking apple,
Pinch of salt	peeled, cored and
1 teasp baking powder	sliced
4 oz butter	Milk to mix
4 oz lard	4 oz icing sugar, sifted
2 eggs, beaten	A little water
2 oz currants	1 tart eating apple
2 oz raisins, seeded	(red), cored and sliced

Dip the fruit in a little lemon juice as soon as prepared, to prevent discoloration.

Sift together the flour, salt and baking powder. Rub in the fat, mix in the beaten egg, currants, raisins, cooking apple and milk. Mix well. Turn into a 1-lb lined loaf tin, and bake in a moderate oven at 190°C, 375°F, Gas 5 for 40–45 min, or until springy and browned. When cool, spread the loaf with a thin icing made with icing sugar and water, and decorate with sliced eating apple. Serve for high tea, especially when salads are scarce.

6–8 helpings

GUGELHUPF (without yeast)

7 eggs	1 tablesp sultanas
7 oz sugar	Rind and juice of $\frac{1}{2}$
6 oz flour	lemon
1 teasp baking powder	

Apple loaf

NUT AND RAISIN BREAD

Separate the egg yolks from the whites and beat the egg yolks. Add the sugar and continue beating until thick and creamy. Sift in the flour and baking powder and mix lightly. Beat the egg whites to a stiff snow and fold into the mixture. Add the sultanas, finely-grated lemon rind and lemon juice. Pour into a greased 8–9 in 'Gugelhupf' tin and bake in a fairly hot oven (190°C, 375°F, Gas 5) for about 45 min.

6–10 helpings

NUT AND RAISIN BREAD (Wholemeal)

¾ lb wholemeal flour	2 oz sugar
¼ teasp salt	2 oz sultanas
2 oz lard	4 oz chopped nuts
2 round teasp baking powder	1 egg
	½ pt milk

Rub the fat into the sifted flour and salt. Add remaining dry ingredients and mix to a fairly soft dough with egg and milk. Put into a well-greased bread or cake tin and bake in a fairly hot oven (200–190°C, 400–375°F, Gas 6–5).

1 loaf   Cooking time 1 hr

SOUR MILK BREAD

1 lb plain flour	½ pt sour milk or buttermilk (approx)
1 teasp salt	
1 round or 2 level teasp bicarbonate of soda	2 oz lard may be rubbed in; this makes a better keeping bread
1 round or 2 level teasp cream of tartar	

Sift the flour and salt, and, if you wish, rub in the fat. Add the soda and tartar, making quite sure that all the lumps are sifted out of the soda. Mix to a light spongy dough with the milk. Divide the dough and form into two round cakes. Place on a greased baking sheet and bake in a hot oven (230–220°C, 450–425°F, Gas 8–7).

2 loaves   Cooking time 30 min

YEAST BREADS AND BUNS

BASIC WHITE BREAD

3½ lb white flour	1 teasp sugar
3½ teasp salt	1¾ pt warm water
1 oz yeast	

Grease 3–4 loaf tins and put them to warm. Mix salt and flour well together, cream yeast with the sugar and add to warm water. Make a well in the centre of the flour, pour the liquid into the well and sprinkle on or mix in a little of the flour to form a pool of batter and allow to stand in a warm place for 20 min. Mix to an elastic dough, using more water if required; knead well till the dough leaves the basin clean, and put to rise in a warm place until the dough has doubled its size. Then turn on to a floured board, knead again not too heavily but until there are only small holes in the dough, and put into the prepared tins. Put to prove until the dough is well up the sides of the tin then bake in a hot oven (220°C, 425°F, Gas 7).

3–4 loaves   Cooking time 1 hr

NUT BREAD

Make like white bread. Add 8 oz chopped raisins when kneading the dough for the second time.

RAISIN BREAD

Make like white bread. Add 8 oz chopped nuts (walnuts, peanuts, etc).

SULTANA BREAD

Make like white bread. Add 8 oz sultanas when kneading the dough for the second time.

LARDY CAKE

1 lb white bread dough which has risen once	4 oz currants or sultanas
6 oz lard	A little spice, if liked
6 oz granulated sugar or a little less	Sugar syrup to glaze (see Cherry Bread)

Roll out the dough on a floured board, and put on half the lard in dabs, to cover two thirds of the surface, as in making flaky pastry. Sprinkle with the sugar, fruit and spices to your taste. Fold the dough into three, folding the unlarded piece over first. Turn to the right, and repeat the sugaring, larding and folding. Turn to the right again, and roll once more. Fold again. Roll, this time to fit a Yorkshire pudding tin about 12 × 7 in. Put to rise in a warm place, and cover with a clean tea towel. Due to the sugar, it will take longer than usual, but need only rise half its height. This will take about ¾ hr.

Bake in the centre of the oven at 200°C, 400°F, Gas 6 for about ¾ hr, until brown and crisp. When cooked (or before), brush with a thick sugar syrup to give a glistening top.

1 The cake looks better if you score the top with a sharp knife into diamond shapes before putting it to rise.

2 It is better eaten hot.

3 This is a traditional recipe, which used to be made on the day bread was baked, or from a piece of dough kept in the cold larder until the next day.

BASIC MILK BREAD

1 lb plain flour	2 oz lard or margarine
1 teasp salt	½ pt warm milk (approx)
½ oz yeast	
½ teasp sugar	1 egg (optional)

Mix the salt with the warmed flour, cream the yeast with the sugar. Rub fat into flour and mix with the yeast, milk and egg if used, to a fairly soft, light dough. Beat until mixture is smooth and leaves the sides of the basin clean. Allow to stand in a warm place till twice its original size. Proceed as for White Bread.

BREAD PLAIT

Roll risen dough into two strips, each 10 in long by 5 in or 6 in wide. Cut each strip almost to the top in three even-sized pieces and plait them as if plaiting hair. Damp and seal the ends neatly but firmly and place on a greased baking sheet. Allow to prove 10–15 min. Brush with egg wash and place in a hot oven (230°C, 450°F, Gas 8). Bake 20–30 min, reducing heat after first 10 min to 200°C, 400°F, Gas 6 or 190°C, 375°F, Gas 5.

2 loaves   Cooking time 20–30 min

CHERRY OR CURRANT BREAD

1 lb plain flour	2 teasp sugar
1 teasp salt	6 oz roughly chopped glacé cherries or currants
2 oz lard	
½ oz yeast	
½ pt warm milk (approx)	Sugar syrup to glaze (see recipe below)
1–2 eggs	

Grease two 6-in cake tins and put them to warm. Make the dough as for Milk Bread, and mix in the fruit. When the dough has risen to double its size, knead very lightly, shape into two loaves and place in the prepared tins. Allow to prove for 15 min or till well risen in the tins. Bake in a hot oven (220°C. 425°F, Gas 7). Reduce the heat after 10 min to 190°C. 375°F, Gas 5. Bake for a further 15–20 min or until loaves are firm. Glaze on removing from oven. To make the glaze, boil 1 dessertsp sugar and 1 tablesp water until slightly syrupy.

2 loaves   **Cooking time 30 min**

WHOLEMEAL BREAD

3½ lb wholemeal flour	1 oz yeast
3½ teasp salt	2 oz lard
1 teasp sugar	1¾ pt warm water

Mix salt well with flour and make warm in a large basin. Cream the yeast with the sugar, add the warm water, together with the melted fat, and mix with the flour to an elastic dough. Knead well until smooth, cover with a cloth, to prevent surface

Lardy cake

SCOTTISH BROWN BREAD (Wholemeal)

3¼ lb wholemeal flour	2 level teasp bicar-
¼ lb oatmeal	bonate of soda
3½ teasp salt	1½–1¾ pt warm water
1 teasp sugar	(approx)
1 oz yeast	

Mix the wholemeal flour and oatmeal and proceed as for wholemeal bread below, adding soda dissolved in a little water. Prepare tins by greasing and dusting very thickly with flour. Oval-shaped tins give an attractive-looking loaf. Divide the dough into pieces and put in tins. Press well into shape and smooth on top. Prove for 15 min or until well risen, with a baking-sheet on top. Bake in a very hot oven (230°C, 450°F, Gas 8) with a baking sheet and weight on top, reducing the heat after 20 min to fairly hot (190°C, 375°F, Gas 5). The finished bread should be floury on the outside.

3–4 loaves   **Cooking time 45–60 min**

evaporation, and set in a warm place to rise to double its size—about 1 hr. When the dough is sufficiently risen it has a honeycombed appearance. The first kneading distributes the yeast and softens the gluten of the flour. Knead the dough a second time to distribute the carbonic acid gas which has formed. Continue kneading until, when the dough is cut, there are no large holes in it, but do not knead too heavily. Divide into the number of loaves required. Place in warmed greased tins, making the top round. Prick and allow to prove or recover for 20 min or just until the dough is well up to the top of the tin and no longer. Bake in the middle of a very hot oven (230°C, 450°F, Gas 8) for 10–15 min, then reduce heat to fairly hot (190°C, 375°F, Gas 5), baking in all about 1 hr. When ready the loaf should have a hollow sound when knocked on the bottom, and should be well risen and nicely browned with a crisp crust.

4 loaves   **Cooking time 1 hr**

FANCY BREAD ROLLS

BASIC DOUGH

½ lb plain flour	**1 heaped teasp castor sugar**
1 level teasp salt	**¼ pt skim milk made from milk powder**
1 oz margarine	
½ oz fresh yeast *or* ¼ oz dried yeast	

Sift the flour and salt into a large bowl. Leave to stand in a warm place for 10–15 min. Rub in the margarine. Cream the yeast and sugar together until liquid. Warm the milk and stir it into the yeast mixture. Make a well in the centre of the flour, pour in the liquid and mix to a soft dough. Knead for 5–10 min on a floured surface, until the dough is smooth and glossy. Place in a greased bowl, turn over to grease the whole surface of the dough, cover with a damp cloth, and leave to rise until doubled in size. Shape as required.

Trefoils

Divide the basic dough into 8 pieces, then divide each piece into 3 bits. Form these into balls and cluster 3 together in a patty tin. Fill 8 tins, then leave in a warm place until doubled in size. It will take about 15 min. Brush with beaten egg yolk and skim milk to glaze, and scatter on a few poppy seeds. Bake in a fairly hot oven, at 200°C, 400°F, Gas 6 for 15–20 min.

Bread Knots

Divide the dough into 8 pieces and roll each into a tube shape about 10-in long. Tie in a loose knot. Prove and glaze as above, place on a greased baking sheet, and bake like trefoils.

Baby cottage loaves

Divide the basic dough into 8 pieces. Cut each piece into a smaller and larger piece. Shape into rounds. Place the larger rounds on a greased baking sheet, and put the smaller ones on top. Make a dip in the centre of each with your finger. Prove and glaze like trefoils, and bake in the same way.

Ginger twists

Knead 2 level teasp ground ginger into the dough (or sift in with the flour). Divide the dough into 16 pieces and roll each out 6-in long. Twist 2 pieces together, and place on a greased baking sheet. Prove, glaze and bake like trefoils. When cooked and cool, brush over with icing made from sifted icing sugar and water.

BRIOCHE ROLLS

1 lb plain flour	**4 eggs**
½ teasp salt	**1 oz castor sugar**
½ oz yeast	**6 oz margarine**
2–3 tablesp tepid water	

Sift the warmed flour and salt into a basin, make a well in the middle and pour in the creamed yeast and tepid water. Mix in a little flour. Allow this sponge to set in a warm place for about 30 min. Add the eggs, sugar and slightly warmed margarine and mix all together with additional tepid water to make a soft pliable dough. Allow dough to rise 1–2 hr, until it has doubled its size. Take ⅔ and divide it into 20–24 large balls. Divide the remaining ⅓ into 20–24 small balls. Grease patty tins, place a large ball on each tin and flatten slightly, make a small depression, damp it and fix a small ball on top. Put your little finger through the centre. Leave the rolls in a warm place to prove for 20 min. Brush with egg and sprinkle with salt, or if wanted sweet, with sugar. Bake in a hot oven (220°C, 425°F, Gas 7).

20–24 rolls **Cooking time 15–20 min**

BATH BUNS

1 lb plain flour	**Good ½ oz yeast**
½ teasp salt	**3 oz sugar**
3 oz fat (margarine and lard)	**2 eggs**
	1½–2 gills warm milk

SUGAR SYRUP GLAZE

1 tablesp water	**1 dessertsp sugar**

Mix salt with warmed flour and rub in fat. Mix in most of the sugar. Mix to a light dough with yeast creamed with remainder of sugar, egg and milk. Put to rise till double its size, then knead lightly. Divide into 24 pieces and shape each 3½–4-in long and 1-in wide. Place fairly close together (so that they join up in baking) on greased baking sheets and prove 15 min. Bake in a hot oven (220°C, 425°F, Gas 7) 10–15 min.

To make the glaze—boil together the water and sugar until slightly syrupy. Brush the buns immediately they come from the oven so that the syrup dries on.

Dredge thickly with castor sugar. Break buns apart before serving.

NOTE. 2 oz sultanas and 1 oz chopped peel can be worked into the dough after it has risen.

24 buns **Cooking time 10–15 min**

Croissants

CHELSEA BUNS

½ lb plain flour	**½ oz currants *or* sultanas**
¼ teasp salt	**½ oz chopped candied peel**
1 oz lard *or* margarine	**1 oz sugar**
½ oz yeast	
1 gill warm milk	

Mix flour and salt; rub in fat, cream yeast and add to flour, with warm milk. Beat well and put to rise to double its size. Knead risen dough lightly and roll out in a square of about 10 in. Sprinkle with the fruit and sugar and roll up like a Swiss roll. Cut roll into 9 pieces and put cut side uppermost. Place buns in a greased 8 in sandwich cake tin so that they will join together when cooked and allow to prove till up to the top of the tin. Brush with milk or egg. Bake in a hot oven (220°C, 425°F, Gas 7) for 20–25 min. When cooked, glaze and dust with sugar like Bath Buns.

9 buns   Cooking time 20–25 min

CROISSANTS

1 lb plain flour	1 egg, beaten
2 level teasp salt	4–6 oz hard margarine
1 oz lard	

YEAST MIXTURE

1 oz fresh yeast blended into $\frac{1}{2}$ pt (less 4 tablesp) water *or* 1 level tablesp dried yeast sprinkled on the same amount of water warmed to 43°C, 110°F, with 1 teasp sugar

Rub the 1 oz lard into the flour. Make a dough with the yeast mixture after letting it stand for 10 min. Mix the beaten egg in with the yeast mixture. Knead the dough on a lightly floured board for 10–15 min until smooth. Roll into a strip about 20 × 8 in and $\frac{1}{4}$ in thick, taking care to keep the edges straight and corners square. Soften the margarine with a knife, and divide it into 3 parts. Dot one part in flakes over two-thirds of the dough, leaving a small border clear. Fold in 3, folding over the unflaked portion first. Turn the dough so that the fold is on the right hand side. Seal the edges with a rolling pin. Re-shape into a long strip by gently pressing the dough at intervals with a rolling pin. Repeat the flaking and folding process twice more. Place the finally shaped dough in a polythene bag, and let it rest in the refrigerator for $\frac{1}{2}$ hr. Roll out as before, and repeat the folding process 3 times more. Let the dough rest in the fridge for 1 hr this time.

Roll the dough into a rectangle about 23 × 14 in. Let it rest for 10 min. Then trim it with a knife to 21 × 12 in and divide the strip in half lengthways. Cut each strip into 6 triangles 6 in high with a 6 in base. Make an egg wash with 1 egg, a little water and $\frac{1}{2}$ teasp sugar. Brush the croissants. Roll up each triangle loosely towards its point from the opposite side, ending with the tip underneath. Curve each into a crescent moon shape.

Put the shaped croissants on an ungreased baking sheet. Brush the tops with egg wash, put the sheet into a lightly greased polythene bag and leave at room temperature for about $\frac{1}{2}$ hr, until the croissants are light and puffy. Brush yet again with egg wash, and bake in the centre of a hot oven at 220°C, 425°F, Gas 7, for 20 min.

DOUGHNUTS

$\frac{1}{2}$ lb plain flour	$\frac{1}{2}$ oz yeast
$\frac{1}{4}$ teasp salt	$\frac{1}{2}$–$\frac{3}{4}$ gill warm milk
$\frac{3}{4}$ oz lard and 1 oz margarine	1 egg
1 oz castor sugar	Cinnamon sugar for coating
	Fat for deep frying

Rub the fat into the warmed flour and salt; add sugar, having taken out $\frac{1}{2}$ teasp to cream the yeast. Add the warm milk and egg to the creamed yeast and pour into the flour. Mix well (do not make too soft as the dough is to be cut out), and put to rise to double its size. Knead lightly and roll out $\frac{1}{2}$ in thick. Cut into rings, using $2\frac{1}{2}$–$2\frac{3}{4}$-in cutter for outside and $1\frac{1}{2}$–$1\frac{3}{4}$-in for inner ring, and prove on a warm tray for 5 min. Drop into very faintly smoking fat and cook 5 min; drain well and toss in castor sugar *or* sugar

mixed with ground cinnamon to taste.

Alternative method Divide dough into 12. Roll each piece into a ball and place a glacé cherry or a little jam in the middle. Prove 10 min and proceed as above.

14–16 doughnuts

HOT CROSS BUNS

1 lb plain flour	$\frac{1}{2}$ oz yeast
$\frac{1}{2}$ teasp salt	1–2 eggs
2 oz margarine *or* margarine and lard	$1\frac{1}{2}$–2 gills milk
4 oz sugar	2 oz currants *or* 2 oz raisins and peel
1 teasp mixed spice *or* cinnamon	Short crust pastry trimmings

Mix salt with warmed flour. Rub in fat. Add sugar, spice, creamed yeast, and eggs with the warm milk. Mix to a soft, light dough, beat well and put to rise. When well risen, knead the dough lightly, working in the fruit, and divide into 20–24 pieces. Form into round shapes, flatten slightly and put to prove for 15 min. Cut narrow strips of pastry $1\frac{1}{2}$–2-in long, brush tops of buns with egg wash *or* milk, place pastry crosses on top and bake in a hot oven (220°C, 425°F, Gas 7).

20–24 buns   Cooking time 15–20 min

Doughnuts made with yeast

PIKELETS
PIKELETS or CRUMPETS

½ lb plain flour
½ teasp salt
½ oz yeast
½ teasp sugar

½ pt milk and water
Pinch of bicarbonate of
    soda

Warm the flour and mix with the salt. Cream yeast with sugar, add to the warmed milk and water and mix with flour to the consistency of a soft batter. Cover and leave to rise 30–45 min. Dissolve the soda in 1 tablesp warm water, add to the mixture, beating well, and put to rise again for 30 min. Grease a griddle, thick frying-pan or electric hot-plate and heat until fairly hot. Grease pikelet rings or large plain cutters (3½–4-in), place on the griddle and pour in enough batter to cover the bottoms of the pikelet rings or cutters to a depth of ¼-in. When top is set and bubbles burst, turn and cook on underside. Serve hot with butter.

8–10 pikelets

SCANDINAVIAN TEA RING

6 oz plain flour
¼ teasp salt

Small ½ oz yeast
½–¾ gill warm milk

½ oz sugar

½–1 egg

FILLING

1 oz ground almonds
1 oz castor sugar

Hot water to mix to a
    spreading
    consistency

ICING

3 oz sifted icing sugar

Warm water to mix

DECORATION

½ oz blanched and
    chopped almonds

Mix flour and salt; add most of the sugar. Cream yeast with remainder of sugar, add warm milk and egg and mix with flour to a light but workable dough. Put the dough to rise and when well risen roll out in an oblong shape. Spread with the almond mixture; damp edges with water and roll up. Form into a ring or horseshoe shape; prove 10–15 min. Bake in a hot oven (220°C, 425°F, Gas 7), reducing the heat after 10 min to fairly hot (190°C, 375°F, Gas 5). When cold, spread with icing and sprinkle with chopped almonds.

Cooking time 20–30 min

Preserving farm and garden produce was vital in the past when people's only source of food was their local countryside. They dared not waste a scrap of summer bounty, in places where lean winter months would surely come when food would be scarce and boring in its sameness.

We, too, dare not waste food, but mainly because there are now too many of us to feed. As peoples multiply and industries spread, our food resources shrink, and the areas fit for growing and rearing foodstuffs and stock shrink too. We must use all the resources we have to the best advantage. In the Western world, most malnutrition is caused by simple over-eating; but we also eat too much food which provides little nourishment. So we must concentrate on the most nourishing foods, and take care to preserve all their goodness and flavour. We need and desire less bulk if our food is interesting.

Today, a very high proportion of our food is processed by a manufacturer in some way, usually to preserve it or make it easier to use. So, while this section deals with preserving flavoursome home-grown produce as jams, jellies, preserves, pickles and ketchups, and with home freezing, a great many recipes in this book can use ingredients and products processed by manufacturers.

Many of these are what we call 'convenience' foods; that is, foods highly processed so they are almost ready for use. They include frozen foods, from shelled peas to whole, ready-cooked meals, and ice creams; canned foods; and dried foods in packets or sachets. Sometimes these are partly cooked (such as rice), sometimes concentrated (such as canned soups) and sometimes in a brand-new form with no natural counterpart, such as 'instant' coffee or corn flakes.

We spend more than 20 per cent of our total food budget on these foods; so it is good to know that many still have a high food value when they reach us, certainly much better than the foods preserved by our forebears by drying in the fields and by salting.

JAM AND JELLY MAKING

Because fruit varies so much in quality, and the type of pan you use affects its cooking, the same jam or jelly recipe can have different results from household to household. The following recipes have been tested thoroughly, but the yields may vary slightly.

The fruits from which jams and jellies are made contain different amounts of sugar, acid and pectin (a natural gum-like substance). All three are essential to the 'set' of a jam or jelly, and fruits can be divided into:

1 Fruits which make a well-set jam or jelly, e.g. apples, blackcurrants, damsons, gooseberries, plums and redcurrants.

2 Fruits of medium setting quality, e.g. apricots, blackberries, raspberries and loganberries.

3 Fruits which set poorly, e.g. cherries, strawberries.

If you doubt the pectin content of a given crop of fruit, use the Pectin Test below. But in the following recipes pectin is already added to medium and poor-setting fruits either by adding pectin-rich fruit (as in Blackberry and Apple jam) or juice (e.g. lemon juice) or commercial pectin (such as is found in whole strawberry jam).

CHOICE OF FRUITS
FOR JAMS AND JELLIES

Choose firm ripe fruit, or just ripe and under-ripe fruit. Over-ripe fruit will not set as jam. (Gooseberries must be under-ripe and hard.)

PRESERVING PANS

CHOICE OF PRESERVING PAN FOR JAMS

Choose a pan which is large enough. It should not be more than half full when the fruit and sugar are in because they must boil together rapidly without risk of boiling over. A pressure cooker must never be more than half filled when ready for pressure cooking jams.

Use a preserving pan, or a large pan of aluminium, stainless steel or unchipped enamel (it should be unchipped, otherwise the jam may stick and burn, or the iron may spoil its colour). Copper or brass preserving pans can be used as long as any metal polish used for cleaning is thoroughly removed; but jam made in these pans may contain less vitamin C. Do not use iron or zinc pans; the fruit acid will attack the metal, and the colour and flavour of the jam will be spoiled. To prevent the jam sticking and to help avoid scum, the inside of the pan can be rubbed before use with glycerine or a small piece of butter or margarine.

TESTING FOR SETTING POINT

There are several tests for setting point including the simple methods given below. Unless otherwise stated in a recipe, jams are usually tested when high frothing ceases and boiling becomes noisy, with heavy plopping bubbles. If the jam is not set, continue testing at frequent intervals.

1 Cold plate test

Remove the pan from the heat (otherwise setting point may be missed while this test is being made). Spoon a little jam on to a cold plate or saucer, and allow it to cool. If setting point has been reached, the surface will set firm and will wrinkle when pushed with the finger.

2 Temperature test

For this an accurate thermometer marked in degrees up to and above 104°C (220°F) is required. Put the thermometer in hot water before and after use. Stir the jam thoroughly so that it is an even temperature throughout. Insert the thermometer holding it well in. Provided a reliable recipe which gives sufficient acid and sugar is being used, a good set should be obtained when the jam reaches 104°C (220°F). Occasionally a temperature of 105–106°C (221–222°F) will give better results. Use this test in conjunction with the Flake Test.

3 Flake test

Dip a clean wooden spoon into the jam, remove it and twirl it around until the jam on it has cooled slightly. Then tilt the spoon to allow the jam to drop from it; if it has been boiled sufficiently, the jam will partially set on the spoon and the drops will run together to form flakes which will fall cleanly and sharply.

4 Volume test

In a good recipe it is generally reckoned that 5 lb of jam should be obtained for every 3 lb of sugar used. To test the volume of the jam:

(*a*) Before making the jam, fill a 1 lb jam jar with water five times, pouring the water into the preserving pan. See that the pan is perfectly level.

(*b*) carefully hold the handle of a wooden spoon upright in the centre of the pan, and mark on it the level of the water. Then empty the pan and make the jam.

(*c*) when the jam is to be tested, remove it from the heat so that the bubbling will subside, then hold upright in it the handle of the wooden spoon.

A good setting jam should be obtained when the level has been boiled down to the mark on the spoon handle. (It follows that, when making 10 lb of jam, the level of 10 filled jam jars should be marked on the spoon.)

It is an excellent plan to have another wooden spoon marked off in this way permanently, to

Left, *plate test for setting of jam*
Right, *flake test for setting jam*

give the level in the centre of your pan *for each pint* of liquid it contains. Then, if a recipe calls for the addition of 1 lb sugar to every 1 pint jam or marmalade, you can easily measure how many pints the pan contains. Use a pint measure in place of the jam jar, to pour the water in.

TEST FOR PECTIN

After the fruit has cooked till tender, squeeze out a teasp of juice. Place to cool in a cup or glass. Then add 3 teasp methylated spirits. Shake gently and leave 1 min. If there is plenty of pectin in the fruit, a transparent jelly-like lump will form. If there is only a moderate amount of pectin there may be two or three lumps, not very firm. If there is insufficient pectin, the lump will break into many small pieces and the fruit should be simmered for a little longer before another pectin test is made. It is a waste of effort to attempt to make jam or jelly if there is only a poor amount of pectin. It is wiser to mix the fruit with another which is known to be a good setter, e.g. apple.

SPECIAL POINTS IN JELLY MAKING

1 Use fresh fruit, not over-ripe.

2 Simmer gently in water (the amount varies with the recipe) till the fruit is tender and thoroughly broken down (usually $\frac{3}{4}$–1 hr). If in any doubt about its setting properties, test for pectin at this stage, as a good set depends upon the amount of acid, pectin and sugar present.

3 After cooking, strain the fruit through a jelly bag, first scalding the bag by pouring boiling water through it. Hang the bag on a special frame, or suspend it from the legs of an upturned stool *or* chair with a basin below to catch the drips.

4 Never hurry the straining of the juice by squeezing the bag; this may make the jelly cloudy. Some people leave the juice to drip overnight, but do not leave it too long before completing the jelly, certainly not more than 24 hr. Fruit which is very rich in pectin can be strained twice. The two juices can be mixed together, or two grades of jelly can be made, one from the first and another from the second.

5 Measure the juice into a preserving pan. Bring to the boil. Add the sugar. Strained juice rich in pectin needs 1 lb sugar to each pint of juice. Juice with only a fair pectin content needs only $\frac{3}{4}$ lb sugar to each pint. A thick, sticky juice is almost certain to contain plenty of pectin, but many people prefer to be sure by using the Pectin Test above.

6 After dissolving the sugar, boil rapidly till setting point is reached (about 10 min). Test by

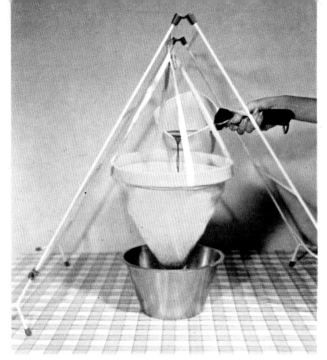

Simple device for straining jelly

any of the methods for Jam. The Flake Test, used with the Temperature Test, is probably the most satisfactory.

7 Skim, removing the last traces of scum from the surface with the torn edge of a piece of kitchen paper. Pour into warm jars, 1 lb size or smaller, at once, before it has time to begin setting in the pan. Put on waxed circles (waxed side down) immediately. Cover when hot or cold. Do not tilt the jars until the jelly has set. Store in a cool, dry, dark place.

The exact yield of jelly from each recipe cannot be given because of varying losses in straining the juice, but usually about 10 lb of jelly can be made from each 6 lb sugar used.

APPLE JELLY

4 lb well-flavoured crab-apples *or* cooking apples (windfalls can be used)	Flavouring: lemon peel *or* root ginger .Sugar

Wash the apples and cut up without peeling or coring; just remove any bad portions. Barely cover with about 2–3 pt water and simmer with the chosen flavouring till tender and well mashed. This will take about 1 hr. Strain through a scalded jelly bag. Bring the strained juice to the boil and test for pectin. Add the sugar (usually 1 lb sugar to every pint of juice). Stir to dissolve. Boil briskly till setting point is reached.

APPLE AND QUINCE JAM OR JELLY

3 lb apples, quartered	1½ pt water
3 lb quinces, quartered	Granulated sugar

Place fruits in a preserving pan and add water. Stew gently until fruit is well pulped. For jam use the same weight in sugar as fruit. For jelly, strain through a scalded jelly cloth leaving juice to drip through undisturbed. Measure the juice and place it

Apple jelly and mint jelly

in a pan over low flame; add sugar, allowing 1 lb sugar to each pint of juice. In either case, dissolve the sugar slowly. Skin jelly frequently during cooking. Boil rapidly until setting point is reached. Pour into small warmed jars. Seal when cool.

APPLE OR PEAR SPICE BUTTER

6 lb apples *or* pears	2 level teasp allspice
2 pt cider *or* perry	½ teasp nutmeg
Granulated sugar	2 level teasp cloves
Lemon juice and grated rind	

Wash and cut up the fruit. Put in a pan with the cider or perry, and cook over a low heat until tender. Pass through a sieve. Weigh the pulp and allow 1 lb sugar and the rind and juice of 1 lemon for every 1 lb of pulp. Add the remaining ingredients and cook over a low heat for 40–60 min, until thickened. Turn into hot sterilised jars. Seal when cold.

APRICOT JAM—(Fresh Fruit with added pectin)

2 lb ripe apricots	3 lb sugar
¼ pt water	½ bottle pectin
3 tablesp lemon juice	

Use only ripe fruit. Wash, stone and cut the apricots into slices. Do not peel. Place the fruit in a preserving pan with the water and lemon juice. Cover and simmer for 20 min until the fruit is tender.

Add the sugar, stir over a low heat until it has dissolved. Bring to a rolling boil and boil rapidly for 1 min, stirring occasionally. Remove from the heat. Stir in the pectin. Cool 5 min. Pot and put on waxed discs immediately. Cover and label.

A few blanched kernels may be added to the fruit.

Yield 5 lb

APRICOT or PEACH JAM (Dried Fruit)

This is a popular jam for making in the winter when most other fruits are scarce.

1 lb dried apricots *or* peaches	Juice of 1 lemon
	3 lb sugar
2–3 pt water (2 pt for peaches, 3 pt for apricots)	2–3 oz blanched and finely shredded almonds (optional)

Wash the fruit and put in a basin with the water. Soak for 24–48 hr. Transfer the fruit and water to the preserving pan and simmer for 30 min, stirring occasionally. Add the sugar, lemon juice and the shredded almonds. Stir over a low heat until the sugar is dissolved. Boil rapidly until setting point is reached. Skim, pot and cover.

Yield approx. 5 lb

BLACKBERRY AND APPLE JAM

¾ lb sour apples (weighed when peeled and cored)	½ pt water
	2 lb blackberries
	3 lb sugar

Slice the apples and stew them till soft in ¼ pt of the water. Pick over the blackberries, add the other ¼ pt of water and stew slowly in another pan till tender. Mix the 2 cooked fruits together. Add the sugar, heat gently until dissolved, then boil rapidly until setting point is reached. Skim, pour into warm, dry jars and cover.

Yield 5 lb

BLACKCURRANT JAM

2 lb blackcurrants	3 lb sugar
1½ pt water	

Remove currants from the stalks. If the fruit is dirty, wash it thoroughly and drain. Put into the preserving pan with the water, and stew slowly till the skins are soft. *This will take at least ½ hr, probably more.* As the pulp thickens, stir frequently to prevent burning. Add the sugar, stir over a low heat until dissolved, then boil rapidly till setting point is reached. (Test for set at intervals after about 10 min rapid boiling.) Skim, pour into dry, warm jars and cover.

NOTE. This is a good jam for beginners—it sets very easily. But beware of adding the sugar too soon, otherwise hard, 'boot-button' currants will result. Try adding 1 tablesp blackcurrant jam when cooking curry; it helps to darken the curry and gives a good flavour.

Yield 5 lb

CHERRY (BLACK) JAM (with added pectin)

2½ lb black cherries (after stoning)	6 tablesp lemon juice
	3 lb sugar
¼ pt water	1 bottle pectin

Place the washed and stoned cherries in a preserving pan with the water and lemon juice. Cook gently with the lid on for 15 min. Remove lid. Add the sugar and stir over gentle heat until it has dissolved. Bring to a full rolling boil and boil rapidly for 3 min. Remove from the heat, stir in the pectin, return to the heat, bring to the boil and boil for 1 min only. Cool for 15 min to prevent fruit rising. Pot and put on waxed discs immediately. Cover and label.

Yield 5 lb

DAMSON JAM

2½ lb damsons	3 lb sugar
¾–1 pt water	

Remove the stalks, wash the damsons and put into the pan with the water. Stew slowly until the damsons are well broken down. Add the sugar, stir over a low heat till dissolved, bring to the boil, then boil rapidly. Remove the stones as they rise to the surface (a stone-basket clipped to the side of the pan is useful for holding the stones, and allows any liquid to drip back into the pan). (Test for set after about 10 min boiling.) Continue boiling rapidly until setting point is reached. Skim, pour into dry, warm jars and cover.

Yield 5 lb

GOOSEBERRY JAM—GREEN OR RED

2¼ lb gooseberries	3 lb sugar
¾–1 pt water	

Pick or buy the gooseberries while still green. Top and tail and wash them, and put in a pan with the water. Simmer gently until the fruit is soft; this may take ½ hr or longer. Then add the sugar and stir over a low heat until dissolved. Bring to the boil and boil rapidly for 10 min. Remove from the heat to test for the set. Boil until setting point is reached. Skim, pour into dry, warm jars and cover.

Most gooseberry jam turns a reddish colour as it cooks. It can be kept green by taking the following steps:

1 Choose a variety of gooseberry which is green when ripe, e.g. 'Careless', 'Green Gem' or 'Keepsake'.

2 Use a copper or brass preserving pan.

3 Give the jam the shortest possible boil in which it will set once the sugar has been dissolved.

For 'Muscat Flavoured' Gooseberry Jam, put the flowers from 8 heads of elderflowers in a muslin bag, and cook them with the gooseberries. Squeeze out the juice and remove the bag before the sugar is added.

This is a good jam for beginners, because it is a notoriously good setter. It is specially good served on scones with whipped cream.

LEMON OR ORANGE CURD

FOR LEMON CURD USE

3 eggs	Rind and juice of 2
3 oz butter	lemons
8 oz sugar	

FOR ORANGE CURD USE

4 eggs	Rind and juice of
2 oz butter	2 oranges and
8 oz loaf sugar	1 lemon

Whisk the eggs and put into a basin with the butter, sugar, finely-grated lemon rind (or orange rind) and the strained juice. Place the basin over a pan of boiling water, stir until the mixture is thick

Selection of apple jams

and smooth. Pour into clean, warm jars and cover.

MARROW AND GINGER PRESERVE

4 lb marrow (weighed	2 oz root ginger
after preparation)	3 tablesp lemon juice
3 lb sugar	

Peel the marrow and cut into cubes, removing the seeds. Place the cubes in a colander over a pan of boiling water, put the pan lid on top of the marrow and steam until just cooked and tender. Place in a basin, cover with the sugar and leave overnight. Next day, bruise the root ginger (bang it with a hammer or weight) and tie it in muslin. Put the bag of ginger into a preserving pan with the marrow and lemon juice. Cook slowly for about 1 hr until the marrow is clear and transparent. This jam does not give a firm set, so do not hopefully go on cooking it. Stop cooking when the correct yield (5 lb) is obtained. By this time the marrow should be transparent and the syrup thick. Remove the bag of ginger just before the end. Pour into dry, warm jars and cover.

Yield 5 lb

MINT JELLY

3 lb green apples	Sugar
1⅛ pt water	3 level tablesp chopped
A small bunch of fresh	mint
mint	A few drops of green
1⅛ pt vinegar	colouring

Wash the apples, cut in quarters and place in a preserving pan with the water and the bunch of mint. Simmer until the apples are soft and pulpy, then add the vinegar and boil for 5 min. Strain overnight through a cloth, measure the juice and to each pint, allow 1 lb sugar. Put the juice and sugar into the pan and bring to the boil, stirring until the sugar is dissolved. Boil rapidly until setting point is nearly reached, add the chopped mint and colouring, then boil until setting point is reached. Pour into hot jars and cover immediately with waxed discs. When quite cold, tie down with parchment or transparent covers, label and store.

MULBERRY AND APPLE JAM—SIEVED

2½ lb mulberries	1 lb apples (peeled
½ pt water	and cored)
	3 lb sugar

Stew the mulberries in some of the water till soft. Rub through a sieve. Stew the apples in the rest of the water. When soft, stir in the sieved mulberries and the sugar. Stir over a low heat till the sugar is dissolved. Bring to the boil and boil till 5 lb jam are obtained.

Yield 5 lb

PEACH (FRESH) JAM
(with added pectin)

2 lb yellow flesh	6 tablesp lemon juice
peaches	3 lb sugar
¼ pt water	½ bottle pectin

Stone and skin the peaches and cut into slices. Place in a large preserving pan with the water and the lemon juice. Cover the pan and simmer gently for 15–20 min until the fruit is tender. Add the sugar and stir over a low heat until the sugar has dissolved. Bring to a rolling boil and boil rapidly for 1 min stirring occasionally. Remove from the heat and stir in the pectin. Cool 5 min. Pot and put on waxed discs immediately. Cover and label.

Yield 5 lb

PLUM JAM

3 lb plums	¼–¾ pt water (¼ pt for
3 lb sugar	ripe, juicy dessert
	plums, ¾ pt for
	cooking varieties)

Remove stalks and put the washed plums into the pan with the water. Stew slowly until the fruit is well broken down. Ripe fruit or very juicy varieties will need only a small quantity of water and will be cooked in a few min. Firmer varieties may take about 20 min to break down, and will need the larger quantity of water. Add the sugar, stir over a low heat till dissolved, then boil rapidly, remove the stones as they rise to the surface (a stone-basket clipped to the side of the pan is useful for holding the stones, and allows any liquid to drip back into the pan). Keep testing for setting point after about 10 min rapid boiling. Skim, pot and cover.

If desired, a few of the raw plums may be stoned;

crack the stones, remove the kernels, blanch them by dipping in boiling water and add the halved kernels to the pan.

For plum and apple jam, use 1½ lb plums and 1½ lb apples. Proceed as above.

Yield 5 lb

QUINCE JELLY

Quinces	Sugar
Water	

Wipe the fruit carefully. Do not peel but cut into quarters and put into the preserving pan with sufficient cold water to cover. Bring slowly to the boil and simmer gently until the quinces are tender. Strain through a scalded jelly bag. Do not squeeze or the jelly will not be clear. Add 1 lb of sugar to each pint of juice and boil till setting point is reached.

RASPBERRY JAM. Quick Method

This jam does not set very firmly, but it has a delicious fresh flavour. Do not wash the raspberries unless absolutely necessary; if they have to be washed, drain very thoroughly.

2½ lb raspberries	3 lb granulated sugar

Bring the fruit gently to the boil, then boil rapidly for 5 min. Remove from the heat, add the warmed sugar and stir well over a low heat until all the sugar has dissolved. Bring to the boil and boil rapidly *for 1 min*. Skim quickly, pour the jam at once into dry, warm jars and cover.

Yield 5 lb

REDCURRANT JELLY

6 lb large, juicy red	Sugar
or red and white	
currants mixed	

Remove the leaves and only the larger stems. Place the cleaned fruit in the preserving pan, without any water, and heat very gently until the currants are softened for about ¾ hr and well cooked. Mash, then strain the pulp through a scalded jelly bag, leaving it to drip undisturbed. Measure the juice into the cleaned pan. Add 1¼ lb of sugar to each pint of juice. Bring to the boil, stirring constantly, and boil, without stirring, for 1 min. Swiftly skim the jelly and immediately pour it into the warmed jars, before it has a chance to set in the pan.

ROSE HIP JELLY (PRESSURE COOKER)

2 lb rose hips	Sugar
1½ pt water	Tartaric acid

Rose hip jelly

Five fruit marmalade

Choose firm but well ripened fruit. Wash and top and tail. Remove the trivet from the pressure cooker. Put in the fruit and water. Bring to 10 lb pressure over a medium heat and pressure cook for 30 min. Reduce pressure at room temperature and stir well with a wooden spoon through a wire sieve. Strain the pulp again through a scalded jelly bag. Add 1 lb sugar and ½ teasp of tartaric acid to each pint of juice. Return to heat in open cooker. Stir over low heat until sugar is dissolved. Bring to boil and boil until setting point is reached.

This method can be used for other pressure cooker jams and jellies, although most fruit will need only 5–10 min cooking under pressure.

WHOLE STRAWBERRY JAM
(with added pectin)

2¼ lb small straw- berries	A little butter *or* margarine
3 lb sugar	½ bottle pectin
3 tablesp lemon juice	

Hull the strawberries and put in a preserving pan with the sugar and lemon juice. Stand for 1 hr, giving the contents of the pan an occasional stir. Place over a low heat and, when the sugar has dissolved, add a small piece of butter or margarine to reduce foaming. Bring to a rolling boil and boil rapidly for 4 min. Remove from the heat and add the pectin. Stir well. Allow to cool for at least 20 min to prevent the fruit rising. Stir gently, then pour into clean, warm, dry jars. Put on waxed discs immediately. Cover and label when cold.

Yield 5 lb

MARMALADE MAKING

Marmalade-making is similar to jam-making and nearly all the same rules apply. As in jam-making, the fruit is first simmered gently, usually in an open pan, until it is thoroughly softened. During this long, slow cooking, in the presence of acid, the jellying substance—pectin—is brought into solution. After this, the sugar is added and stirred over a gentle heat till dissolved. Then the marmalade is boiled rapidly, with a full, rolling boil, until setting point is reached. The tests for setting point are the same as for jam-making.

These are the essential differences:

(*a*) The peel of citrus fruit takes longer to soften than the fruit used for jams.

(*b*) Because most of the pectin is present in the pips and the pith, rather than in the fruit pulp or fruit juice, these are important ingredients of marmalade recipes. The pips and pith should not be discarded (unless they are being replaced by commercial pectin) but should be tied loosely in muslin and cooked with the fruit until the pectin has been extracted. If the muslin bag is tied to the handle of the pan, it can easily be removed before adding the sugar.

MAKING MARMALADE

Cutting up oranges

Adding measured water

Measuring sugar

Putting into pots

FURTHER POINTS TO NOTE FOR MAKING MARMALADE

1 All citrus fruits should be only just ripe, and must be used as soon as possible; if possible, order the fruit in advance and ask the greengrocer to tell you as soon as it reaches him.

2 It is not usually easy for the layman to distinguish between the true Seville orange and other imported bitter oranges. Sevilles are considered to have a superior flavour, but ordinary bitter oranges can replace them in the recipes below.

3 If the recipe tells you to peel the citrus fruit, try soaking the fruit in boiling water first for 1–2 min. This helps the skin to peel off easily.

4 It is necessary to use a very sharp stainless knife to cut the peel into shreds. Remember that the peel will swell slightly during the cooking. If large quantities of marmalade are made, it may be worth-while buying a special machine which cuts the peel swiftly and easily.

Many recipes recommend soaking the peel, etc, for 24–48 hr to soften it before cooking. If time is limited, this is not essential. But if the soaking is omitted, you may have to cook the peel a little longer to make sure that it is sufficiently softened.

The sugar must not be added until the pulp is considerably reduced and the peel will disintegrate when squeezed. This takes $1\frac{1}{2}$–2 hr. Given this, setting point is generally reached after about 15–20 min rapid boiling.

HOW TO POT AND COVER MARMALADES

Always remove the scum from marmalade as soon as the setting point is reached. Use a hot metal spoon. If the scum is not removed immediately, it subsides gently on the peel and is then extremely difficult to skim off.

To prevent the peel rising to the top of the pots, leave the skimmed marmalade to cool undisturbed in the pan until a thin skin begins to form on the surface. Then stir it to distribute the peel (but do this gently to avoid air bubbles, and do not stir clear jelly marmalades).

Pour into the pots, using a small jug or cup.

Waxed discs should be placed on the marmalade immediately, taking care to avoid air bubbles under the disc. Some recipes advise putting on the outer cover when the marmalade is quite cold. Alternatively, the outer covers can be put on while the marmalade is still very hot. But do not put them on when it is only warm, as warm marmalade makes moisture condense on the underside of the cover and the heat from the marmalade is not sufficient to dry it. Moulds grow easily on damp preserves.

CLEAR SHRED ORANGE MARMALADE

3 lb Seville oranges	6 pt water
2 lemons	Sugar
1 sweet orange	

Wash the fruit, dry and cut in half. Squeeze out the juice and strain, keeping back pulp and pips. Scrape all the white pith from the skins, using a spoon, and put pips, pulp and white pith into a bowl with 2 pt water. Shred the peel finely with a sharp knife and put this into another bowl with 4 pt water and the juice. Leave to stand for 24 hr. Strain the pips, etc, through a muslin bag and tie loosely. Put the bag and strained liquor, the peel and juice into the preserving pan and bring to simmering point. Simmer for 1½ hr until the peel is tender. Remove from the heat and squeeze out the muslin bag gently. For a very clear jelly, allow to drip only. Measure 1 lb sugar to each pint juice and allow the sugar to dissolve completely over a low heat. Bring to the boil and boil rapidly for about 20 min until a set is obtained. Remove from the heat and cool until a skin forms on the surface. Pour into hot jars and cover immediately.

Yield approx. 10 lb

DARK COARSE-CUT MARMALADE

2 lb Seville oranges	6 lb sugar
1 lemon	1 tablesp black treacle
7 pt water	

Wash the fruit, cut in half and squeeze the juice. Tie the pips loosely in a muslin bag. Slice the skins into medium-thick shreds. Put the juice, muslin bag, sliced peel and water into a preserving pan and simmer until the peel is tender and the liquid reduced by *at least* ⅓. This will take about 1½ hr. Remove the bag of pips, after squeezing the juice out gently. Remove the pan from the heat then add the sugar and the treacle; return the pan to the heat and stir over a low heat till the sugar is dissolved. Then boil rapidly till setting point is reached.

Yield 10 lb

FIVE FRUIT MARMALADE

2 lb fruit: 1 orange,	3 pt water
1 grapefruit, 1	3 lb sugar
lemon, 1 large apple,	
1 pear	

Wash and skin orange, grapefruit and lemon and shred the peel finely. Cut this fruit coarsely. Put the pips and coarse tissue in a basin with ½ pt water. Place the peel and cut citrus fruit in a bowl with 2½ pt water. Soak for 24 hr. Strain the pips and tissue, tie in a muslin bag and place in a preserving pan with the fruit, the peel and the liquid. Peel and dice the apple and pear and add to the rest of the fruit. Bring to the boil, simmer for 1¼ hr and until reduced by ⅓. Remove the muslin bag. Add the sugar, stir over low heat until dissolved. Bring to the boil and boil rapidly until set. This takes about 30 min. Cool slightly, then pot into clean warm jars. Seal and label in the usual way.

You can make Three or Four Fruit Marmalade by using fewer kinds of fruit, e.g. 2 grapefruit, 2 lemons and 1 large sweet orange, or 2 oranges, 1 grapefruit, 1 apple and 1 pear.

Yield 5 lb

SEVILLE ORANGE MARMALADE

1½ lb Seville oranges	Juice of 1 lemon
4 pt water	Sugar

Wash the fruit and cut it in half. Squeeze out the juice and the pips. Cut the peel into shreds. Tie the pips in a muslin bag and put into a bowl with the

orange and lemon juice, water and peel. Soak for 24–48 hr, covered to keep it clean. Transfer to the pan and cook for approx 1½ hr until the peel is soft. Remove the bag of pips, squeezing it gently. Take the pan from the heat, add 1 lb sugar to each pint and stir till dissolved. Return pan to heat, bring to the boil; boil rapidly until setting point is reached.

Yield about 6½ lb

WHOLE FRUIT PRESERVES

Whole or sliced fruits can be preserved for later use in various ways. They can be bottled in water or syrup for use in desserts, or pickled in brine. They can also be preserved in alcohol, or can be candied or crystallised for use as sweetmeats or on cakes. Some whole fruit preserves with syrup are very like jams; others,

Fruit bottled in brandy

QUEENSLAND HONEY FRUIT COMPOTE

using sliced fruits preserved in brine, are more like chutneys. All are useful additions to the store-cupboard.

QUEENSLAND HONEY FRUIT COMPOTE

½ lb dried prunes	1 pt water
½ lb dried apricots	10 oz clear honey
½ lb dried figs	Thinly pared rind of 1
½ lb dried peaches	lemon

Soak the dried fruits for 8 hr. Drain. Dissolve the honey in the water and boil, together with the rind, for 5 min. Remove the rind.

Pack the fruits into sterilised preserving jars. Cover with syrup to within ½ in of the top of the jars. Stand the jars on a rack in a deep preserving pan and add warm water to come level with the neck of the jars. Bring to the boil and boil for 3 min to expel the air from the jars. Cover with the lids, and screw down to seal. Continue boiling for 25 min.

Remove jars to a cooling rack to cool. Label and store.

PEARS AND CHERRIES IN WHITE PORT

1 pt white port *or*	1 lb Morello cherries
white wine	4 lb pears, peeled,
2 lb sugar	cored and halved
1 pt water	A little yellow *or*
Piece of cinnamon	orange colouring
stick	

Bring the port, sugar, water and cinnamon stick to the boil. Add the cherries (unstoned) and simmer until the syrup is thick and the cherries almost tender. Add the pear halves and bring the syrup to the boil once more. Simmer for 2–3 min, but do not allow the pears to soften. Pour immediately into sterilised jars, until syrup is about to overflow, and seal.

PEACHES PRESERVED IN BRANDY

Peaches	Water
Sugar	Brandy

Dip peaches in hot water, one at a time, and rub off the 'fur' with clean towel. Weigh. For each lb fruit allow ¾ lb sugar and 8 oz (in a measuring jug) water. Boil the sugar and water together for 10 min without stirring. Add the peaches to the syrup and cook (only a few at a time to prevent bruising) for about 5 min until tender. Remove the peaches from the syrup with a strainer and pack firmly into hot sterilised jars. Continue cooking the syrup, after removing peaches, until thick. Cool and measure. Add equal quantity of brandy. Bring to boiling point and fill jars of peaches to overflowing. Seal.

FRUIT BOTTLING

From many successful bottling methods, we have chosen two to give in detail. The *Quick Deep Pan* method is probably the most useful for a busy housewife who wishes to complete a large amount of bottling in the shortest possible time. The *Slow Deep Pan* method is recommended for those who wish to display for exhibitions—this method is more likely to produce jars which are perfect in appearance.

PREPARING AND TESTING JARS

There are two main types of preserving jar—one which fastens with a screw-band and the other fastening with clips or grips. Some are straight sided, for easy packing, others have a 'shoulder'. Jam jars can also be used, if fastened with special covers.

Always examine jars before use to see that they are unchipped. If the lid or the rim of the jar is chipped, discard it since it will not have an air-tight seal. Do not use metal covers if they are bent or if the lacquer has been attacked by the fruit acid. It is not advisable to use rubber rings a second time. Test unused rubber rings by stretching them: if they are good, they feel elastic and should return to normal size.

Before filling the jars, wash them thoroughly and drain—do not wipe dry.

PREPARING SYRUP OR BRINE

Fruit can be preserved in plain water, but a sugar syrup gives a better flavour and colour. The quantity of sugar used for a sugar syrup may be varied according to taste, but the usual quantity for most fruits is 8 oz granulated or loaf sugar to each 1 pt of water. Heat together and, when dissolved, bring to boiling-point and boil for 1 min. (If the syrup is to be used cold, save cooling time by heating the sugar with half the water and then adding the rest of the water cold.) If it is to be kept hot for long, put the lid on the pan to prevent evaporation.

If you prefer, substitute equal weights of *golden syrup* or *honey* for sugar. You can also add spices such as cinnamon or nutmeg.

To prepare brine for bottling tomatoes—add ½ oz salt to each 1 qt of water. Bring to the boil and boil for 1 min.

CHOOSING, PREPARING AND PACKING THE FRUIT

Choose fresh, firm, ripe fruit (except gooseberries, which should be green and hard). It is a waste of time and labour to bottle damaged or over-ripe fruit. Grade according to size, so that fruit of the same size is packed into each jar. If necessary, use the handle of a wooden spoon to help to place firm fruit in position. To ensure a tight pack for soft fruit, tap the filled jars on a folded cloth or on the palm of your hand.

Deal with the fruits below, as follows:

Apples Peel, core, cut into slices, or rings ¼ in thick. To prevent discoloration drop them into brine (1 oz salt to 4 pt water), keeping them under the surface with a plate. Drain, rinse and pack immediately.

Apples (Solid Pack): After draining from

brine as above, scald in boiling water for 2–3 min. This shrinks the fruit so that the jar can be tightly filled, with no air-spaces and little or no added liquid. A mixed pack of alternate layers of apples (solid pack) and blackberries (unscalded) is recommended.

Apricots Choose fully ripe fruit, not too soft. Stalk and rinse. Pack whole, *or* halve by slitting and twisting the fruit; stone and pack quickly to avoid browning. A few cracked kernels can be added to each jar.

Blackberries Choose large juicy, fully ripe berries. Remove stalks, leaves and unsound fruit.

Cherries Choose Morello if you can. Should have small stones and plump flesh. Stalk and rinse. Can be stoned, but take care not to lose the juice.

Currants (Black, Red, White) Choose large, firm, juicy and well-flavoured currants. They should be evenly ripened and unbroken. Remove stalks, rinse. Red and white currants have large seeds and are best mixed with raspberries.

Damsons Choose ripe, firm, purple fruit. Stalk and rinse.

Bottled gooseberries and jam

Greengages Choose firm, ripe fruit. Remove stalks. After processing, the fruit will turn greenish-brown and the syrup may be cloudy. But if a pressure cooker is used the fruit should keep a good colour due to the short cooking time.

Gooseberries Choose green, hard and unripe berries. Top and tail and, if preserving in syrup, cut off a small slice at either end with a stainless steel knife (this prevents shrivelling and toughening; it is not necessary when preserving in a pressure cooker).

Peaches and pears in brandy—a dessert for a special occasion

FRUITS FOR BOTTLING

Peaches Choose a free-stone variety (e.g. Hale) just fully ripe. Halve and stone by slitting and twisting the fruit. Dip in a pan of boiling water for 1 min, then put into cold water: the skin should then peel off easily. Pack quickly.

Pears Choose one of the best dessert varieties, e.g. Williams' Bon Chrétien, Conference, Doyenné du Comice, just fully ripened. Peel, halve and scoop out cores and fibres with a sharp-pointed teaspoon. Place in an acid brine (4 pt water; 1 oz salt; $\frac{1}{2}$ oz citric acid), keeping below surface with a plate. Rinse when ready for packing. Pack quickly.

Pears—cooking Prepare like the dessert varieties. Then stew till tender in a sugar syrup (4–6 oz sugar to 1 pt water). Drain, pack and cover with the syrup in which they were cooked. Sterilise as for other pears. These cooking pears will be darker in colour than the dessert varieties.

Plums Choose Victoria plums when they are fully grown but still firm and just turning pink. Choose purple varieties before the colour has developed, when still bright red, and yellow ones when they are still firm and lemon-yellow. Remove stalks, and rinse in cold water. Wipe to remove the bloom. Free-stone varieties can be halved, others must be packed whole. Prick whole plums before preserving in a pressure cooker.

Raspberries Choose large, firm, bright red and well-flavoured berries. Pick carefully, putting the fruit gently in shallow baskets to prevent squashing. Remove plugs and damaged fruit. Preserve as soon as possible; it is not usually necessary to rinse the fruit first.

Rhubarb Choose Champagne or Linnaeus rhubarb and bottle it in the spring when it is tender and needs no peeling. Wipe the stalks and cut in short lengths. Pack straight away (in water or syrup) *or* after soaking. *To soak* pour a hot syrup (8 oz sugar to 1 pt water) over the prepared rhubarb. Leave to soak and shrink for 8–12 hr. Pack, cover with the syrup.

To avoid a white deposit (unsightly but harmless) use previously boiled or softened water.

Strawberries Hull the berries. Rinse fruit in cold water.

Tight Pack for small soft fruit, e.g. elderberries, blackberries, raspberries, strawberries, mulberries: Roll the fruit in castor sugar, then pack into the jars tightly, without any added liquid. Process by either Deep Pan method.

Tomatoes *Tomatoes in their own juice:* Dip into boiling water for up to 30 seconds (according to ripeness) then into cold water; the skins should then peel off easily. Leave whole, or pack in halves or quarters if large. Press tightly into the jars, sprinkling the layers with sugar and salt—use 1 teasp sugar and 2 teasp salt to each 2 lb tomatoes. No additional liquid is either needed or desirable.

Whole, unskinned tomatoes: Remove stalks, rinse tomatoes and pack into jars. Use a brine ($\frac{1}{2}$ oz salt to 1 qt water) in place of syrup or water.

QUICK DEEP PAN METHOD

1 Pack prepared fruit tightly into tested jars. Put rubber rings to soak in warm water.

2 Fill jars to overflowing with hot (about 60°C, 140°F) syrup or water. For tomatoes use hot brine.

3 Dip the rubber rings in boiling water and put them on the jars, with the lids. Fasten with screwbands, clips or other grips.

4 If using screwbands, tighten them, then unscrew $\frac{1}{4}$ turn to allow for expansion.

5 Stand jars in the pan on wooden slats or on a thick piece of towelling or cardboard. See that they do not touch each other or the side of the pan. Cover completely with warm (about 38°C, 100°F) water. Put on the lid of the pan.

6 Bring up to simmering point (100°C, 190°F) in 25–30 min. Simmer for time indicated below. Then remove jars one at a time on to a wooden surface (use tongs to lift jars *or*, using a cup, empty out sufficient water to enable you to lift the jars with a cloth).

7 Tighten screwbands. Cool for 24 hr, tightening screwbands further if necessary. Clips should hold properly without attention.

8 Next day, remove screwband or clip. Lift each jar by lid. If properly sealed the lid will stay on securely. Label with date and other details and store in a cool, dark, dry place. Wash, dry and grease screwbands and clips and store till next year.

Processing times

Simmer for time indicated below:

2 min Apple Rings, Blackberries, Currants (Black, Red, White), Gooseberries (for pies), Raspberries, Rhubarb (for pies), Strawberries.

10 min Apricots, Cherries, Damsons, Gooseberries (for dessert), Greengages, Plums (whole), Rhubarb (for dessert), Tight pack of soft Fruit (except Strawberries).

20 min Apples (solid pack), Nectarines, Peaches, Pineapples, Plums (halved), Tight pack of Strawberries.

40 min Pears, Tomatoes (whole).

50 min Tomatoes (in own juice).

SLOW DEEP PAN METHOD

This is the same as the quick deep pan method, with the following exceptions:

At step 2, the jars are filled with cold syrup, water or brine.

At step 5, the fastened jars are covered with cold water.

At step 6, the water is raised gradually (i.e. in 90 min) to the temperature indicated below, and kept at that temperature for the time stated.

Processing times

Raise to 70°C, 165°F and maintain at that temperature for 10 min.

Apple rings, Blackberries, Currants (Black, Red, White), Gooseberries (for pies), Loganberries, Mulberries, Raspberries, Rhubarb (for pies), Strawberries, Whortleberries.

Raise to 80°C, 180°F and maintain at that temperature for 15 min.

Apples (solid pack), Apricots, Cherries, Damsons, Gooseberries (for dessert), Greengages, Nectarines, Plums (whole or halved), Peaches, Pineapples, Rhubarb (for dessert). Tight pack of soft Fruit.

Raise to 100°C, 190°F and maintain at that temperature for 30 min.

Pears, Tomatoes (whole).

Raise to 100°C, 190°F and maintain at that temperature for 40 min.

Tomatoes (in their own juice).

BOTTLING PULPED OR PURÉED FRUIT AND TOMATO JUICE

Pulped Fruit Soft and stone fruit, e.g. blackcurrants, apples, tomatoes, plums. Do not use copper or iron utensils. Remove fruit skins if necessary, and any stems and diseased or bruised portions. Peel and core apples. Stone plums. Stew any fruit with just sufficient water to prevent burning. When cooked right through, pour quickly (while still boiling) into hot, clean preserving jars. Seal immediately with hot lids and rubber rings dipped in boiling water. Process, using a pan with a false bottom or lined with a cloth.

To process: Cover the jars with hot water, raise to boiling-point and boil for 5 min. Remove from water. Test for seal next day.

Apple purée Cut unpeeled apples into slices, removing bruised or diseased portions. Stew apples till soft in just sufficient water to prevent burning. Rub through a sieve. Add a paring of lemon rind and sugar to taste. Immediately return the pulp and rind to the pan, bring to the boil, stirring to dissolve the sugar, pour into hot preserving jars and seal at once. Process as for pulp above.

Tomato purée Rinse the ripe tomatoes. Heat in a covered pan with a little salt and water. When soft, rub through a hair or nylon sieve. Reheat, and fill quickly into hot preserving jars. Fasten and process, using a pan with a false bottom or lined with a cloth.

To process: Cover the jars with hot water, raise to boiling-point, and boil for 10 min. Remove from water. Test for seal next day.

Tomato juice Rinse and heat the ripe tomatoes in a covered pan till they are soft. Sieve through a hair or nylon sieve. To each quart of pulp add: $\frac{1}{2}$ pt water, 1 teasp salt, 1 oz sugar and a pinch of pepper. Re-heat, fasten and process as for Tomato Purée above.

PICKLES, CHUTNEYS AND KETCHUPS

1 You can often save money by cutting up mis-shapen vegetables and fruits for pickles,

Pickled apples and pears

Mixed pickles

chutneys and sauces. But they should, be fresh, not over-ripe or in poor condition.

2 When making vegetable pickles, either soak the vegetables in brine or cover them with layers of salt. This draws out some of the water. When they are covered with spiced vinegar, they should be covered by at least $\frac{1}{2}$ in and the jars should be covered tightly so that none of the vegetables are left uncovered by subsequent evaporation.

3 When making chutneys, make a trial batch first because tastes vary and it may be necessary to adjust the spices in the recipe. But remember when tasting that chutneys are always spicier when first made: they mellow on keeping.

4 Use aluminium or unchipped enamel-lined pans, not brass, copper or iron.

5 If sieving is necessary, use a hair or nylon sieve, since a metal one may give an unpleasant taste.

6 Cover the jars with one of the following:

a A cork, boiled to be thoroughly clean, and covered with greaseproof paper.

b Synthetic skin.

c A well-lacquered metal cap, lined with a layer of cork, waxed cardboard or vinegar-proof paper. The vinegar must not come in contact with the metal otherwise it may cause corrosion and rusting.

d Greaseproof paper, covered with a circle of cotton material dipped in melted paraffin wax.

Spiced pickling vinegar

Buy only the best bottled vinegar for pickling; it should have an acetic acid content of at least 5 per cent. It is false economy to buy cheap barrelled vinegar: if—as is often the case—the percentage of acetic acid is too low the pickles will not keep.

For exhibition, white vinegar is often recommended because it shows off the colour and texture of the pickle, but for home use, the flavour of malt vinegar is usually preferred.

To make spiced vinegar, add to 1 qt of vinegar: $\frac{1}{2}$ oz cloves, $\frac{1}{2}$ oz allspice, $\frac{1}{2}$ oz ginger, $\frac{1}{2}$ oz cinnamon, $\frac{1}{2}$ oz white pepper.

NOTE: All these spices should be whole, not ground. Buy them fresh. If you find this spice too strong, reduce the quantities.

Steep the spices in the unheated vinegar for 1–2 months. Shake the bottle occasionally. Then strain and re-cork the bottle until needed.

Quick method If the spiced vinegar is wanted immediately, put the spices and vinegar into a basin. Bring the basin with a plate and stand it in a saucepan of cold water. Bring the water to the boil, remove the pan from the heat, and allow the spices to remain in the warm vinegar for about 2 hr. Keep the plate on top of the basin so that no flavour is lost. Strain the vinegar and use, either cold or hot according to the recipe.

224

PICKLED BEETROOT

Beetroots are obtainable most of the year and, like all the root crops, require cooking before pickling. Wash off any soil still clinging to the roots, taking care not to break the skin, for beetroot bleeds easily. If pickling for immediate use, simmer for 1½–2 hr. When cold, skin and cut into squares or slices, and cover with unspiced or spiced vinegar, whichever is preferred.

If pickling for storage, bake the roots in a moderate oven (180°C, 350°F, Gas 4) until tender and, when cold, skin and cut into squares—it packs better that way for keeping; cover with spiced vinegar to which has been added ½ oz salt to each pint.

Beetroot contains a good deal of sugar, and fermentation is more likely than with other vegetables, so seal thoroughly to exclude air.

PICKLED CUCUMBER

The easiest way to pickle cucumbers is to quarter them lengthways, cut into smaller pieces, brine with dry salt for 24 hr, then pack and cover with spiced vinegar. Like most vegetables they are best mixed with others.

PICKLED GHERKINS

The small immature cucumbers that are known as dills or gherkins require a longer process, especially if their deep green colour is to be fixed. They need partial cooking.

Select gherkins of a uniform size, place in a saucepan and cover with standard brine (½ lb salt to 3 pt water). Bring to near boiling-point; do not actually boil, but simmer for 10 min.

Drain until cold, then pack into jars and cover with spiced vinegar, preferably aromatic.

A great many people prefer gherkins sweet; they are particularly popular at cocktail parties. These are quite easy to prepare from the ordinary pickled fruit.

A spoonful of sugar added to the jar and shaken up, then allowed to stand for 24 hr, is all that is needed. Do not do this too long in advance as sugar added to a cold pickle in this way may very easily start to ferment. Another way is to turn the gherkins out on to a shallow dish, the one in which they will be served, and sprinkle with sugar an hour or two before serving.

MIXED PICKLES

Make a selection of available vegetables. Any of the following are suitable: small cucumbers, cauliflower, small onions, French beans. Prepare the vegetables: only the onions need be peeled, the rest should merely be cut into suitably sized pieces.

Put all into a large bowl, sprinkle with salt, and leave for 24 hr. Drain thoroughly and pack into jars. Cover with cold spiced vinegar, seal, and leave for at least a month before using.

PICKLED NASTURTIUM SEEDS

Nasturtium seeds when pickled are a good substitute for capers, and add variety to salad dressings. They are rather too small to be popular on the table, but go well in clear mixed pickles.

Gather seeds whilst still green on a dry day and steep in brine (½ lb salt to 3 pt water) for 24 hr. Pack in small jars, warm in the oven for 10 min and cover with hot spiced vinegar. It is best to use a hot spice mixture for these, and a few leaves of tarragon, if available.

The only important thing to remember is to use small jars or bottles, so that they are consumed at once when opened.

PICKLED ONIONS

Use small even-sized pickling onions. Peel with a stainless knife and drop them into a basin of salted water until all have been peeled. Remove from water and allow to drain thoroughly before packing into jars or bottles. Cover with cold spiced vinegar and keep for at least 1 month before using.

PICKLED WALNUTS

Use walnuts whose shells have not begun to form. Prick well with a silver fork; if the shell can be felt, do not use the walnut. The shell begins to form opposite the stalk, about ¼ in from the end.

Cover with a brine (1 lb salt to 1 gal water) and leave to soak for about 6 days. Drain, make fresh brine, and leave to soak for a further 7 days.

Drain, and spread in a single layer on dishes, leaving exposed to the air, preferably in sunshine, until the nuts blacken (1–2 days). Pack into jars and cover with hot spiced vinegar. Tie down when cold and leave for at least a month before using.

Wear gloves when handling walnuts.

APPLE CHUTNEY

6 lb apples	3½ lb sugar
2 lb sultanas	1 oz salt
¾ lb preserved ginger	1 teasp allspice
3 pt vinegar	

Peel, core and chop the apples into small pieces and chop up the sultanas and ginger. Mix the vinegar, sugar, salt and spice together and bring to the boil, then add the apples and simmer for 10 min

Pickled onions and beetroot

BRISBANE CHUTNEY

before adding the ginger and sultanas. Simmer until the mixture becomes fairly thick, then pour into the jars.

BRISBANE APRICOT AND SULTANA CHUTNEY

1 lb dried apricots	1½ pt cider vinegar
1½ lb onions	1 dessertsp salt
1 lb granulated sugar	2 cloves garlic, crushed
Grated rind and juice	1 teasp mustard
of 2 oranges	½ teasp powdered
½ lb sultanas	allspice

Soak the apricots overnight, then drain and chop them. Finely chop or mince the onions. Put the apricots and onions in a preserving pan with the sugar, rind and juice of the oranges, the sultanas and the cider vinegar. Add the salt, garlic, mustard and allspice. Simmer until soft, stirring occasionally to prevent sticking. Pour into hot jars, cover and seal.

5–6 lb chutney

GREEN TOMATO CHUTNEY

5 lb green tomatoes	1 lb sugar
1 lb onions	1 qt vinegar
½ oz peppercorns	½ lb raisins
1 oz salt	½ lb sultanas

Slice the tomatoes and chop the onions and mix together in a basin with the peppercorns and salt. Allow this to stand overnight. Next day boil up the sugar in the vinegar, then add the raisins (which may be chopped) and the sultanas. Simmer for 5 min, then add the tomatoes and onions, and simmer till thick.

MINCEMEAT

1¼ lb cooking apples	1 level teasp ground
(prepared weight)	nutmeg
1 lb currants	¼ level teasp ground
1 lb seedless raisins	cloves
½ lb sultanas	¼ level teasp ground
¼ lb candied peel	cinnamon
1 lb beef suet	½ level teasp salt
1 lb sugar	⅛ pt brandy (see note
Grated rind and juice	below)
of 2 lemons or 1	
orange and 1 lemon	

Peel and core the apples. Put these with the fruit, candied peel and suet through the mincer. Add the other ingredients and mix well. Cover in jars and use as required.
NOTE. If the mincemeat is to be used within a few days the brandy may be omitted.

QUEENSLAND FRUIT CHUTNEY

4 lb apples	2 qt vinegar
2 lb pears	1 level teasp cayenne
3 lb tomatoes	pepper
1 level teasp mace	1 teasp cloves
½ lb sultanas	1 teasp peppercorns
½ lb seedless raisins	2 tablesp salt
4 lb sugar	1 teasp ground ginger

Peel the apples and pears, core them and cut them into small pieces. Skin the tomatoes and add them to the apples and pears. Add the remainder of the ingredients, and simmer for two hours. Bottle while hot, and seal when cold.

About 10 lb chutney

BENTON KETCHUP OR SAUCE

¼ pt vinegar, pre-	1 teasp mixed mustard
ferably wine	1–2 teasp castor sugar
2 tablesp grated	
horseradish	

Mix all the ingredients well together. This sauce will keep for a month. Serve with beef.

TOMATO KETCHUP

6 lb ripe tomatoes	½ teasp cloves
1 pt vinegar	½ teasp cinnamon
½ lb sugar	½ teasp cayenne
1 oz salt	pepper
½ teasp allspice	

Cut the tomatoes into quarters, place them in a preserving pan with the salt and vinegar and simmer until the tomatoes are quite soft and broken up. Strain the mixture through coarse muslin or a nylon sieve, then return the purée to the preserving pan and add the sugar. Continue to simmer till the ketchup starts to thicken, and then add the spices a little at a time, stirring thoroughly until the flavour is to taste.

When the ketchup is reasonably thick, fill into hot bottles and seal immediately, or allow it to cool slightly, then fill the bottles and sterilise at 80°C, 170°F for 30 min.

Remember it will be thicker when cold than hot, so don't reduce it too far.

Bottling Queensland fruit chutney

Mincemeat

HOME FREEZING

Quick freezing is becoming an increasingly popular way of preserving foods.

Most refrigerators now have an ice-making compartment big enough for short-term storage of a fair amount of frozen food. Many compartments are marked with one, two or three stars, indicating how long foods can be stored safely (i.e. how low the interior temperature of the compartment is). But none is cold enough for quick-freezing unfrozen foods safely. For this, one needs a special freezer unit which can have an interior temperature of between minus 17°C, 0°F, and minus 12°C, 10°F, or colder. (Real 'deep freezing' is only possible commercially; commercial frozen-food stores are kept at about minus 30–35°C, minus 22–31°F.)

A refrigerator is, however, a vital adjunct to a freezer, since foods can be chilled in it before freezing, and most foods are better if thawed slowly at refrigerator temperature (1–10°C or 35–50°F).

Careful use of a freezer will fairly soon offset the capital outlay on the machine. Large quantities of home-grown and reared products can be preserved, at their prime, in glut periods. Moreover, when cooking meals 'make two and freeze one' saves time, labour and fuel, and prevents wastage of ingredients and money.

In addition to freezing poultry, meat, fruit and vegetables, many small quantities or por-tions of cooked food can be frozen and kept in the freezer until required. For instance, game or poultry, especially turkey, can be enjoyed so much more in smaller amounts at more frequent intervals. Even small quantities of stock or soup which are not required for immediate consumption can be safely stored in the freezer until required. Such things as sponge cakes, genoese pastries (decorated with butter cream) mince pies, etc, can be prepared in readiness for Christmas three or four weeks ahead if necessary, which can be a great convenience. Larger quantities of yeast breads and rolls may be mixed up at one time and some of the unbaked doughs may be frozen for as long as two weeks. Freshly baked breads may be wrapped and frozen as soon as they are cool. This will keep them fresh for two or three weeks.

Besides home-grown and home-made products, a freezer keeps ready for use the whole range of frozen foods which can now be purchased in bags or packets. Some of these contain single ingredients, such as peas. Sometimes mixed vegetables or fruits are packaged. Pastry is available, both in slab form and as ready-cut vols-au-vent or tartlets. Made-up dishes can also be bought, which only need brief cooking or re-heating; some of the better ones come in linked 'boil-in-the-bag' packs, one holding a starchy vegetable, the other a meat or fish mixture.

There is no need to use a whole packet or bag

227

FREEZER CONTAINERS

of many frozen goods at one time. If vegetables or fruits are bought in loose packs, a suitable quantity can be shaken out for use, and the bag can be re-fastened and re-stored. The same applies to goods like hamburgers, fish fillets and vol-au-vent cases.

CHOICE OF FOOD

Many fruits and vegetables freeze very well. But all should be nearly ripe, firm, in good condition and freshly picked. Freezing cannot improve poor food. Try to freeze produce as soon as it is picked or bought, but if this is not possible, keep it in a cool place, preferably a refrigerator not longer than 24 hr.

CHOICE OF CONTAINERS

All foods to be frozen must be suitably wrapped or packed to avoid drying out in the freezer. If even-sized containers are carefully stacked, it is often possible to pack about 20 lb of solid food into 1 cubic foot of storage space. Make up packages of a size most suitable to serve for one meal; this avoids leftover defrosted food. Food must not be re-frozen once it has thawed.

If possible, choose square or rectangular cartons rather than irregular shaped containers which take up more space. They must be airtight. Wrapping materials must be moisture-vapour-proof, and greaseproof. Large articles such as chicken, turkeys, joints, etc can be over-wrapped with mutton cloth or paper after they have been sealed. This is to protect the container from being torn by another package in the freezer. Wax tubs, rigid containers, polythene bags, low-temperature resistant glass jars without shoulders, aluminium foil and self-stick transparent wrapping can all be used if properly tied or sealed. The air inside must be pressed out as far as possible, and all projecting

Selection of food for a freezer

edges on the food should be wrapped up, before sealing. (See sealing below)

Label all packages with a felt pen marker and keep a list of the goods stored.

Fruits may be frozen, unsweetened. But for the best flavour, colour and texture, it is advisable to freeze them with granulated sugar or cover them with a syrup.

Syrup Prepare this in advance and use when quite cold. It can be stored for a week or so in a refrigerator.

The amount of sugar used can be varied according to taste. The recommended strengths are:

2 oz sugar dissolved in water and made up to 1 pt = 10%

4 oz sugar dissolved in water and made up to 1 pt = 20%

6 oz sugar dissolved in water and made up to 1 pt = 30%

PACKING FOR THE FREEZER

Beef   **Chicken**   **Vegetables**   **Fruit**

Fruit	Method of Preparation	Type of Pack
Apple slices (good cooking variety)	Peel, core and slice. *Scald or blanch for 3 min. (Work quickly to prevent discoloration. If cutting up large quantities, scald them in batches.)	Pack plain *or* cover completely with 20% syrup.
Apple purée (good cooking variety)	Stew, then rub through a sieve.	Mix 1 lb granulated sugar with 4–5 lb pulped apple, *or* freeze without sugar.
Apricots	Wash, cut in halves, stone, peel.	Cover with 40% syrup.†
Blackberries	Sort and stem. If really necessary, rinse gently in ice-cold water and drain well.	Pack plain (sugar can be added at the cooking stage) *or* cover with 50% syrup *or* mix 1 lb granulated sugar with 3–4 lb fruit.
Blackberry and Apple	Clean the blackberries, Peel, core and slice the apples, working quickly to avoid browning. Mix in required quantities.	Mix 1 lb granulated sugar with 4–5 lb fruit.
Cherries (a well-flavoured black variety)	Stem. Rinse gently in ice-cold water. Stone if desired.	Cover with 30% syrup.
Currants (black or red)	Stem. If really necessary, rinse gently in ice-cold water and drain well.	Cover with 30% syrup, *or* mix 1 lb granulated sugar with 3 lb currants.
Gooseberries	Pick just before fully ripened. Top and tail. Wash in ice-cold water. Drain.	Pack plain if for cooking, or with sugar if desired.
Grapes (delicate flavour, tender skins)	Stem. Wash in ice-cold water. Drain. Cut in half and take the pips out. Grapes need careful defrosting.	Cover with 30% syrup.
Grapefruit, oranges, tangerines	Chill. Wash, peel and remove all pith. Remove segments by cutting along membrane (or halve and remove the fruit pulp with a grapefruit spoon). Remove pips. (Work quickly, preparing one or two packages at a time.)	Pack in own juice without sugar *or* mix 1 part granulated sugar with 4 parts fruit segments by weight *or* cover with 50% syrup for grapefruit and 30% for oranges.
Juice of grapefruit, oranges, tangerines, lemons	Extract the juice and strain it through a double thickness of muslin. Fill into the containers to within ½ in of the lid.	Freeze plain, immediately.
Loganberries, raspberries	Look over carefully. Do not wash them unless necessary. If essential, rinse a few at a time in ice-cold water. Drain.	Pack without sugar *or* cover with 40% syrup *or* mix 1 lb granulated sugar with 3–4 lb fruit.
Loganberry *or* raspberry purée	After sorting and rinsing if necessary, rub fruit through a sieve.	Mix 1 part sugar with 4–5 parts sieved fruit.
Peaches	Peel, stone and slice.	Cover with 40% syrup.†
Plums (dark variety)	Stem. Rinse in ice-cold water. Drain.	Cover with 40% syrup.
Rhubarb	Wash, trim and cut stalks into 1 in lengths.	Pack plain *or* cover with 30% syrup *or* mix 1 lb granulated sugar with 5 lb rhubarb.
Strawberries (firm, ripe, well-coloured)	Remove calyx. Rinse a few at a time in ice-cold water. Drain. Slice or leave whole. Weigh.	Mix 1 lb granulated sugar with 4–5 lb fruit *or* cover with 40% syrup. Best unsweetened as they are apt to go pulpy.
Strawberry purée	Remove calyx. See Loganberry, raspberry purée.	

* *See* below for method.

† To help preserve the natural colour, slice apricots and peaches into a citric acid solution (¼ teasp citric acid dissolved in 1 qt water. Leave 1–2 min, drain and pack with syrup). *Or* add ¼ teasp ascorbic acid to each teacup of syrup before pouring it over the sliced fruit.

VEGETABLES AND THE FREEZER

8 oz sugar dissolved in water and made up to 1 pt = 30%

10 oz sugar dissolved in water and made up to 1 pt = 40%

Method: Bring the sugar and water just to the boil. Cover to prevent evaporation and put to one side until quite cold. Allow about 1 pt of syrup to each 2 lb fruit. This should be sufficient to cover the fruit.

VEGETABLES

In order to keep the colour, flavour and food value during storage, it is essential to blanch vegetables before packing and freezing.

To blanch

Do not blanch more than 1–2 lb of vegetables at a time. After preparing the vegetables, bring some water to a rolling boil in a large saucepan (allow 8 pt of water for 1–2 lb of non-leafy vegetables; for leafy vegetables, allow 12 pt of water).

Place the vegetables in a wire basket or in a muslin bag. Immerse them in the boiling water, note the time, and bring the water rapidly to the boil again. Move the vegetables around in the water for the time given in the table below. Remove *immediately* the time is up, and chill thoroughly in ice-cold water. Drain, pack into a moisture-vapour-proof container and seal. A moisture-vapour-proof bag is an easy container to use in freezing vegetables.

The same water may be used for successive batches of the same vegetable. Do not add any salt to the water. Salt should not be added until the frozen vegetables are removed from their packets for cooking.

FILLING THE CONTAINERS WITH FRUITS AND VEGETABLES

1 Just as water expands when turning into ice, so fruit purée or fruit in syrup expand when

Vegetable	Method of Preparation	Scalding Time
Asparagus	Grade into thick and thin stems. Wash, scrape off bracts, cut so that stems measure 6 in from the tips.	Thin stems: 2 min Thick stems: 4 min
Broad beans (young, tender)	Remove pods.	1½ min
Beans—French *or* Runner (small, tender)	Wash, top and tail, string if necessary. Leave small beans whole; slice larger ones.	2–3 min
Broccoli, Purple Sprouting	Cut into even lengths, about 2–3 in long. Wash carefully.	4 min
Brussels Sprouts (small, tight "button" sprouts)	Wash carefully	4 min
Carrots (young, even sizes)	Wash, scald, then cool and rub off the skins. Leave whole or slice or dice before packing for freezing.	3 min
Cauliflower and Broccoli (Winter Cauliflower)	Break into florets 2 in across	3 min
Corn-on-the-cob (just mature)	Cut off tough skin, strip off the outer green leaves and the silky threads, and cut off any immature grains. Wash.	Small: 4 min Large: 6 min
Whole grain sweet corn	Prepare as for corn-on-the-cob, cut off the grain with a sharp knife. After scalding and cooling, pack into containers for freezing.	
Peas (good cooking variety, just mature)	Remove pods.	1–2 min
Potatoes (new—avoid potatoes which tend to blacken when cleaned)	Wash, scrape.	4–5 min
Spinach	Wash very thoroughly in several changes of water until free of dirt. Remove tough stems. Divide into batches each weighing about 3 oz.	2 min
Vegetable Purées (asparagus, beetroot, carrots, parsnips, peas, spinach *or* turnips)	Cook in boiling water or steam till tender. Mash with a potato ricer so that the purée is smooth without having air whipped into it, or use a kitchen utensil made specially for puréeing foods. Chill, then pack into the container, label and freeze.	

frozen. Therefore the container should never be completely filled. Leave $\frac{1}{2}$–$\frac{3}{4}$ in head space, according to the size of the carton.

2 If the fruit is packed plain or in dry sugar, there is no need to leave space. It is the water which expands, not the fruit.

3 Vegetables are packed without added liquid, so they can come almost to the brim of the container, or can be wrapped tightly in suitable material.

4 Avoid wetting the seal edges of packets. A wide-mouthed funnel is useful for filling neatly.

POULTRY

Choose only the best-quality, healthy, well-formed birds for quick freezing. Clean and wash well in running water, and drain.

For freezing, truss the bird as for the table. Wrap the well-washed giblets in greaseproof paper, moisture-proof cellophane or plastic material and place by the side of the bird.

Package the bird in a moisture-vapour-proof container, a bag being the most suitable for quick handling. If the bones of the legs are sharp and pointed, wrap small pieces of foil round them so that they do not pierce the bag. Label, mark weight of bird and date frozen.

The bag should now be carefully sealed either by heat-sealing or with a bag fastener, or with special sealing tape; see below.

Jointed birds Wrap each piece separately in greaseproof paper, moisture-proof cellophane, or polythene, in either a waxed carton, a moisture-proof bag or fibre tray.

Giblets are wrapped in the same way.

MEAT

Choose only good-quality meat for freezing. Protect all cuts from loss of moisture during the freezing and storing process by proper packaging.

When preparing roasting joints, etc, each piece of meat must be wrapped individually, eliminating as much air as possible from the package by pressing and wrapping material close to the meat. Meat can be wrapped in a variety of ways; the easiest is to use a bag which can be filled, sealed by heat or with a bag fastener or special sealing tape. When emptied it can be washed thoroughly and put away for future use.

When preparing chops, fillets, etc, first trim off excess fat. When packing two or more pieces of meat in one container, the portions should be separated by placing two small pieces of grease-proof paper or cellophane between them. (By doing this it is quite easy to take out any piece of meat while still solidly frozen.) The meat should then be packed in a suitable container

Blanching cauliflower

for quick freezing and storing.

Each package should be marked with the date, weight of the meat or any other remarks required.

When meat is packed in polythene bags or sheets of moisture-vapour-proof materials, it is wise to overwrap it with strong paper or mutton cloth.

BAKED AND DAIRY GOODS

Most baked goods freeze extremely well. Dairy produce is less successful. Cream should be pasteurised and cooled rapidly and contain 40 per cent butter fat; if it has a lower content it tends to separate. Milk may curdle. Hard cheeses can freeze well, but softer cheeses may crumble. It is inadvisable to freeze cakes with fillings as these tend to go soggy. So does meringue. Gelatine goes cloudy, but is fine for opaque dishes.

Many ready-prepared desserts (including, obviously, ice creams) freeze well, and a selection of recipes for making them and freezing them is given in this book.

SEALING

Special waxed containers should be sealed with adhesive tape sold for this purpose. Tubs have lids which seal into a groove, or screw tops.

When using bags made of moisture-vapour-proof materials they need to be heat-sealed with a warm iron, curling tongs or a bag fastener; squeeze out as much air as possible before sealing. Some materials need to be protected from direct contact with the iron by a piece of paper. Before wrapping meat, poultry or game, cover

LABELLING AND STACKING

all sharp ends of bone with several thicknesses of clean kitchen paper, to avoid piercing the wrapper.

LABELLING AND STACKING

Do not attempt to use ordinary stick-on labels in the freezer, or to write in ink. Mark the container with a chinagraph pencil or felt pen. Note the variety, quantity and the amount of sugar or syrup (if used) and the date, e.g. 'Whole strawberries, 15 oz; in 40% syrup; July 20, 19—'.

Stack the containers closely (once food is frozen, the closer it is stacked the better. It is in the freezing process that they must not touch). Tubs are most economically stacked with every other one upside down. Do not over-load the freezer at the actual time of freezing fresh produce. Freezer manufacturers issue pamphlets stating the maximum freezing load.

STORAGE

1 Once frozen, it is a good idea to keep similar varieties together, either with coloured paper or tapes, or in string nets, or cardboard boxes or special baskets provided with some freezers. (These can be purchased separately and used in other models.) Keep a plan showing where the produce is stored—this saves keeping the freezer open while you search for a particular packet.

2 It is best not to store frozen food for longer than a year. Plan to have a quick turnover of stock, with as much variety as possible.

3 If there is a short power cut, do not open the cabinet unless it is really necessary. It should remain at a temperature sufficiently low not to harm the food. Food kept like this should be all right for 12–36 hours, depending on the type, size and the insulation of the freezer. If you are moving house and the freezer has to be emptied, pack the food with dry newspaper for transport.

4 To defrost, follow the manufacturers' instructions carefully. With careful handling defrosting will probably only be necessary about once a year. But do not leave it too long because too much ice round the inside of the compartment takes up space and impairs the efficiency of the freezer.

TO USE FROZEN FOODS

Fruits To preserve the best appearance allow fruit to thaw gradually when required for dessert use. Do not open the packet while the food is thawing; merely leave it at room temperature for 3–4 hr per 1 lb weight, or leave it (still unopened) in a domestic refrigerator for 5–6 hr per 1 lb weight.

If you are in a hurry for the fruit, place an unopened pack in cold water allowing the tap to run slightly, so changing the water.

Fruit to be used for cooking need not be defrosted first.

Vegetables Corn on the cob should be thawed before it is cooked, or the outside will be overcooked before the heat can penetrate properly to the inside.

It is unnecessary to thaw any other deep-frozen vegetables before cooking. As a general rule, allow about $\frac{1}{2}$ pt water and $\frac{1}{2}$ teasp salt to a 1 lb pack, adding any other seasoning to taste. Bring the salted water to the boil, add the frozen vegetables, and as they heat, break up the block with a fork to help it to thaw quickly. Boil for only about $\frac{1}{2}$ the time needed to cook fresh vegetables. Cooking time is counted from the time the water begins to boil again.

Meat or poultry Joints of meat or poultry must be fully thawed before cooking. Allow 5–6 hr per lb if thawed in a domestic refrigerator or 2–3 hr per lb if thawed at room temperature. If more rapid thawing is necessary, place the sealed package in a warm place or in the draught from an electric fan, allowing about 45 min per lb in weight. The meat should be left in the unopened package while thawing. Cook the food as soon as possible after it has been completely thawed, as at this stage it keeps less well than fresh food; once it has been cooked, however, it will keep for the same time as similarly cooked fresh meat.

Chops, sausages and thin portions of meat can be cooked without thawing, but will take longer to cook than usual.

Well-stocked fridge

ANCHOVY SAUCE

To $\frac{1}{2}$ pt basic white sauce (see below) made from fish stock *or* water *or* $\frac{1}{2}$ milk and $\frac{1}{2}$ water add 1 *or* 2 teasp anchovy essence to taste and a few drops lemon juice and a few drops of cochineal to tint the sauce a dull pink.

APPLE AND RICE STUFFING FOR TURKEY

1 chicken stock cube	1 lb cooking apples,
6 oz long grain rice	finely grated
3 medium-sized onions,	3 oz fresh white
finely chopped	breadcrumbs
6 oz frozen peas	1 egg to bind
Salt and pepper	Butter or margarine
4–5 oz medium fat soft	
cheese	

Dissolve the stock cube in one pt of water and bring to the boil. Add the rice and onions. Simmer gently for 10 min until all the stock has been absorbed. Stir in the peas and allow the mixture to cool. Season carefully. Mix the cheese and grated apple together, and add carefully to the rice. Sprinkle on the breadcrumbs and stir in. Add the egg to bind the mixture. (This quantity is enough to stuff a 13 lb turkey, leaving enough mixture over to make 7 or 9 forcemeat balls.) Bake the forcemeat balls separately in foil with butter or margarine to baste, for about 20 min at 170°C, 325°F, Gas 3.

APPLE SAUCE FOR ROAST PORK

1 lb apples	Rind and juice of $\frac{1}{2}$
2 tablesp water	lemon
$\frac{1}{2}$ oz butter *or*	Sugar to taste
margarine	

Stew the apples very gently with the water, butter and lemon rind until they are pulpy. Beat them quite smooth or rub them through a hair or nylon sieve. Re-heat the sauce with the lemon juice and sweeten to taste.

For Apple Raisin sauce, add $\frac{1}{2}$ tablesp chopped parsley and 1 oz seedless raisins before reheating.

APRICOT OR REDCURRANT GLAZE

2 tablesp apricot jam *or*	1 tablesp water
redcurrant jelly	

Sieve apricot jam or redcurrant jelly and water and bring to boiling point.

APRICOT SAUCE

$\frac{1}{2}$ lb apricots, fresh *or*	Lemon juice
canned	1 teasp Maraschino
$\frac{1}{4}$ pt water *or* syrup	(optional)
from can	1 level teasp arrowroot
1–2 oz brown sugar	

Stone the apricots and stew them till soft in the water. When soft rub them through a hair or nylon sieve. Meanwhile crack the stones, scald and skin the kernels. Add sugar, lemon juice, liqueur (if used) and kernels to the sauce. Re-heat the sauce, stirring in the arrowroot blended with a little cold water. Bring to the boil and serve.

See also Queen's Pudding

ASPIC JELLY

1 qt jellied veal stock	2 egg whites and shells
1 oz gelatine	1 glass sherry
Bouquet garni (parsley,	(optional)
thyme, bay leaf)	$\frac{1}{4}$ pt vinegar
2 sticks of celery	

Let the stock become quite cold, and remove every particle of fat. Put it into a stewpan with the gelatine, herbs, celery cut into large pieces, the egg whites previously slightly beaten and the shells previously washed and dried. Whisk over heat until nearly boiling, then add the wine and vinegar. Continue the whisking until quite boiling, then reduce the heat and simmer for about 10 min, strain till clear, and use.

FOR ASPIC JELLY SET WITH GELATINE, USE

2 egg whites and shells	1 carrot
1 lemon	2–3 sticks celery
1 qt stock	Bouquet garni
2 oz gelatine	10–12 peppercorns
$\frac{1}{4}$ pt white vinegar	1 teasp salt
1 onion	

Whisk the egg whites slightly. Wash the shells. Peel the lemon rind thinly, and strain the juice. Strain the stock. Put all the ingredients into a pan, whisk over medium heat until boiling. Lower heat and simmer gently for about 20 min. Strain.

FOR ASPIC CREAM, USE

1 gill double cream	Pinch of white pepper
$1\frac{1}{2}$ gills aspic jelly	Pinch of castor sugar
1 teasp lemon juice	

Put the cream into a basin, stir it with a whisk, and gradually add the aspic, which must be liquid.

BROWN SAUCE

Aspic

Aspic cream

Add the lemon juice and seasoning and pass through a tammy cloth or fine strainer.

To use aspic as a glaze, cool it until thick and syrupy. Brush on as required. If necessary, chill the dish being glazed until the aspic is firm, then brush on a second coat. Repeat the process if a darker, thicker coating is desired.

To chop aspic when set, use a knife dipped in hot water.

FOR ASPIC MAYONNAISE, USE

¼ pt mayonnaise   ¼–½ pt aspic jelly

Have the mayonnaise really stiff and the jelly liquid but cold. Fold the jelly carefully into the mayonnaise. Use the aspic mayonnaise when it is beginning to thicken.

Note: The smaller proportion of jelly gives a mixture which may be piped through a forcing tube and bag; the higher proportion of jelly gives a mixture for coating cold foods served with salad.

For Aspic Jelly without meat, use vegetable stock set with gelatine.

BASIC BROWN SAUCE

1 small carrot   1 oz flour
1 onion   1 pt brown stock
1 oz dripping   Salt and pepper

Thinly slice the carrot and onion. Melt the dripping and in it slowly fry the onion and carrot until they are golden-brown. Stir in the flour and fry it even more slowly till it is also golden-brown. Stir in the stock, bring to simmering point, season, then simmer for ½ hr. Strain the sauce before use. As the frying of the flour is a long process extra colour may be given to the sauce by adding a piece of brown onion skin, or a little gravy browning or a little meat or vegetable extract which will also add to the flavour.

Cooking time 40 min–1 hr

BASIC WHITE SAUCE
FOR A COATING SAUCE

2 oz butter *or* margarine   1 pt milk *or* stock (fish,
2 oz flour   meat *or* vegetable to
Pinch of salt   suit dish), *or* a
                                mixture of stock and
                                milk

FOR A POURING SAUCE

1½ oz butter *or*   1 pt of liquid as for
  margarine   coating sauce
1½ oz flour   Pinch of salt

Melt the fat in a deep saucepan, large enough to hold the amount of liquid with just enough room to spare for beating the sauce. Stir the flour into the fat and allow it to bubble for 2–3 min over a gentle heat. On no account allow it to change colour; this is a white roux. Remove from heat and stir in ½ the liquid gradually. Return to moderate heat and stir the sauce briskly until it thickens, then beat it vigorously. Season and use it at once. If the sauce must be kept hot, cover it with wet greaseproof paper and a lid, and before use beat it again in case skin or lumps have formed.

A coating sauce should coat the back of the wooden spoon used for stirring, and should only just settle to its own level in the pan.

A pouring sauce should barely mask the spoon; it should flow freely, and easily settle to its own level in the pan.

For Melted Butter sauce, whisk in 2 extra oz butter, a nut at a time, just before serving.

Cooking time 15 min

VARIATIONS

To ½ pt basic white sauce made with stock, or ½ milk and ½ stock, add, just before serving:

Caper sauce 1 tablesp capers and 1 teasp vinegar from caper pickle.

Cucumber sauce ¼ medium cucumber, diced.

Horseradish sauce 1 rounded tablesp grated horseradish, 1 teasp vinegar and ½ teasp sugar.

Maître d'hôtel sauce Juice of ½ lemon, 1 rounded tablesp finely-chopped parsley and 1 oz extra butter.

Parsley sauce 1 tablesp finely-chopped parsley and 1 oz extra butter.

BATTERS FOR COATING

Notes and standard recipes are given under Sweet Fritter Coating Batters, in the Desserts section. These recipes can be used equally well for savoury mixtures. Simply omit the sugar from the ingredients.

BÉCHAMEL SAUCE

1 pt milk	Salt
1 small onion	6 peppercorns
1 small carrot	A small bunch of herbs
2 in celery stick	2 oz butter
1 bay leaf	2 oz flour
1 clove	⅛ pt cream (optional)
¼ teasp mace	

Warm the milk with the vegetables, herbs, salt and spices, and bring it slowly to simmering point. Put a lid on the pan and stand it in a warm place on the cooker to infuse for ½ hr. Strain the milk, melt the butter, add the flour. Cook this roux for a few minutes without browning it. Stir the flavoured milk gradually into the roux. Bring the sauce to boiling point, stirring vigorously. If cream is used, add it to the sauce just at boiling point and do not reboil it.

Béchamel sauce can be made with ½ white stock and ½ milk; the result will have a good flavour but will be less creamy.

BIGARADE SAUCE

½ pt Espagnole sauce	⅛ pt red wine (optional)
½ Seville orange	Salt
½ lemon	Cayenne pepper
	Pinch of sugar

Remove the outer orange rind, avoiding the pith, and cut the rind in neat, thin strips. Cover it with a little cold water; stew till just tender; then strain. Squeeze the orange and lemon juice into the sauce, add the orange rind, reheat, add the wine, if used, season and add sugar to taste. Serve with roast duck, goose, wild duck, pork or ham.

BOUQUET GARNI or BUNCH OF FRESH HERBS or FAGGOT OF HERBS

1 sprig of thyme	1 small bay leaf
1 sprig of marjoram	A few stalks of parsley
1 small sage leaf (optional)	A few chives (optional)
1 strip of lemon rind (optional)	Sprig of chervil (optional)

Tie all the herbs into a bunch with thick cotton or fine string. Alternatively the herbs may be tied in a small square of muslin.

BRANDY or RUM SAUCE

¼ pt single cream	1 dessertsp brown sugar
2 egg yolks	⅛ pint brandy or 2 tablesp rum

Mix all the ingredients in a basin. Set the basin over a saucepan of hot water, and whisk until the mixture thickens.

Rum sauce can also be made like Brandy Butter

or as described under Savarin.

BRANDY BUTTER (Hard sauce)

3 oz butter	1 teasp–1 tablesp brandy
6 oz icing sugar or 4½ oz icing sugar and 1 oz ground almonds	1 whipped egg white (optional)

Cream the butter till soft. Sift the icing sugar and cream it with the butter till white and light in texture. Mix in the almonds if used. Work the brandy carefully into the mixture. Fold the stiffly whipped egg white into the sauce. Serve with Christmas or other steamed puddings.

This sauce may be stored for several weeks in an airtight jar. It makes an excellent filling for sweet sandwiches.

BREAD SAUCE

1 large onion	2 oz dry white bread-crumbs
2 cloves	½ oz butter
Pinch of ground mace	Salt and pepper
1 bay leaf	2 tablesp cream (optional)
4 peppercorns	
1 allspice berry	
½ pt milk	

Put the onion and spices into the milk, bring them very slowly to boiling point. Cover the pan and infuse over a gentle heat for ½–1 hr. Strain the liquid. To it add the crumbs and butter, and season to taste. Keep the mixture just below simmering point for 20 min. Stir in the cream if used, serve the sauce at once. Serve with roast chicken or turkey.

BROWN STOCK MADE WITH MEAT FOR CLEAR GRAVIES, ETC

At least 2 lb veal & beef bones, mixed	Salt and pepper
1–2 lb shin beef (lean only)	1 carrot
3 qt cold water	1 stick of celery
	1 onion
	Bouquet garni

Scrape the bones, remove every scrap of fat and marrow and wash well in hot water. Wipe the meat with a damp cloth and cut it into small pieces, after removing any fat. Put all the bones and meat into a pan and add the cold water and seasoning. Soak for ½ hr. Bring very slowly to simmering point and simmer for 1 hr. Add the vegetables whole, including a piece of outer, brown skin of onion, and the bouquet garni, and simmer for a further 3 hr. Strain the stock through a metal sieve.

To clear the stock, beat 3 egg whites until frothy. Put into a pan with the strained stock, and simmer very gently for 1 hr. Strain slowly through a finely woven cotton cloth.

If jellied stock is wanted, 2 oz dissolved gelatine can be added to the stock and well stirred in before cooking. For a rich stock, reduce to the strength required.

CANDIED ANGELICA AND OTHER FRUITS

The amounts needed for trimmings and decorations are usually so small that it is not worth while preparing them at home. Use bought products.

To use angelica, cut in thin strips, then cut these into diamond or leaf shapes.

To use candied peel, scrape off the sugar, then shred, chop or slice into slivers. Use citron peel to

Decorated apple foam parfait with candied angelica

decorate plain cakes.

Glacé cherries make a gay decoration. They are heavy, so cut in halves or quarters before using.

CARAMEL SAUCE

2 oz sugar or golden syrup	½ pt custard sauce
⅛ pt water	Lemon juice or vanilla essence

Put the sugar and 2 tablesp water in a small pan; dissolve the sugar over gentle heat, then boil the syrup so made until it is a deep golden-brown. Add to the caramel the rest of the water and leave it in a warm place to dissolve. If golden syrup is used heat it without water until of a golden-brown colour, then dissolve it in the water. Add the dissolved caramel to the custard sauce and flavour to taste.

CHOCOLATE SAUCES

(1) RICH

¼ lb chocolate	1 teasp rum
½ pt milk	Sugar, if required
2–3 egg yolks	1 egg white (optional)
Vanilla essence	

Dissolve the chocolate in the milk. Make a custard with the egg yolks and the chocolate-flavoured milk —*see* custard sauce. Flavour and sweeten to taste. If liked one egg white may be whipped to a stiff froth and folded into the finished sauce.

(2) CHOCOLATE SAUCE (COCOA)

2 rounded dessertsp cocoa	3 rounded dessertsp sugar
1 rounded dessertsp cornflour	½ pt water
½ oz butter	3 drops vanilla essence

Blend together the cornflour, cocoa and sugar with a little of the water. Boil remaining water and pour on to blended mixture. Return to pan and boil for 2 min, stirring all the time. Add vanilla and butter. Serve hot or cold.

(3) CHOCOLATE SAUCE WITH RUM

See Chocolate Soufflé Omelet.

CRANBERRY SAUCE

½ lb cranberries	Sugar to taste
¼–½ pt water	

Stew the cranberries till soft, using ¼ pt water and adding more if needed. Rub the fruit through a hair or nylon sieve. Sweeten to taste. For economy, half cranberries and half sour cooking apples make an excellent sauce. Serve with roast turkey, chicken or game.

CREAM SALAD DRESSING (1)

½ level teasp mixed English mustard *or* French mustard	4 tablesp double cream
1 level saltsp salt	1 tablesp vinegar (wine *or* malt with a little tarragon)
1 saltsp castor sugar	

Mix the mustard, salt and sugar smoothly together. Stir in the cream. Add the vinegar drop by drop, beating mixture all the time.

If you prefer, use only 2 tablesp cream and add 1 tablesp oil. In this case, use only a dessertsp vinegar, and add the oil, drop by drop, to the cream mixture before adding the vinegar.

CREAM SALAD DRESSING (2)

¼ pt thick soured cream *or* 3 oz rich full-fat soft cheese *and* 2 dessertsp milk *and* juice of ½ lemon	Salt and pepper Mixed English mustard *or* French mustard Castor sugar

If using cheese, mix it with the milk and lemon juice until smooth. Flavour the cream or soft cheese mixture with salt, pepper, mustard and sugar. Add a little top of the milk if too thick.

CREAM SAUCE

½ pt Béchamel sauce	Lemon juice to taste
Cayenne pepper	⅛ pt cream
Salt	

Heat the sauce; add the cayenne, salt and lemon juice. Stir cream into seasoned sauce, just below boiling point. On no account allow sauce to boil or it will curdle. Serve at once.

CROÛTES AND CROÛTONS

A croûte is a fried or toasted slice of bread (round, square, etc) used as a base, usually for a savoury item such as a roast game bird or a meat mixture. Many hors d'œuvres and snacks are served on small round croûtes or fingers of bread. Croûtes are also used as a garnish for a rich dish such as a salmi, their crispness contrasting with the sauce.

Croûtes should be cut from bread at least one day old, and should be $\frac{1}{4}$–$\frac{1}{2}$-in thick.

TO MAKE CRESCENTS OR FLEURONS

Cut bread slices (or pastry) into circles with a pastry cutter. Then cut crescent moon shapes from these, with the same or a slightly smaller cutter.

TO FRY CROÛTES

Use clarified butter or oil, and make sure that the first side is crisp and golden before turning.

TO MAKE TOASTED CROÛTES

Toast whole bread slices, and cut to shape after toasting, using a sharp knife or scissors.

TO MAKE CROÛTONS

Croûtons are small squares or dice of fried or toasted bread usually served with soups. Cut the crusts off $\frac{1}{4}$–$\frac{1}{2}$-in slices of day-old bread, cut into dice and fry until golden on all sides. Alternatively, bake until golden.

Fried bread and watercress as garnishes

CUMBERLAND SAUCE

1 orange	$\frac{1}{4}$ teasp mixed
1 lemon	mustard
$\frac{1}{8}$ pt water	Salt
$\frac{1}{8}$ pt port wine	Cayenne pepper
2 tablesp vinegar	6–8 glacé cherries
$\frac{1}{4}$ lb redcurrant jelly	

Grate the rind of the orange and lemon, carefully avoiding the pith. Simmer the rinds in the water for 10 min. Add the wine, vinegar, jelly and mustard and simmer them together until the jelly is completely melted. Add the juice of the orange and lemon, season to taste and cool. Chop the glacé cherries and add them to the sauce.

CURRY SAUCE, MILD

1 medium-sized onion	$\frac{1}{2}$ pt pale stock,
1 oz butter or	coconut infusion (see
margarine	below) or water
1 small cooking apple	$\frac{1}{2}$ teasp black treacle

$\frac{1}{4}$–$\frac{1}{2}$ oz curry powder	1–2 teasp lemon juice
$\frac{1}{2}$ oz rice flour or	1 dessertsp chutney
flour	Salt

Chop the onion, put it into a saucepan and fry it very gently in the butter for 10 min. Chop the apple and cook it in the butter with the onion for a further 10 min. Stir in the curry powder and heat it for a few minutes. Add the flour and then stir in the liquid. When boiling, add all the other ingredients and simmer the sauce for at least $\frac{1}{2}$ hr, or better $1\frac{1}{2}$ hr.

To make the coconut infusion Soak 1 oz desiccated or fresh grated coconut in $\frac{1}{2}$ pt water for a few minutes, bring slowly to boiling point and infuse it for 10 min. Wring the coconut in a piece of muslin to extract all the liquid.

CUSTARD (AS) SAUCE

1 dessertsp sugar	$\frac{1}{2}$ pt milk
2 egg yolks or 1	Flavouring (see
whole egg	Flavourings)

Curry sauce with turkey duchesse

ESPAGNOLE SAUCE

Beat the egg yolks *or* whole egg slightly and beat in the sugar gradually. Warm the milk to about blood heat. Stir the milk into the egg mixture, return to the pan or place in the top of a double boiler, and heat very gently until the egg thickens. The mixture must not boil, or the egg will curdle. As soon as it thickens, pour the mixture through a strainer into a sauceboat or jug. Flavour and add extra sweetening if required.

If the custard *should* curdle, whisk it briskly with a fork just before serving.

ESPAGNOLE SAUCE

1 onion	2 oz flour
1 carrot	1 pt brown stock
2 oz mushrooms *or*	Bouquet garni
mushroom trimmings	6 peppercorns
2 oz lean raw ham *or*	1 bay leaf
bacon	$\frac{1}{4}$ pt tomato pulp
2 oz butter *or*	Salt
dripping	$\frac{1}{8}$ pt sherry (optional)

Slice the vegetables, chop the ham. Melt the fat and fry the ham for a few minutes and then, very slowly, the vegetables until they are golden-brown. Add the flour and continue frying very slowly till all is a rich brown. Add the stock, herbs and spices and stir till the sauce simmers; simmer for $\frac{1}{2}$ hr. Add the tomato pulp and simmer the sauce for a further $\frac{1}{2}$ hr. Wring the sauce through a tammy cloth or rub it through a fine hair or nylon sieve. Season, add the sherry, if used, and re-heat the sauce.

For demi-glace sauce, boil together $\frac{1}{2}$ pt Espagnole sauce, $\frac{1}{4}$ pt roast meat juices or stock and 1 teasp meat glaze. Reduce well, and skim off any fat.

FLAVOURINGS

Flavourings may be
1 Powdered or grated, e.g. ground cinnamon, grated lemon peel, grated cheese
2 In plant form, e.g. bay leaf, onion
3 Concentrated, e.g. essences, various liqueurs
4 Liquid, e.g. lemon juice, wine

Powdered or grated flavourings are usually sifted into other dry ingredients or are sprinkled into, or on top of liquid ones.

Leaf, stem and root flavourings can be infused in the liquid to be flavoured, e.g. in milk; or they may be included in a dish such as a stew while it cooks, and removed before serving.

Concentrated essences and fruit juices are usually added to a dish or sauce shortly before completing it; in the case of liqueurs, the alcohol is driven off if, for instance, it is overheated or heated for long. Some liqueured dishes are flambéed or flamed, the alcohol being poured over the dish and set alight, to give a distinctive flavour.

Liquid flavourings such as cider or wine can be used as the cooking medium for a dish such as a stew, or may be added near the end of the cooking time.

Lists of common herbs and spices used for flavouring are given below.

FRENCH DRESSING

2–3 tablesp olive oil	1 tablesp wine vinegar
Pepper and salt	

Mix the oil and seasoning. Add the vinegar gradually, stirring constantly with a wooden spoon so that an emulsion is formed.

Alternatively, make the sauce in a bottle with a tight stopper. Keep it in the fridge, and shake vigorously before use. French dressing will keep for several days if chilled.

Lemon juice can be used in place of vinegar. Where suitable, orange or grapefruit juice can also be used.

A pinch of sugar, a little mustard and one or two drops of Worcester sauce can be added.

FRUIT SAUCE

Fruits suitable are: Damsons, Plums, Raspberries, Redcurrants, Blackberries.

1 lb bottled *or* fresh	Lemon juice, if liked
fruit	1 teasp (rounded)
A very little water to	arrowroot to each
stew	$\frac{1}{2}$ pt purée
Sugar to sweeten	

Stew the fruit in the water till soft, then sieve it. Sweeten, flavour and thicken the sauce with arrowroot blended with a little cold water or fruit juice.

Red fruit sauce on pears

Note: Fruit syrup from a can can be used as a sauce for some desserts, e.g. Timbale of Semolina. Heat gently if desired, and stir in any extra flavouring required, such as lemon juice. A little wine can be added, and a few drops of food colouring.

FRUIT PURÉES

These can be used as sauces for many hot and cold puddings. They give more balanced nourishment than a starch-based sauce when the pudding itself is starchy.

FRUIT SYRUP SAUCE (RASPBERRY)

6 lb sound ripe raspberries	$\frac{1}{2}$–$\frac{3}{4}$ lb loaf sugar to each pt of juice

Crush the fruit in a jar standing in a pan of boiling water. Cook gently for about 1 hr to extract all the juice. Strain through a fine nylon sieve. Measure the juice and add the sugar. Bring back to the boil and cook for 15 min, removing the scum as it rises. Let stand until quite cold, then pour into bottles. Lock, seal, store and use as required.

Gooseberries, cranberries or strawberries can be used in the same way.

GLAZES

To glaze is to make shiny. Pastry can be glazed with egg, sometimes called egg wash. Apricot or redcurrant glaze is used to brush over fruit tartlets, etc. Aspic jelly is used on hors d'œuvres, cold fish dishes, etc, and meat glaze on both hot and cold meat dishes. Ham is sometimes glazed with syrup or jam. Icings such as Chocolate Glaze are used on cakes.

DEMI-GLAZE

Use clear stock suitable for consommé. Reduce it until slightly thick and 'tacky'.

GLAZE FOR MEAT DISHES, OR MEAT GLAZE

Strictly, you should reduce about 4 qt clear stock to about $\frac{1}{4}$ pt by continued boiling, uncovered. It is cheaper and quicker to add enough gelatine to strong stock to set it almost firm.

IMITATION MEAT GLAZE

Add 1$\frac{1}{4}$ oz gelatine to $\frac{1}{4}$ pt cold water. Warm gently, stirring until dissolved. Without boiling, add 1 level teasp each of meat and yeast extract, and a little browning. Use hot to brush galantines, etc. Use ·soon; it does not keep well.

GLAZE FOR VEGETABLES

Make like Meat Glaze, using strong vegetable stock and yeast extract.

GLAZED VEGETABLES AS TRIMMINGS

Diced vegetables, slightly undercooked	Butter *or* margarine Granulated sugar
The cooking liquid	

Drain the vegetables and put the cooking liquid into a saucepan. Melt the butter and sugar in it gently. Reduce if necessary, until there is just enough liquid to coat the vegetables. Add the vegetables, and toss. Simmer for a few minutes until they are well coated and beginning to colour.

GLAZES FOR PASTRY

(a) Egg wash or egg white glaze. Brush pastry with well-beaten egg or slightly beaten egg white before baking. For a deeper colour, use the yolk only, or the yolk and a little milk. Use for meat pies,

patties, sausage rolls, etc.

(b) Sugar glazes. Fruit tarts, flans, puffs, etc can be brushed lightly with cold water and dredged with castor sugar just before baking. Sugar syrup can also be used. For a thin coat of icing, brush with beaten egg white and dredge with castor sugar when nearly baked, or use thin glacé icing after baking. Buns and plain cakes can also be glazed with egg white and fine or coarsely crushed sugar.

GRAVIES, SAUCES AND SOUPS, TO THICKEN

Gravies, sauces and soups can be thickened by adding any smooth vegetable purée, creamed potato or other cereal, or roux (white or brown as appropriate). A panada can also be used.

Luxury white sauces and soups are sometimes thickened with egg yolks mixed with cream. Stir in, when the liquid is very hot but not boiling. Do not let the mixture boil afterwards.

The most economical way to thicken gravies, sauces and soups is with beurre manié or butter and flour kneaded together, usually in equal amounts. Work these together until smoothly blended. Drop small nuts of the mixture, one by one, into the near-boiling liquid. Whisk the sauce until it boils, by which time the thickening should be smoothly blended in.

Beurre manié will keep for several weeks in the fridge.

GRAVY BROWNING

$\frac{1}{4}$ lb sugar	$\frac{1}{4}$ pt water (approx)

Dissolve the sugar very slowly in 1 tablesp water, then boil it quickly till it is a dark brown. Add a little water and warm this gently till the caramel dissolves, then add enough water to make a thin syrup. Bring this to boiling point, cool and bottle it.

GRAVY—for any Roast Joint except Pork

Meat dripping from the roasting tin	Water in which vegetables have been boiled *or* stock
Flour	
Essences from the joint	Salt and pepper

Drain most of the fat from the roasting-tin, carefully saving any sediment and meat juices. Dredge into the thin film of dripping sufficient flour to absorb it all. Brown this flour slowly till of a nut-brown colour. Stir in water in which green vegetables or potatoes have been cooked, or stock, allowing $\frac{1}{2}$ pt for 6 persons. Boil the gravy and season it to taste.

To obtain a brown colour without browning the flour, add a few drips of gravy browning from the end of a skewer.

For giblet gravy for poultry, use chicken fat and stock made with giblets.

GRAVY for Game

Bones, giblets *or* trimmings of game	1 clove 6 peppercorns and 1
Cold water to cover	piece of onion to
1 bay leaf	each pt of water
Thyme	Salt

Make stock from the above ingredients. Drain all the fat from the roasting-tin and rinse the tin with the game stock, using no flour. Boil the gravy and skim it.

GREEN SALAD AS GARNISH

GRAVY (thickened)
(for a Stuffed Joint or for Roast Pork)

Bones and trimmings from the joint	Cold water Salt

To each pint of gravy:

1 oz dripping	1 oz flour

Make a stock from the bones, allowing at least 2 hr simmering—longer if possible.

Melt dripping and sprinkle in the flour. Brown the flour slowly until a nut-brown colour. Stir in the stock, boil up and season to taste.

GREEN SALAD AS GARNISH
See **Lettuce Salad**

Note that you can use endive for a green salad in the same way as lettuce.

HARLEQUIN APPLES FOR ROAST PORK

4 dessert apples, skin removed in strips, dipped in lemon juice	Juice of $\frac{1}{2}$ lemon 1 tablesp raisins
2 large cooking apples, peeled, cored and sliced, cooked with: $\frac{1}{2}$ oz sugar	

Cook the cooking apples until soft and fork briskly. Remove the flesh from the centres of the dessert apples, and refill with the apple purée, mixed with the lemon juice and raisins. Serve immediately.

HOLLANDAISE SAUCE

2 tablesp wine vinegar	Salt and pepper
2 egg yolks	Lemon juice
2–4 oz butter	

Boil the vinegar till it is reduced by half; allow to cool. Mix the cool vinegar with the egg yolks in a basin and place this over hot water. Whisk the egg yolks till they begin to thicken, then whisk in the butter gradually until all is absorbed. Season, add lemon juice to taste and serve immediately.

HORS D'ŒUVRE VEGETABLES AS TRIMMINGS

Celery Curls Cut celery in 2-in lengths. Shred lengthwise over a coarse grater. Put shreds into iced water and leave for $\frac{1}{2}$ hr.

Gherkin Fans Make about 6 cuts from the top almost to the base of the gherkins. Spread into fan shapes.

Radish Roses Cut off the roots of the radishes. Make 4–6 cuts in each, almost to the base. Put into iced water; they will open like roses.

Tomato Slices and Lilies Slice *un*skinned tomatoes with a sharp knife. To make lilies, use a stainless steel knife to make zigzag cuts all round the tomato, into the centre. Pull the 2 halves apart.

To skin tomatoes, drop into hot water for a moment. The skins should peel off easily.

HERBS COMMONLY USED IN COOKERY

Herb	Part Used	Used for
Angelica	Leaf stalks	These can be candied and used for flavouring and decorating cakes and fruit
Aniseed	Seeds	Flavouring drinks, sweetmeats
Basil	Leaves	In salads or for flavouring soups and sauces. Good with tomatoes and green beans
Bay	Leaves	Flavouring stock, sauces, puddings and custards
Borage	Leaves and flowers	In salads, and for flavouring fruit cups and other drinks
Caraway	Seeds	Flavouring cakes, soups and sauces. Good with red cabbage, beans
Chervil	Leaves	As a garnish, in salads or for flavouring soups, entrees and sauces. Good with fish, veal and chicken
Chives	Leaves	In salads or for flavouring soups, omelettes and entrees
Coriander	Seeds	In pickles or for flavouring cakes, sauces and drinks
Dill	Leaves	Flavouring soups and sauces. Good with cabbage, potatoes and cauliflower; also with fish
	Seeds	In preserves or pickles
Fennel	Leaves	As a garnish or for flavouring sauces. Popular for use with fish
Garlic	'Clove' (bulb)	In salads or for flavouring soups and stews
Horseradish	Root	Flavouring sauces. Traditionally served with beef
Marjoram	Leaves	In stuffings or for flavouring soups, stews or sauces. Good with mushrooms, tomatoes, veal, pork and sausages
Mint	Leaves	As a garnish or for flavouring sauces, soups or vegetables. Traditionally served with lamb, green peas
Parsley	Leaves	As a garnish, in salads or for flavouring soups and sauces. Used with everything
Rosemary	Leaves and shoots	In salads or for flavouring stews, sauces and fruit cups. Good with lamb, in apple jelly and with game
Sage	Leaves	In stuffings or for flavouring soups, sauces and stews. Good with pork and duck, cheese and as 'tea'
Savory	Leaves	As a garnish, in stuffings or for flavouring stews, sauces and vegetables
Tarragon	Leaves	In salads, for making Tarragon vinegar or flavouring omelettes, sauces and stews. Good with artichokes, mushrooms, chicken and egg dishes, fish dishes, and in mayonnaise
Thyme	Leaves	In stuffings or for flavouring soups and stews. Good with tomatoes, cheese, chicken and veal, rich meats

ITALIAN SAUCE

½ pt Espagnole sauce	⅛ pt white wine
4 shallots	(optional)
6 mushrooms	Parsley stalks
1 tablesp olive oil	Sprig of thyme
⅛ pt stock	1 bay leaf
	Salt and pepper

Chop the shallots and mushrooms and cook them very gently for 10 min in the olive oil. Add the stock, wine (if used), herbs and spices and simmer gently until reduced by half. Add the Espagnole sauce and cook gently for 20 min. Season, and lift out the herbs.

JAM SAUCE

4 good tablesp jam	1 heaped teasp
½ pt water	arrowroot

Mix and heat gently until thick.

LEMON SAUCE (CLEAR)

Rind of ½ lemon	Juice of 2 lemons
½ pt water	1 heaped teasp
4 oz sugar or golden	arrowroot
syrup to sweeten	

Infuse the thinly cut lemon rind in the water for 15 min, then remove it. Add sugar or syrup to flavour water and boil for 5 min. Add the lemon juice and thicken the sauce with the arrowroot blended with a little cold water.
Note: If desired richer, a small glass of sherry and an egg yolk may be added to the above a few minutes before serving, but the sauce must not be allowed to boil again once the egg yolk has been added.

Make Orange Sauce in the same way, but with less sugar.

MACEDOINE OF VEGETABLES

Carrots	Cauliflower
Turnips	French or runner beans
Peas	Salt

Wash and scrape or peel the carrots and turnips. Dice them very neatly or cut out small balls with a vegetable scoop. Wash and divide cauliflower into neat sprigs. Cut beans into diamond shapes. Cook each vegetable separately in the minimum of boiling salted water until just tender. Drain well. Use one vegetable only as a garnish or mixtures of any or all of the above.

MADEIRA SAUCE

½ pt demi-glace	1 teasp meat glaze or
sauce	good beef extract
⅛ pt Madeira wine	Salt and pepper

Simmer the sauce, wine and extract (if used) together until well reduced. Season to taste, put in the meat glaze (if used), stir until dissolved: strain and use as required. Serve with meat, poultry and game.

MARZIPAN FRUIT, e.g. APPLES

Marzipan (see below)	Food colouring, green,
	brown, red and
	yellow
	Angelica, cloves, etc

Divide the marzipan into portions, and colour each portion differently. Use green marzipan to make rounded 'apples' and brush lightly with red colour-

ing; use a whole clove for a stalk, and cut 'leaves' from a strip of angelica or split pistachio nuts. Make other fruit in a similar way.

FOR THE MARZIPAN USE

1 lb loaf sugar	2 egg whites
1½ gills water	3 oz sifted icing sugar
12 oz ground almonds	Flavouring

Boil the loaf sugar and water to 110°C, 240°F, then draw the sugar boiler or pan aside, and when the syrup has cooled slightly add the almonds and egg whites. Stir over a low heat for a few minutes, then turn on to a slab, stir in the icing sugar, and work with a palette knife until cool enough to handle. Knead with the hands until perfectly smooth, add flavouring and mould into shapes.

Marzipan balls are the traditional decoration to place round the top of a Simnel Cake.

MAYONNAISE, HAND-MADE

1–2 egg yolks	Mixed vinegars to
Salt and pepper	taste—if possible, 4
Mustard	parts wine, vinegar or
¼–½ pt best olive oil	lemon juice, 2 parts
	tarragon and 1 part
	chilli vinegar

The eggs and oil should be at the same temperature and not too cold. In summer it is easier to make a good mayonnaise beginning with 2 egg yolks.

Remove every trace of egg white from the yolks. Put the yolks in a thick basin which will stand steady in spite of vigorous beating. Add to the egg yolks the pepper, salt and mustard to taste. Drop by drop, add the olive oil, beating or whisking vigorously all the time. As the mayonnaise thickens, the olive oil can be poured in a thin, steady stream but whisking must never slacken. When the mixture is really thick a few drops of vinegar or lemon juice stirred in will thin it again. Continue whisking in the oil, alternately with a little vinegar until the whole amount is added.

If the mayonnaise should curdle, break a fresh egg yolk into a clean basin and beat into this the curdled mixture just as the oil was added originally.

Various other ingredients are often added to mayonnaise, to give a different flavour and colour. They are useful when making a mixed hors d'œuvre or any other dish of mixed products coated with mayonnaise, for they identify the different ingredients, and emphasise their variety.

Some variations are complex sauces in their own right. But it is hardly worth making these for light savoury dishes where, as a rule, only a small amount of each sauce is needed. So the following simple additions to plain Mayonnaise are suggested instead.

To ¼ pt mayonnaise, add:

1 2 tablesp concentrated tomato purée and 1 sweet red pepper, chopped (Andalusian Sauce)
2 1 tablesp cooked spinach purée and 2 tablesp single cream (Green Mousseline Sauce)
3 ½ teasp horseradish cream, 1 teasp each chopped parsley and chervil (Escoffier Sauce)
4 1 tablesp yogurt (or sour cream), ½ teasp chopped chives and a few drops each of Worcester Sauce and lemon juice (Gloucester Sauce)
5 1 oz mixed chopped fresh herbs, as many as you can get (Green Mayonnaise)

An electric blender makes almost foolproof mayonnaise. Use a whole **egg** instead of yolks and 2 tablesp

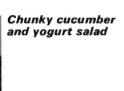

vinegar. Put these into the goblet with the seasoning and whisk at high speed for 10 seconds. Still whisking, trickle in the oil gradually. The mixture will start to thicken after ¼ pt has gone in, and will not 'take' more than ½ pt.

White wine can be used instead of wine vinegar, and wine vinegar with a drop or two of Tabasco Sauce can replace the chilli vinegar.

MEAT GLAZE *See* Glazes

MELBA SAUCE

To make Melba sauce pass the required quantity of fresh raspberries through a nylon sieve and sweeten with icing sugar. The sauce is not cooked. Use as required.

MINT SAUCE

3 heaped tablesp finely chopped mint	2 tablesp boiling water
A pinch of salt	¼ pt vinegar
2 teasp sugar	

The mint should be young and freshly gathered if possible. Wash well, pick the leaves from the stalks and chop the leaves finely.

Mix the mint, salt and sugar in the sauceboat. Pour on to them the boiling water and leave the mixture to cool. Add the vinegar and if possible leave the sauce for 1 hr to infuse the flavour of mint into the vinegar. Serve with roast lamb.

MUSHROOM SAUCE (BROWN)

½ pt basic brown sauce	2–4 oz mushrooms (field if possible)

Chop the mushroom stalks and fry with the other vegetables when making the brown sauce. Add the mushrooms with the stock when making the sauce, and simmer until tender. Strain the sauce, chop the mushrooms and return them to the sauce.

MUSHROOM SAUCE (WHITE)

½ pt basic white sauce	½–1 oz butter
2–4 oz mushrooms	

Cook the thinly sliced mushrooms very gently in the butter for 15–20 min. Stir the mushrooms with the butter and their juice into the hot sauce.

ONION SAUCE—WHITE

To ½ pt white sauce made from ½ milk and ½ liquor in which onions were boiled, add 2 chopped, cooked onions and a few drops of lemon juice.

ORANGE SAUCE, SAVOURY

½ pt Espagnole sauce	2 tablesp redcurrant
½ orange	jelly
½ lemon	Salt
⅛ pt red wine (optional)	Cayenne pepper
	Pinch of sugar

Remove the outer orange rind without the pith, and cut it in neat, thin strips. Cover the orange rind with a little cold water; stew till just tender; then strain. Squeeze the orange and lemon juice into the sauce, add the orange rind. Re-heat, add the wine (if used), the redcurrant jelly, season with salt, pepper and sugar to taste.

PARSLEY AS GARNISH

Parsley is perhaps the commonest trimming or garnish for all kinds of savoury dishes.

To blanch Bring a saucepan of water to the boil. Place the washed parsley sprigs in a strainer, dip it in the boiling water for a moment, then withdraw it and shake the parsley to dry it.

To Chop Blanch the parsley so that it keeps its greenness and Vitamin C. Wring it in a cloth to dry it. Cut off the stalks, and chop finely with a sharp knife, using a downward, not a 'sawing' stroke. Blanched parsley will not stain the chopping board.

To fry Immerse the washed and dried parsley in deep, hot fat for a few moments only. You can fry

Filling and decorating tarts or tartlets

The pastry edge of a tart or tartlet looks best glazed with egg; fruit fillings need a jam glaze

the sprigs only, in a strainer, or tie the stalks together with string, leaving a dangling loop by which to hold the parsley while dipping it in the hot fat.

PASTRY. GENERAL HINTS

1 Light pastry depends on how much cold air is incorporated into the mixture when making it. The air expands when heated, making the pastry light. It may be trapped in tiny spaces throughout the mixture or (in flaky, rough puff and puff pastry) lie in thin layers between layers of dough, so that special care must be taken not to squeeze it out when rolling.

2 Plain flour is best for pastry, although self-raising can be used for plain short crust and suet crust. Butter, or butter mixed with lard, or white cooking fat, should be used if possible. When the amount of fat is less than ½ the amount of flour, add 1 level teasp baking powder for each 8 oz flour.

3 Keep tools and hands cool. Use chilled or cold liquid, and not too much (it hardens the pastry). Use a little lemon juice for lighter pastry.

4 Always sift flour and any spices used with it. Rub in fat with the finger tips only, raising them so as to catch air in the mixture as it falls back into the bowl. Handle pastry as little and as lightly as possible. Let it 'rest' in a cool place after making, before rolling it.

5 Roll pastry evenly, with short strokes, using only a little flour on the board. Do not roll off the edge of the pastry. When rolling a circle, use radiating strokes from the centre, giving the pastry a quarter-turn clockwise when necessary. Always roll away from yourself, never from side to side. Let flaky, rough puff and puff pastry 'rest' for 15 min between rollings. After final rolling, brush off surplus flour with a pastry brush.

6 Lift pastry on the rolling pin. Use the rolled side for the outside of a crust. When placed in position, cut to shape with a sharp knife held vertically. To cut a lid for a pudding basin, roll a circle of pastry

and cut out ¼ as segment. Make a cone of the ¾ piece, fit it into the basin as lining, then re-roll the segment to make the lid.

7 Rich pastry requires a hotter oven than plain pastry. If the oven is too cool, the fat runs out before the starch grains swell to hold it. (This does not apply to Hot Water Crust, Choux and Genoese pastry.)

8 To glaze pastry, see Glazes above.

TO TRIM AND DECORATE PASTRY

Various ways of decorating pies, flans and tarts are shown in the illustrations in this book.

Remember that savoury pies containing liquid should have a hole or slits in the crust to let steam escape; the pie is re-filled with additional liquid after baking. The pastry removed for a hole can be baked separately and re-inserted after baking.

Trimmings of pastry can be re-rolled into a strip and cut into diamond or 'leaf' shapes.

A pastry 'rose' (e.g. to cover a hole) is made by rolling a narrow short strip from the thinner end. Roll over once or twice tightly, then 2 or 3 times more loosely.

TYPES OF PASTRY (for pastry for sweet dishes see Index)

FLAKY PASTRY

1 lb flour	**Cold water to mix**
Pinch of salt	**½ teasp lemon juice**
10 oz butter *or* butter	
and lard	

Sift the flour and salt into a basin. Divide the butter into 4 equal pieces and rub ¼ of it (1 piece) into the flour. If butter and lard are used, blend them together well before dividing into 4 pieces. Mix to a soft dough with cold water and lemon juice, making it the same consistency as the remaining butter.

Roll out into an oblong strip and flake another ¼ piece of the butter on the ⅔ of the pastry farthest from you. Dredge lightly with flour, fold the uncovered ⅓ of the pastry over, on to the fat and then fold over it the fat-flaked top ⅓ of pastry. Press the

edges of the pastry 'packet' together lightly with the rolling pin, to prevent butter or air being squeezed out. Half-turn the pastry, so that the folded edges are right and left when rolling. With the rolling pin, press ridges in the pastry to distribute the air evenly. Roll out. Allow the dough to relax in a cool place for 10 min.

Repeat the process twice to incorporate the remaining two $\frac{1}{4}$ pieces of the butter.

Put flaky pastry into a very hot oven (230°C, 450°F, Gas 8) until set, then reduce heat to 190°C, 375°F, Gas 5 for as long as required.

TO MAKE PATTY CASES

Roll out puff or flaky pastry to a thickness of $\frac{1}{8}$ in and cut into rounds with a $2\frac{1}{2}$-in or 3-in cutter. Remove the centres from half of these rounds with a $1\frac{1}{4}$-in or $1\frac{1}{2}$-in cutter. Turn the pastry upside down after cutting. Moisten the plain halves and place the ringed halves evenly on top. Prick the centres. Place on a baking-tray and allow to stand for at least 10 min in a cold place. Glaze the ringed halves and the small lids and bake in a very hot oven (230°C, 450°F, Gas 8). When baked, remove and scoop out any soft inside part. If liked the cases can be made as vol-au-vent cases.

TO MAKE HORN OR CORNET CASES

Roll out pastry thinly, then cut into strips $\frac{1}{2}$-in wide and 12–14 in long. Moisten strips with water and wind round cornet mould from the point upwards with moist surface on outside. Finish final overlap on underside of tin and trim neatly. Brush with milk and bake in the middle of a very hot oven (230°C, 450°F, Gas 8). Cooking time 10–15 min.

HOT WATER CRUST PASTRY *(See also page 120)*
For Pork, Veal and Ham or Raised Game Pies

10 oz plain flour	3 oz lard
$\frac{1}{2}$ teasp salt	$\frac{1}{4}$ pt milk *or* water

Sift the flour and salt into a warm bowl, make a well in the centre, and keep in a warm place. Heat the lard and milk *or* water together gently until boiling then add them to the flour, mixing well with a wooden spoon, until cool enough to knead with the hands. Knead thoroughly, use as required. Leave covered for $\frac{1}{2}$ hr.

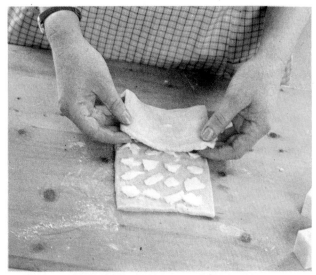

Throughout the processes of mixing, kneading and moulding, the pastry must be kept warm. But if it is too warm it will be so soft and pliable that it cannot retain its shape, or support its own weight.

Bake in a hot oven (220°C, 425°F, Gas 7), reducing heat to moderate (180°C, 350°F, Gas 4) as soon as pastry is set.

TO RAISE A PIE

The pastry must be raised or moulded whilst still warm. Reserve $\frac{1}{4}$ for the lid and leave in the bowl in a warm place covered with a cloth. Roll out the remainder to about $\frac{1}{4}$-in thickness in a round or oval shape. Gently mould the pie with the hands; if this proves too difficult mould it over an inverted, greased and floured jam jar.

When cold, remove the pastry case from the jar, put in the filling. Roll the ¼ of pastry reserved for the lid, damp the rim of the case, put on the lid and press edges firmly together.

Three or four folds of greased paper should be pinned round the pie to preserve its shape during baking and to prevent it becoming too brown.

Note: If the pie is raised without using a jar, when the lower part of the pie has been raised to the required shape and thinness, moulding can be facilitated by pressing in firmly some of the filling to support the lower part of the pie.

PUFF PASTRY, FRENCH

For Tartlets, Patties, Vol-au-Vents, etc

1 lb butter	2 egg yolks
1 lb plain flour	⅓ pt cold water
½ teasp salt	(approx)

Squeeze the butter in a floured cloth to remove as much moisture as possible. Put 2 oz aside and form the remainder into a flat cake. Keep in a cool place. Sift the flour and salt and rub in the 2 oz butter. Mix to a firm dough with the egg yolks and water, and knead quickly and lightly till smooth. Roll out into an oblong about ½-in thick, keeping the ends square, and enfold the cake of butter in the pastry. Press lightly with the rolling-pin until the butter is flattened. Roll out into a strip as thinly as possible without allowing the butter to break through, fold in 3, seal the edges using the rolling-pin, and put aside in a cool place for about 15 min to allow the pastry to become sufficiently cool and firm. Roll and fold it twice, half turning the pastry between each rolling and again leave in a cool place for 15 min. After the pastry has been rolled and folded seven times it is ready for use.

TO MAKE A VOL-AU-VENT CASE

Roll out the puff pastry to about ¾-in thickness, and with a cutter previously dipped in flour, cut into a round or oval shape as desired. Cut cleanly without dragging or twisting the pastry. Place on a baking-sheet, brush over the top of the pastry with beaten egg. With a smaller, floured cutter cut an inner ring, cutting the pastry to about ½ its depth. Bake in a very hot oven (230°C, 450°F, Gas 8). When baked, remove the lid and scoop out the soft inside.

ROUGH PUFF PASTRY

½ lb plain flour	½ teasp lemon juice
Pinch of salt	Cold water to mix
6 oz butter *or* butter and lard	

Sift the flour and salt. Add the butter cut up into pieces the size of a walnut and mix lightly with the flour. Make a well in the centre, put in the lemon juice and gradually add sufficient water to mix to an elastic dough. Roll into a long strip, keeping the corners square, fold into three. With the rolling-pin seal the edges and give the pastry a half-turn, so that the folded edges are on the right and left. Repeat until the pastry has been rolled and folded 4 times, if possible leaving for 15 min in a cool place between the second and third rollings.

Use as required. Bake in a very hot oven (230°C, 450°F, Gas 8).

SUET CRUST PASTRY

For Meat puddings, Fruit puddings, Jam Roly Poly, Suet Puddings, etc

3-4 oz suet	1 teasp baking powder
½ lb plain flour	Cold water to mix
¼ teasp salt	

Chop the suet finely with a little flour or use shredded suet. Sift the flour, salt and baking-powder, and mix in the suet. Mix to a firm dough with cold water.

SHORT CRUST PASTRY, ALL-PURPOSE

½ lb plain flour	2 oz lard
Pinch of salt	Cold water
2 oz butter	

Sift the flour and salt. Rub in the fat, add baking-powder and using a knife, mix to a stiff dough with cold water. Use as required.

Bake in a very hot oven (230°C, 450°F, Gas 8), lower later to cook filling.

For savoury tarts, a little spice or a few finely chopped herbs can be added.

SHORT CRUST PASTRY—PLAIN

½ lb plain flour	1 teasp baking powder
Pinch of salt	Cold water to mix
3 oz lard, clarified fat *or* dripping	

Sift together the flour and salt. Rub the butter and lard lightly into the flour using the fingertips. Mix to a stiff paste with cold water.

Note: Recipes for Crumb Crust Pastry, Choux Pastry, Pâté Sucrée, Puff, Short and Rich Short and Sweet Pastry for use in sweet dishes are in the section on Desserts.

PIQUANT SAUCE

½ pt basic brown sauce	1 tablesp chopped gherkins
1 onion *or* 2 shallots	
1 oz mushrooms	1 dessertsp mushroom ketchup
1 bay leaf	
¼ teasp mace	½ teasp sugar (optional)
2 tablesp vinegar	
1 tablesp halved capers	

Finely chop the onion or shallots and chop the mushrooms coarsely. Simmer the onion or shallots, the bay leaf and mace in the vinegar for 10 min. Add this mixture and the chopped mushrooms to the brown sauce and simmer till the mushrooms are soft. Add all the other ingredients. Do not strain the sauce but lift out the bay leaf and mace. Serve with pork, mutton or vegetables.

This sauce may also be made with an Espagnole foundation.

PORT WINE SAUCE

1 tablesp redcurrant jelly	⅛ pt port wine
¼ pt good mutton *or* venison gravy	

Heat all the ingredients together until the jelly is melted. Serve with roast mutton or venison.

PRAWN OR SHRIMP SAUCE

To ½ pt white stock made with ½ fish stock and ½ milk, add ¼ pt cooked shelled prawns (fresh or frozen), a few drops of anchovy essence and lemon juice to taste. Colour very lightly with a drop or two of pink colouring. Season with a little cayenne pepper, and re-heat very gently without boiling.

SAGE AND ONION STUFFING

$\frac{1}{4}$ lb onions	2 oz breadcrumbs
4 sage leaves *or*	1 oz butter
$\frac{1}{2}$ teasp powdered sage	Salt and pepper
	1 egg (optional)

Slice the onions thickly, parboil them for 10 min in very little water. Scald the sage leaves. Chop both. Mash all the ingredients together and season to your taste.

SAUSAGE MEAT STUFFING

$\frac{1}{2}$ lb lean pork	Salt and pepper
2 oz breadcrumbs	Grated nutmeg to taste
$\frac{1}{2}$ teasp mixed fresh herbs *or* $\frac{1}{4}$ teasp dried herbs	The liver of the bird to be stuffed
2 small sage leaves	Stock

Mince the pork. Chop the liver. Mix all the ingredients, using enough stock to bind the mixture. Season to taste.

Use for turkey or chicken.

A good bought pork sausage meat mixed with the liver of the bird makes a quick stuffing for poultry.

SAVOURY BUTTERS

General Method

Scald any herbs to be used, then chop all the ingredients. Crush and pound flavouring materials, or process in an electric blender. Cream butter, add the other items and mix until fully blended. Vary the amounts to suit your taste. Sieve the mixture if a smooth butter is required for piping, rosettes, curls etc; or spread $\frac{1}{4}$–$\frac{1}{2}$ in thick on a plate and chill until firm, then cut out in round pats with a pastry cutter, or shape into balls.

Use 2 oz butter, and salt and pepper to taste, with the ingredients below:

Anchovy Butter 6 bottled anchovies, lemon juice to taste (use no salt).

Curry Butter $\frac{1}{2}$ teasp curry powder, $\frac{1}{4}$ teasp lemon juice.

Devilled Butter $\frac{1}{4}$ teasp each, cayenne pepper, white pepper, curry powder and ground ginger.

Garlic Butter 1–3 cloves blanched garlic, chopped parsley.

Herb Butter Good pinch each of dried thyme and parsley.

Lobster Butter 1 oz lobster coral and spawn (raw if to be used in a sauce or soup).

Maître D'Hôtel Butter 2 teasp finely chopped parsley, $\frac{1}{2}$ teasp each chopped chervil and tarragon (optional), $\frac{1}{2}$ teasp lemon juice. Spread on a plate and chill after making, cut out round pats and use to top fish, steaks etc.

Meunière or Noisette Butter Lemon juice. (Heat the butter until golden-fawn, add the lemon juice, and use hot.)

Mustard Butter 1–2 teasp French mustard.

Shrimp Butter $\frac{1}{4}$ pt cooked, shelled shrimp, pounded, lemon juice.

Tarragon Butter 1 teasp fresh tarragon, lemon juice.

Watercress Butter $\frac{1}{4}$ bunch finely chopped watercress.

SHALLOT SAUCE

6 shallots	$\frac{1}{2}$ teasp lemon juice
1 oz butter	Salt and pepper
$\frac{1}{2}$ pt good gravy *or* demi-glace sauce	$\frac{1}{2}$ teasp finely chopped parsley
1 glass sherry	

Chop the shallots finely, melt the fat in a sauté pan, fry them lightly then drain well. Cool them slightly. To the gravy or demi-glace sauce, add the sherry, lemon juice, well-drained shallots, seasoning and parsley. Boil well until reduced, season to taste and keep hot until needed.

SHERRY OR WINE SAUCE, SWEET

$\frac{1}{8}$ pt water	Sugar to taste
$\frac{1}{8}$ pt sherry *or* sweet white wine	Lemon juice to taste
2 tablesp any jam *or* jelly	

Apples coated with cloves

Boil all the ingredients together for 5 min. Rub through a hair or nylon sieve or strain the sauce. Adjust the flavour, re-heat if necessary. If you wish, this sauce can be thickened like Jam Sauce.

SOUBISE SAUCE

½ pt Béchamel sauce	Salt and pepper
½ lb onions	Sugar
1½ oz butter	Nutmeg
1–2 tablesp stock	

Peel and slice the onions and cook them gently in ½ oz of the butter and just enough stock to moisten them. When they are tender, sieve them or process in an electric blender. Have the sauce very thick, add to it the onion purée, re-heat, season and add sugar and nutmeg to taste. Whisk the remaining 1 oz butter into the sauce at boiling point, adding a small pat at a time. Do not allow the sauce to boil.

SPICES COMMONLY USED IN COOKERY

Allspice The berry of a tree growing in the West Indies, Mexico and parts of South America. Called 'allspice' because its smell and flavour are very like a combination of cloves, cinnamon and nutmeg. Can be used whole or ground.

Capsicums The red chilli, always part of mixed pickles, is the pod of the capsicum, and chilli vinegar is made by infusing capsicum pods in vinegar. Cayenne pepper is obtained from the pods and the seeds. Capsicums owe their stimulating power to an active principle called capsicine, and when used in moderation produce no injurious effects.

Cinnamon The dried, inner bark of cinnamon is sold in stick form and in powdered form. It is used extensively for culinary purposes.

Cloves The dried flower buds of a native tree of the Molucca Islands. They form a well-known spice, and are much used in cookery both in sweet and savoury dishes.

Curry Curry is composed of various condiments and spices, which include cardamom seed, coriander seed, cumin seed, dried cassia leaves, dried chillies, cayenne, ginger, mustard seed, turmeric, cinnamon, mace and cloves. It owes its peculiar smell and bright colour to the presence of turmeric, a variety of ginger. Thorough cooking is absolutely necessary to develop the full flavour of the various ingredients comprising curry powder; the directions given in the respective recipes for preparing the curry sauce before adding to it other substances should therefore be strictly followed.

Garlic A pungent, strong-scented bulb, of the onion family, composed of smaller bulbs called 'cloves'.

Ginger A tropical Asian plant. The root is dried and then preserved in syrup, or it is crystallised, or ground. Ginger is an important ingredient in curry powder, and in gingerbreads and spiced cakes. It is also a pungent sweetmeat. Green ginger is usually available in cans for use in pickles, chutneys, etc.

Mace Mace is the outer shell or husk of the nutmeg.

Mustard Commercial mustard is composed of the seeds of both common and white mustard ground and mixed together. Its pungency is not fully developed until moistened with water; its flavour is best when freshly prepared. A pinch of salt added to mixed mustard will prevent it from becoming dry.

Nutmeg Seeds of the tropical nutmeg tree. Nutmeg is largely used as a flavouring: but it should be added sparingly to cereal dishes.

Paprika One of the capsicums. Paprika pepper is made from the bright red pod. Its pleasant flavour is less pungent than cayenne.

Pepper Seed of the plant *Piper nigrum*. (The same plant produces both white and black pepper.) The berries when ripe, are bright in colour, and each contains a single seed which changes to nearly black when dried. This is the commercial black pepper, white peppercorns being produced by further treatment. It is sold as whole peppercorns or ground pepper.

Salt The importance of salt as a condiment, as an antiseptic, and as food cannot be overestimated. It is used in all savoury dishes, and a pinch improves most sweet ones, especially icings.

Vanilla Vanilla is the fruit of a tropical orchid plant. It is extensively used as a flavouring for cakes, custards, puddings, chocolate, liqueurs, etc.

A vanilla pod can be stored in the icing sugar jar.

Vinegar The best vinegar is made from white wine. Ordinary vinegar is made chiefly from malt, cheap wine and cider. Any vinegar can be used as the bases of chilli, tarragon, or shallot vinegar, the ingredients from which they take their name being steeped in the vinegar.

Vinegar serves many useful purposes in cookery: it is an ingredient in many sauces, and helps to soften the fibres of tough meat.

FISH STOCK

Bones, skin and heads from fish which have been filleted *or* fish trimmings *or* cods' or other fish heads	Peppercorns
	1 onion
	1 stick of celery
	¼ teasp mace
	1 bay leaf
Salt	Bouquet garni

Wash the fish trimmings and break up the bones. Cover them with cold water, add salt and bring slowly to simmering point. Add the other ingredients and simmer gently for no longer than 40 min. Strain and use the same day if possible. If cooked for longer the fish stock will taste bitter. Fish stock does not keep and should be made as required.

POULTRY OR GAME STOCK

Carcass of chicken, duck *or* game bird, with giblets if available	Salt
	Cold water to cover
	1 onion
Cleaned feet of bird	White peppercorns
Giblets	

Make like Brown Stock. Made with Meat.

STOCK MADE WITH BONES

Cooked *or* raw bones of any kind of meat	Salt
	1 outside stick of celery
Cooked or raw skin, gristle and trimmings of lean meat	1 onion
	1 bay leaf
Clean peelings of carrots, turnip, mushrooms	Peppercorns

Break or chop the bones to 3-in pieces and put them with the skin and trimmings into a strong pan. Cover with cold water and add ½ teasp salt to each quart of water. Bring slowly to simmering point. Add the vegetables, including a piece of outer brown skin of onion, if a brown stock is required. Simmer for at

SUET DUMPLINGS

least 3 hr, without a lid on top heat, or covered in a slow oven. Bones may be cooked until they are porous and so soft that they crumble when crushed, but they should be strained and cooled at the end of each day, the vegetables removed at once, and fresh water added next day. If the stock is not required at once it must be cooled quickly, kept cold—preferably in a fridge—and used within 24 hr even in cool weather or within 3 days if kept in a fridge.

Before use, skim the fat from the top of the stock. This may be clarified with other meat fat, or used as needed in meat cookery.

Quantity—1½ pt from each 1 lb bones, etc.

SUET DUMPLINGS

3–4 oz suet	1 teasp baking powder
½ lb flour	Cold water
¼ teasp salt	

Make like suet crust pastry; form into small balls and drop into boiling stock; after 3 min reduce heat and simmer for 15–20 min.

SUGAR SYRUP SAUCE

Sugar syrup used for freezing fruit can be used up as a sauce. Treat like a canned fruit syrup. *See Fruit Sauce.*

Use with steamed or baked puddings, or as a base for fruit salad.

SUPRÊME SAUCE

½ pt Velouté sauce	Nutmeg to taste
2 tablesp—⅛ pt cream	Lemon juice
1 egg yolk	Salt and pepper
½–1 oz butter	

Heat the Velouté sauce, preferably in a double boiler. Mix the egg yolk and cream, and stir into the sauce. Cook without boiling until the egg yolk thickens. Whisk in the butter, a small pat at a time. Add a pinch of nutmeg, a few drops of lemon juice, season and use the sauce at once.

SWEET SAUCE

4 egg yolks *or* 2 whole eggs	¼ pt milk
4 oz castor sugar	Grated rind of 1 orange
	¼ pt cream

Beat the egg yolks or whole eggs with the sugar and milk until well mixed. Add the orange rind and cream and cook over very gentle heat or in a double boiler until the sauce thickens. It must not boil.

TARTARE SAUCE, QUICK

1 4-oz can cream	1 dessertsp castor sugar
2 tablesp chopped capers	1 tablesp white vinegar
2 tablesp chopped gherkins	¼ pt bottled *or* home-made mayonnaise (optional)
1 tablesp lemon juice	

Chill the cream. When cold, open the can, and pour off the whey. Mix with the other ingredients in a bowl. Chill for an hour before use.

TARTARE SAUCE

¼ pt mayonnaise	A little French mustard
1 teasp each of chopped gherkin, chopped olives,	1 dessertsp wine vinegar
chopped capers, chopped parsley, chopped chives	A little dry white wine (optional)

Mix the chopped ingredients into the mayonnaise, add the mustard. Thin to the required consistency with the vinegar and wine. Use this sauce for light, cold fish and meat first courses as well as hors d'œuvres.

TOMATO SAUCE

1 onion	½ oz cornflour
1 small carrot	½ pt white stock *or* liquid from canned *or* bottled tomatoes
1 oz bacon scraps *or* bacon bone *or* rinds	Salt and pepper
½ oz butter *or* margarine	Lemon juice
4 medium-sized tomatoes, fresh, bottled *or* canned	Sugar
	Grated nutmeg

Slice the onion and carrot. Put them into a saucepan with the bacon and fry them in the fat without browning them for 10 min. Slice and add the tomatoes and cook them for 5 min. Sprinkle in the corn flour, add the stock or juice, stir till the sauce boils. Simmer the sauce for 45 min. Rub the sauce through a hair or nylon sieve. Re-heat, season and add lemon juice, sugar and nutmeg to taste.

VEAL FORCEMEAT OR FORCEMEAT BALLS

4 oz breadcrumbs	Nutmeg
2 oz chopped suet *or* margarine	Grated rind of ½ lemon
1 tablesp chopped parsley	Salt and pepper
½ teasp chopped mixed herbs	1 beaten egg

Mix all the ingredients well together, using the egg to form a stiff paste. If liked, roll into balls and fry in deep or shallow fat until golden-brown all over.

VEGETABLE STOCK AND GRAVY

2 large carrots	½ teasp vegetable extract
½ lb onions	Bouquet garni
3 sticks celery	1 teasp salt
2 tomatoes	½ teasp peppercorns
¼ small cabbage	Pinch of ground mace
1 oz butter *or* margarine	1 bay leaf
2 qt boiling water	

Wash, peel and cut up the vegetables. Fry the roots gently in the fat until golden brown. Add the tomatoes and fry a little. Add all the other ingredients except the cabbage and simmer for 1 hr. Add the cabbage and simmer another 20 min. Strain and use as soon as possible.

For gravy use 1 pt of this stock with 1 tablesp mushroom ketchup and 1 teasp walnut ketchup (optional). Mix the ketchups smoothly with 1 teasp arrowroot, and browning if desired. Add a few drops of sherry (optional). Stir the arrowroot mixture into the stock, bring to simmering point and stir. Simmer until the desired consistency and flavour is reached.

VELOUTÉ SAUCE

2 oz butter	1 pt good vegetable stock (*see above*)
6 button mushrooms *or* mushroom trimmings	Salt and pepper
12 peppercorns	Lemon juice
A few parsley stalks	⅛–¼ pt cream
2 oz flour	

Melt the butter in a saucepan and gently cook the mushrooms, peppercorns and parsley for 10 min. Add the flour and cook for a few minutes without browning it. Stir in the stock, bring the sauce to simmering point and simmer for 1 hr. Wring the sauce through a tammy cloth or damp muslin. Season, add lemon juice, and re-heat. Just at boiling point stir in the cream. The mushrooms may be rinsed and used as garnish for the dish.

For fish dishes, use fish stock.

VINAIGRETTE SAUCE

This consists of a simple French dressing to which the following are added:

1 teasp finely chopped gherkin
½ teasp finely chopped shallot *or* **chives**
½ teasp finely chopped parsley
1 teasp finely chopped capers
½ teasp finely chopped tarragon and chervil (if available)

WHITE ITALIAN SAUCE

½ pt Béchamel sauce	**½ glass dry white wine**
2 shallots	**(optional)**
2 oz button	**Salt and pepper**
mushrooms	**Lemon juice to taste**
½ oz butter	**1 dessertsp chopped**
¼ pt fish or vegetable	**parsley**
stock	**2 tablesp cream**

Chop the shallots and mushrooms very fine. Melt the butter and in it cook the mushrooms and shallots very gently for 10 min. Add the sauce, the stock and wine if used. Stir all well together and simmer the sauce steadily until the mushrooms are soft and the whole sauce is reduced to a creamy texture. Season, add the lemon juice and chopped parsley and, just before serving, stir in the cream.

WHITE SAUCE *See* **Basic White Sauce**

WHITE STOCK

2 lb knuckle of veal	**1 stick of celery**
2 qt cold water	**½ teasp white pepper-**
1 teasp salt	**corns**
1 dessertsp white	**Small strip of lemon**
vinegar or lemon juice	**rind**
1 onion	**1 bay leaf**

Make like Brown Stock, Made with Meat.

Quantity about 3 pt

WHITE WINE SAUCE

½ pt white stock *or*	**⅛ pt white wine**
fish stock	**1–2 egg yolks**
2 oz butter	**Juice of ½ lemon**
1 oz flour	**Salt and pepper**

Make a white sauce with the stock, ½ the butter and the flour. Add the wine to this and simmer it for 10 min. Whisk in the remaining butter just below boiling point, then stir in the egg yolks mixed with lemon juice; season. Thicken the egg yolks without letting the sauce boil again.

Acknowledgements

WE, THE EDITORS, wish to thank the many people whose work and personal goodwill have helped towards the making of this book. We want to include all those who have generously supplied materials and afforded facilities for the many photographs taken by our photographers, and the organisations which have contributed original and other pictures of their own taking. Their patience and co-operation have contributed a great deal towards making our book a reality.

We would like to mention the following, in particular, for supplying photographs, materials, settings or expert information for the text: Australian Recipe Service; Bacofoil Ltd; Bentley's Restaurant; Birds Eye Foods Ltd; J. Bourne & Sons Ltd; British Bacon Curers' Federation; British Meat Service; British Turkey Federation; Bulmer's Ltd; Cadbury Schweppes Foods Ltd; The Canned & Packaged Foods Bureau; The Cheese Bureau; Coffee Promotion Council; Convenient Cooks; Danish Food Centre, London; Floris Chocolates Ltd; The Flour Advisory Bureau; Fowler Ltd; Fruit Producers' Council; Harrods; H. J. Heinz Company Ltd; Herring Industry Board; Hungarian Wines by F. & E. May; John West Products; The Kraft Kitchen; Lard Information Bureau; MacDougall's Foods Ltd; Max Redlich Ltd; Michael Dyer Associates; Milk Marketing Board; Mushroom Growers' Association; The Nature Conservancy; The Nestlé Company Ltd; New Zealand Lamb Information Bureau; Mrs. Mary Norwak; Old Hall Tableware Ltd; Potato Marketing Board; Pyrosil Ltd; Ravenhead Advisory Service; R.H.M. Foods Ltd; Rice Information Service; Royal Society for the Protection of Birds; Scott's Restaurant; Simpson's-in-the-Strand; St Ivel English Curl Butter; St Ivel Golden Meadow Butter; Swiss Cheese Union; Tabasco Ltd; Unigate Foods Ltd–St Ivel Country Cheeses; Walls Ice Cream Recipe Service; Walls (Meats) Ltd; White Fish Kitchen; Young's Seafoods.

Ernest Greenwood and John Dixon, the photographers who took most of our own photographs, deserve a special mention. So does Miss Jean Whitcombe for her artwork. We should also like to thank our Home Economists, Miss Nikki Moore and Miss Judith Batson, for their unflagging help.

Index

INDEX

INDEX